Introduction to RESEARCH

in Health, Physical Education, Recreation, and Dance

Jerry R. Thomas, EdD
Jack K. Nelson, EdD
Louisiana State University

Human Kinetics Publishers, Inc.
Champaign, Illinois

Library of Congress Cataloging in Publication Data

Thomas, Jerry R.
Introduction to research in health, physical education, recreation, and dance.

Bibliography: p.
Includes index.
1. Physical education and training—Research.
2. Health—Research. 3. Recreation—Research.
4. Dance—Research.
I. Nelson, Jack K. II. Title.
GV361.T47 1985 613.7′072 84-25251
ISBN 0-931250-93-5

Production Director: Karen Morse
Developmental Editor: Susan Wilmoth, PhD
Typesetters: Sandra Meier and Yvonne Sergent
Text Layout: Lezli Harris
Cover Design and Layout: Jack Davis

ISBN: 0-931250-93-5

Printed in the United States of America

10 9 8 7 6 5

Human Kinetics Books
A Division of Human Kinetics Publishers, Inc.
Box 5076, Champaign, IL 61825-5076
1-800-747-4HKP

Contents

PREFACE

Introduction to Research in Health, Physical Education, Recreation, and Dance is intended primarily for graduate students. The concepts and methodology, however, should also have widespread application for other professional personnel engaged in research.

We have presented the research concepts, techniques, and processes in a simple and logical manner, drawing from our considerable experience in conducting, advising, and reviewing research studies. Although we provide examples of research studies from health, physical education, recreation, and dance, space does not permit equal representation for all fields with all research techniques. Because the types of research are used with varying frequencies in different areas and because of our professional backgrounds, we have included more illustrations from research in physical education than from the other areas.

Our book is divided into five sections. Section I provides an overview of the research process: Chapter 1 describes the nature of the research process and the four main types of research; Chapter 2 pertains to the literature review, its uses, the search strategy, and ways of organizing and presenting the literature; Chapter 3 presents the various aspects involved in defining and delimiting the problem, including the statement of the problem, the research hypotheses, operational definitions, assumptions, limitations, and the significance of the study; and Chapter 4 gives a detailed description of the methods used in the research study.

Section II is devoted to statistical concepts in research. The three chapters in this section pertain to the need for statistics, basic statistical concepts, characteristics of data, relationships among variables, and differences among groups. We make every effort to present the statistical concepts and methods in a clear and straightforward manner, emphasizing general understanding and interpretation of statistics rather than computation, although we do provide the necessary information for the calculations of basic statistical techniques as well. In addition, we have included computer programs in Appendix B (in BASIC for the Apple II, II+, or IIe) for many of the techniques.

Section III, types of research in HPERD, contains five chapters: Chapter 8 (Historical Research) and Chapter 9 (Meta-analysis) are types of analytical research; Chapter 10 pertains to descriptive research; Chapter 11 discusses experimental research; and Chapter 12 concerns creative research. In each of the chapters we explain the specific research techniques and provide examples of research problems.

Section IV (Chapters 13, 14, and 15) cmphasizes the role of measurement in research, featuring the basic concepts of reliability and validity as they apply to the measurement of fitness parameters, psychomotor performance, motor behavior, and biomechanical analysis. We also consider measurement problems in research in the affective domain and cover the different types of response modes and item analysis.

The last section pertains to writing the research report: Chapter 16 explains the research proposal, its purpose, content, and format; Chapter 17 discusses the preparation of results and discussion sections, including descriptions of, suggestions for, and examples of tables, figures, and illustrations. Finally, Chapter 18 outlines various ways of reporting research, including the thesis and dissertation, journal articles, abstracts, oral reports, and poster presentations.

Our book is aimed at graduate students (beginning at the master's level). We have organized the material in a sequential manner; thus, we assume in later parts that you have read and understood the material in the previous parts. This pertains particularly to the information presented in Section II (Statistics) prior to its use in Section III (Types of Research) and Section IV (Measurement). Therefore, we recommend that you read and use the book serially from front to back, rather than skip around to various sections.

Give particular attention to Appendix B which includes a series of statistical computer programs for use on a microcomputer. These programs should prove useful for reasonable size data sets. While they are written in BASIC for the Apple II+, minor alterations make them adaptable for any micro that uses BASIC as a language.

As in most endeavors, we have had a little help from our friends. As often as possible, we give credit through citation to the published literature.

> But how about the many ideas and procedures that one has picked up from discussions with colleagues? After the passage of time, one can no longer remember who originated what idea. After the passage of even more time, it seems to me that all of the really good ideas originated with me, a proposition which I know is indefensible. (Day, 1979, p. vii)

Thus, we want to thank our friends who have inadvertently contributed their ideas for which we now receive credit, specifically, Helen Fant who wrote Chapter

8 on historical research and Terry Worthy, who contributed Chapter 12 on creative research. Without the excellent contributions of these two colleagues at Louisiana State University, two important areas would have been inadequately presented. We also extend our gratitude to Dr. Joseph E. Steinmetz from the Department of Psychology at Stanford University for allowing us the use of the statistical computer programs appearing in Appendix B. In addition, Dr. Steve Silverman from the University of Texas, Austin (formerly of Louisiana State University) wrote the random numbers program, and Dr. Tim Lee from McMaster University in Canada wrote the Omega squared program.

We belive this book provides the necessary information for both the consumer and producer of research. While no amount of knowledge about the tools of research can replace expertise in the content area, it is unlikely that good scholars in HPERD can function apart from effective use of research tools. Professionals in HPERD (whether they are teachers, researchers, technicians, counselors, or coaches) need to understand the research process. If they do not, they are forced to accept information on face value or on the recommendation of others. While neither is necessarily bad, the ability to carefully evaluate and reach a valid conclusion is the mark of a professional.

We firmly believe that the topic of research does not have to be presented in a dry, pompous manner. As in any human enterprise, there are humorous occurrences. In fact, attempts at being overly dignified and scholarly lead to amusing and sometimes ludicrous results. Therefore, we have interjected a few anecdotes and sketches as well as some "laws and corollaries," emphasizing various points which we hope you will find enjoyable. Our attempts at humor are designed to enliven the reading but not distract from the content. Research processes are not mysterious events that graduate students should fear: On the contrary, research processes are useful tools to which every professional should have access—they are, in fact, the very basis by which professionals make competent decisions.

Jerry R. Thomas
Jack K. Nelson

Section I

OVERVIEW OF THE RESEARCH PROCESS

This section will provide you with an overall perspective of the research process. The introductory chapter defines and reviews the various types of research done in health education, physical education, recreation, and dance (HPERD), and gives you some examples. In particular, the scientific method of problem solving is stressed. This logical method answers the following four questions (Day, 1979, p. 4) that comprise a typical thesis report:

1. What was the problem? Your answer is the *Introduction*.
2. How did you study the problem? Your answer is the *Materials and Methods*.
3. What did you find? Your answer is the *Results*.
4. What do these findings mean? Your answer is the *Discussion*.

In addition, Chapter 1 includes a brief history of research in HPERD in the United States and concludes with ways of locating and identifying research problems.

Suggested in Chapter 2 are ways of using the literature to identify the research problem, to specify hypotheses, and to develop the methodology. In particular, a system for searching, reading, analyzing, synthesizing, organizing, and writing the review of literature is proposed.

Presented in the final two chapters in Section I is the format of the research proposal with examples. This information is typically required of the master's or doctoral student prior to data collection for the thesis/dissertation. Chapter 3 defines and delimits the research problem, including the introduction, statement of the problem, research hypotheses, operational definitions, assumptions and limitations, and significance. Chapter 4 covers methodology or how to do the research. Included are the topics of subject selection, instrumentation or apparatus, procedures, and design and analysis. The emphasis is on the value of pilot work prior to the research and the protection of human subjects.

Once you have completed Section I, you should better understand the research process. Then comes the tricky part—learning all the details. These details are presented in Section II, Statistical Concepts; Section III, Types of Research; and Section IV, Measurement.

Chapter 1

Introduction to Research in HPERD

THE NATURE OF RESEARCH

Research implies a careful and systematic means of solving problems and has five characteristics (Tuckman, 1978).

1. *Systematic.* Problem solving is accomplished through the identification and labeling of variables, followed by the design of research which tests the relationship among these variables. Then data are collected which, when related to the variables, allow for the evaluation of the problem and hypotheses.
2. *Logical.* Examination of the procedures used in the research process allows researchers to evaluate the conclusions that are drawn.
3. *Empirical.* The researcher collects data on which to base decisions.
4. *Reductive.* Research takes many individual events (data) and uses them to establish more general relationships.
5. *Replicable.* The research process is recorded, enabling others to test the findings by repeating the research or to build future research on previous results.

Problems to be solved come from many sources. For example, goals have been found to enhance performance. Suppose we want to investigate more specifically how setting goals influences the performance and retention of a motor skill. Because many motor tasks involve learning to time a movement, our research question is "What are the effects of varying the levels of goal difficulty on the acquisition and retention of a timed movement sequence?" We establish three

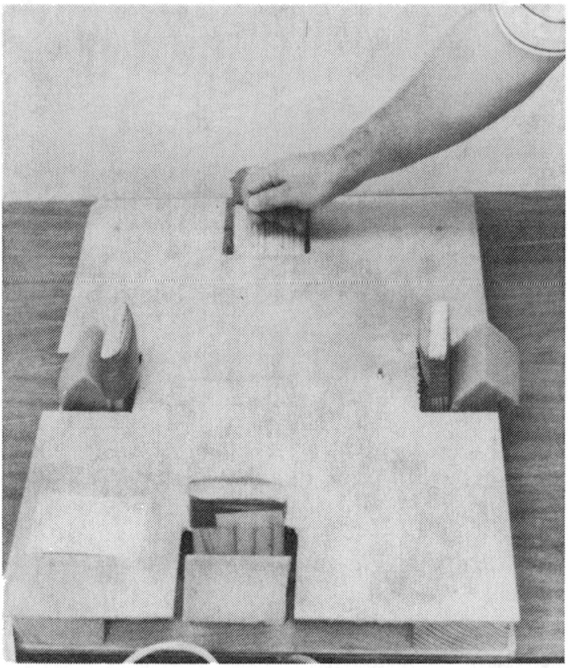

Figure 1.1 Knock-down barrier task. Photo courtesy of Motor Behavior Laboratory, Louisiana State University.

levels of goal difficulty (a) a 20% improvement on each block of trials (easy goal); (b) a 50% improvement on each block of trials (hard goal); and (c) a no-goals condition (do your best). The task is to learn a timed movement of 1500 msec. The timed movement involves releasing a start button and moving 20 cm to the right at a 45° angle to knock over a barrier, moving 40 cm to the left at a 30° angle to knock over a second barrier, moving 35 cm to the right at a 40° angle to knock over a third barrier, and finally, moving 25 cm to the center at a 30° angle to hit a stop key (see Figure 1.1). Subjects are given knowledge about their amount of error (1500 msec minus movement time) after each trial.

A total of 30 female subjects are randomly assigned to three equal groups consisting of 10 subjects. All three groups receive 30 trials on the task. The differences among the groups are in what they are told after each block of three trials. Each subject in the hard-goal group is asked to reduce her error from the past block of three trials by 50% during the next block of three trials. So if a subject had errors of 500, 470, and 380 msec on the first three trials, the average, (500 + 470 + 380)/3 = 450 msec, would be determined. Then her goal for the next trial block (3 trials) would be to reduce the 450 msec average error by 50%, or to average no more than 225 msec in error (450 × .5 = 225, 450 − 225 = 225). This procedure would be applied for all 10 trial blocks. The same procedures would be used with the easy-goal groups except a 20% improvement would be used. The no-goal group would rest for a brief time after each trial block.

When each subject completed the 30 acquisition trials, a 5-minute rest would be given and then 9 retention trials (3 blocks of 3 trials) would be administered. No goals or knowledge of performance would be provided during these 9 trials. To answer our research question, a statistical analysis of this data would first focus on the question of acquisition of the timing task. Did the three groups acquire the timing skill at different rates over the 10 blocks of trials? The second question would focus on retention. Was there any difference in how well the skill was retained depending on which acquisition group the subjects were in?

This type of research falls within the motor-learning area and has both theoretical and applied benefits. Insight may be gained into the nature of goals and their difficulty. In addition, physical education teachers might find this knowledge useful in the daily instruction of students.

Research in HPERD can be placed on a continuum with *applied* research at one extreme and *basic* research at the opposite extreme. The research extremes have certain characteristics (Figure 1.2) generally associated with them. Applied research tends to address immediate problems, to use real world settings, to use human subjects, to have limited control over the research setting, and to have results that are of direct value to practitioners. At the other extreme, basic research usually deals with theoretical problems, has the laboratory as the setting, frequently uses animals as subjects, has carefully controlled conditions, and produces results that have limited direct application.

The strengths of applied research are the weaknesses of basic research and vice versa. Considerable controversy exists in the literature (psychology, education, physical education [for an example from physical education see Martens, 1979; Siedentop, 1980; & Thomas, 1980]) about whether research in HPERD should be more basic or applied. This issue, labeled ecological validity, deals with two concerns: Is the research setting perceived by the subject in the way intended by the experimenter? and Does the setting have enough of the "real world" characteristics to allow for generalizing to reality? Of course, most research is neither absolutely applied nor basic, but to some degree between the two. We believe systematic efforts are needed to produce research from sound theoretical frameworks in carefully controlled settings that are followed by studies with more of the characteristics of applied research. An example of this type of an effort can be found in the research of Smoll, Smith, and colleagues (Thomas, 1984)

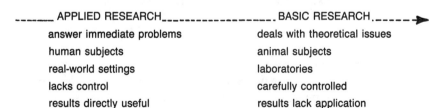

APPLIED RESEARCH	BASIC RESEARCH →
answer immediate problems	deals with theoretical issues
human subjects	animal subjects
real-world settings	laboratories
lacks control	carefully controlled
results directly useful	results lack application

Figure 1.2 Characteristics of studies at the extremes of the research continuum. Adapted from *A student guide for educational research* (2nd edition) by R.L. Hoenes and B.S. Chissom, 1975, Statesboro, GA: Vog Press. Adapted and reprinted with permission.

on the effects of coaching behaviors on youth league baseball players. Smoll and Smith went from developing and testing a theoretical base for assessing and influencing coach-player interactions to developing and evaluating a training program for coaches. More efforts of this type are needed in HPERD. While the research base has grown tremendously in HPERD over the past 20 years, much remains to be done. For example, within *health education* studies of the effectiveness of preventative education programs on disease control, drug use, stress, alcohol abuse, obesity, and other areas are now being undertaken. In *physical education* scholars are beginning to understand the biochemical basis for exercise benefits, the acquisition and control of motor skills, the psychosocial factors influencing sport performance, and the effectiveness of teachers in promoting gains in motor skills and physical fitness. Research in *recreation* has begun to evaluate how equipment selection and arrangement promotes vigorous activity on playgrounds, the psychosocial benefits derived from effective use of leisure, the need for recreational programming for senior citizens, and so on. *Dance* researchers are developing increasingly effective ways to record and evaluate choreographic research, studying common features in ballet and modern dance performance and various other efforts in creative dance research.

Thus, a great need exists in HPERD to prepare proficient consumers and producers of research. To be proficient at either or both requires a thorough understanding of the appropriate knowledge base (e.g., choreography, exercise physiology, teaching effectiveness, leisure planning, health science) as well as the necessary tools of research methodology. In this book we attempt to provide an understanding of the tools necessary to consume and to produce research. Much of the methodology is common across the various areas of HPERD (as well as other areas such as psychology, sociology, education, physiology). Quality research efforts always involve some or all of the following components: identification and delimitation of a problem; searching, reviewing, and effectively writing about relevant literature; specifying and defining testable hypotheses; designing the research to test the hypotheses; selecting, describing, testing, and treating the subjects; analyzing and reporting the results; and discussing the meaning and implications of the findings.

WAYS OF PROBLEM SOLVING

While there are many definitions of research, nearly all of them characterize research activity as some sort of structured problem solving. The word *structured* refers to the fact that a number of research techniques can be used as long as the techniques are considered acceptable by scholars in the field. Thus, research is concerned with solving problems which lead to new knowledge.

The problem-solving process involves several steps whereby the problem is developed, defined, and delimited, hypotheses are formulated, data gathered and analyzed, and the results are interpreted with regard to the acceptance or rejection of the hypotheses. These steps are often referred to as the *scientific method of problem solving*. The steps also basically constitute the chapters or sections of the thesis or research paper. Consequently, much of this text is devoted to the specific ways these steps of obtaining knowledge are accomplished.

SOME UNSCIENTIFIC METHODS OF PROBLEM SOLVING

Before going into more detail concerning the scientific method of problem solving, it is important to recognize some other ways by which humankind has acquired knowledge. All of us have used these methods so they are recognizable. Helmstadter (1970) labeled the methods as *tenacity, intuition, authority,* the *rationalistic* method, and the *empirical* method.

Tenacity. People sometimes cling to certain beliefs regardless of the lack of supporting evidence. Our superstitions are good examples of this "method" called tenacity. Coaches and athletes are notoriously superstitious. A coach may wear a particular sport coat, hat, tie, or shoes because the team won before when he wore it. Athletes frequently have a set pattern which they consider "lucky" for dressing, for warming-up, and for entering the stadium. Even though they acknowledge that there is no logical relationship between the game's outcome and the particular routine, they are afraid to break the pattern.

Take for example the man who believed that black cats brought bad luck. One night when returning to the ranch, a black cat started to cross the road. The man swerved off onto the prairie to keep the cat from crossing in front of him, hitting a hard bump that caused the headlights to go off. Unable to see the black cat in the dark night, he sped frantically along over rocks, mounds, and holes until he came to a sudden stop in a ravine, wrecking his car and sustaining moderate injuries. Of course, this just confirmed his staunch belief that black cats do indeed bring bad luck.

Obviously, tenacity has no place in science. It is the least reliable source of knowledge.

Intuition. Intuitive knowledge is sometimes considered "common sense" or "self-evident." However, a number of self-evident truths are subsequently found to be false. That the earth is flat is a classic example of the intuitively obvious; that the sun is farther away in the winter than the summer is self-evident; that no one could run a mile in less than 4 minutes once was self-evident. Furthermore, for anyone to throw the shot put over 70 feet or to pole vault over 18 feet, or for a woman to run distances over a half mile was impossible. One of the fundamental tenets of science is that we must be ever cognizant of the importance of substantiating our convictions with factual evidence.

Authority. Reference to some authority has long been used as a source of knowledge. While this is not necessarily invalid, it of course depends on the authority and the rigidity of adherence. However, the appeal to authority has been carried to absurd lengths. Even personal observation and experience have been deemed unacceptable when they disputed authority. Supposedly, people actually refused to look in Galileo's telescope when he disputed Ptolomy's explanation of the world and of the heavens. Consequently, he was later jailed and forced to recant his beliefs. Bruno also rejected Ptolomy's theory and was burned at the stake. (Ptolomy's book on astrology and astronomy was read and believed for 1200 years after his death!) In 1543, Vesalius wrote a book on anatomy, much of which is still correct today. However, because his work clashed with Galen's theories, he met with such scorn and ridicule that he gave up his study of anatomy.

Perhaps the most crucial aspect of the appeal to authority as a means of obtaining knowledge is the right to question, to accept, or to reject the information. Furthermore, the qualifications of the authority and the methods by which the authority acquired the knowledge also determine the validity of this source of information.

Rationalistic Method. In this method, knowledge is derived through reasoning. A good example is the classical syllogism:

> All men are mortal. (major premise)
>
> The emperor is a man. (minor premise)
>
> Therefore, the emperor is mortal. (conclusion)

While you probably would not argue with this reasoning, the key to this method is the validity of the premises and their relationship to each other. For example,

> Basketball players are tall.
>
> Tom Thumb is a basketball player.
>
> Therefore, Tom Thumb is tall.

In this case, however, Tom Thumb is a dwarf. The conclusion is trustworthy only if derived from reliable premises. Also, the premises may not, in fact, be premises but actually descriptions of events or statements of fact. The statements are not connected in a cause-and-effect manner, such as,

> There is a relationship between achievement in mathematics and shoe size in young children.
>
> Herman has big feet.
>
> Therefore, Herman is good in mathematics.

Of course, in the first statement the factor common to both mathematics achievement and shoe size is age. Older children tend to be bigger and thus have bigger feet than younger children. Older children also have higher achievement scores in mathematics, but there is no cause-and-effect relationship. You must always be cognizant of this when dealing with correlation. Reasoning is fundamental in the scientific method of problem solving, but it cannot be used by itself to arrive at knowledge.

The Empirical Method. The word empirical denotes experience and the gathering of data. Certainly, data gathering is part of the scientific method of solving problems. However, the over-reliance on your own experience (or data) can be very unscientific. First of all, your own experience is very limited. Furthermore, your retention depends substantially on how the events agree with your past experience and beliefs, on whether things "make sense," and on your state of motivation to remember. Nevertheless, the use of data (and the empirical method) is high on the continuum of methods of obtaining knowledge, as long as you are aware of the limitations of leaning too heavily on this method.

THE SCIENTIFIC METHOD OF PROBLEM SOLVING

The methods of acquiring knowledge previously discussed lack the objectivity and control that characterize the scientific approach to problem solving. Several basic steps are involved in the scientific method. Some authors list seven or eight steps, and others condense these steps into three or four. Nevertheless, all of the authors are in general agreement as to the sequence and process which are involved. The steps are briefly described next. Greater detail concerning the basic processes will be covered in other chapters.

Step 1. Developing the Problem (Defining and Delimiting It). This may sound a bit contradictory, for how could the development of the problem be a part of solving it? Actually, the discussion here is not about finding a problem to study (ways of locating a problem will be discussed later in this chapter); the assumption is that the researcher has already selected a topic. However, in order to design and execute a sound investigation, the researcher must be very specific about what is to be studied and to what extent.

Many ramifications constitute this step. One very important aspect is the identification of the *independent* and *dependent* variables. The independent variable(s) is what the researcher is manipulating. If, for example, two methods of teaching a motor skill are being compared, then the teaching method is the independent variable; this is sometimes called the *experimental* or *treatment* variable.

The dependent variable is the effect of the independent variable. In the comparison of teaching methods, the measure of skill is the dependent variable. If you think of an experiment as a cause-and-effect proposition, the cause is the independent variable and the effect is the dependent variable. The latter is sometimes referred to as the *yield*. Thus, the researcher must define exactly what is going to be studied and what is going to be the measured effect. When this is resolved, the experimental design can be determined.

Step 2. Formulating the Hypotheses. A hypothesis is an expected result. When a person sets out to conduct a study, he or she generally has an idea as to what the outcome will be. This anticipated solution to the problem may be based on some theoretical construct, from the results of previous studies, or perhaps even from the experimenter's past experience and observations. The last source is probably least likely or defensible because of the weaknesses of the unscientific methods of acquiring knowledge which were discussed previously. In any event, the researcher should have some experimental hypothesis about each of the subproblems in the study.

One of the essential features about a hypothesis is that it must be "testable." The study must be designed in such a way that the hypothesis can be either supported or refuted. It should be obvious to the reader, then, that the hypothesis cannot be some type of value judgment or some abstract phenomenon that cannot be observed.

For example, you might hypothesize that success in athletics is dependent solely on fate. In other words, if a team wins, it is because it was meant to be; and, similarly, if a team loses, it was just not meant to be. There is no way to refute this hypothesis because there is no evidence that could be obtained to test it. A good example is the story of the pilgrim who believed wholeheartedly in fate. He proclaimed to anyone who would listen that if one's "number was up" no actions or precautions could alter the course of fate. A skeptic in the crowd asked, "If this is so, why do you carry a musket when you go into the forest?" The pilgrim replied, "Oh, every once in a while, I meet an Indian whose number is up."

Step 3. Gathering the Data. Of course, before this step can be accomplished, the researcher must decide upon the proper methodology in acquiring the necessary data to be used in testing the research hypotheses. The reliability of the measuring instruments, the controls that are employed, and the overall objectivity and precision of the data-gathering process are crucial to the solution of the problem.

In terms of difficulty, the actual data gathering may be the easiest of the steps, because in many instances, it is mostly routine. However, the planning of the method is one of the most difficult steps. Good methods attempt to maximize both the internal and external validity of the study.

The terms *internal validity* and *external validity* relate to the research design and controls that are used. Internal validity refers to the extent to which the results can be attributed to the treatments used in the study. In other words, the researcher must try to control all other variables which could influence the results. For example, Jim Nasium wants to scientifically assess the effectiveness of his physical education program in developing physical fitness. He tests his students at the first of the year and at the end of the year and thus concludes that the program brought about significant improvement in fitness. What is wrong with Jim's conclusion? His study contains several flaws. The first is that Jim gave no consideration to maturity. Nine months of maturation produce significant changes in size and in accompanying strength and endurance. Also, what else were the students doing during this time? and How do we know that their other activities were not responsible or partly responsible for the changes in their fitness? Chapters 4 and 11 will deal with these threats to internal validity.

External validity pertains to the generalizability of the results. To what extent can the results apply to the "real world"? This often produces a paradox for research in the behavioral sciences because of the controls required for internal validity. In motor-learning studies, for example, the task is usually something novel so as to control for past experience. Furthermore, it is desirable to be able to measure the performance objectively and reliably. Consequently, the learning task is frequently a maze, a rotary pursuit meter, or a linear positioning task which may meet the demands for control with regard to internal validity. But, then you are faced with the question of external validity: How does performance in a laboratory setting with a novel, irrelevant task apply to learning gymnastics or basketball? These questions are important and sometimes vexing but not insurmountable and will be discussed later.

Step 4. Analyzing and Interpreting Results. The novice researcher finds this step to be the most formidable for several reasons. For one thing, this step usually involves some statistical analysis, and the novice researcher (particularly the master's student) has a rather limited background and a fear of statistics. Secondly, analysis and interpretation require considerable knowledge, experience, and insight, which, of course, the novice is lacking.

That analysis and interpretation of results is the most challenging step is without question. It is here that the researcher must provide evidence for the support or the rejection of the research hypotheses. In doing this, the researcher also compares the results with those of others and perhaps attempts to relate and integrate the results into some theoretical model. Inductive reasoning is employed in this step (whereas deductive reasoning is primarily used in the statement of the problem). The researcher attempts to synthesize the data from his or her study along with the results of other studies to contribute to the development or substantiation of a theory.

TYPES OF RESEARCH IN HPERD

Research is a structured way of solving problems. There are different kinds of problems in the fields of health education, physical education, recreation, and dance; hence, there are different types of research used to solve these problems. This text concentrates on four types of research: analytical, descriptive, experimental, and creative. A brief description of each follows:

TABLE 1.1

TYPES OF RESEARCH IN HPERD

Analytical	Descriptive	Experimental	Creative
Historical	Survey:	Pre-designs	Choreography
Philosophical	Questionnaire	True designs	Sculpture
Reviews	Interview	Quasi-designs	Music
Meta-analysis	Normative		Art
	Case study		
	Job analysis		
	Documentary analysis		
	Developmental		
	Correlational		

ANALYTICAL RESEARCH

As the name implies, this type of research involves in-depth study and evaluation of available information in an attempt to explain complex phenomena. The different types of analytical research are historical, philosophical, reviews, and meta-analysis.

Historical Research. Obviously, historical research deals with events which have already occurred. The researcher endeavors to locate as many pertinent sources of information as possible concerning the specific problem, and then analyzes the information as to its authenticity and accuracy. Sources are collected and classified as primary or secondary, and the material is scrutinized for internal and external validity; that is, the source is evaluated to determine if it is genuine, and the information is criticized as to whether it is accurate and reliable.

Historical research focuses on events, organizations, institutions, and people. In some studies, the researcher is mostly interested in preserving the record of events and accomplishments of the past. In other investigations, the writer attempts to discover facts which will provide more meaning and understanding of past events in order to explain the present state of affairs. Some historians have even attempted to use information from the past to predict the future. The research procedures associated with historical studies will be addressed in considerable detail in Chapter 8.

Philosophical Research. Critical inquiry characterizes the philosophical method of research. The researcher establishes hypotheses, examines existing facts, analyzes them and synthesizes the evidence into a workable theoretical model. Many of the most important problem areas must be dealt with by the philosophical method. Problems dealing with objectives, curricula, course content, requirements, and methodology are but a few of the important issues that can only be resolved through the philosophical method of problem solving.

Although some authors stress the differences between science and philosophy, the philosophical method of research follows essentially the same steps as other methods of scientific problem solving. The philosophical approach utilizes scientific facts as the basis for formulating and testing research hypotheses.

The philosophical approach to the solution of problems is greatly influenced by the cultural confines in which the problem is studied and by the time and the facts available. Consequently, principles developed through philosophical research can be expected to change as the culture and the available facts change.

There have been several philosophical research studies in the fields of HPERD. An excellent example of philosophical research procedures was Arthur A. Esslinger's dissertation (1938) in which he established principles upon which the selection of the content of the physical education program could be based. Esslinger used information related to growth and development, child interests, and capacities, and facts from the fields of anatomy, physiology, education, and psychology. He also examined the social trends at the time. Through analysis and synthesis, Esslinger developed principles concerning the selection of activities and the formulation of the overall curriculum. Practical implications were then proposed for the physical education program based on the principles that had been established.

In philosophical research, the breadth of experience and education are essential, because as in any type of research, the formulation of hypotheses and the suggested solutions to problems are a function of experience, imagination, and intelligence. The logical thinking, the scrupulous regard for the limitations and scope of the data, and the recognition of personal biases are all implicit factors in the philosophical method.

Having an opinion is not the same as having a philosophy. In philosophical research, beliefs must be subjected to rigorous criticism in light of the basic underlying assumptions. Academic preparation in philosophy plus a solid background in the fields from which the facts are derived are necessary.

Another example of sound philosophical research in physical education was Morland's study (1958) in which he analyzed the educational views held by leaders in American physical education and categorized them into educational philosophies of reconstructionism, progressivism, essentialism, and perennialism.

Reviews. A review paper is a critical evaluation of recent research on a particular topic. The author must be very knowledgeable about the available literature as well as the research topic and procedures. A review paper involves analysis, evaluation, and integration of the published literature, often leading to important conclusions concerning the research findings up to that time.

Certain publications consist entirely of review papers, such as the *Psychological Review*, the *Annual Review of Physiology*, and the *Review of Educational Research*. A number of journals publish reviews periodically, and some occasionally devote an entire issue to reviews. For example, the Fiftieth Anniversary Issue of the *Research Quarterly for Exercise and Sport* (Safrit, 1980) contains some excellent review papers on various topics.

Meta-analysis. Reviews of literature are difficult to write because they require that a large number of studies be synthesized to determine common underlying findings, agreements, or disagreements. To some extent this is like attempting to make sense of data collected on a large number of subjects by just looking at the data. Glass (1977; Glass et al., 1981) has proposed a mathematical means of analyzing the findings from numerous studies called *meta-analysis*. Findings between studies are compared by changing results within studies to a common metric called effect size (ES). Glass et al. (1981) provide numerous formulas for transforming means and standard deviations and other statistics to ES. Effect size may then be treated with standard statistical techniques for summarizing and analyzing the data points (findings from various studies). A few examples of meta-analysis have been reported in the physical education literature (Feltz & Landers, 1983; Sparling, 1980). This technique will be discussed in more detail in Chapter 9.

DESCRIPTIVE RESEARCH

Descriptive research studies are concerned with status. Of the several descriptive research techniques, the most prevalent is the questionnaire. Other forms of descriptive research include the interview, the normative survey, the case study, job analysis, documentary analysis, developmental, and correlational studies.

Chapter 10 provides detailed coverage of descriptive research procedures. The following paragraphs give a brief identification of the different types of descriptive research techniques:

The Questionnaire. The main justification of a questionnaire is the need to obtain responses from persons from a wide geographical area. The questionnaire usually strives to secure information about present practices, conditions, and demographic data. Occasionally, a questionnaire asks for opinions or knowledge. Questionnaires have been used in HPERD to gather information on numerous topics such as recreation directors' perceptions of recreation services for the mentally retarded (Decker, 1980) and attitudes toward and knowledge of medical self-care of college students (Dunn, 1980).

The researcher must take great care in preparing the questionnaire in order to obtain valid and reliable responses. The importance of the cover letter, pilot study, and follow-up(s) is discussed in Chapter 10. However, the questionnaire has acquired an unfavorable reputation as a research tool in some fields. This has been largely the result of poorly designed and overused questionnaires.

The Interview. The interview and the questionnaire are essentially the same technique insofar as their planning and procedures. Obviously, the interview has certain advantages over the questionnaire in that the researcher can rephrase questions and ask additional ones to clarify responses and to secure more valid results. Becoming a skilled interviewer requires training and experience. Telephone interviewing has become increasingly more common in recent years. One of the principal reasons is cost. Telephone interviewing costs about half as much as face-to-face interviews. The telephone interview also has the advantage of being able to cover a wide geographical area which is generally a limitation in personal interviews. Some other advantages of the telephone interview technique will be discussed in Chapter 10.

The Normative Survey. There have been a number of notable surveys in the fields of physical education and in health education. The normative survey generally seeks to gather performance or knowledge data on a large sample from a population and present the results in the form of comparative standards, or norms.

The development of the norms for the *AAHPERD Youth Fitness Test* (1958) is an outstanding example of a normative survey. Thousands of boys and girls ages 10 to 18 throughout the United States were tested on a battery of motor-fitness items. Percentiles were then established to provide information for students, teachers, administrators, and parents as to comparative performances. Actually, the Youth Fitness Test was developed in response to another survey, the Kraus-Weber test which revealed that American children scored dramatically lower on a test battery of minimum muscular fitness when compared with European children.

The Case Study. The case study is used to provide detailed information about an individual (or some institution, community, etc.). In order to better understand the subject or condition, the case study aims to determine unique characteristics about it. This descriptive research technique is used widely in many fields such as medicine, psychology, counseling, and sociology.

The researcher attempts to gather and analyze as much information about the "case" as possible. Sometimes subjects who are high achievers are studied, and often the lower performer serves as the subject for a case study. For example, Popp (1959) compared case studies of boys with the 20 lowest and the 20 highest physical fitness scores as to medical records, nutritional status, living habits, and personal problems.

The Job Analysis. The objective of the job analysis is to describe in detail the various duties, procedures, responsibilities, preparation, advantages, and disadvantages of a particular job. Used widely in vocational training and counseling, the job analysis research procedures require time, attention to details, and a variety of data-gathering techniques. The job analysis has not been used to a great extent in HPERD, but some studies have been done dealing with the duties of the athletic director, intramural director, and the physical education teacher.

Documentary Analysis. In some respects, the documentary analysis could be classified under analytical research because it is used in literature reviews, historical studies, and other areas. However, the form of documentary analysis included in descriptive research is directed primarily at establishing the status of certain practices, areas of interest, and prevalence of certain errors, usage of terms, and space counts.

For example, newspapers or magazines might be studied to determine the extent of coverage (and thus public interest) devoted to certain sports or recreational activities. A study to ascertain the frequency of use of various statistical procedures in a research journal also falls under the category of documentary analysis.

Developmental Studies. In developmental research, the investigator is usually concerned with the interaction of learning or performance with maturation. For example, a researcher may wish to assess the extent to which processing information can be attributed to maturation as opposed to strategy; or the researcher may desire to determine the effects of growth on some physical parameter such as aerobic capacity.

Developmental research can be undertaken by what is called the *longitudinal* method, whereby the same subjects are studied over a period of years. Obvious logistical problems are associated with longitudinal studies; thus, an alternative is to select samples of subjects from different age groups in order to assess the effects of maturation. This is called the *cross-sectional* approach.

Correlational Studies. The purpose of the correlational study is to examine the relationship between certain performance variables, such as between heart rate and ratings of perceived exertion; or the relationship between traits such as anxiety and pain tolerance; or the correlation between attitudes and behavior as in the attitude toward recreation and the amount of participation in leisure activities.

Sometimes, correlation is employed to predict performance. For example, a researcher wishes to predict percent body fat from skinfold measurements. First, the correlation between percent body fat (as measured by some method such as underwater weighing) and skinfold measurements is established with a sample of subjects. Based on this relationship, percent fat can then be predicted for other subjects just by using skinfold measurements.

Correlational research is descriptive in that you cannot presume a cause-and-effect relationship. All that can be established is that there is an association between two or more traits or performances.

EXPERIMENTAL RESEARCH

Experimental research is usually acknowledged as being the most scientific of all the types of research because the researcher can manipulate treatments in order to cause things to happen (i.e., a cause-and-effect situation can be established); this is in contrast to other types of research where already existing phenomena or data from the past are observed and analyzed.

For an example of an experimental study, assume that Virginia Reel, a dance teacher, hypothesizes that students would learn more effectively through the use of a videotape. First, she randomly assigns students to two sections: One section is taught by the so-called traditional method (explanation, demonstration, practice, critique); the other section is taught in a similar manner except the students are filmed while practicing and can thus observe themselves at the same time the teacher critiques their performance. After 9 weeks, a panel of dance teachers evaluates both sections. In this study, method of teaching is the independent variable and dance performance (skill) is the dependent variable. After the groups' scores are compared statistically, Virginia can then conclude whether her hypothesis can be supported or refuted.

In experimental research, the researcher attempts to control all factors except the experimental (or treatment) variable. If the extraneous factors can be successfully controlled, then the researcher can presume that the changes in the dependent variable are due to the independent variable.

Several research designs are used in experimental research. Not all designs are truly experimental in that the independent variable cannot always be manipulated. In a study of learning strategies of brain-damaged children and normal children, the researcher certainly would not take a sample of children and cause brain damage to half of them; instead, children with brain damage would be chosen for the study. Similarly, a researcher wishing to compare training responses of men and women has to select subjects from each sex and then compare their responses. Thus, when there are preexisting differences such as sex, race, age, and personality traits, the independent variable is not truly independent, it is *categorical*. Such a design is an example of a *quasi-experimental* design. Experimental research procedures and the different types of designs are discussed in detail in Chapter 11.

CREATIVE RESEARCH

Creative research is different in many respects from the other types of research already mentioned. In this text, creative research is confined to the field of dance, although it is also used in other fields such as art, sculpture, and music.

An original choreography is an example of creative research. As with other types of research, the first step deals with the development of the problem. Then the literature is reviewed, the idiom and format are selected, and the scope of the work is determined. Next, the choreographic process is developed. The various movements and sequences are planned and rehearsed, which is somewhat analogous to the gathering of data in other forms of research.

The choreography is evaluated in terms of its artistic merit and the manner by which it "interprets the results" in its portrayal and expression of the chosen theme, which is the presentation. This presentation is comparable to the written report in other types of research; therefore, it must meet the critical evaluation of the viewers in much the same way that a thesis or research article is judged acceptable. For a thesis or dissertation, a written account is usually required in addition to the public presentation. Sometimes films or videotapes are also made to preserve the creative work. Consequently, creative research demands the same rigorous attention to detail and the same scholarly approach to the solution of the problem as any other type of research.

A BRIEF HISTORICAL OVERVIEW OF RESEARCH IN HPERD IN THE UNITED STATES[1]

PHYSICAL EDUCATION

The beginnings of systematic research in physical education in the United States closely followed the establishment in 1854 of the first Department of Hygiene and Physical Education at Amherst College. Although John Hooker was actually the first director of this department, the appointment of Edward Hitchcock, M.D. (1853, Harvard Medical School) as director in 1861 represents the beginnings of research efforts in physical education. Dr. Hitchcock frequently made anthropometric measurements and used chin-ups to assess arm strength. Over the next 20 years, the list of measurements taken was extended considerably. The tabulation of these measurements was first published in the *Anthropometric Manual* (1887, revised editions in 1889, 1893, and 1900) and represents one of the first data-based research publications in physical education in the United States.

Then Dudley Sargent, who received his M.D. from Yale Medical School in 1878, established a private gymnasium in New York where he began applying a series of bodily measurements to participants. Two years later, he was appointed assistant professor at Harvard and made director of the new Hemenway Gymnasium. All entering freshmen were given an examination, including both strength tests and anthropometric measures. Dr. Sargent collected more than 50,000 anthropometric measures on individuals during his career. In fact, lifelike statues of typical American youths were constructed based upon his measurements and displayed at the 1893 Chicago World's Fair: This might be listed as the first formal research presentation in physical education in the United States. Sargent was also a leader in the development of strength testing and used these tests to determine membership of Harvard's athletic teams. Following the lead of Sargent, several women's colleges (Bryn Mawr, Mount Holyoke, Radcliffe, Rockford, Vassar, and Wellesley) in the 1880s established programs of anthropometric measurements and strength tests of students.

When a new gymnasium was constructed at Johns Hopkins in 1883, Dr. Edward Hartwell (Ph.D., Johns Hopkins; M.D., the Medical College of Ohio) was appointed its director. There, in 1897, he began the use of survey research in physical education through his evaluations of gymnastics in the United States.

To measure throwing, running speed, and distance jump, Dr. Luther Gulick devised in 1890 the very first achievement test. This test, called the Pentathlon Test, was initially created for the Athletic League of the YMCAs of America but was further developed in the early 1900s for the Public School Athletic League in New York.

---

[1]This brief history has relied upon several secondary sources (Hackensmith, 1966; Lee, 1983; Leonard & Affleck, 1947; Van Dalen & Bennett, 1971). In particular, Lee's summaries of research in Chapters 6, 9, 13, and 16 were helpful.

Then in the late 1800s and early 1900s, several books appeared which either reported, summarized, or influenced early research in physical education. Among those were Blaikie's *How to Get Strong and How to Stay So* (1879) which reported Sargent's early work and influenced Harvard (Blaikie was a Harvard alumnus) to employ Sargent. DuBois-Reymond published *Physiology of Exercise* in Berlin in 1885 which was translated into English in *Popular Science Monthly*. Following Sargent's lead in anthropometric measurement, Seaver published *Anthropometric and Physical Examinations* in 1896.

The beginning of the 20th century saw a continuing interest in research in physical education. In particular, an interest arose in tests of physical achievement and cardiovascular efficiency. Physicians (both within and outside the profession of physical education) showed increased interest in classifying people for exercise intensity based upon cardiovascular function. At Springfield College (MA), James McCurdy (1895-1935) began studying changes occurring over the adolescent years in heart function and blood pressure. The first of the widely used cardiovascular efficiency tests was developed in 1917 by Schneider at Connecticut Wesleyan College and was used in World War I for the evaluation of fitness of aviators.

Physical achievement testing advanced considerably in the early 1900s, and in 1922, the American Physical Education Association set up a committee under McCurdy's direction to develop motor ability tests. The two most recognized tests of the 1920s were Sargent's Physical Test of Man, and Roger's Physical Fitness Index (PFI). By the 1930s many schools and colleges were administering physical achievement tests. In fact, this increase in motor performance and fitness testing probably led to the establishment in 1930 of *The Research Quarterly* by the American Physical Education Association. (For a review of the history of *RQ*, see Park, R.J. *The Research Quarterly* and its antecedents. *Research Quarterly for Exercise and Sport*, **51**, 1-22.) This was the first journal established specifically to report research in physical education.

Beginning in the 1930s, tests and measurements became the most active research area in physical education. Many physical fitness and motor ability tests were developed and widely used in public schools and in colleges and universities. Names of particular importance in test development were David Brace and C.H. McCloy.

The Progressive Education Movement (1930s), frequently characterized as teach what the child wants to learn, had a significant impact on both education and physical education. Physical educators began to concentrate on making the curriculum fun. This resulted in questionnaire research designed to discover what children liked to do. However, a statement by C.H. McCloy (1960, p. 91) seemed to put everything into perspective:

> I hope the next fifty years will cause physical education to . . . seek for facts, proved objectively; to question principles based on average opinions of people who don't know but are all anxious to contribute their average ignorance to form a consensus of uninformed dogma.

As testing became more popular in the schools during the 1930s, the use of true-false knowledge tests for physical education activities increased considerably. With the advent of new statistical techniques, both physical and knowledge tests were provided with increased scientific rigor and standards for physical education. However, sometimes the emphasis upon numbers got out of hand:

> We lived in one long orgy of tabulation . . . Mountains of fact were piled up, condensed, summarized and interpreted by the new quantitative technique. The air was full of normal curves, standard deviations, coefficients of correlation, regressive equations. (Rugg, 1941, p. 182)

The outbreak of World War II brought renewed interest in physical fitness as large numbers of the men drafted did not meet minimum standards for physical fitness. In fact, one third of the men examined were found unfit for service, and even those accepted generally lacked adequate levels of physical fitness. Many physical education leaders were placed in roles in which they were responsible for the testing and conditioning of servicemen. Thus, a considerable number of advances were made in both testing and training in exercise physiology.

World War II also led to the development of the area known today as motor learning and control. Many psychologists were involved in the development of training programs for pilots. The motor coordination involved in learning to control an airplane is considerable and led to many studies of motor skill performance and learning. Unfortunately, when the war ended, most of the interest in motor skill acquisition was lost as experimental psychologists returned to their interest in cognitive performance.

The 1950s brought a renewed interest in physical fitness. The 1953 publication of the Kraus-Weber test results revealed the poor record of American children when compared to European children. While the test does not assess many of the factors considered important in fitness today (e.g., cardiovascular endurance, strength), the fact that nearly 60% of the American children failed compared to less than 9% of the European children attracted national attention. As a result, President Eisenhower called a special White House Conference in 1956. This conference and several subsequent ones led to the establishment of the President's Council on Youth Fitness and the development of the AAHPERD Fitness Test. This emphasis gave a considerable boost to research in exercise physiology and tests and measurements.

Beginning in the 1960s, research in physical education began to expand rapidly. Franklin Henry's (Henry & Rogers, 1960) historic memory drum theory launched a renewed interest in motor learning and control. Henry (1964) contributed still further to the promotion of research with his paper about physical education being a discipline. This led to the identification of a knowledge base for physical education frequently called human movement. Research expanded dramatically as exercise physiology, biomechanics, motor learning and control, motor development, sports psychology, and sport sociology began to produce knowledge about movement. The *Research Quarterly* was expanded and new journals such as *Medicine and Science in Sport* and the *Journal of Motor Behavior* began publication.

The 1970s saw a continued interest in research in the discipline of human movement, but renewed interest evolved in research within the professional base of physical education. Observational techniques were developed and refined that allowed accurate assessment of teaching behavior and student-teacher interaction. The area of classroom observation called "research on teaching" in education was developed for use in the gymnasium and playing fields in physical education. Research on curriculum theory in physical education, measurement and evaluation, and the history of sport and physical education received renewed attention.

Many researchers from the discipline of human movement began to establish specific professional groups outside of the traditional affiliations these researchers had held in the American Alliance for Health, Physical Education, Recreation, and Dance. Such groups as the American College of Sports Medicine, North American Society for Sport History, North American Society for the Psychology of Sport and Physical Activity, and several others became major contributors to the research base. AAHPERD responded to these inroads into membership and activities with the creation of various academies, elevation of the Research Consortium to the research arm of the Alliance, and an increased focus on and name change of *Research Quarterly* to *Research Quarterly for Exercise and Sport*. The first issue under the new name was the 50th anniversary issue (Safrit, 1980) where the editor and the advisory committee had solicited papers from the various subdisciplines in physical education: biomechanics, exercise physiology, psychology of sport, measurement and research design, sociology of sport, motor development, and motor behavior.

This increased emphasis upon research in both the discipline of human movement and the professional base of physical education can only lead to higher standards and more physically educated students during the 1980s. Physical education is now basing the refinement of its unique goals (development of physical fitness and development of motor skills) upon a solid knowledge of human movement and upon increased sophistication in planning and teaching physical education to children and adults.

DANCE, HEALTH EDUCATION, AND RECREATION

These three areas, which are frequently associated with physical education, all enjoy a history of their own in the United States. However, until recent years, research efforts have been sporadic and sometimes difficult to separate from physical education.

Dance has used many of the measurement techniques and paradigms for research found in physical education. For example, studies of the biomechanics of dance movements may be found in the literature. Energy expenditure for certain dances or dance techniques is reported. However, dance has also developed its own type of research (under the general label of creative research presented in Chapter 12) that involves the planning, development, and recording of original choreography. Techniques of recording movements include Laban notation, videotape, and film. Thus, while dance has a long and illustrious history of performance, formal documentation for research purposes has only been used for about 20 years.

Health education was conceived jointly with physical education from the very beginning in the United States. (Note that the name of the first college unit established at Amherst in 1854 was the Department of Hygiene and Physical Education.) However, beginning in the 1960s health education established a separate identity and began its own research programs. Clearly, school and community health education appear to function cooperatively if not always together. Researchers in school health education usually concentrate efforts on the effectiveness of behavioral programs in altering knowledge and attitudes about health problems (e.g., inappropriate drug use, obesity). Researchers in community health education have conducted many large-scale surveys identifying health problems and have sometimes attempted to intervene to actually change behaviors. In the late 1970s and early 1980s, the two areas appear to be joining efforts to create effective models for promotion of good health, opposed to past practices which have tried to remedy already existing health problems.

Recreation has been identified as being separate from physical education since the 1920s, although many of the personnel and facilities have been shared. Much of the early research was survey in nature, identifying activities and facilities people needed and wanted. Increased amounts of leisure time from 1960 onward have developed the need for more recreational services. Research efforts have also increased and branched into a variety of areas. For example, numerous studies exist about aging and leisure time use, playground development, values of recreational sports programs, as well as many other areas drawn from research paradigms in psychology and sociology.

Thus, the history of research in physical education, dance, health education, and recreation are somewhat intertwined but are also independent. One of the more creative and humorous overviews of this history is given in a short paper presented by Earle Zeigler at the AAHPER convention in St. Louis in 1968 and published in the *Journal of Health, Physical Education and Recreation* (1968).

A TALE OF TWO TITLES

> Blank, sometimes designated as __________, but who really should be called tnemevom (which is quite difficult to pronounce), has had both a glorious and a shameful existence. He is a part of the very nature of the universe. He is involved with both the animate and inanimate aspects of the cosmos. He is a basic part of the fundamental pattern of living of every creature of any type that has ever lived on earth. Early man knew he was important, but he was often not appreciated until he was gone, or almost gone. The first civilized men used him extensively in their societies, as did the Greeks and the Romans. Some used him

vigorously, but others used him carefully and methodically. He was used gracefully by some, ecstatically by others, rigorously by many when the need was urgent, and regularly by most who wanted to get the job done. He was called many things in various tongues. But strangely enough, he was never fully understood.

The time came when he was considered less important in life, although people still admired him on innumerable occasions. Some seemed to understand him instinctively, while others had great difficulty in employing him well. He was eventually degraded to such an extent that well-educated people often did not think that he had an important place in their background and preparation for life. Many gave lip service to the need for him, but then would not give him his due. Others appreciated his worth, but felt that he was less important than many aspects of education. But he persisted despite the onset of an advanced technological age. Some called him calisthenics. Others called him physical training. A determined group called him gymnastics. A few called him physical culture, but they turned out to be men of ill repute. Others felt that he had been neglected in the preparation of man for life. So, they did him a favor and called him physical education.

He prospered to a considerable degree with this name, although it caused him some embarrassment because it classified him as a second-class citizen. But he struggled on. Then a strange thing happened. As a result of this modicum of prosperity, he developed offshoots. (Two of his brothers had, of course, been with him for thousands of years. They were known as dance and athletics.) One offshoot was known as recreation; another was called health and safety education. Our hero helped them develop and they, in their gratitude, helped him too.

Then one day after some great wars and other strong social forces had their influence on society, physical education, who was still a second-class citizen among educators, discovered that his offshoots had grown large and important in the world. They were anxious to become first-class citizens, and they made loud noises on occasion to inform all men that they deserved priority in life—and men recognized that they were right. But times change slowly, and the education of men was not yet greatly affected by this recognition.

At the same time physical education received another shock. His brothers, athletics and dance, had somehow grown strong and powerful as well. Athletics (and sport) looked at him and said, "What a dull clod art thou!" What athletics meant was that physical education, or blank, or __________, or tnemevom (which is quite difficult to pronounce), wasn't very exciting, as it usually involved dull exercises which promoted muscular strength and cardiovascular efficiency. Sadly enough, his other brother, dance, seemed to feel the same way. He proclaimed that he was an art, and he wanted to join his brother arts who were quite respectable, although at times a bit odd.

Physical education, or blank, or __________, or tnemevom felt very sad, and he became worried. He looked back at his long heritage, and he recounted to himself the tale that has just been told to you. He felt important—at least to himself. He figured that he had been misjudged, since his motives were pure. He wondered if he had been stupid, because people often seemed to treat him as such. He knew that all people still needed him (hadn't a great president been shocked by his absence?) but his very name—physical education—made many seemingly intelligent people's lips curl. What should he do?

And then he began to think deeply. His identical twin sister, the lowly female creature who was really part of him (but who often made different noises as she went her own way), had been telling him for some time that he couldn't see the forest for the trees. She said "Physical education, blank, sometimes designated as __________, but who really should be called tnemevom (which is quite difficult to pronounce), we have really been fools and we merit our plight. We have been so stupid that we haven't been able to spell what we really should have been called. We have been spelling it backwards."

With a rising sense of elation, tnemevom came to life all at once. He saw the light, as explained to him by his identical twin sister. He took a deep breath, tensed his muscles, and executed a back somersault with a half twist. He assumed a new dignity almost immediately as he realized that he now had a new name (that was quite simple to pronounce) and it was MOVEMENT! From that day forward, he vowed to carry out his function purposefully. He recognized that he could still relate effectively to his brothers and to his offshoots, as well as to his own identical twin sister. But, more importantly, he realized that there was more to him than push-ups and jogging, as truly important as these parts of him might be. He sensed that he had physiological aspects, anatomical aspects, historical aspects, philosophical aspects, psychological aspects, sociological aspects, and so many other aspects that he couldn't count them on the fingers of his two hands.

This was an important realization for MOVEMENT, but he didn't rush off blindly to proclaim his glory to the world. He had learned his lesson. This time he would spell his name correctly, and he would rest his case for recognition on a sound scientific base. He looked around for his twin sister (that lowly female creature who was really part of him) and said, "It's a hard road that lies ahead, but together we will traverse it. If we deserve to reach the goal we have dreamed of we may get there someday. But let's not debate the issue for long since the sun is already quite high in the sky."[2]

THE RESEARCH PROCESS

IDENTIFYING THE RESEARCH PROBLEM

The identification of a research problem is one of many major issues facing the graduate student. Problems may arise from real-world settings or be generated from theoretical frameworks. Regardless, a basic requirement for proposing a good research problem is in-depth knowledge about the area of interest. To some extent, this seems ironic because the research methods course is typically taken in the first semester (or quarter) of graduate school before the student has had the opportunity to acquire the necessary in-depth knowledge. The usual result is that research problems selected are trivial, lack a theoretical base, and frequently only replicate earlier research. While this is a considerable shortcoming, the advantages of taking the research methods course early in the program are substantial with regard to success in other graduate courses because the student learns

- to approach and solve problems in a scientific way;
- to search the literature;
- to write in a clear scientific fashion;
- to understand basic measurement and statistical issues;
- to use an appropriate writing style;
- to be an intelligent consumer of research; and
- to appreciate the wide variety of research strategies and techniques used in HPERD.

How, then, does a student without much background select a problem? It seems that the harder you try to think of a topic, the more you are inclined to think that all of the problems in the field have already been solved. Adding to this frustration is the pressure of time.

To help alleviate the topic-finding problem, we offer the following suggestions: One is to be aware of the research being done at your institution, for research spawns other research ideas. Often, a researcher will have a series of studies planned. Another suggestion is to be alert for any controversial issues in some area of interest. Lively controversy prompts research in efforts to resolve the

---

From "A Tale of Two Titles" by E.F. Zeigler, 1968, *Journal of Health, Physical Education and Recreation*, **39**, p. 53, AAHPERD, Reston, VA. Reprinted with permission.

TABLE 1.2

CRITERIA IN SELECTING A RESEARCH PROBLEM

1. *Workability.* Is the contemplated study within the limits and range of your resource and time constraints? Will you have access to the necessary sample in the numbers required? Is there reason to believe you can come up with an "answer to the problem"? Is the required methodology manageable and understandable?

2. *Critical mass.* Is the problem of sufficient magnitude and scope to fulfill the requirement that has motivated the study in the first place? Are there enough variables? enough potential results? enough to write about?

3. *Interest.* Are you interested in the problem area, specific problem, and potential solution? Does it relate to your background? to your career interest? Does it "turn you on"? Will you learn useful skills from pursuing it?

4. *Theoretical value.* Does the problem fill a gap in the literature? Will others recognize its importance? Will it contribute to advancement in your field? Does it improve the "state of the art"? Is it publishable?

5. *Practical value.* Will the solution to the problem improve educational practice? Are practitioners likely to be interested in the results? Will education be changed by the outcome? Will your own educational practices be likely to change as a result?

Note. From *Conducting educational research* (2nd ed.) (pp. 24-25) by B.W. Tuckman, 1978, New York: Harcourt Brace Jovanovich. Reprinted with permission.

issue. In any case, be sure to talk to professors and advanced graduate students in your area of interest and use their suggestions to focus upon a topic. Then locate and read a review paper (possibly in a review journal, in a research journal, or in a recent textbook). From there, read several of the research studies on the reference list of the review paper and locate other more current research papers on the topic. Using all this information, list either research questions that appear unanswered or logical extensions of the material you have read. At that point, apply the criteria for choosing a problem as listed in Table 1.2.

Of course, no single problem will necessarily meet all of the criteria perfectly. For example, some theoretical problems may have limited direct application; however, theoretical problems should be directed toward issues that may ultimately prove useful to practitioners. By honestly answering the questions in this table, a practical evaluation of the selected problem is possible.

INDUCTIVE AND DEDUCTIVE REASONING

The means for identifying specific research problems comes from two methods of reasoning: *inductive* and *deductive*. Figure 1.3 provides a schema of the inductive-reasoning process.

Individual observations are tied together into specific hypotheses. These hypotheses are grouped into more general explanations which are united into theory. To move from the level of observations to theory requires many individual studies that test specific hypotheses. But even beyond the individual studies, someone

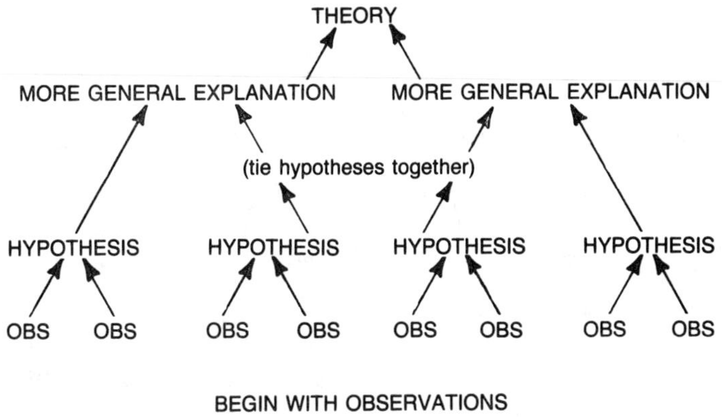

Figure 1.3 Inductive reasoning. From *A student guide for educational research* (2nd edition), p. 22, by R.L. Hoenes and B.S. Chissom, 1975, Statesboro, GA: Vog Press. Reprinted with permission.

must see how all the findings relate and offer a theoretical explanation that encompasses all the individual findings.

An example of this process can be found in the motor learning and control area. In 1971, Adams proposed a *closed loop* theory of motor skill learning. Basically, a closed loop theory is one in which information received as feedback from a movement is compared to some internal reference of correctness (assumed to be stored in memory); then the discrepancies between the movement and the intended movement are noted; and, finally, the next attempt at the movement is adjusted to approximate the movement goal more nearly. Adams' theory was developed to tie together many previous observations about movement response. The theory was tightly reasoned but limited to slow-positioning responses. This limitation really makes it a "more general explanation" according to Figure 1.3. In 1975, Schmidt proposed a *schema* theory which extended Adams' reasoning to include more rapid types of movements, frequently called *ballistic tasks*. Schema theory also deals with several other limitations of Adams' theory that are not important to our discussion here. The point is that schema theory proposed to unify two more general explanations, one about slow movements and the other about ballistic (rapid) movements, under one theoretical explanation—clearly an example of inductive reasoning.

However, reasoning must be careful, logical, and causal, otherwise one of our examples of inappropriate induction (Thomas, 1980, p. 267) may result:

> A researcher spent several weeks training a cockroach to jump. The bug became well trained and would leap high in the air on the command "Jump." The researcher then began to manipulate his independent variable which was to remove the bug's legs one at a time. Upon removing the first leg, the researcher said "Jump," and the bug did. He then removed the second, third, fourth, and fifth leg and said "Jump" after each leg was removed, and the bug jumped every time. Upon removing

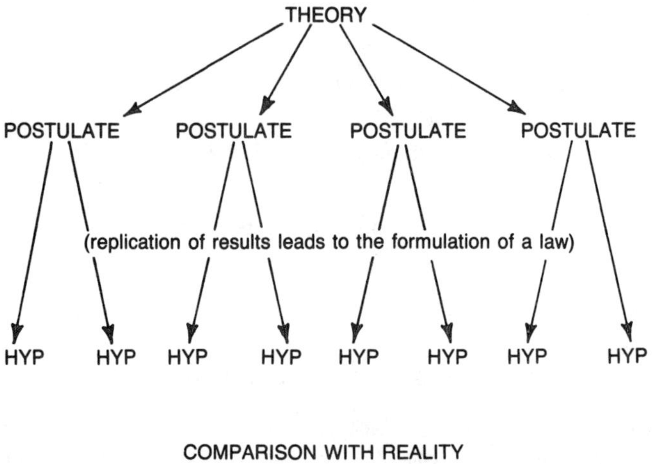

Figure 1.4 Deductive reasoning. From *A student guide for educational research* (2nd edition), p. 23, by R.L. Hoenes and B.S. Chissom, 1975, Statesboro, GA: Vog Press. Reprinted with permission.

> the sixth leg and giving the "Jump" command, the bug just lay there. The researcher's conclusion from this research was: "When all the legs are removed from a cockroach, the bug becomes deaf."

In Figure 1.4 a model of deductive reasoning is presented. Deductive reasoning moves from a theoretical explanation of events down to specific hypotheses which are tested against (or compared to) reality to evaluate if the hypotheses are correct. Using the previously presented notions from schema theory (to avoid explaining another theory), Schmidt advanced a hypothesis frequently called *variability of practice*. Essentially this hypothesis (reasoned or deduced from the theory) says that practice of a variety of movement experiences (within a movement class), when compared to practicing a single movement, facilitates transfer to a new movement (but still within the same class). This hypothesis, identified by deductive reasoning, has since been tested by a number of studies and found viable.

In fact, within any given study, both inductive and deductive reasoning are useful. In Figure 1.5 the total research spectrum is presented. Notice how the deductive and inductive processes operate: That is, at the beginning of a study, the researcher deduces hypotheses from relevant theories and concepts and induces hypotheses from relevant findings in other research.

A nice overview of the research methods course as well as an introduction to this book is provided in Figure 1.5. This flow chart provides a linear way to think about planning a research study. Once the problem area is identified, reading and thinking about relevant theories and concepts as well as a careful search of

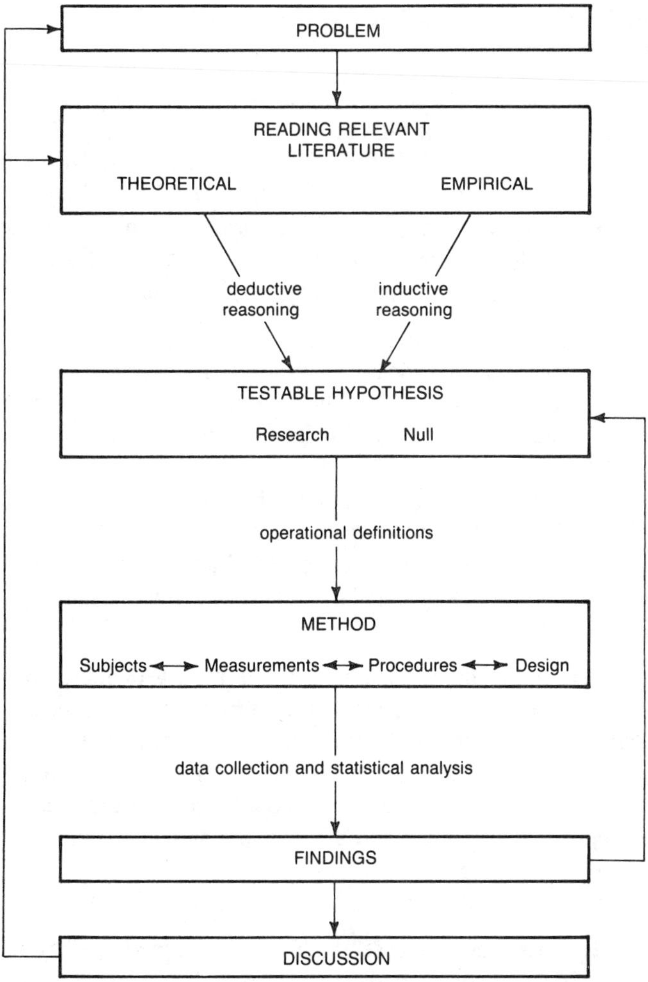

Figure 1.5 The total research setting.

the literature for relevant findings leads to the specification of hypotheses. Operational definitions are needed in a research study so that the reader knows exactly what the researcher means by certain terms. Operational definitions are observable phenomena which enable the researcher to empirically test whether or not the predicted outcomes (hypotheses) can be supported. The study is designed and the measuring devices selected and made operational; the data are collected and analyzed and the findings identified; and finally, results are related back to the original hypotheses and discussed in relation to theories, concepts, and previous research findings.

THE PARTS OF A THESIS: A REFLECTION OF THE STEPS IN THE RESEARCH PROCESS

In this chapter, you have been introduced to the research process. The theme of the chapter has been the scientific method of problem solving. Generally speaking, a thesis or research article has a rather standard format. This is for the purpose of expedience in that the reader knows where to find the different information such as purpose, methods, and results. The format also reflects the steps in the scientific method of problem solving. Let's look at a typical thesis format and see how the chapters account for the steps in the scientific method.

Chapter 1. Introduction. In the first chapter, the problem is defined and delimited. The researcher specifically identifies the problem and states the research hypotheses. Certain terms critical to the study are operationally defined for the reader and limitations are acknowledged as well as perhaps some basic assumptions.

The literature review may be in the first chapter, or it may warrant a separate chapter. When it is in the first chapter, it more closely adheres to the steps in the scientific method of problem solving. The literature review is instrumental in the formulation of hypotheses and the deductive reasoning leading to the statement of the problem.

Chapter 2. Method. Often, Chapter 2 is the review of literature. However, because the purpose here is to make the thesis format parallel to the data-gathering steps, Chapter 2 relates to the scientific method. First, the researcher explains how the data were gathered. The subjects are identified; the measuring instruments are described; the measurement and treatment procedures are presented; the experimental design is explained; and the methods of analyzing the data are summarized. The major purpose of the method chapter is to describe the study in such detail and with such clarity that you could duplicate it.

Chapter 3. Results. The results section presents the pertinent findings from the analysis of the data. It corresponds to the step in the scientific method in which the results are scrutinized as to their meaningfulness and their reliability.

Chapter 4. Discussion and Conclusions. In this last step in the scientific method, the researcher employs inductive reasoning in an effort to analyze the findings, to compare these findings with previous studies, and to integrate them into a theoretical model. In this chapter (step), the research hypotheses are judged as to their acceptability. Then on the basis of the analysis and discussion, conclusions are usually made. The conclusions should address the purpose and subpurposes that were specified in the first chapter or step.

Chapter 2

Using the Literature in Developing the Problem

THE LITERATURE REVIEW

Reviews of literature serve many purposes. Frequently, they are used as a basis for inductive reasoning. A scholar may seek to locate and synthesize all the relevant literature on a particular topic in order to develop a "more general explanation" or a theory to explain certain phenomena. An interesting new way of analyzing the literature, mentioned in Chapter 1, meta-analysis (Glass, McGraw, & Smith, 1981), will be discussed in some detail in Chapter 9 on Analytical Research.

The major problem of literature reviews is "How can all those studies be related to each other in an effective way?" Most frequently, authors will attempt to relate studies by similarities/differences in theoretical frameworks, problem statements, methodologies (subjects, instruments, treatments, designs, and statistical analyses), and findings. Then results are determined by "vote counting." For example, from the eight studies with similar characteristics, five found no significant difference between the treatments; thus, this treatment has no consistent effect.

This procedure is most easily accomplished through use of a summary sheet (see Table 2.1 as an example). This table could be used to relate the frequency and intensity of exercise to the percentage of change in body fat. The conclusion from looking at these studies might be that exercising 3 days/week, 20 minutes per day for 10-14 weeks at 70% of maximum heart rate produces moderate losses of body fat (4-5%). However, more frequent exercise bouts produce minimal increases, but less frequent or intense exercise decreases the fat loss substantially. Techniques of this type lend themselves to the development of the literature review around central themes or topics. Not only does this approach allow synthesis of the relevant findings, but it also makes the literature review interesting to read.

TABLE 2.1
SAMPLE FORM FOR SYNTHESIZING STUDIES
(A HYPOTHETICAL EXAMPLE)

	Characteristics of Studies				
Studies	Problem Statement	Subject Description	Instruments	Procedures and Design	Finding
Smith 1974	Effects of exercise on body fat	30 college age males	Underwater weighing	Exercise 3 days /wk at 70% of (220 – age) for 12 wks	4% reduction in body fat
Johnson 1978	Effects of exercise on body fat	45 college age males	Underwater weighing	Jog 3 days/wk at 70% or 50% of (220 – age) for 10 wks	5% for 70% gp 2% for 50% gp
Andrews 1979	Effects of frequent and intense exercise on body fat	36 college age males	Skinfold calipers	Jog 2, 4, 6 days /wk at 75% of (220 – age) for 12 wks	1% for 2 days 4% for 4 days 5% for 6 days
Mitchell 1980	Effects of work load on body fat	24 high school males	Skinfold calipers	Peddled at 30, 45, 60 RPM with 2 kp resistance/20 min/3 day/wk/ 14 wks	1% at 30 RPM 3% at 45 RPM 4% at 60 RPM

IDENTIFYING THE PROBLEM

As discussed in Chapter 1, the literature review is useful in identifying the specific problem. Of course, the first task, after locating a series of studies, is to decide which studies are related to the topic area. This can frequently be accomplished by reading the abstract and, if necessary, some specific parts of the paper. Once a few key studies are identified, a careful reading will usually produce several ideas and unresolved questions. The student will find it useful to discuss these questions with a professor or advanced graduate student in his or her area of specialization. Doing so can eliminate unproductive approaches or dead ends. After the problem is specified, an intensive library search process begins.

DEVELOPING HYPOTHESES

Hypotheses are deduced from theory or induced from other empirical studies and real-world observations. These hypotheses are based upon logical reasoning and, when predictive of the outcome of the study, are labeled *research hypotheses*. For example, after spending a good deal of time at registration as undergraduates, graduate students, and faculty members, we are able to put forth the following hypothesis for you to test:

> The shortest line at registration will always be the slowest. If you change lines, the one you left will speed up and the one you enter will suddenly stop.

DEVELOPING THE METHOD

While considerable work is involved in identifying the problem and specifying hypotheses, one of the more creative parts of research is developing the method to test the hypotheses. If the method is planned and pilot tested appropriately, the outcome of the study will allow the hypotheses to be evaluated. *We believe that the researcher fails when the results of a study are blamed on methodological problems.* Post-hoc methodological blame results from lack of (or poor) planning and pilot work prior to undertaking the research.

The review of literature can be extremely helpful in identifying methods that have been successfully used to solve particular types of problems. Valuable elements from other studies may include the characteristics of the subjects, data collection instruments and testing procedures, treatments, designs, and statistical analyses. All or parts or combinations of previously used methodologies are quite helpful as the researcher plans the study. However, previous methodologies should not limit the researcher in designing the study. Creative methodology is a key to good hypothesis testing. However, neither other scholars' research nor creativity ever replaces the need for careful and thorough pilot work prior to the study.

THE LITERATURE SEARCH

The prospect of beginning a literature search can sometimes be frightening or depressing to some people. How and where do you begin? What kind of sequence or strategy should you use in locating relevant literature? What services does the library offer to assist you in canvassing the literature?

SEARCH STRATEGIES

Authors of research texts have advanced various strategies for finding pertinent information on a topic. There is no "right" way of doing it. The search process depends considerably on your initial familiarity with the topic. In other words, if you have virtually no knowledge about a particular topic, your starting point and sequence would be different from that of someone already quite familiar with the literature.

Haag (1979) presents a logical, comprehensive strategy, applicable to any subject area, for literature searching in physical education. This system has merit

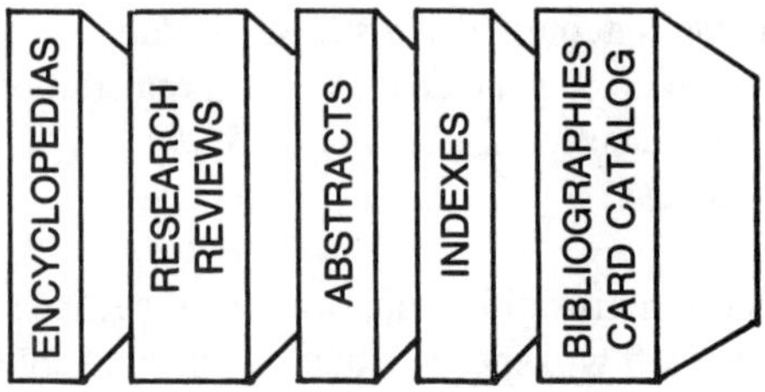

Figure 2.1 The continuum for a literature search strategy.

because it provides a search strategy for the person totally unfamiliar with the information on a subject; furthermore, those with more knowledge about the subject can "enter" the structure at different points along the continuum. In this strategy, you proceed from sources which provide an overview of information about the subject to sources which are mostly location devices. Figure 2.1 illustrates the continuum. Because topics differ and because each search has unique characteristics, you do not always proceed in the same step-by-step manner. Instead, you will often move back and forth along the continuum.

LIBRARY RESOURCES

Encyclopedias. Encyclopedias provide an overview of information on research topics and summarize knowledge about subject areas: General encyclopedias provide broad information about an entire field; and specialized encyclopedias pertain to much narrower topics, such as *The Encyclopedia of Sport Sciences and Medicine, The Encyclopedia of Physical Fitness,* and the *Encyclopedia of Physical Education, Fitness, and Sports*.

Because of a rather lengthy period (years) from the time the authors submit their contributions until the publication date, you should be aware that the information in an encyclopedia is dated. Still, you can get important background information about a subject and become familiar with basic terms and note references to some of the pertinent research journals.

Reviews of Research. Reviews of research are an excellent source of information for three reasons: (a) some knowledgeable person has spent a great deal of time and effort in canvassing the latest literature on the topic; (b) the author has not only located the relevant literature but has also *critically* reviewed and synthesized it into an integrated summarization of what is known about the area; and (c) the reviewer often suggests areas of needed research, which the graduate student greatly appreciates.

Some actual review publications are the *Annual Reviews of Medicine*, the *Annual Review of Psychology*, the *Review of Educational Research, Physiological Reviews*, the *Psychological Review*, the *Recreation Review*, the *College Health Review*, the *Annual Review of Public Health*, and *Exercise and Sport Science Reviews*.

The AAHPERD publishes a number of reviews: One is a series called *What Research Tells the Coach* and is about different sports such as baseball, football, sprinting, distance running, swimming, tennis, and wrestling; two other series are *What Research Says to the Recreation Practitioner* and *Kinesiology Reviews I, II, and III*. Many other research journals regularly publish reviews and some occasionally devote entire issues to research reviews.

Abstracts. Concise summaries of research studies are valuable sources of information in the literature search on a topic. Abstracts of papers presented at research meetings are available at national, district, and most state conventions. *Abstracts of Research Papers* is also sold through AAHPERD Publications.

Completed Research in Health, Physical Education, Recreation and Dance, a publication sponsored by the Research Consortium of the AAHPERD, publishes hundreds of abstracts of theses and dissertations each year. In addition to the abstracts, it contains a bibliography section of titles of research articles from over 160 periodicals.

Other abstract sources are *Dissertation Abstracts International* which contains abstracts of dissertations from a large majority of the colleges and universities in the United States, and the *Index and Abstracts of Foreign Physical Education Literature* which provides abstracts from journals outside the United States. Furthermore, there are sources of abstracts in related fields such as *Biological Abstracts, Psychological Abstracts, Sociological Abstracts*, and *Resources in Education (RIE)*, which is a part of the ERIC system.

Microform Publications, a project conducted by the College of Human Development and Performance at the University of Oregon, provides a special type of resource to researchers in HPERD. The emphasis is placed on producing unpublished research materials on microfiche, particularly dissertations and theses, as well as scholarly books and journals now out of print.

Indexes. There are several indexes which provide references to magazine and journal articles concerning specific topics. Some of the indexes which are commonly used in HPERD are the *Current Index to Journals in Education (CIJE)*, which is part of ERIC, *Index Medicus, Education Index, Reader's Guide to Periodical Literature, New York Times Index*, and the *Physical Education Index*. Despite the title, this last source provides a comprehensive subject index to domestic and foreign periodicals in the fields of dance, health education, recreation, sports, physical therapy, and sportsmedicine.

ERIC. We have mentioned ERIC with regard to abstracts and the *Resources in Education (RIE)* and the *Current Index to Journals in Education (CIJE)*. ERIC stands for Educational Resources Information Center and is an information system that collects, sorts, classifies, and stores thousands of documents on various topics concerning education and related fields.

The basic indexes of ERIC are the *RIE* and the *CIJE*. Besides containing the abstracts, *RIE* provides information on how you can obtain an article: whether you can purchase it on microfilm, order an ERIC copy, or request the original copy from the publisher. The *RIE* and the *CIJE* provide valuable assistance in the search for information on specific topics. In addition, ERIC produces a *Thesaurus* containing thousands of index terms which can be used in locating references and in conducting a computer search for information.

Bibliographies. Bibliographies list books and articles relevant to specific topics. They come in many different forms as to how the information is listed. Basically, all contain the author(s), title of book or article, journal name, and publishing information. Some bibliographies are annotated meaning that a brief description of the nature and scope of the article or book is included with each reference.

The bibliography of a recent study on the topic in question is an invaluable aid to the researcher. Some authors have made the statement that one of the most valuable, if not the most valuable, contributions of a dissertation is the review of literature and bibliography. However, you cannot simply "lift" the literature review from a previous study. Just because someone else has reviewed pertinent sources doesn't relieve you from the responsibility of reading each of the sources and of making an evaluation yourself. Keep in mind the following two things: (a) The previous author may have been careless and cited the source(s) incorrectly; and (b) the previous author may have taken the results of a study out of context or from a different point of view than the original author's or than your own. We have found incorrect bibliographic entries on numerous occasions.

A good search strategy is to look for the most recent sources of information and work backward. You will save much time by consulting the most recent studies, profiting from the searches of others.

Some examples of bibliographies are *Annotated Bibliography on Movement Education, Completed Research in Health, Physical Education, Recreation and Dance, Bibliography of References for Intramural and Recreational Sports, Bibliography of Research Involving Female Subjects, Research in Dance, Bibliography on Perceptual Motor Development, Health Education Completed Research, Annotated Bibliography in Physical Education, Recreation and Psychomotor Function of Mentally Retarded Persons*, and *Social Sciences of Sports*.

Card Catalog. Use the card catalog when you are looking for a specific title or author. The card catalog immediately identifies if the work is available and, if so, its location in the library.

SOME PERIODICALS IN HPERD

Within the last 20 years, the number of periodicals available in the fields of HPERD has increased tremendously. More specialization within the fields is one reason for this increase, the so-called "generalist" giving way to the specialist.

Consequently, the vast amount of research and development of new knowledge about the special areas of interest has led to new audiences with common interests. Following is a compilation of many journals in the fields of health, physical education, recreation, and dance.

References in Health Education

Annual Review of Public Health
Archives of Sexual Behavior
Chemical Newsletter
Child Study Journal
College Health Review
Death Education
Educational Gerontology
Health Education
International Journal of the Addictions
International Journal of Health Education
Journal of American College Health Association
Journal of the American Medical Association (JAMA)
Journal of American School Health Association
Journal of Environmental Health
Journal of Mental Deficiency Research
M.D.
Physician and Sports Medicine
Research in Community and Mental Health
Research Quarterly for Exercise and Sport
Royal Society of Health Journal
Society of Public Health Education Monographs

References in Physical Education

Acta Physiologica Scandinavica
Adapted Physical Activity Quarterly
American Corrective Therapy Journal
American Journal of Physical Anthropology
American Journal of Physical Medicine
American Journal of Physiology
American Journal of Sports Medicine
Athletic Administration
Athletic Training
Australian Journal of Sports Medicine
British Journal of Physical Education

British Journal of Sports Medicine
Canadian Journal of History of Sport and Physical Education
Child Development
Educational and Psychological Measurement
Human Factors
International Journal of Sport Biomechanics
International Journal of Sport Sociology
Journal of Applied Physiology
Journal of Biomechanics
Journal of Comparative and Physiological Psychology
Journal of Educational Psychology
Journal of Experimental Psychology
Journal of Learning Disabilities
Journal of Motor Behavior
Journal of Physical Education
Journal of Physical Education, Recreation and Dance
Journal of Physiology
Journal of Sport History
Journal of Sports Medicine and Physical Fitness
Journal of Sport Psychology
Journal of Teaching Physical Education
Journal of the Philosophy of Sport
Medicine and Science in Sport and Exercise
Perceptual and Motor Skills
Physical Educator
Physical Therapy
Physician and Sportsmedicine
Physiological Reviews
Psychological Reviews
Psychology in the Schools
The Olympian
Quest
Research Quarterly for Exercise and Sport
Sociological Abstracts
Sociology of Sport Journal

References in Recreation

Journal of Leisure Research
Journal of Physical Education, Recreation and Dance
Leisure Sciences
Managing the Leisure Facility
National Parks and Conservation Magazine
Outdoor Recreation Action
Park Maintenance
Parks and Recreation
Recreation Management
Recreation Review
Research Quarterly for Exercise and Sport
Therapeutic Recreation Journal

References in Dance

CORD
Dance Magazine
Dance Observer
Dance Perspectives
Dance Research Annual
Dance Research Journal
Dancing Times
Research Quarterly for Exercise and Sport

Additional Dance References

Drama Review
Horizon
The New Yorker
Saturday Review
Tulane Drama Review
Village Voice

COMPUTER SEARCHING

If computer service facilities are available, the literature search can be greatly expedited. Automated searching provides a more effective and efficient access to indexes and information than does manual searching. There is a fee for a computer search, and the more extensive the search, the more costly. However, the fee usually isn't prohibitive, especially if the searcher is careful in selecting pertinent descriptors and in limiting the number of most recent and relevant documents.

ERIC provides a computer search. The *Thesaurus of ERIC Descriptors* contains all descriptors that ERIC uses. A listing of all titles in the file classified according to a given set of descriptors can be provided by the computer search. Remember, a computer search cannot judge or screen as to quality, which again relates to the selection of a number of descriptors for simultaneous searching.

Today, more and more colleges and universities have access to some sort of computer retrieval systems. Data bases are predominantly in the sciences and social sciences. Numerous data bases are available; among the most common are the Lockheed Information Systems, the System Development Corporation, Bibliographic Retrieval Services, and the National Library of Medicine.

Most data bases are machine-readable indexes which provide comprehensive bibliographies. Remember, the key to a successful literature search is careful planning. Therefore, succinctly write down your statement of the problem and then formulate cogent descriptors and key indexing terms. Printed indexes and abstracts are helpful in this regard. It is also beneficial to find one or more journal articles pertaining to your topic to assist you in the search strategy.

Searches are scheduled through your library. You will complete a form on which you specify the research statement and keywords (descriptors). The library personnel will be extremely helpful in the literature search process, which usually takes about a week. The resulting bibliography, in most cases, is well worth the expense, especially in light of the comprehensiveness and in the short amount of time and energy you expend.

OTHER LIBRARY SERVICES

The library services available obviously depend mostly on the size of the institution in that larger schools generally provide more financial support for the library. However, some relatively small institutions have excellent library resources which provide outstanding support for the institutional and research aspects of the school.

Besides the usual services of card catalogs, reference department, circulation department, bibliographic collection and stack areas, libraries also offer resources and services such as copy services, interlibrary loan (where materials may be borrowed from other libraries), newspaper rooms, microform files and "readers," government document sections, and many other special features and services.

Many libraries offer guided tours, short courses for orientation to the library, or self-guided tour information. Get acquainted with your library: It will be the wisest investment of time spent as a graduate student.

USE OF THE MICROCOMPUTER FOR LITERATURE STORAGE AND RETRIEVAL

In addition to the vast and versatile library resources and services, the reader should be aware of the capabilities of microcomputers for storing bibliographic entries, abstracts, and even reprints of studies. A number of commercial programs are available for this purpose. The information can be retrieved by the use of pertinent keywords. Additions, changes, and deletions are easily accomplished, and hundreds of items can be stored on a single disk. Each new entry is automatically stored in alphabetical order, and the complete bibliography is always instantly accessible.

READING THE LITERATURE

Collecting all the related literature is a major undertaking, but the next step is even more time consuming—you must read, understand, and record the relevant information from the literature, keeping in mind the famous (anonymous) quote:

> No matter how many years you save an item, you will never need it until after you have thrown it away.

Without question the person originating this quote was a researcher working on a literature review. You may count on the fact that if you throw away one note from your literature search, that paper will be cited incorrectly in your text or reference list; or if you throw away your notes on an article because you don't believe it is relevant to your research, your major professor, a committee member, or the journal to which you submit the paper will request inclusion of the article. Then when you go back to locate the article in the library, either it will be ripped out of the journal, the whole journal will be missing, or a professor will have checked it out, never to return it (and the librarian will not reveal the professor's name). Therefore, when you find a particular paper, take careful and complete notes including accurate and exact citation information.

To help you understand the literature you read, Table 2.2, "A Key to Scientific Research Literature," lists each scientific phase. Once you understand what each scientific phase really means, you should have little difficulty in understanding the literature you read.

In particular, you, as researcher, should note the following information from your research:

- Statement of the problem (and maybe hypotheses)
- Characteristics of the subjects
- Instruments and/or tests used (including reliability and validity information, if provided)
- Testing procedures
- Independent and dependent variables
- Treatments applied to subjects (if experimental study)
- Design and statistical analyses

- Findings
- Questions raised for further study
- Check for citations to other relevant studies not located.

TABLE 2.2

A KEY TO SCIENTIFIC RESEARCH LITERATURE

What He Said	What He Meant
1. It has long been known that . . .	I haven't bothered to look up the original reference but . . .
2. Of great theoretical and practical importance . . .	Interesting to me . . .
3. While it has not been possible to provide definite answers to those questions . . .	The experiment didn't work out, but I figured I could at least get a publication out of it.
4. The W-PO system was chosen as especially suitable to show the predicted behavior . . .	The fellow in the next lab had some already made up.
5. Three of the samples were chosen for detailed study . . .	The results on the others didn't make sense.
6. Accidentally strained during mounting . . .	Dropped on the floor.
7. Handled with extreme care throughout the experiment . . .	Not dropped on the floor.
8. Typical results are shown . . .	The best results are shown.
9. Agreement with the predicted curve	
is: excellent	fair
good	poor
satisfactory	doubtful
fair	imaginary
10. It is suggested that . . . It is believed that . . . It may be that . . .	I think
11. It is generally believed that . . .	A couple of other guys think so too.
12. It is clear that much additional work will be required before a complete understanding . . .	I don't understand it.
13. Unfortunately, a quantitative theory to account for these results has not been formulated . . .	Neither does anybody else.
14. Correct with an order of magnitude . . .	Wrong
15. Thanks are due to Joe Glotz for assistance with the experiments and to John Doe for valuable discussion.	Glotz did the work and Doe explained what it meant.

Furthermore, when studies are particularly relevant to the proposed research, make a photocopy. Include the *complete citation* on the title page (if the journal does not provide this, write in the citation yourself). Also, indicate the studies that are photocopied on a note card.

Another of the more useful ways to learn to read and to understand related literature is to critique a few studies. Table 2.3 includes a series of questions to use when critiquing a study. Table 2.4 is a sample form that we use and includes suggestions for reporting critiques. A few critiquing attempts should aid you in focusing on the important information contained in research studies.

TABLE 2.3

CRITERIA FOR CRITIQUING A RESEARCH PAPER

A. Overall (most important)
   1. Is the paper a significant contribution to knowledge about the area?
B. Introduction and Review of Literature
   1. Is the research plan developed within a reasonable theoretical framework?
   2. Is current and relevant research cited and properly interpreted?
   3. Is the statement of the problem clear, concise, testable, and derived from the theory and research reviewed?
C. Method
   1. Are relevant subject characteristics described and are the subjects appropriate for the research?
   2. Is the instrumentation appropriate?
   3. Are testing/treatment procedures described in sufficient detail?
   4. Are the statistical analyses and research design sufficient?
D. Results
   1. Do the results evaluate the stated problem?
   2. Is the presentation of results complete?
   3. Are the tables and figures appropriate?
E. Discussion
   1. Are the results discussed?
   2. Are the results related back to the problem, theory, and previous findings?
   3. Is there excessive speculation?
F. References
   1. Are all references in the correct format and are they complete?
   2. Are all references cited in the text?
   3. Are all dates in the references correct and do they match the text citations?
G. Abstract
   1. Does it include: a statement of the purpose; description of subjects, instrumentation, and procedures; and a report of meaningful findings?
   2. Is the abstract the proper length?
H. General
   1. Are key words provided?
   2. Are running heads provided?
   3. Does the paper provide for use of nonsexist language, protection of human subjects, and appropriate labeling of human subjects?

TABLE 2.4
FORM FOR A CRITIQUE

I. Basic information
   1. Name of journal
   2. Publisher of journal
   3. How many articles in this issue?
   4. Are there publication guidelines for authors? Which issue?
   5. Who is editor?
   6. Is there a yearly index? Which issue?
   7. What writing style is used? (APA, Index Medicus, etc.)
   8. Complete reference in APA style for article you will review.

II. Summary of the article

III. Critique of the article
   1. Introduction and Review
   2. Method
   3. Results
   4. Discussion
   5. References
   6. Overall

IV. Attach 1 photocopy of the article

V. Information about critique
   1. It must be typed, double-spaced in APA style.
   2. Do not put it in any type of folder; just staple the pages in upper left-hand corner.
   3. Use a cover page identifying course, purpose, and yourself.
   4. Critique may not exceed 5 typewritten pages exclusive of cover page.

To summarize, the best system for recording relevant literature is probably a combination of note taking and photocopying. By using index cards (4'' x 6'' are usually big enough), the important information about most studies can be recorded and indexed by topic. Always be sure to record the complete and correct citation on the card with the appropriate citation style used by your institution (e.g., APA, Index Medicus, etc.).

WRITING THE LITERATURE REVIEW

The literature review has three basic parts: the introduction, the body of the review, and the summary and the conclusions. The introduction should explain the purpose of the review and the how and why of its organization. The body of the review should be organized around important topics. Finally, the literature review should conclude with a summary, important implications, and the direction for future research. The purpose of the review is to demonstrate that your problem needs investigation and that you have considered the value of relevant past research in developing your hypotheses and method. That is, you know and understand what other people have done and how that relates to and supports what you plan to do.

The introduction to the review (or to topical areas within the review) is *very important*. If these paragraphs are not well done and interesting, the reader may skip the entire section. Attempt to attract the reader's attention by identifying in a provocative way the important points to be covered.

The body of the literature review requires considerable attention. Relevant research must be organized, synthesized, and written in a clear, concise, and interesting way. There is no unwritten law dictating that reviews of the literature must be boring and poorly written, although we suspect graduate students work from that assumption. Part of the problem stems from graduate students' perceptions that they must find a way to make their scientific writing complex and wonderful as opposed to simple and straightforward. Apparently the rule is, Never use a short and simple word when a longer more complex one can be substituted. While Table 2.5 is humorous, Day (1979) has provided a useful aid to potential research writers. In fact, we strongly recommend Day's book, which can easily be read in 4-6 hours. It provides many excellent and humorous examples which are valuable in writing for publication and for theses/dissertations.

TABLE 2.5

WORDS AND EXPRESSIONS TO AVOID

Jargon	Preferred Usage
a majority of	most
a number of	many
accounted for by the fact	because
along the lines of	like
an order of magnitude faster	10 times faster
are of the same opinion	agree
as a consequence of	because
as a matter of fact	in fact (or leave out)
as is the case	as happens
as of this date	today
as to	about (or leave out)
at an earlier date	previously
at the present time	now
at this point in time	now
based on the fact that	because
by means of	by, with
completely full	full
definitely proved	proved
despite the fact that	although
due to the fact that	because
during the course of	during, while
elucidate	explain
end result	result

TABLE 2.5 (Cont.)

Jargon	Preferred Usage
fabricate	make
fewer in number	fewer
finalize	end
first of all	first
for the purpose of	for
for the reason that	since, because
from the point of view of	for
give rise to	cause
has the capability of	can
having regard to	about
in a number of cases	some
in a position to	can, may
in a satisfactory manner	satisfactorily
in a very real sense	in a sense (or leave out)
in case	if
in close proximity	close, near
in connection with	about, concerning
in my opinion it is not an unjustifiable assumption that	I think
in order to	to
in relation to	toward, to
in respect to	about
in some cases	sometimes
in terms of	about
in the event that	if
in the possession of	has, have
in view of	because, since
inasmuch as	for, as
initiate	begin, start
is defined as	is
it has been reported by Smith	Smith reported
it has long been known that	I haven't bothered to look up the reference
it is apparent that	apparently
it is believed that	I think
it is clear that	clearly
it is clear that much additional work will be required before a complete understanding	I don't understand it
it is doubtful that	possibly
it is evident that *a* produced *b*	*a* produced *b*
it is of interest to note that	(leave out)
it is often the case that	often
it is suggested that	I think
it is worth pointing out in this context that	note that
it may be that	I think
it may, however, be noted that	but
lacked the ability to	couldn't

TABLE 2.5 (Cont.)

Jargon	Preferred Usage
large in size	large
let me make one thing perfectly clear	a snow job is coming
militate against	prohibit
needless to say	(leave out, and consider leaving out whatever follows it)
of great theoretical and practical importance	useful
on account of	because
on behalf of	for
on the basis of	by
on the grounds that	since, because
on the part of	by, among, for
our attention has been called to the fact that	we belatedly discovered
owing to the fact that	since, because
perform	do
pooled together	pooled
prior to	before
protein determinations were performed	proteins were determined
quite unique	unique
rather interesting	interesting
red in color	red
referred to as	called
relative to	about
smaller in size	smaller
subsequent to	after
sufficient	enough
take into consideration	consider
terminate	end
the great majority of	most
the opinion is advanced that	I think
the question as to whether	whether
there is reason to believe	I think
this result would seem to indicate	this result indicates
through the use of	by, with
ultimate	last
utilize	use
was of the opinion that	believed
ways and means	ways, means (not both)
we wish to thank	we thank
whether or not	whether
with a view to	to
with reference to	about (or leave out)
with regard to	concerning, about (or leave out)
with respect to	about
with the possible exception of	except
with the result that	so that

Note. From *How to write and publish a scientific paper* (pp. 144-147) by R.A. Day, 1979, Philadelphia: ISI Press. Reprinted with permission.

In addition to removing as much jargon as possible (using Day's suggestions), scientific writing should be clear and to the point. We advocate use of the KISS Principle (Keep It Simple, Stupid) as a basic tenet for writing. Many grammatical errors can be avoided by use of simple declarative sentences. Proper syntax (the way words and phrases are put together) is the secret of successful writing. We always enjoy receiving a questionnaire which includes one or more items like the following:

> Indicate your degree of success in placing your graduate students, broken down by sex.

In questioning our graduate students, none will admit that they are, although we have observed a few professors who appear to be. The following is another excerpt of improper syntax from a thesis draft: ". . . responses pertaining to suicide and death by means of a questionnaire." We are aware that some questionnaires can be ambiguous, irrelevant, and trivial, but we had no idea they were fatal.

In Table 2.6, Day (1979) rephrases a list from the Council of Biology Editors *Newsletter* (1968). The first 10 items are Day's, but we've included a few of our own comments as well.

TABLE 2.6

THE TEN COMMANDMENTS OF GOOD WRITING—PLUS A FEW OTHERS

1. Each pronoun should agree with their antecedent.
2. Just between you and I, case is important.
3. A preposition is a poor word to end a sentence with. (Incidentally, did you hear about the streetwalker who violated a grammatical rule? She unwittingly approached a plainclothesman, and her proposition ended with a sentence.)
4. Verbs has to agree with their subjects.
5. Don't use no double negatives.
6. A writer mustn't shift your point of view.
7. When dangling, don't use participles.
8. Join clauses good, like a conjunction should.
9. Don't write a run-on sentence it is difficult when you got to punctuate it so it makes sense when the reader reads what you wrote.
10. About sentence fragments.
11. Don't use commas, which aren't necessary.
12. Its' important to use apostrophe's right.
13. Check to see if you any words out.
14. As far as incomplete constructions, they are wrong.
15. "Last but not least, lay off cliches."

As mentioned previously, the literature review should be organized around important topics. These topics serve as subheadings in the paper to direct the reader's attention. The best way to organize the topics and the information within topics is to *develop an outline*. The more carefully the outline is planned, the easier the writing will be. A good task is to select a review paper from a journal or a thesis/dissertation review of literature and construct the outline the author must have used. In looking at older theses/dissertations, the literature review tends to be a historical account, often presented in chronological order. We suggest that you *not* select one of these older studies as this style is cumbersome and usually poorly synthesized.

To write a literature review effectively, write as you like to read. No one wants to read abstracts of study after study presented in chronological order. A more interesting and readable approach is to present a concept and discuss the various findings about that concept, documenting findings by the various research reports related to it. In that manner, consensus and controversy can be identified and discussed in the literature review. More relevant and important studies can be presented in greater detail while several studies with the same outcome can be covered in one sentence.

In a thesis or dissertation the two important aspects of the literature review are *criticism* and *completeness*. The various studies should not just be presented relative to a topic, but the theoretical, methodological, and interpretative aspects of the research should be criticized—not necessarily on a study-by-study basis but rather across studies. This criticism not only demonstrates the writer's grasp of the issues, but identifies problems that should be overcome in the study you are planning. Frequently, these problems identified by criticism of the literature may provide justification for your research.

Completeness, not in the sense of the length of the review, but reference completeness, is the other important aspect of the literature review. You should demonstrate to your committee that you have located, read, and understood *all* of the related literature. Many studies may be redundant and only need appropriate citing, but they must be cited. The thesis/dissertation is your passport to graduation because it demonstrates your competence; therefore, *never fail to be thorough and complete*. This, however, applies only to the thesis/dissertation. Writing for publication or the use of alternate thesis/dissertation formats does not emphasize the thoroughness and completeness of the literature cited (note *cited*, not read). Journals do not have the necessary space and usually want the Introduction and Literature Review integrated and relatively short.

SUMMARY

There are no shortcuts to locating, reading, and indexing the literature and then writing the literature review. If you follow our suggestions, however, you can do it effectively, but much hard work is still required. A good scholar is careful and thorough. Do not depend on secondary sources because they are often incorrect. *Look it up yourself.*

No one can just sit down and write a good literature review. A carefully thought-out plan is necessary. First, outline what you propose to write, then write it, and, finally, write it again. When you are convinced that the review represents your best effort, have a knowledgeable graduate student or faculty member read it, welcoming their suggestions. Then have a friend who is not as knowledgeable read it. If your friend can understand it, then your review is probably in good shape. Of course, your research methods professor will find something wrong, or at least something he or she thinks should be different. Just remember, professors feel obligated to find errors in graduate students' work. This obligation comes from years of reading examples of unclear writing such as those depicted in Table 2.7.

TABLE 2.7
EXAMPLES OF UNCLEAR WRITING

Sentences taken from actual letters received by the Welfare Department in applications for support:

1. I am forwarding my marriage certificate and six children. I had seven but one died which was baptized on a half sheet of papers.
2. I am writing the Welfare Department to say that my baby was born two years old. When do I get my money.
3. Mrs. Jones has not had any clothes for a year and has been visited regularly by the clergy.
4. I cannot get sick pay. I have six children. Can you tell me why.
5. I am glad to report that my husband who is missing is dead.
6. This is my eighth child. What are you going to do about it.
7. Please find for certain if my husband is dead. The man I am now living with can't eat or do anything until he knows.
8. I am very much annoyed to find that you have branded by son illiterate. This is a dirty lie as I was married a week before he was born.
9. In answer to your letter, I have given birth to a boy weighing ten pounds. I hope this is satisfactory.
10. I am forwarding my marriage certificate and my three children; one of which is a mistake as you can see.
11. My husband got his project cut off two weeks ago and I haven't had any relief since.
12. Unless I get my husband's money pretty soon, I will be forced to lead an immortal life.
13. You have changed my litle boy to a girl. Will this make any difference.
14. I have no children as yet as my husband is a truck driver and works night and day.
15. In accordance with your instructions, I have given birth to twins in the enclosed envelope.
16. I want money as quick as I can get it. I have been in bed with doctor for two weeks and he doesn't do me any good. If things don't improve, I will have to send for another doctor.

PROBLEMS

Throughout this chapter we have made several suggestions for exercises that will help you in locating, synthesizing, organizing, critiquing, and writing the literature review. These suggestions are summarized below. You will need to return to various points in the chapter to read about these exercises and to refer to the necessary tables.

1. Do the library assignment (see Table 2.8).

TABLE 2.8
LIBRARY ASSIGNMENT

Choose a topic in which you are interested in the areas of health, physical education, recreation, or dance. In the sources listed below find the required information concerning your topic. Limit your selections to the past 3 years if possible. Use APA style for references (or style required by your professor).

Source	
1. *Current Index to Journals in Education (CIJE)*	1 article—author, title, periodical, date, page number(s)
2. *Reader's Guide to Periodical Literature*	1 article—author, title, periodical, date, page number(s)
3. *Completed Research in Health, Physical Education, Recreation and Dance*	1 article—in Bibliography Section—author, title, source, 1 study in Theses—author, title, periodical or school, date
4. *Cumulative Book Index*	1 book—author, title, publisher, date, number of pages, price
5. *Book Review Digest*	1 book—author, title, publisher, date
6. *Index Medicus*	1 article—author, title, periodical, date, page number(s)
7. Card catalog	1 book—author, title, publisher, date, call number
8. A thesis from your institution	1 study—author, title, date
9. A dissertation from your institution	1 study—author, title, date
10. *Health, Physical Education and Recreation Microform Publications Bulletin*	1 study—author, title, date, school
11. *Resources in Education* (*RIE*)	1 study—author, title, date, location
12. *Dissertation Abstracts International*	1 study—author, title, date, school
13. *Research Quarterly for Exercise & Sport*	1 study—author, title, date

14. Look up call numbers and library location (floor level) for each of the references listed in this chapter in your area (health, PE, etc.).
15. Get information (author, title, journal, date) from the most recent issue of 3 publications in your specific area. Try to avoid using any journal that has already been cited.

2. Critique a research study in your area of interest. Use the questions in Table 2.3 as the basis for the critique. Report the critique in the form suggested by Table 2.4.
3. Select a review paper from a journal or the literature review from a thesis/dissertation. Construct the outline the author probably used to write this paper.

Chapter 3

Defining and Delimiting the Problem

In a thesis or dissertation, the first chapter is titled *Introduction*. Its purpose is to do just that—to inform the reader about the problem being studied. There are several sections in the first chapter which serve to convey the significance of the problem and to set forth the dimensions of the particular study.

Not all thesis advisors subscribe to the same thesis format, for there is no universally accepted format. Moreover, because of the nature of the research problem, there will be differences in format. For example, a historical study would not adhere to the same exact format as an experimental study. We are merely presenting sections each with a purpose and specific characteristics typically found in a first chapter.

THE TITLE

While it may seem logical to discuss the title first, it might surprise you to learn that the choice of the title is often not determined until after the study is written. However, at the time of the proposal meeting, you must have a title, even though it may be provisional, so we will discuss it first.

The length of titles has changed, generally getting shorter. Years ago, the title was, in essence, the statement of the problem (in fact, some even threw in the methods section). Here is an example of a too lengthy title:

> An investigation of a survey and analysis of the influence of PL 94-142 on the attitudes, teaching methodology, and evaluative techniques of randomly selected male and female physical education teachers in public high schools in Cornfield County, State of Confusion.

(Note: The examples we use as representing poor practices are fictional. Frequently, they have been suggested by actual studies, but any similarity to a real study is purely coincidental.)

Simply too much information is in such a title. Day (1979, p. 9) humorously responds to this problem by reporting a conversation between two students. When one asked if the other had read a certain paper, the reply was, "Yes, I read the paper, but I haven't finished the title yet."

The purpose of the title is of course to convey the content, but this should be done as succinctly as possible; for example, *The twelve minute swim as a test for aerobic endurance in swimming* (Jackson, 1978) is a good title because it tells the reader exactly what the study is about. It defines the specific purpose, which is, the validation of the 12-minute swim, and it delimits the study to the assessment of aerobic endurance for swimmers.

However, do not go to the other extreme in striving for a short title either. A title such as *Professional preparation* is not very helpful. It does not include the field or the aspects of professional preparation that were studied. The key to the effectiveness of a short title is whether it reflects the content of the study. A title which is specific is more easily indexed and is more meaningful for a potential reader who is searching for literature on a certain topic.

Avoid waste words such as "An investigation of," "An analysis of," and "A study of," for they simply increase the length of the title, contributing nothing to the description of content. Consider this title: *A study of three teaching methods*. Half of the title consists of waste words, "A study of." The rest of the title isn't specific enough to effectively index: Teaching what? What methods?

Furthermore, always be aware of your audience. You can assume that your audience is reasonably familiar with the field, the accepted terminology, and the viable problem areas. An outsider can question the relevance and importance of studies in any field. Some titles of supposedly scholarly works are downright humorous. For a rousing good time, peruse the titles of theses and dissertations completed at a university in any given year, for example, *The phospholypid distribution in the testes of the house cricket*. How weird can you get? We are joking of course. The point is that there is a tendency to criticize studies done in other disciplines simply because the critic is ignorant about the discipline.

INTRODUCTION

The introductory portion of a thesis or research article is designed to stimulate reader's interest as to the significance of the problem. The introduction is used to acquaint the reader with the problem, provide some background and necessary information, bring out areas of needed research, and then skillfully and logically lead to the specific purpose of the study.

A good introduction requires literary skill because it should flow smoothly yet be reasonably brief. Be careful not to overwhelm the reader with technical jargon, for the reader must be able to understand the problem in order to have an interest in the solution. Therefore, an important rule is, Do not be too technical. A forceful, simple and direct vocabulary is more effective for purposes of communication than scientific jargon and worship of polysyllables. Day (1979, pp. 123-124) tells a classic story of the pitfalls of scientific jargon.

> This reminds me of the plumber who wrote the Bureau of Standards saying he had found hydrochloric acid good for cleaning out clogged drains. The Bureau wrote back "The efficacy of hydrochloric acid is indisputable, but the corrosive residue is incompatible with metallic permanence." The plumber replied that he was glad the Bureau agreed. The Bureau tried again, writing "We cannot assume responsibility for the production of toxic and noxious residues with hydrochloric acid and suggest that you use an alternative procedure." The plumber again said that he was glad the Bureau agreed with him. Finally, the Bureau wrote to the plumber "Don't use hydrochloric acid. It eats the hell out of pipes."

Audience awareness is very important. Again, you can assume that the reader is reasonably informed about the topic (or he or she probably wouldn't be reading it in the first place). However, even an informed reader needs some "refresher" background information to understand the nature of the problem, to be sufficiently interested, and to fully appreciate the author's rationale for studying the problem. You must remember that your audience has not been as completely and recently "immersed" in this particular area of research as you have been.

The introductory paragraphs must create interest in the study; thus, your writing skill and knowledge of the topic are especially valuable in the introduction. The narrative should introduce the necessary background information quickly and explain the rationale behind the study. A smooth, unified, well-written introduction should lead to the statement of the problem with such clarity that the reader could state the purpose of the study before specifically reading it.

The following introductions were selected from a research journal for their brevity of presentation (ours) as well as for their effectiveness. This is not to say that brevity, in itself, is a criterion for some topics require more comprehensive introductions than others. For example, studies developing or validating a theoretical model usually necessitate longer introductions than an applied research topic. Furthermore, theses and dissertations almost always have longer introductions than journal articles simply because of the page cost considerations in the latter.

In the following examples, some of the desirable features in an introduction such as general introduction, background information, gaps in the literature and areas of needed research and logical progression leading to the statement of the problem are specified.

Example from Blattner and Noble (1979)

General Introduction	Vertical jumping ability is of considerable importance in numerous athletic events, and coaches and physical educators have used various training methods to improve this ability. Two of the most recent training methods are isokinetic and plyometric exercises. The purported advantage of isokinetic exercises is that they allow the muscles to work at maximal force throughout the entire range of motion for each and every repetition, thereby providing a greater training stimulus. The effectiveness of such exercises in improving vertical jumping performance has been demonstrated in several studies during the past decade (Hunter, 1976; Knight & George, 1972; Tanner, 1971; Testone, 1972; Van Oteghan, 1975).
Background Information	Plyometric exercise is a relatively new concept of training that applies the specificity principle regarding the preset stretch condition of the muscle prior to explosive contraction (Wilt, 1975). The effects of plyometric exercises in increasing vertical jumping performance have been studied experimentally (Herman, 1976; Parcells,
Lead In	1976; Scoles, 1978), but no attempt has been made to determine if they are more effective than isokinetic exercises.

You should be able to state the purpose of this study at this point. What is it? Another example of an introduction is as follows:

Example from Byrd and Thomas (1983)

General Introduction	Interest in the determination of body composition in athletes and in the general population has increased in the last ten years. The two most widely used methods are anthropometric techniques and hydrostatic weighing (HW), with the latter considered the more accurate (Behnke, 1961; Buskirk, 1961). Body weight, underwater weight, and lung volume are variables which are measured to compute HW body density. Investigators have observed that a significant change in body weight alone, due to varying hydration levels, does affect the determination of body density (Girandola, Wiswell & Romero, 1977; Thomas & Etheridge, 1979).
Background Information	Previous research indicates that body weight increases due to fluid retention may occur during the normal menstrual

cycle. For example, Keates and Fitzgerald (1976) reported that a rise in leg volume occurred at midcycle in 30 females due to peripheral blood flow and venous distensibility. Weekly changes in leg volume were found in all of the cycles, the changes varying between 30 and 100 ml of water in different individuals. Bruce and Russel (1962) reported a premenstrual body weight increase which seldom exceeded 0.5 kg in 10 subjects on a fixed intake of food, water, and sodium, as well as a controlled amount of exercise. Thorn, Nelson, and Thorn (1938) noted an average weight gain of 1.0 kg during the ovulation stage of the menstrual cycle in 38 women. Therefore, the HW

Lead In

method of determining body density may have varying reliability depending on the time during the menstrual cycle when the woman is measured.

Again, see if you can write out the purpose of this study.

STATEMENT OF THE PROBLEM

The statement of the problem follows the introduction. We should point out that the review of literature is often included in the introductory section and thus precedes the statement of the problem. If this is the case, then a brief statement of the purpose should appear fairly soon in the introductory section before the review of literature.

The statement of the problem in the first example from Blattner and Noble is, *To compare the effects of isokinetic and plyometric training on the vertical jumping performance of college males*. The statement of the problem in the Byrd and Thomas study is also obvious from the introduction. The purpose was stated as being, *To determine if weight fluctuations during the menstrual cycle are great enough to affect body density and percent fat as assessed by hydrostatic weighing*.

The statement of the problem should be rather brief and to the point. However, when the study has a number of subpurposes, this is not always easily accomplished. The statement of the problem should identify the different variables in the study including the independent variable, the dependent variable, and the categorical variable (if any). Usually, some control variables can also be identified in the statement of the problem.

The independent and dependent variables have already been mentioned in Chapter 1. The independent variable is the experimental or treatment variable; it is the "cause." The dependent variable is what is measured to assess the effects of the independent variable; it is the "effect."

A *categorical* variable is sometimes referred to as a *moderator* variable (Tuckman, 1978). This variable is a kind of independent variable, except that it cannot be manipulated because it is categorized, such as to different age, race, sex, and so on. It is studied to determine whether the cause-effect relationship of the independent-dependent variables is different in the presence of the categorical variable(s).

The following is an actual study in which the independent, dependent, and categorical variables can be identified. Anshel and Marisi (1978) studied the effect of synchronized and asynchronized movement to music on endurance performance. One group performed an exercise in synchronization to background music; one group exercised with background music which was not synchronized to the pace of the exercise; and a third group exercised with no background music.

The independent variable was the background music condition. There were three levels of this variable: synchronized music, asynchronized music, and no music. The dependent variable was endurance performance which was reflected by the amount of time the subject could exercise on a cycle ergometer until exhaustion.

In this study, the endurance performances of men and women under the synchronized, asynchronized, and absence of music conditions were compared. The authors thus sought to determine whether men responded differently from women to the exercise conditions. Gender, then, represented a categorical variable. Not all studies have categorical variables. In the isokinetic-plyometric study (Blattner & Noble, 1979), referred to in the introduction, there was no categorical variable. The independent variable was type of training (one group used isokinetic exercises, one group used plyometric exercises, and the control group did not train). The dependent variable was vertical-jumping performance. If, for example, the authors thought it important to compare training effects of athletes and nonathletes, then this would be a categorical variable.

Control variables are factors which might influence the results which are kept out of the study. The researcher chooses not to assess a variable's possible effect on the relationship between the independent and dependent variables, so this variable is controlled. For example, suppose a health educator is comparing the effectiveness of different educational programs on students' attitudes toward death and dying. The age of the students might have a bearing on their responses to the programs, so the researcher controls the variable of age by having the subjects all the same age.

A control variable could become a categorical variable if the experimenter wishes to study it. In the above example, if half of the students were 10-year-olds and half were 16-year-olds, then age would be a categorical variable. Of course, other ages would be controlled.

In the study on the effects of synchronized music on endurance (Anshel & Marisi, 1978), the factor of fitness level was controlled by giving all of the subjects a physical-working capacity (PWC) test. Then, on the basis of the PWC test, each subject exercised at a workload which would bring about a heart rate of 170 bpm. Thus, even though the ergometer resistance settings would be different from subject to subject, all would be exercising at approximately the same relative workload; the differences in fitness were controlled in this manner. Another way of controlling fitness as a variable would be to test subjects on a fitness test and just select those subjects of a certain level.

Extraneous variables refer to those factors which could affect the relationship between the independent and dependent variables but which are not included or controlled. The possible influence of an extraneous variable is usually brought out in the discussion. In the Anshel and Marisi study, the authors speculated that some of the differences in the performances of men and women might be due to the reluctance of the females to really exhibit maximum effort in the presence of a male experimenter. Consequently, this would be an extraneous variable.

All of the variables will be discussed in more detail in Chapter 11. Rarely are the variables labeled as such in the actual statement of the problem. Occasionally, the researcher will identify the independent and dependent variables, but mostly these variables are just implied. One or two sentences often will be all that are necessary to state the problem. In the study by Blattner and Noble in the introduction section, the statement of the problem following the introduction was, *To compare the effects of isokinetic and plyometric training on the vertical jumping performance of college males*. We have already identified the independent and dependent variables, and we have observed that there were no categorical variables. Can you identify any control variables? If you answered age and sex, you are correct. Age was controlled by using only college-age subjects and gender was controlled by using only males.

In summary, an effectively constructed introduction leads smoothly to the purpose of the study. This purpose is expressed as the statement of the problem and should be as clear and concise as the subpurposes, or variables, allow it.

To achieve clarity in the statement of the problem, a final but important aspect you must consider is sentence structure, or syntax. For example, in the previously mentioned health education study, the statement of the problem might be, *To compare the effects of two health education programs on the expressed attitudes of high school sophomores toward death and dying*. Observe the problem faulty syntax could create in a statement structured as, *To compare the effects of two health education programs on the expressed attitudes toward death and dying of high school sophomores*. You can see where it would be difficult to get subjects for that study.

THE RESEARCH HYPOTHESIS

The formulation of hypotheses has been discussed in Chapter 1. The discussion here is about the statement of the hypotheses and the distinction between research hypotheses and the null hypothesis.

Remember, research hypotheses are the expected results. In the study by Anshel and Marisi, a research hypothesis would be that endurance performance would be enhanced by exercising to synchronized music. The introduction produces rationale for that hypothesis. Another hypothesis might be that exercise to asynchronized music would be more effective than exercising with no background music (because of the pleasurable sensory stimuli blocking the unpleasant stimuli associated with the fatiguing exercise).

As a further example, a researcher in recreation might hypothesize that white-collar workers have a more positive attitude toward the benefits of recreation than do blue-collar workers. In the example given in the first chapter, a dance teacher hypothesized that the use of videotape in the instructional program would enhance the learning of dance skills.

In contrast, the *null hypothesis* is primarily used in the statistical test for the reliability of the results. The null hypothesis says that there are no differences between treatments (or no relationship between variables); for example, any observed difference or relationship is just due to chance (see Chapter 7).

The null hypothesis is usually not the research hypothesis. Generally, the researcher expects one method to be better than others or anticipates that there will be a relationship between two variables. In other words, a person does not embark on a study if nothing is expected to happen. On the other hand, a researcher sometimes hypothesizes that one method is just as good as another. For example, in the multitude of studies done in the 1950s and 1960s on isometric versus isotonic exercises, it was often hypothesized that the ''upstart'' isometric exercise was just as effective as the traditional isotonic exercise, provided there was regular specific knowledge of results. In a study on recreation of mentally retarded children, Matthews (1979) showed that most research in this area, which reported differences between retarded and nonretarded children, failed to consider socioeconomic status. Subsequently, he hypothesized that there were no differences in frequency of participation in recreation activities between mildly mentally retarded and nonretarded children when socioeconomic status was held constant.

Furthermore, sometimes the researcher doesn't expect differences in some aspects of the study but does expect a difference in others. For example, in a study of age differences in the strategy for recall of movement (Thomas, Thomas, Lee, Testerman, & Ashy, 1983), the authors hypothesized that since location is automatically encoded in memory, there would be no real difference between younger and older children in remembering location (where an event happened during a run). However, they hypothesized that there would be a difference in remembering distance because the older child spontaneously uses strategy for remembering and the younger child does not.

The formulation of the hypotheses is a very important aspect of defining and delimiting the research problem.

OPERATIONAL DEFINITIONS

In the planning of any study, there are certain terms which must be operationally defined so that the researcher and the reader are able to adequately evaluate the results. It is imperative that the dependent variable be operationally defined.

So what is an operational definition? It is an observable phenomenon as opposed to a synonym definition or dictionary definition. To illustrate, a study such as Anshel and Marisi's (1978) which investigated the effects of music on forestalling fatigue must operationally define fatigue. The author cannot use a synonym, such as exhaustion, because that is not concrete enough. We all might have our own concepts of what fatigue is, but if we are going to say that some independent variable has an effect on fatigue, we must supply some observable evidence of changes in fatigue. Therefore, *fatigue* must be operationally defined. In Anshel and Marisi's study the term fatigue was not actually used, but from their description of procedures, we can "infer" an operational definition of fatigue as being when the subject was unable to maintain the pedaling rate of 50 rpm for 10 consecutive seconds.

Another researcher might define fatigue as being when maximal heart rate was achieved; still another might define fatigue as the point of maximal oxygen consumption. In all cases, though, it must be an observable criterion.

A study dealing with dehydration must provide an operational definition such as a loss of 5% of body weight. The term *obesity* could be defined as having 25% body fat (for males). A study of different teaching methods on learning must operationally define learning. To use the old "change in behavior" definition is meaningless in providing evidence of learning. Learning might be demonstrated by five successful maze traversals or some other observable performance criterion.

You may not always agree with the investigator's definitions, but at least you know how a particular term is being used. A common mistaken notion with novice researchers is to think that every term needs to be defined. (We have seen master's students define terms not even used in their study!) An example of unnecessary definition would be in a study dealing with the effects of strength training on changes in self-concept. Self-concept would have to be defined, probably as represented by some scale, but the term strength would not have to be operationally defined. The strength training program used would be described in the methods section. Basically, operational definitions are directly related to the research hypotheses, because if you predict that some treatment will produce some effect, you must define how that effectiveness will be manifested.

BASIC ASSUMPTIONS AND LIMITATIONS

ASSUMPTIONS

Every study has certain fundamental premises without which it could not proceed. In other words, you have to assume that certain conditions will exist, and that the particular behaviors in question can be observed and measured, along with various other basic suppositions. A study in health education which compares teaching methods has to assume that the teachers involved are capable of promoting learning; if not, the whole study is worthless. Furthermore, in a learning study, the researcher must assume that the sample selection (e.g., random selection) results in a normal distribution with regard to learning capacity.

A study designed to assess the attitude toward recreational activities is based on the assumption that this attitude can be reliably demonstrated and measured. Furthermore, you can assume that the subjects will respond truthfully—at least for the most part. If you cannot assume those things, you might as well not waste your time conducting the study.

Of course, the experimenter does everything possible to increase the credibility of the premises. The researcher takes great care in the selection of the measuring instruments, in the sampling, and in the data gathering with regard to such things as standardized instructions and motivating techniques. Nevertheless, the researcher still must rely on certain basic assumptions.

Consider the following studies: Johnson (1979) investigated the effects of different levels of fatigue on visual recognition of previously learned material. Among his basic assumptions were that (a) the mental capacities of the subjects were within the normal range for university students; (b) the subjects understood the directions; (c) the mental task was representative of the type of mental tasks encountered in athletics; and (d) the physical task demands were representative of the levels of exertion commonly experienced in athletics.

Lane (1983) compared skinfold profiles of black and white girls and boys and tried to determine which skinfold sites best indicated total body fatness with regard to race, sex and age. Among her assumptions were (a) the skinfold caliper is a valid and reliable instrument for measuring subcutaneous fat; (b) that skinfold measurements taken at the body sites in this study are indicative of the subcutaneous fat stores in the limbs and trunk; and (c) that the sum of all skinfolds represents a valid indication of body fatness.

In some physiological studies, the subjects are instructed (and agree) to fast, or refrain from smoking or drinking liquids for a specified period of time prior to testing. Obviously, unless the study is conducted in some type of prison environment, the experimenter cannot physically monitor the subjects' activities. Consequently, a basic assumption is that the subjects will follow instructions.

CHARACTERISTICS OF LIMITATIONS

Every study also has limitations. Some refer to the scope of the study, which is usually imposed by the researcher. These are sometimes called *delimitations*. Kroll (1971) describes delimitations as choices the experimenter makes to affect a workable research problem, such as the use of one particular personality test in the assessment of personality characteristics. Moreover, in a study dealing with individual sport athletes, the researcher may choose to restrict the selection of subjects to just two or three sports obviously because all individual sports could not be included in one study. Thus, the researcher delimits the study.

You probably notice that these delimitations are very similar to operational definitions. Although they are similar, they are not actually alike. For example, the size of the sample is a delimitation, but it would not be included under operational definitions.

You can also see that basic assumptions are entwined with delimitations as well as operational definitions. The researcher must proceed on the assumption that the restrictions which are imposed on the study will not be so confining as to destroy the external validity (the generalizability of results).

Remember, theses or dissertations do not have one "correct" format. An examination of studies will find numerous variations in organization. You will see some studies which have delimitations and limitations described in separate sections: Some will use a combination heading; some will only list one heading but include both in the description, and so on. As with all aspects of format, much depends on how the advisor was taught. Graduate Schools often allow great latitude in format as long as the study is internally consistent. You will even find considerable differences in format within the same department.

Limitations are possible shortcomings or influences which either cannot be controlled or are the results of the delimitations imposed by the investigator. In the example Kroll used of delimiting the scope of the study to just two sports to represent individual sport athletes, there is an automatic limitation with respect to how well these represent all individual sports. Moreover, if the researcher is studying personality traits of these athletes and delimits the measurement of personality to just one test, this results in a limitation. Furthermore, there is a limitation(s) in all instruments in which the subject responds to questions about his or her behavior or likes or interests as to the truthfulness of the responses.

Thus, you can see that limitations also accompany the basic assumptions to the extent that the assumptions fail to be justified. And, as with assumptions, the investigator tries as much as possible to reduce limitations that might stem from faulty procedures. In Johnson's study (1979) of fatigue effects on visual recognition of previously learned material, he had to have the subjects first learn the material. He established criteria for learning (operational definition) and tried to control for overlearning (i.e., differences in the level of learning). However, he recognized that despite his efforts, a limitation was that there may have been differences in the degree of learning which could certainly influence recognition.

In the skinfold profiles study by Lane (1983), she had to delimit the study to a certain number of subjects in one part of Baton Rouge, Louisiana. Consequently, a limitation was that the children were from only one geographical location. She also recognized that there are changes in body fatness associated with the onset of puberty, but she was unable to obtain data on puberty or other indices of maturation, and this, therefore, posed a limitation. Still another limitation was the inability to control possible influences on skinfold measurement such as dehydration and other diurnal variations. Finally, since there are no internationally recognized standard body sites for skinfold measurement, generalizability may be limited to the body sites used in this study.

You should not be overzealous in "searching" for limitations or you can apologize away the worth of the study. For example, one of our advisees who was planning to meet with his proposal committee was overapologetic with these anticipated limitations:

1. The sample size may be too small.
2. The tests may not represent the parameter in question.
3. The training sessions may be too short.
4. The investigator lacks adequate measurement experience.

As a result, there was a major revision in the proposal, plus a reassessment of the method.

Remember, no perfect study exists. You must carefully analyze the delimitations to determine whether the resulting limitations outweigh them. In addition, careful planning and painstaking methodology will increase the validity of the results, thus greatly reducing possible deficiencies in a study.

SIGNIFICANCE OF THE STUDY

The inevitable question you face at both the proposal meeting and the final orals deals with the worth or significance of the study, which may be asked in different ways, such as "So what?" or "What good is it?" or "How does this affect the price of tea in China?" Regardless of the manner in which the question is asked, it can be unsettling and must be dealt with. Perhaps because of the inevitability of the question, most students are required to include a section in the first chapter titled "Significance of the Study," or sometimes, "The Need for the Study."

BASIC AND APPLIED RESEARCH REVISITED

To a large extent the worth of the research study is judged by whether it is basic or applied research. In Chapter 1, we explained that basic research does not have immediate social significance; it usually deals with theoretical problems and is conducted in a very controlled laboratory setting. Applied research addresses immediate problems for improving practice. There is less control but ideally more real-world application. Consequently, basic and applied research cannot be evaluated by the same criteria.

The significance of basic research studies obviously depends upon the specific purpose(s) but usually the criteria focus on the extent to which the study contributes to the formulation or validation of some theory. The worth of applied research has to be evaluated on the basis of its contribution to the solution of some immediate problem.

WRITING THE SIGNIFICANCE OF THE STUDY SECTION: CONTINUITY WITH THE INTRODUCTION

The significance section is often a difficult one to write probably because the student thinks only in terms of the practicality of the study; for example, how can the results be immediately used to improve some aspect of the profession? Frantic to find some application from a rather theoretical study, one of our students suggested that the results could possibly be used in the space program. (Talk about far out!)

Kroll (1971) stresses the importance of maintaining continuity of the significance section with the introduction. Too often the sections are written with different frames of reference instead of a continuous flow of thought. The significance section should stress such things as contradictory findings of previous research and gaps in knowledge in particular areas. Difficulties in the measurement of aspects of the phenomenon in question are sometimes stressed. Rationale for the need to verify existing theories may be the focus of the section in some studies, while in others, the practical application is the main concern.

Just as the length of the introduction varies, the length of the significance section varies considerably from study to study. A sample of a significance section in a study referred to previously (Lane, 1983) may serve to illustrate an approach which focuses on some conflicts between previous research findings and present practice.

> Since the measurement of body composition has become an important aspect of physical fitness testing, the validity, reliability, and administrative feasibility of the measurements are of paramount concern. Adult formulas for estimating percent fat are not considered valid for children, thus skinfolds are in themselves used as measures of body composition.
>
> The *AAHPERD Health Related Physical Fitness Test Manual* (1980) contains two skinfold measurements: the triceps and subscapula. Norms for the total of these two measures are provided for boys and girls ages 6 to 17 years. Abbreviated norms are also given for the triceps skinfold only. Norms were taken from HES data (Johnston et al., 1974). There is minimal evidence as to why these two body sites were selected, especially when one, the subscapula, poses some problem with regard to modesty. If the triceps and subscapula were selected as representing one from the limbs and one from the trunk, are they the most predictive of total fatness as indicated by the sum of several skinfolds from the limbs and trunk? Furthermore, if some sites are equally predictive, the ease of administration needs to be considered.
>
> Of major significance in this study is whether the skinfolds which best represent body fatness in white children are equally suitable for black

> children. Authors (Cronk & Roche, 1982; Harsha et al., 1974; Johnston et al., 1974) have reported that there are differences in skinfold thicknesses between black and white children, yet the AAHPERD norms make no distinction. If norms are to be of value they must be representative of the population for which they are intended. Moreover, there may be greater differences in fatness between blacks and whites at different ages.
>
> Similarly, it may be that a different combination of skinfolds would be more valid for girls than boys. It does not seem to be of any great administrative advantage to use the same sites for both sexes if other sites are equally valid indicators of total fatness.

A final word of warning: In being asked the inevitable question in the proposal and in the final orals about the significance of the study, do not reply with "it was necessary to get my degree." The stony silent response will only serve to unnerve you.

DEFINING AND DELIMITING THE PROBLEM: THE DIFFERENCE IN THESIS FORMAT AND THE RESEARCH ARTICLE

A mere glance at research articles in journals reveals that a number of the sections described in this chapter are missing. At least two reasons account for this: One is financial; periodicals are concerned about publishing costs, so brevity is stressed. Second, a kind of novice-master ritual seems to be in operation. The novice is required to explicitly state the hypotheses, define terms, state assumptions, recognize limitations, and justify the worth of the study in writing. Certainly these steps are all part of defining and delimiting the research problem, and it is, undoubtedly, a worthwhile experience to address each step formally.

The research journal author, on the other hand, does not have to explain the step-by-step procedure in developing the problem. Typically, a research journal has an introduction which includes a short review of literature. The length varies considerably; however, some journals insist on very brief introductions.

The purpose of the study is nearly always given, but it usually is not designated by a heading; rather it is often the last sentence(s) in the introduction. For example, in 30 articles in the *Research Quarterly for Exercise and Sport*, 24 had sentences at the end of the introduction which began with the words, "The purpose of the study was"; 1 had a section titled "Purpose of the Study"; 4 indicated the purpose with sentences such as, "This study was designed to," "The intent of the study was," for example; and 1 study did not state the purpose at all. In such cases, the author(s) and editors feel that the purpose is evident from the title and introduction.

Research hypotheses are sometimes given, but with little uniformity. Of course, journals may vary, but we would estimate that the hypotheses are stated in less than 30% of the articles. Operational definitions, assumptions, limitations, and significance of the study are virtually never stated in research articles. Apparently, for the "master" researcher, these steps that were accomplished in the development of the problem are understood (and/or obvious) and need not be stated. If the article is well written, you should be able to discern the operational definitions, the assumptions and limitations, and the independent, dependent, categorical, and control variables even though they are not specifically stated. Moreover, the significance of the study should be implicitly obvious if the author has written a good introduction.

In summary, the development of the problem involves all of the steps and processes we have described in this chapter. The extent to which the investigator formally describes these aspects of problem development varies, depending upon requirements set forth by the advisor, by the institution, and by the research journal or other type of publication.

PROBLEMS

1. For each of the following titles, write the purpose(s) and some possible research hypotheses.
   a. Trait and state anxiety and motor performance under conditions of competition and audience.
   b. Effects of guided and discovery learning strategies on learning and retention of a gross motor task.
   c. Comparison of isometric, isotonic, and isokinetic strength training on the development of muscular power.
   d. Learning and performance in a motor task as influenced by the precision and delay of knowledge of results.
2. Locate five articles from research journals, and for each, try to determine (a) hypotheses, if not stated, (b) operational definitions, (c) limitations, and (d) assumptions.

Chapter 4

Formulating the Method

The previous chapter provided an overview of the *Introduction* chapter in the proposal for a thesis or dissertation. As already indicated, some formats include the literature review (Chapter 2) in the first chapter while others have the literature review as a separate chapter. Regardless, once the introduction has been completed, the researcher must describe the methodology for the research. Typically, this chapter is labeled *Method*.

The purpose of the method chapter is to explain how to conduct the study. The standard rule is, *The description should be thorough enough for a competent researcher to reproduce the study*. Dissertations and theses differ considerably from published articles in the methodological details provided. Journals are trying to conserve space, but space is no issue in a dissertation/thesis. Thus, where standard techniques in a journal article are only referenced to another published study (in an easily obtainable journal), a thesis or dissertation should provide considerably greater detail. Note that we indicated a technique could be referenced to an "easily obtainable journal." When writing for publication use common sense in this regard, for example, consider this citation:

> Farke, F.R., Frankenstein, C., & Frickenfrack, F. (1921). Flexion of the feet by footfetish feet feelers. *Research Abnormal: Perception of Feet*, **22**, 1-26.

By most standards, this citation would not be considered easily obtainable. Therefore, if you are in doubt, give the details.

Furthermore, because a thesis/dissertation has appendices, much of the detail that would clutter and extend the Method chapter may be placed there. Examples include exact instructions to subjects, samples of tests and answer sheets, diagrams and pictures of equipment, sample data recording sheets, and informed consent agreements.

The Method chapter has four sections: subjects, instruments or apparatus, procedures, and design and analysis. The purpose of this planning is to eliminate any alternate or rival hypotheses. This really means when you design the study correctly and the results are as predicted, the only explanation is what you did in the research. Using an earlier example to illustrate, our hypothesis is that "shoe size and mathematics performance are positively related during elementary school." To test this hypothesis, we go to an elementary school, measure the shoe size, and obtain mathematics performance scores of the children in grades 1-5. When we plot these scores, they appear as in Figure 4.1, each dot representing a single child. If you move from the dot to the *Y* axis, you can read their mathematics performance score. By referring to the *X* axis, you can see their shoe size. *Look*, we say, we are correct—as shoe size gets larger, the children's mathematics performance increases. *Eureka!* All we need to do is stretch the children's feet and their mathematics performance will improve. But wait a minute! Thomas and Nelson have overlooked two things. The obvious one is that there

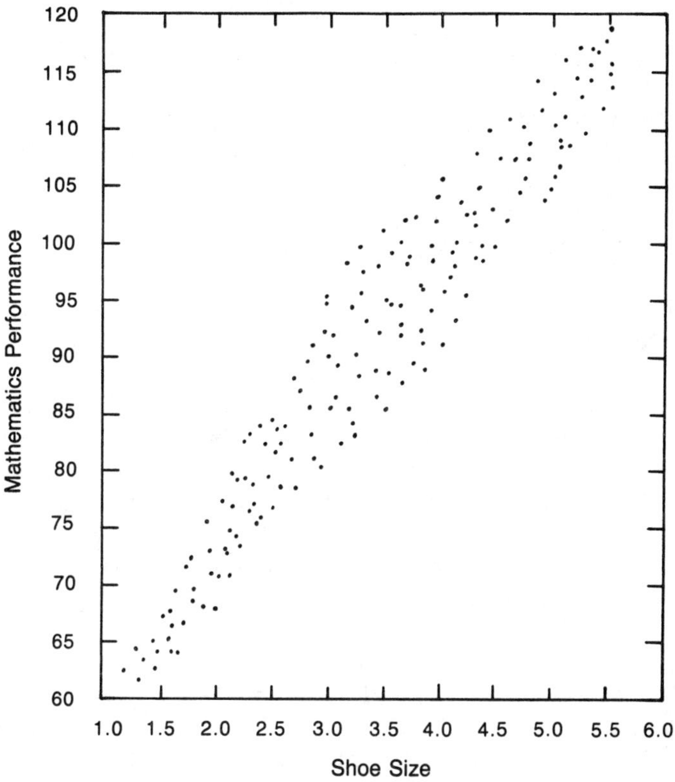

Figure 4.1 Relationship of academic performance and shoe size of children grades 1 through 5.

is a rival explanation—both shoe size and mathematics performance are related to age. That really explains the relationship. As the kids get older, their feet get bigger and they perform better on mathematics tests. In addition, we made another error which we will discuss in a later chapter: Because two things are related does not mean one causes the other. *Correlation does not mean causation.* Obviously, we can not improve children's math performance by stretching their feet.

In research we want to use the *maxicon principle: maximize true variance*, that is, increase the odds that the real relationship or explanation will be discovered; we want to *minimize error variance*, or reduce all the mistakes that could creep into the study to disguise the true relationship; and we want to *control extraneous variance*, that is, make sure that rival hypotheses are not the real explanation of the relationship.

SUBJECTS

This section describes how and why the subjects were selected and what characteristics they have that are pertinent to the study. The exact number of subjects should be given as well as any loss of subjects during the time of study. In the proposal for the study, some of this information may not be exact. For example, the following might describe the potential subjects:

> *Subjects.* For this study 48 males, ranging in age from 21-34 years, will be randomly selected from a group (N = 147) of well-trained distance runners (max $\dot{V}O_2$ = 55 ml • kg • min^{-1} or higher) who have been competitive runners for at least 2 years. Subjects will be randomly assigned into one of four groups (n = 12 per group).

Once the study is completed, details would be available on the subjects, so now this section might read:

> *Subjects.* In this study 48 males, ranging in age from 21-34 years, were randomly selected from a group (N = 147) of well-trained runners (max $\dot{V}O_2$ = 55 ml • kg • min^{-1} or higher) who had been competitive runners for at least 2 years. The subjects selected had the following characteristics, M (SD): age, M = 26 yr (3.3); height, M = 172.5 cm (7.5); weight, M = 66.9 kg (8.7); and max $\dot{V}O_2$, M = 61 ml • kg • min^{-1} (4.2). Subjects were randomly assigned to one of four groups (n = 12 per group).

The characteristics listed might be extremely pertinent in an exercise physiology study but are not at all the subject characteristics of interest in a study of equipment usage by children on the playground. The nature of the research dictates the subject characteristics of interest to the researcher. Carefully think through the important characteristics you will report in your research. Look at other related studies for ideas as to important characteristics to report.

The characteristics about subjects you identify and report must be clearly specified. Note in the example, "well-trained runners" were exactly defined: Their max VO_2 must be equal to 55 ml • kg • min^{-1} or higher. Where subjects of different ages are to be used is another good example. Just to say 7-, 9- and 11-year-old children will be the subjects is not sufficient. How wide an age range is 7 years old—± 1 month, ± 6 months, or what? In the proposal, you may say 7-, 9- and 11-year-old children will be included in the study. At the time of testing, each age will be limited to a ± 6 month age range. Then when the thesis/dissertation is actually written, it may read:

> At each age level 15 children were selected for this study. The ages, *M* (*SD*), for the youngest group was 7.1 years (4.4 months), for 9-year-olds was 9.2 years (3.9 months), and for the oldest group was 11.2 years (4.1 months).

In the proposal the age range is delimited, while in the thesis/dissertation the actual means and standard deviations for each age group are reported.

ETHICS IN RESEARCH

Most of the research in HPERD deals with humans, oftentimes children. Because of this, the researcher must be concerned about any circumstances in the research setting or activity that could harm the participants. Harm should be interpreted to mean to frighten, embarrass, or negatively affect their lives (Tuckman, 1978). Of course, researchers always run the risk of creating a problem. What must be balanced is the degree of risk and the rights of the subjects. The important issue is the potential value of research in contributing to knowledge, to the development of technology, and to the improvement of people's lives. Tuckman (1978) has summarized the subjects' rights that experimenters *must* consider:

1. The right to privacy or nonparticipation including the fact that researchers should not ask for unnecessary information and should obtain direct consent from adults and consent from parents for children (as well as the consent of the children themselves where appropriate);
2. The right to remain anonymous. The researcher should explain that the study focuses on group data and that an ID number (rather than the subject's name) will be used to record data;
3. The right to confidentiality. Subjects should be told who (keep this as few people as possible) will actually have access to original data by which the subject might be identified;
4. The right to expect experimenter responsibility. In particular that the experimenter is well-meaning and that he/she will be sensitive to human dignity. If the subject is not told the purpose of the study (or is misled), the subject must be debriefed immediately after the completion of testing.

For the guidelines on which these ethical considerations are based, see the American Psychological Association's *Ethical principles in the conduct of research with human participants* (1973).

Handicapped subjects are a special issue as research subjects. The fact that the subject is handicapped is protected under the "Right to Privacy Act." Thus, the institution is prohibited from releasing the subject's name as a potential research subject. The researcher must contact the institution about possible subjects. The institution then requests permission from the parents to release the child's name and handicap to the researcher. If the parents approve, the institution then allows the researcher to contact the parents to seek approval for the particular research to be undertaken. While this procedure is rather cumbersome and varies from state to state, individuals clearly have the right not to have their names released as "handicapped" unless they so choose.

PROTECTION OF HUMAN SUBJECTS AND INFORMED CONSENT

Consideration must also be given to *protection of human subjects*. The researcher is required to protect the rights and well-being of subjects in his or her study. Most institutions regulate this protection in two ways. First, researchers are required to complete some type of form about their research. (Table 4.1 is a sample of the form used at Louisiana State University.) The researcher must complete this form, attach an abstract, and have it approved prior to beginning the research, including any pilot work. Second, the researcher is required to obtain informed consent from the subjects. Table 4.2 is a sample of the form frequently used by our graduate students and faculty to obtain informed consent.

The basic elements of informed consent as specified by the *Research Quarterly for Exercise and Sport* Advisory Committee (1983, p. 221) are

1. A fair explanation of the procedures to be followed, including an identification of those which are experimental.
2. A description of the attendant discomforts and risks.
3. A description of the benefits to be expected.
4. A disclosure of appropriate alternative procedures that would be advantageous for the subject.
5. An offer to answer any inquiries concerning the procedures.
6. An instruction that the subject is free to withdraw consent and to discontinue participation in the project or activity at any time. In addition, the agreement should contain no exculpatory language through which the subject is made to waive, or appear to waive, any legal right, or to release the institution or its agents from liability or negligence.

The researcher is required to comply with whatever the institutional guidelines are for protection of human subjects and informed consent. A description of this

TABLE 4.1
HUMAN SUBJECTS FORM

Name ________________________________ Date ______________

Dept. ________________________________

Address (If you want to have your correspondence sent to an address other than the department, please indicate in this space.)

Subject: Request for research approval

Title of research project ________________________________

____

The investigator gives assurances to the Committee on the Use of Humans and Animals as Research Subjects for each of the following:

	Yes	No
1. The human subjects are volunteers.	☐	☐
2. Subjects have the freedom to withdraw at any time.	☐	☐
3. That the data collected will not be used for any purpose not approved by the subjects.	☐	☐
4. The subjects are guaranteed anonymity.	☐	☐
5. The subjects will be informed beforehand as to the nature of their activity.	☐	☐
6. The nature of the activity will not cause any physical or psychological harm to the subjects.	☐	☐
7. Individual performances will not be disclosed to persons other than those involved in the research, those authorized by the subject.	☐	☐
8. If minors are to participate in this experiment, valid consent has been obtained from the parents or guardian.	☐	☐
9. That all questions have been answered to the subjects' satisfaction.	☐	☐
10. All volunteers will consent by signature.	☐	☐

Any exceptions or qualifications to the above assurances are explained below:

____

____

____
Investigator's Name

---

compliance should be included under the Subject section in the Method chapter of the thesis/dissertation. Most journals also require a statement with regard to this issue. The form used for informed consent is normally placed in an appendix of the thesis/dissertation.

TABLE 4.2
EXPERIMENT CONSENT FORM

Date ______________________

To be retained by the investigator:

Experiment Sign-up Form

My signature, on this sheet, by which I volunteer to participate in the experiment on:

____

____

____

Conducted by:

____
Experimenter

indicates that I understand that all subjects in the project are volunteers, that I can withdraw at any time from the experiment, that I have been or will be informed as to the nature of the experiment, that the data I provide will be anonymous and my identity will not be revealed without my permission, and that my performance in this experiment may be used for additional approved projects. Finally, I shall be given an opportunity to ask questions prior to the start of the experiment and after my participation is complete.

____
Subject's signature

INSTRUMENTS

The instruments, apparatus, or tests used to collect the data are described in this section. This information is used to generate the dependent variable(s) in the study. For example, in a health education study, you are interested in the effects of a unit on knowledge about and attitudes toward responsible drug use. In addition, you suspect that the students' attitudes might be modified by certain personality traits, so you select three tests: a drug knowledge test, an attitude inventory about responsible drug use, and a trait personality measure, and give these three tests to all subjects.

In the instrument section, you describe the three tests and probably put complete copies of each in the appendix. You also describe the reliability (consistency) and validity (what does the test measure?) information that is available on each test with appropriate citations. You then explain the scoring sheets (place a sample in the appendix) and also the scoring methods.

Another example might be a motor behavior study in which subjects' reaction times and movement times are measured under various conditions. In this section a description of the reaction and movement time testing apparatus would be provided as well as a diagram or picture. If the apparatus were interfaced with a microcomputer to control the testing situation and data collection, you should describe the microcomputer (brand name and model) and how the interface was made. At least a description of how the computer program operates (if not a complete copy of the program) should be included in the appendix. By appropriate use of both the instrument or apparatus part of the method chapter and the appendix, all necessary information can be presented, allowing the method section to flow smoothly.

PROCEDURES

This section should describe how the data are obtained. All testing procedures for obtaining scores on the variables of interest should be explained. How tests are given and who gives them are important features. The setup of the testing situation and instructions given to the subjects are detailed (although some of this information may be placed in the appendix). If the study is an experimental one, then the treatments applied to the different groups of subjects are described. One of our favorite summaries of the problems encountered and proposed solutions is presented in Table 4.3. These statements are extracted from an article by Martens (1973) called "People errors in people experiments."

TABLE 4.3
ERRORS IN EXPERIMENTS

Sources of Errors in Experiments
Martens's Method
(For Eliminating People Errors in People Experiments)

The Martens's method derives from the basic premise that:

In people experiments people errors increase in disporportionate ratio to the contact people have with people.

It is obvious that the most logical deduction from this premise is:

To reduce people errors in people experiments, reduce the number of people.

While this solution might be preferred for its elegant simplicity, its feasibility can be questioned. Therefore, the following alternative formulation warrants consideration:

The contact between people-testers and people subjects in people experiments should be minimized, standardized and randomized.

Note. From "People errors in people experiments," by R. Martens, 1973, *Quest*, **20**, pp. 331-332, Champaign, IL: Human Kinetics Publishers, Inc. Reprinted with permission.

The procedures section is where most of the detail that allows another researcher to replicate the study is given. Details generally include:

> (1) the specific order in which steps were undertaken, (2) the timing of the study (for example, time for different procedures and time between different procedures), (3) instructions given to subjects, and (4) briefings, debriefings, and safeguards (Tuckman, 1978).

Table 4.4 called "Quirk Theory" provides a humorous view of all the things that go wrong in the procedures. Unless you carefully pilot all your procedures, "Quirk Theory" will apply to your research. *No single item in this book is more important than our advice to pilot all your procedures.* HPERD has produced thousands of studies in which the discussion centers on methodological faults which caused the research to lack validity. We are aware that we are repeating ourselves, but placing post hoc blame on the methodology for inadequate results is unacceptable. Every thesis/dissertation proposal should present pilot work that verifies that *all* instruments and procedures will function as specified on the type subjects for which the research is intended. In addition, you must demonstrate that you can use these procedures and apparatus accurately and reliably.

During our years as editors and researchers, we have seen abstracts of thousands of master's theses and doctoral dissertations. More than 75% of these research efforts are unpublishable and make no contribution to theory or practice because of major methodological flaws that could have been easily corrected with pilot work. Sadly, this reflects negatively, not only on the profession, but on the graduate students who conducted the research as well as the faculty who directed it. Yet, nearly all of the problems could be corrected by increased knowledge about the topic, better research design, and pilot work on the procedures.

TABLE 4.4
"QUIRK THEORY"
OR
THE UNIVERSAL PERVERSITY OF MATTER

Law of Experiment

First Law—In any field of scientific endeavor, anything that can go wrong will go wrong.

- Corollary One—Everything goes wrong at one time.
- Corollary Two—If there is a possibility of several things going wrong, the one that will go wrong is the one that will do the most damage.
- Corollary Three—Left to themselves, things always go from bad to worse.
- Corollary Four—Experiments must be reproducible; they should fail in the same way.
- Corollary Five—Nature always sides with the hidden flaw.
- Corollary Six—If everything seems to be going well, you have overlooked something.

Table 4.4 (Cont.)

Second Law—It is usually impractical to worry beforehand about interference; if you have none, someone will supply some for you.

Corollary One—Information necessitating a change in design will be conveyed to the designer after, and only after, the plans are complete.

Corollary Two—In simple cases, presenting one obvious right way versus one obvious wrong way, it is often wiser to choose the wrong way so as to expedite subsequent revisions.

Corollary Three—The more innocuous a modification appears to be, the further its influence will extend, and the more plans will have to be redrawn.

Third Law—In any collection of data, the figures that are obviously correct, beyond all need of checking, contain the errors.

Corollary One—No one whom you ask for help will see the errors.

Corollary Two—Any nagging intruder who stops by with unsought advice will spot it immediately.

Fourth Law—If in any problem you find yourself doing a transfinite amount of work, the answer can be obtained by inspection.

To assist in the research suggested, the following rules have been formulated for the use of those new to this field.

Rules of Experimental Procedure

1. Build no mechanism simply if a way can be found to make it complex and wonderful.
2. A record of data is useful; it indicates that you have been busy.
3. To study a subject, first understand it thoroughly.
4. Draw your curves; then plot your data.
5. Do not believe in luck; rely on it.
6. Always leave room when writing a report to add an explanation if it doesn't work. (Rule of the way out.)
7. Use the most recent developments in the field of interpretation of experimental data.
   a. Items such as Finagle's Constant and the more subtle Bougeurre Factor (pronounced "Bugger") are loosely grouped, in mathematics, under constant variables, or if you prefer, variable constants.
   b. Finagle's Constant, a multiplier of the zero order term, may be characterized as changing the universe to fit the equation.
   c. The Bougeurre Factor is characterized as changing the equation to fit the universe. It is also known as the "Soothing" Factor; mathematically somewhat similar to the damping factor, it has the characteristic of dropping the subject under discussion to zero importance.
   d. A combination of the two, the Diddle Coefficient, is characterized as changing things so that the universe and the equation appear to fit without requiring any change in either.

Note. From "Quirk theory or the universal perversity of matter," 1968, *Illinois Technograph*, Dec. **59**, Urbana, IL: Engineering Publications. Reprinted by permission.

DESIGN AND ANALYSIS

Design is the key to controlling the outcomes from experimental and quasi-experimental research. The independent variable(s) are manipulated in an attempt to judge their effects upon the dependent variable. A well-designed study is one in which the only explanation for change in the dependent variable is how the subjects were treated (independent variable). The design has enabled the researcher to eliminate all rival or alternative hypotheses. The design is a section heading in the method chapter for experimental and quasi-experimental research.

The plans for analysis of the data must also be reported. In most studies some type of statistical analysis is used but there are exceptions, for example in historical or qualitative research.

Typically, the researcher will explain the proposed application of the statistics. In nearly all cases descriptive statistics are provided, such as means (group average) and standard deviation (group variability) for each of the variables. If correlational techniques (relationships among variables) are used, then the variables to be correlated and the techniques are named; for example, "The degree of relationship between two estimates of percent fat will be established by using Pearson *r* to correlate the sum of three skinfolds with underwater weighing." In experimental and quasi-experimental studies, descriptive statistics are provided for the dependent measures and the statistics for establishing differences among groups are reported; for example, "A *t* test was used to determine if modern dancers spend more time than ballet dancers using broad bases of support."

The major problem encountered here is the tendency for graduate students to feel the need to instruct everyone about their knowledge of statistics. Of course, that is not much of a problem for the new graduate student. But if your program of studies is a research-oriented one in which you take several statistics courses, your attitude may change rapidly.

> Hiawatha, who at college
> Majored in applied statistics,
> Consequently felt entitled
> To instruct his fellow men on
> Any subject whatsoever, . . .
>
> (Kendall, 1959, p. 331)

The point of these lines from Kendall's poem is for you to describe your statistical analyses but do not instruct upon their theoretical underpinnings and proper use.

SUMMARY

This chapter is an overview of the method for the research study. We have identified the major parts as subjects, instruments or apparatus, procedures, and design

TABLE 4.5
SUMMARY OF THE METHODS CHAPTER

Total Research Situation
Considerations for Formulating the Study
Subjects
Instruments
Procedures
Design and Analysis
Eliminate Alternate or Rival Hypotheses
Maxicon Principle
Maximize experimental variance
Minimize error variance
Control extraneous variance

Note. From *A student guide for education research* (2nd ed.) by R.L. Hoenes and B.S. Chissom, 1975. Statesboro, GA: Vog Press. Adapted and reprinted with permission.

and analysis. Table 4.5 shows the four parts of the method chapter and their major purpose—to eliminate alternative or rival hypotheses; in other words, to control any explanation for the results except the hypothesis the researcher intends to evaluate. The *Maxicon Principle* shows the way to accomplish this: (1) Maximize the true or planned sources of variation; (2) minimize any error or unplanned sources of variation; and (3) control any extraneous sources of variation. In the following sections, we detail how to do this from a statistical (Section II), design (Section III), and measurement (Section IV) viewpoint.

Section II

STATISTICAL CONCEPTS IN RESEARCH

In the following three chapters some basic statistical techniques are presented which are frequently used in HPERD research. More attention has been given here to the basic statistical techniques than to the more complex methods. A general understanding of the underlying concepts of the statistical techniques has been emphasized rather than any derivation of formulas or extensive computations. Because an understanding of how the basic statistical techniques work facilitates an intuitive grasp of the more advanced procedures, the computational procedures for most of the basic statistics as well as examples of their use have been provided. In addition, Appendix B contains microcomputer programs (for the Apple II) for each of the basic techniques discussed.

Chapter 5 discusses the need for statistics. Different types of sampling procedures are described, and the basic statistics used in describing data, such as measures of central tendency and measures of variation, are summarized. The emphasis here is that statistics can reveal two things about data: their reliability and their meaningfulness. The concepts of probability and significance are explained as they relate to inference or to generalizing the results of a study.

Chapter 6 pertains to relationships among variables. Different correlational techniques are reviewed such as the Pearson *r* for the relationship between only two variables. Partial correlation is explained as a technique in which one can determine the correlation between two variables while holding the influence of a third (or more variables) constant.

The use of correlation for prediction is discussed using just one predictor variable and when using more than one variable to predict a criterion (multiple regression). Lastly, canonical correlation is briefly explained as a means of determining the relationship between two or more dependent variables and two or more independent variables.

Chapter 7 focuses on statistical techniques for comparing treatment effects or groups, such as different training or different samples. The simplest comparison of differences is between two groups—the *t* test. Next, analysis of variance is described as a means of testing the significance of the differences among more than two groups. The use of factorial analysis of variance is discussed in which two or more levels of an independent variable can be compared.

The last part of the chapter is devoted to multivariate techniques. Discriminant analysis is a statistical technique for comparing two or more levels of one independent variable on two or more dependent variables. Multivariate analysis of variance (MANOVA) can be used when there are two or more independent variables and two or more dependent variables.

After reading the three chapters in Section II, you will not be a statistician (unless you were one before you started). However, if you *read* and *study* these chapters carefully and perhaps further explore some of the references, you should be able to comprehend the statistical analysis sections of most research studies.

Chapter 5

The Need for Statistics

Statistics is an objective means of interpreting a collection of observations. Various statistical techniques allow the description of the characteristics of data, testing of relationships between sets of data, and testing of the differences among sets of data. For example, if height and the standing long-jump score were measured for each person in a seventh-grade class, you could sum all of the heights and divide by the number of people. The answer (statistic to represent the average height) is the mean ($\Sigma X/N$, where Σ = sum, X = each person's height, N = number of people; *read this as* sum all Xs and divide by N). This mean (*M*) describes the average height in the class; it is a single characteristic that represents the data.

An example of testing relationships between sets of data would be to measure the degree of association between height and the scores on the standing long jump. You might hypothesize that taller people can jump further. By plotting the scores (Figure 5.1), you can see that in general, people who are taller do jump further. But note that the relationship is not perfect. If it were, the scores would begin in the lower left-hand corner of the figure and proceed diagonally in a straight line toward the upper right-hand corner. One measure of the degree of association between two variables is called Pearson *r* (or simple correlation). When two variables are unrelated, their correlation (*r*) is approximately .00. In the example of Figure 5.1, the two variables (height and standing long-jump score) have a moderately positive correlation (*r* is probably between .40 and .60). Relationships and correlation will be discussed in greater detail in the next chapter, but for now you should see that researchers frequently want to investigate the relationship between variables.

The third category of statistical techniques is used to measure differences among groups. Suppose you believe that weight training of the legs will increase the distance people can jump. So take a seventh-grade class, divide it into two groups,

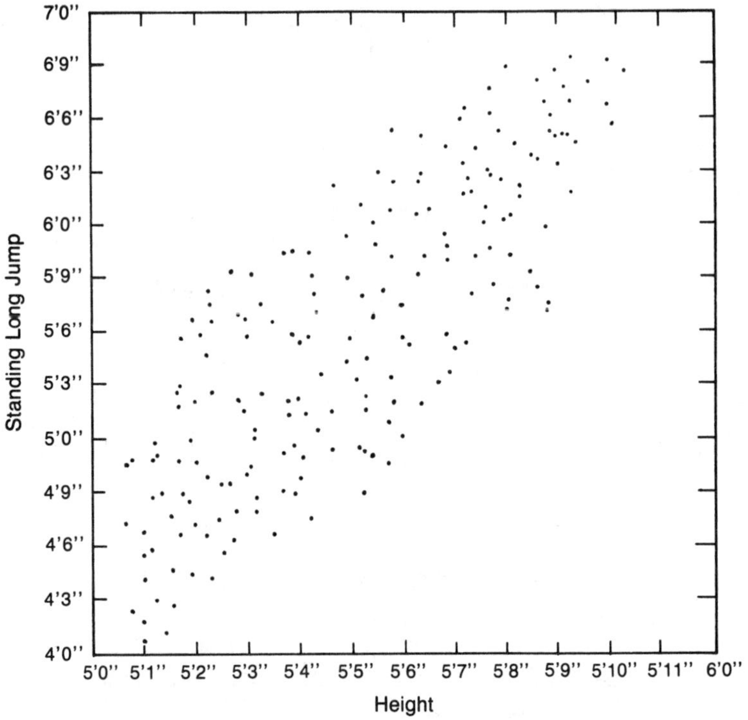

Figure 5.1 Relationship of height and standing long jump.

and have one group participate for 8 weeks in a weight-training program designed to develop leg strength. The other group continues its regular activities. You want to know if the independent variable (weight training versus regular activity) produces a change in the dependent variable (standing long-jump score). Therefore, measure the two groups on standing long-jump scores at the end of the 8 weeks (treatment period) and compare their average performances. In this case, a statistical technique to assess differences between two independent groups called a *t* test would be used. By calculating *t* and comparing it to a value from a *t* table, you can judge if the two groups were significantly different on their average long-jump score. Ways for assessing differences among groups will be discussed in Chapter 7.

COMPUTERS AND STATISTICS

Computers are very helpful in the calculations of statistics. Computers do not make the mistakes that occur in hand calculations and they are many times faster.

Two types of computers will be referred to for statistical analysis in Chapters

5, 6, and 7. First, microcomputers are frequently used in laboratories, offices, and homes for statistical calculations. Micros are small desk-top computers such as the Apple II (II+, IIe), IBMpc, TRS 80, Commodore 64, and others. The computer and its attachments (disk drives, monitors, printers) are called "hardware," and the computer programming is called "software." There are numerous programs written for these computers that will calculate statistics. Included are some sample statistical programs in Appendix B for calculations that are used in Chapters 5, 6, and 7. These specific programs will be referred to as the various statistics are presented. For a particular program, a description, the computer statements in BASIC (a computer language) for an Apple II (or II+ or IIe), and then a sample of the printout from the particular example in the text of the chapter is given. Slight alterations of these programs are required for use with other micros that allow the use of BASIC. All you need to do to use these programs is to type them (exactly as listed) into your Apple II (II+ or IIe with at least 48K and at least one disk drive) and "SAVE" under the appropriate name. When you want to use the program, put in your program storage disk, type "LOAD *program name*," type "RUN," and then follow the instructions.

There are two limitations of micros for statistical analyses. First, some of the sophisticated statistical routines (e.g., Multivariate Analysis of Variance, Canonical Correlation) have seldom been adapted to micros. Second, micros cannot handle large data sets.[1] Both these limitations are due to the limited memory capacity for micros. A greater memory capacity is the major advantage of large mainframe computers.

The second type of computer used for statistical analyses is the large computers (frequently called mainframes) that most colleges and universities have. Several well-known computer packages for these mainframes are available including the UCLA Biomedical Series (BIMED), *Statistical Package for the Social Sciences* (SPSS), and the Statistical Analysis System (SAS).

A brief overview of these three most widely used mainframe statistical packages is included in Appendix C. Most colleges and universities have one or more of these packages which can be used from a terminal, a microcomputer (with proper hardware and software), or through cards on which programming statements and the data are typed by means of a keypunch machine. Your com-

[1]The exact size of the data set a microcomputer can handle cannot be specified in terms the lay reader will understand. It depends on the interaction of the memory capacity of the micro, size of the statistical program to be used, the number of subjects, the number of scores for each subject, and the size of the numbers. For example, the limit is first set by the memory of the micro, which might range from very small (16K) to fairly large (128K). Next, a simple statistical program such as calculating the mean and standard deviation of a measure requires fewer programming statements than a more sophisticated program like a factorial analysis of variance (look at the number of lines each takes in Appendix B). If the memory is smaller and the program is larger, the less memory space remains for data, i.e., number of subjects, number of scores for each subject, and larger (more digits) versus smaller numbers. The above factors are normally not an issue when using mainframe computers.

puter center will have information about equipment and services that are available. Most frequently, you will need to acquire a computer number (and other identification information), which can be obtained easily. Many computer centers provide a "User Services" or "User Consultant Center." They will advise you about the hardware and software available and how to use it. Most institutions also teach statistics courses in which these packages are used. Statistics departments may also offer consulting services on the appropriate use of statistics for research projects. You should carefully investigate the services your institution offers. Senior graduate students and faculty can also advise you on the services that are available.

Reference to the packages for mainframes will not be made again; these packages all include the appropriate programs for techniques presented in these chapters (as well as many other techniques; see Appendix C for an overview). The main advantages of mainframes are that the statistical packages are more sophisticated, well documented, and flexible. In addition, these packages will handle large data sets.

DESCRIPTION AND INFERENCE

These two words, *description* and *inference*, are sometimes confused with statistical techniques. This confusion is the result of saying that correlations describe relationships while cause-effect is inferred by techniques for testing differences among groups. These statements are not necessarily true. The results of any statistic *describe* the sample of subjects for which it was calculated. If the sample of subjects represents some larger group, then the findings can be inferred (or generalized) to the larger group. However, the statistic used has nothing to do with inference. Sampling procedures do or do not allow inference.

SELECTING THE SAMPLE

The sample is the group of subjects on which the study will be conducted. The key issue is how this group is selected. The sample might be randomly selected from some larger group (population). For example, if your college or university has 10,000 students, you could randomly select 200 for a study. You would assign each of the 10,000 students a number-name. The first number-name would be 0000, second 0001, third 0002, up through the last (10,000) who would have the number-name 9999. Then a random number table (see Table A.1, Appendix) would be used. The numbers in this table are arranged in two digit sets so that any combination of rows or columns is unrelated. In this case (number-names from 0000 to 9999) you need to select 200 four-digit numbers. Because the rows and columns are unrelated, you can choose any type systematic strategy to go through the table. Enter the table at random (close your eyes and put your finger on the page). Suppose the place of entering the table is the sixth column of two-digit number on row eight. The number-name here is 9953 (includes column 6 and 7 for four-digit numbers). The subject with that number-name, 9953, is selected, next 9386, and so on. Continue down this column to the bottom of the page, then begin at the top of column 8 with the number-name 2392, and continue until 200 subjects are selected. Column 7 is not used because it was included with column 6 to yield a four-digit number.

The system used in the random number table is not the only one. You can use any systematic way of going through the table. You could read across rows rather than down columns. Of course, the purpose of all this is to select a sample of subjects randomly so that the sample is representative of the larger population; that is, the findings in the sample can be inferred back to the larger population. From an inferential viewpoint, this says that a characteristic, relationship, or difference found in the sample is likely to also be present in the population from which the sample was selected.

In Appendix B is a computer program that will do random selection for you on a microcomputer (Apple II, II+, IIe). Once you have typed and saved the *Random* program, all you need to do is choose the random selection option that will appear on the screen. You then tell the computer the population size and the sample size that is to be selected and the program will list the selected numbers.

Another type of sampling is *stratified random sampling*. The population is divided (stratified) on some characteristic prior to random selection of the sample. Returning to the previous example, the selection was of 200 subjects from a population of 10,000. Suppose your college is 30% freshmen, 30% sophomores, 20% juniors, and 20% seniors. You could stratify on class prior to random selection to make sure the sample was exact in terms of class representation. In this case, you would randomly select 60 subjects from the 3000 freshmen, 60 from the 3000 sophomores, 40 from the 2000 juniors, and 40 from the 2000 seniors. This still yields a total sample of 200.

Stratified random sampling might be particularly appropriate for survey or interview research. Suppose you suspect that attitude toward drug use changed over the college years. You might use a stratified random sampling technique for interviewing 200 college students to test this hypothesis. Another example would be to develop normative data on a physical fitness test for grades four to eight in a school district. Because performance would be related to age, you should stratify the population by age prior to randomly selecting your sample on which to collect normative data.

If the population from which the sample is to be selected is very large, assigning a number-name to each potential subject is time consuming. Suppose you want to sample a town with a population of 50,000 concerning the need for new recreational facilities. An approach would be to use *systematic sampling* from the telephone book. You might decide to call a sample of 500 people. To do so, you would select every 100th name in the phone book. Of course, you are assuming that the telephone book represents the population. Said another way, everyone you need to sample has a telephone. This turned out to be a very bad assumption in the 1948 Presidential election (Dewey versus Truman). The pollsters had predicted Dewey to win by a substantial margin. However, the pollsters had sampled from telephone books in key areas. Unfortunately, for Dewey, many people without telephones voted and Truman won. His victory was called an upset, but it was an upset only because of poor sampling procedures.

Systematic sampling will yield a good sample and should be equivalent to random sampling if the sample is fairly large. However, random sampling is generally preferred.

Sometimes random sampling of subjects is nearly impossible to achieve. This is a particular problem in more field-oriented (applied) research. As an illustration, children are placed in classrooms in schools at the beginning of the year. It may be impossible to randomly select children from classes or schools. In this case, the unit that is randomly selected might change. If three school systems are to participate in a study, each class within a school could be given a number-name and 25 classes randomly selected; or classes could be stratified by grade level prior to random selection. The procedures are the same, only the unit has changed from the individual child to the class. The same idea can be applied to school systems, athletic teams, and physical education activity classes. While random selection of subjects is preferred, any unit of random selection adds to the ability to generalize the results.

RANDOM ASSIGNMENT

In experimental research, groups are formed within the sample. The issue here is *not how* the sample was selected, but *how* the groups are formed within the sample. Chapter 11 will discuss experimental research and *true* experimental designs. All true designs require that the groups within the sample be *randomly assigned* or *randomized*. While this requirement has nothing to do with the selection of the sample, the procedures used for random assignment are the same. Each subject in the sample is given a number-name. If the sample has 30 subjects, the number-names go from 00 to 29. Suppose three equal groups (n = 10 per group) are to be formed. Enter a table of random numbers; the first number-name encountered between 00 and 29 goes in Group 1, the second in Group 2, and so on until each group has 10 subjects.

This process allows the researcher to assume the groups are equivalent at the beginning of the experiment, one of several important features of good experimental design where the purpose of the research is to establish cause-effect.

In Appendix B the same computer program that was mentioned earlier in random selection allows random assignment of subjects to groups. When the menu appears on the screen, select the random assignment option. Respond to the computer's request for your sample size, number of groups, and whether or not the groups will be equal in the number of subjects. The computer program will then list the subject numbers assigned to each group.

POST-HOC EXPLANATIONS

Frequently, the sample for research is not randomly selected, but the researcher will attempt a *post-hoc* justification that the sample is representative of some larger group. A typical example might include showing that the sample does not differ in average age, racial balance, or socioeconomic status from some larger group. Of course, the purpose is to allow the findings on the sample to be generalized to the larger group. A post-hoc attempt at generalization may be better than nothing, but it is not the equivalent of random selection. Random selection allows the assumption that the sample does not differ from the population on the characteristics you measure as well as any other characteristics. In a post-hoc justification, only the characteristics measured can be compared. Whether those are the ones that really matter is open to speculation.

This same justification is used to compare intact groups, which are designs where groups within the sample are not randomly formed. Except in this case, the post-hoc justification is that because the groups did not differ on certain measured characteristics prior to the beginning of study, they can be judged equivalent. Of course, the same point applies—Are the groups different on some unmeasured characteristic that affects the results? The question cannot be answered satisfactorily. But as before, a good post-hoc justification of equivalence does add strength to comparisons of intact groups.

MATHEMATICAL CONCEPTS AND STATISTICAL SYMBOLS

Before beginning a discussion of statistical techniques, a review of basic mathematical concepts may be helpful. The presentation in Table 5.1 is rather basic, so don't hesitate to skip over it if you are competent in its content.

Statistical formulas frequently use symbols in combination with mathematical functions. Table 5.2 explains the symbols to be used and provides some examples of their use in connection with the mathematical functions used in Table 5.1.

MEASURES OF CENTRAL TENDENCY AND VARIABILITY

When you have a group of scores, one number may be used to represent the group. The statistic with which most of you are familiar where this occurs is the *mean* ($\bar{X}$ or M) or average. Formula 5.1 is the formula for the mean.

$$M = \Sigma X/N \quad \textbf{(5.1)}$$

TABLE 5.1
MATHEMATICAL FUNCTIONS

1. + means add
2. − means subtract
3. × or • means multiply
4. ÷ or / or $\overline{)\quad}$ means divide
5. $\sqrt{\quad}$ means take the square root
6. ^{2}superscript or raised number means to multiply the number by itself that many times, $2^2 = 2 \times 2 = 4$; $3^3 = 3 \times 3 \times 3 = 27$
7. ( ) means perform mathematical acts inside parentheses first, $3(2 + 3) = 3(5) = 15$
8. multiply and divide before adding and subtracting unless parentheses indicate otherwise
9. like signs are always added, $-7 - 4 = -11$

Useful examples

Addition of signed numbers	$+3 - 2 = 1$, $-3 + 1 = -2$, $-5 + 4 - 3 = (-5 - 3) + 4 = -8 + 4 = -4$
Subtraction of signed numbers	$-4 - 3 = -7$, $+4 - 3 = 1$, $-4 + 3 = -1$, $(-4) - (-3) = -4 + 3 = -1$
Multiplication of signed numbers	$(-3) \times (-4) = +12$, $(-3) \times 4 = -12$, $+5 \cdot -3 = -15$, $(3)(4)(-2) = -24$
Division of signed numbers	$-12/-4 = 3$, $-24/-3 = 8$, $(9/-3)(-2) = 6$, $4/2 + -8/2 = -2$
Complex cases	$(3 - 4)(-5 - 2) = (-1)(-7) = 7$, $(3 + 5)/(-3 + 1) = 8/-2 = -4$

TABLE 5.2
STATISTICAL SYMBOLS

1. Σ means to sum or add
2. X or Y represents a given number
3. $\overline{X}$ or M represents the mean or average of several numbers
4. *x* or *y* is a deviation score, $x = X - M$
5. *N* is the number of subjects in the sample
6. *n* is the number of subjects within sample subgroups
7. *SD* or *s* represents the standard deviation
8. s^2 represents the variance

Examples

1. $x_1 = 2, x_2 = 4, x_3 = 1, x_4 = 5$
   $\Sigma X = 2 + 4 + 1 + 5 = 12$
2. $Y_1 = 7, Y_2 = 3, Y_3 = 2, Y_4 = 4$
   $\Sigma Y = 7 + 3 + 2 + 4 = 16$
3. $\Sigma X^2 = 2^2 + 4^2 + 1^2 + 5^2 = 4 + 16 + 1 + 25 = 46$
4. $(\Sigma X)^2 = (2 + 4 + 1 + 5)^2 = 12^2 = 144$

Thus, if you have the following numbers—4, −5, 3, 6, −2, −1, 4, −2, 3, −3,—then

$$M = [(4+3+6+4+3) + (-5-2-1-2-3)]/10 = (20-13)/10 = 7/10 = 0.7$$

The number 0.7 is the average or represents this series of numbers.

Sometimes the mean may not be the most representative or characteristic score. Suppose you have the numbers 4, 5, 4, 6, 3, 5, 26, 3, 4, 2. The mean is 6.2, a number larger than all but one of the scores. It is not very representative because one score (26) has made the average high. In this case, another measure of central tendency called the *median* is more useful. The median is the score in the middle. In our example, if you arrange the numbers from lowest to highest—2, 3, 3, 4, 4, 4, 5, 5, 6, 26—the midpoint or middle score is a 4, which is a much more representative score.

Most often you will be interested in the mean of a group of scores. However, you may occasionally be interested in the median or another central tendency measure, the *mode*, which is the most frequently occurring score. In the previous example the mode is also 4 as it occurs three times.

Another characteristic of a group of scores is their variability. An estimate of the variability or spread of the scores can be calculated as the standard deviation (*s* or *SD*).

$$s = \sqrt{\Sigma(X-M)^2/(N-1)} \qquad \textbf{(5.2)}$$

This formula translates as, calculate the *M* by formula 5.1, subtract each subject's score from the mean ($X - M$), square the answer, sum the squared scores, divide by the number of subjects minus one ($N - 1$), and take the square root of the answer. Table 5.3 provides an example.

The *M* and *s* together are good descriptors of a set of scores. If the *s* is large, the *M* may not be a good representation. Roughly 68% of a set of scores fall between $\pm$ 1 *s*, about 95% of the scores fall between $\pm$ 2 *s*, and about 99% of the scores fall between $\pm$ 3 *s*.

Formula 5.2 was used to help you understand the meaning of the *s*. For use with a hand calculator, formula 5.3 is easier.

$$s = \sqrt{N\Sigma X^2 - (\Sigma X)^2/[N(N-1)]} \qquad (5.3)$$

One final point for later consideration, the square of the standard deviation is called the variance, s^2.

Appendix B contains a description of the computer program (Descriptive Statistics), the program itself, and a sample printout. The data analyzed are those from Table 5.3.

Sometimes the *range* of scores may also be reported, particularly when the median is used rather than the mean. The median and mean may be used in connection with each other. For example, 15 subjects might be given 10 blocks of

TABLE 5.3
CALCULATION OF MEAN AND STANDARD DEVIATION

Subjects	X	X − M	(X − M)²
1	2	−2	4
2	4	0	0
3	3	−1	1
4	5	1	1
5	6	2	4
Σ	20	0	10

$M = \Sigma X/N = 20/5 = 4$

$s = \sqrt{\Sigma(X - M)^2/(N - 1)} = \sqrt{10/4} = \sqrt{2.5} = 1.58$

10 trials (100 total trials) on a reaction time (RT) task. The experimenter may decide to use the median RT of a subject's 10 trials as the most representative score in each block. Thus, each subject would have 10 median scores, one for each of the 10 trial blocks. In this situation, the range of scores from which the median was selected should be reported. The *M* and *s* would be reported for the 15 subjects' scores at trial block 1, trial block 2, and so on. Thus, the range is reported for the selection of the median at each trial block, while the standard deviation is reported for the group mean at each trial block.

CHARACTERISTICS OF DATA

The use of various statistical tests depends upon meeting the assumptions for those tests. Tests fall into two general categories. The first, *parametric* statistical tests, has two assumptions about the distribution of the data: (a) the population from which the sample is drawn must be normally distributed on the variable of interest, and (b) the population must have the same variances on the variable of interest. In addition, certain parametric techniques have additional assumptions. The second category, *nonparametric* statistics, is called distribution-free because the two assumptions do not have to be met.

Whenever the assumptions are met, parametric statistics are preferred because they have more *power*. To have power means to increase the chances of rejecting a false null hypothesis. You frequently *assume* that the two assumptions for use of parametric statistics are met. The assumptions can be tested by the use of estimates of *skewness* and *kurtosis*. Only the meaning of these tests will be explained. Any basic statistics book provides considerably more detail.

To explain skewness and kurtosis, first consider the normal distribution in Figure 5.2. In a normal curve the mean, median and mode are at the same point

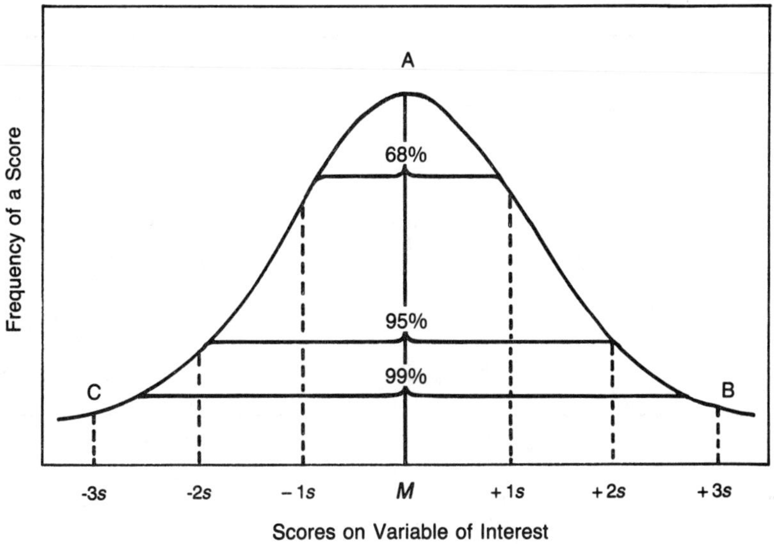

Figure 5.2 The normal curve.

(center of the distribution). In addition, ± 1 *s* includes 68% of the scores, ± 2 *s* includes 95% of the scores, and ± 3 *s* includes 99% of the scores. Thus, data distributed as in Figure 5.2 would meet the two assumptions for use of parametric techniques. Skewness of the distribution describes the direction of the hump of the curve (labeled A) and the nature of the tails of the curve (labeled B and C). If the hump (A) is shifted to the left and the long tail (B) is to the right as in Figure 5.3a, the skewness is positive. If the shift of the hump (A) is to the right and the long tail (C) to the left (Figure 5.3b), the skewness is negative. Kurtosis describes the shape of the curve, for example whether the curve is more peaked or flatter than the normal curve. Figure 5.4a shows a more peaked curve while 5.4b shows a flatter curve.

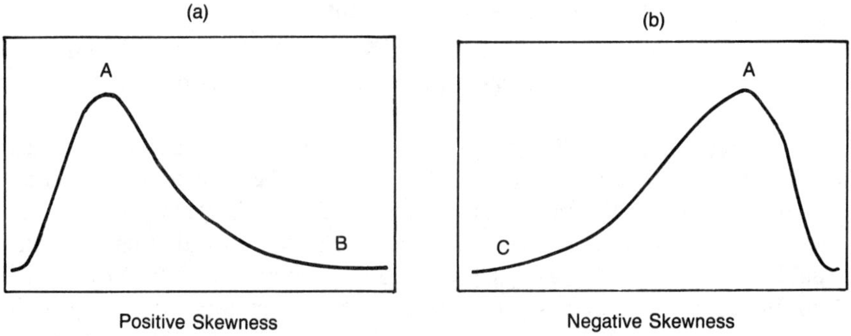

Figure 5.3 Skewed curves.

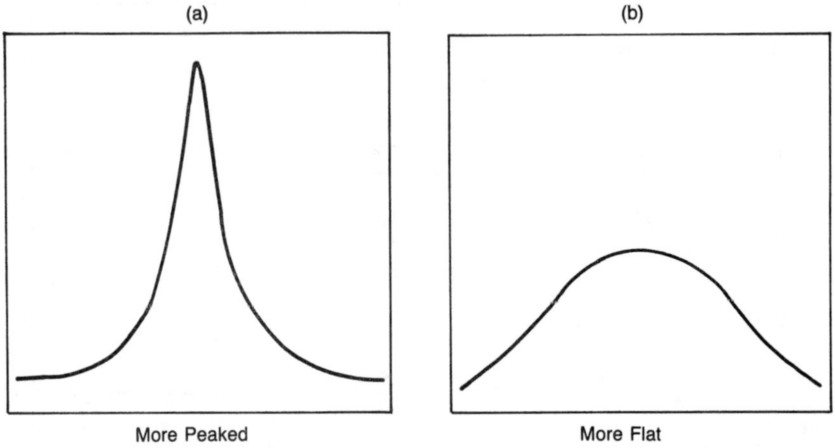

Figure 5.4 Curves with abnormal kurtosis.

In the remainder of this section of the book, consider that the two basic assumptions for parametric statistical tests have been met. This is done for three reasons: First, the assumptions are very robust to violations, meaning that the outcome of the statistical test is relatively accurate even with fairly severe violations of the assumptions; second, most of the research in HPERD uses parametric tests; and third, nonparametric tests are relatively easy to understand. (For a good presentation on nonparametric tests, see Conover, 1971.)

WHAT STATISTICS CAN DO

The statistical techniques presented in the next two chapters tell the following two things about the data to which they are applied:

1. *Is the effect or relationship of interest a reliable one?* That is, can you count on it? Or, if the experiment is repeated, will the effect or relationship be there again—is it significant?
2. *How strong (or meaningful) is the effect or relationship of interest?* This really refers to the magnitude or size of the effect or relationship.

Two facts are important about the two statements listed above: First, statement one always takes precedence over statement two, for the strength of the relationship or effect is not of interest until it is known to be a reliable (significant) one; second, statement two is always of interest if the effect or relationship is significant. Sometimes in elating over the significance of effects and relationships, one loses sight of the need to look at the strength or meaningfulness of these relationships. This is particularly true in research in which differences among groups are compared. The experimenter frequently forgets that relatively small differences can be significant. That only means that the differences are reliable or that the same answers can be obtained if the research is repeated. The experimenter then needs to look at the size of the differences to interpret if the findings are meaningful. For each technique presented in the next two chapters, testing will first emphasize if the relationship or effect is significant (reliable), and then ways to evaluate the strength (meaningfulness) of the relationship or effect will be suggested.

CATEGORIES OF STATISTICAL TECHNIQUES

While it is inaccurate to divide statistical techniques into categories, they are most frequently divided into two distinct groups: statistical techniques used to test relationships between or among several variables in one group of subjects (regression or correlation); and techniques used to test differences between or among groups of subjects (*t*-tests and ANOVA). This division is inaccurate because both sets of techniques are based upon the general linear model and only involve different ways of entering data and manipulating variance components. However, an introduction to research methods is neither the place to reform the "world of statistics according to Thomas and Nelson," nor to confuse you. Thus, the techniques as two distinct groups will be considered. (For a discussion of relationship between analysis of variance and regression techniques, see Pedhazur, 1982.) Chapter 6 discusses relationships between and among variables (simple correlation, multiple correlation, and canonical correlation), while Chapter 7 discusses differences between and among groups (*t*-tests, analysis of variance, discriminant analysis, and multivariate analysis of variance). Teaching you the relatively simple calculations underlying the easier techniques and building on this helps you to intuitively understand the more complex ones. Do not panic because statistics involves manipulating numbers, for you can escape from this section with a reasonable grasp of how, why, and when the various statistical techniques are used in HPERD.

Remember, however, that correlation between two variables does not indicate causation. Causation is not determined from any statistic, correlation, or otherwise. Cause-effect is established by the total experimental situation of which statistics is a part. As summarized from Pedhazur (1982, p. 579).

> "Correlation is no proof of causation." Nor does any other index prove causation, regardless of whether the index was derived from data collected in experimental or in nonexperimental research. Covariations or correlations among variables may be suggestive of causal linkages. Nevertheless, an explanatory scheme is not arrived at on the basis of the data, but rather on the basis of knowledge, theoretical formulations and assumptions, and logical analyses. It is the explanatory scheme of

the researcher that determines the type of analysis to be applied to data, and not the other way around.

PROBABILITY

Probability means "what are the odds certain things will happen?" You use probability in everyday events. What are the chances that it will rain? Or sometimes a number is attached as in the weather report, for example, the probability of rain is 90%. You always wonder if that means it will rain in 90% of the places or more likely, the chances are 90% that it will rain where you are. The terms *subjective* or personalistic probability are used to describe this concept.

A second concept of probability is called *equally likely* events. For instance, if you roll a die, the chances of the numbers from 1 to 6 occurring is equally likely, 1 in 6. The third approach to probability involves *relative frequency*. To illustrate, suppose you toss a coin 100 times. You would expect a head 50 times and a tail 50 times; the probability is .50 or 1/2 or 50%. However, in tossing, you get a head 48 times or .48. That is the relative frequency. You might do this 10 times and never get .50, but the relative frequency would be distributed closely about .50, and you would still assume the probability as .50.

In a statistical test you are sampling from a population of subjects and events. You use probability statements to describe the confidence you place in the statistical findings. Frequently, you will encounter a statistical test followed by a probability statement such as $p < .05$. This interpretation would be that a difference or relationship of this size would be expected less than 5 times in 100 to be due to chance.

In research, the statistical test is always compared to a probability table for that statistic which tells you what the chance occurrence is. The experimeter establishes an acceptable level of chance occurrence (called alpha, α) prior to the study. This level of chance occurrence can be varied from low to high, but can never be eliminated. For any given study, the probability of the findings being due to chance always exists. Or, to quote *Holten's Homily*, "The only time to be positive is when you are positive you are wrong."

In behavioral research, alpha (probability of chance occurrence) is frequently set at .05 or .01 (the odds the findings are due to chance are either 5 in 100 or 1 in 100). There is nothing magic about .05 or .01. They are used to control for Type I error. In a study, the experimenter may make two types of error. A Type I error is to reject the null hypothesis (Ho) when the null hypothesis is true, while a Type II error is not to reject the null hypothesis when the null hypothesis is false. Figure 5.5 is called a truth table and demonstrates Type I and II errors. As you can see, to accept a true Ho or reject a false Ho is the correct decision. Control for Type I error is obtained by setting alpha. For example, if α is set at .05, then if we conduct 100 experiments, a true Ho of no difference or no relationship would only be rejected on 5 occasions. While the chances for error still exist, the experimenter has specified them exactly by establishing alpha prior to the study.

	Ho TRUE	Ho FALSE
ACCEPT	Correct Decision	Type II Error (β)
REJECT	Type I Error (α)	Correct Decision

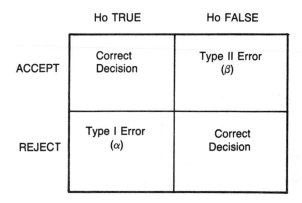

Figure 5.5 Truth table for null hypothesis (Ho).

Although some people disagree, alpha should be specified prior to the research, and findings should be reported at the alpha that has been specified. Results are either significant at the specified alpha or not—not much is in between. It is like being pregnant—one either is or is not. Alpha works the same way. It is established as a criterion and results either meet the criterion or they don't. Although sometimes experimenters may report borderline significance (if α is .05, they label from .051 to .10 as borderline), whether you do this or not reflects the type error you are willing to make. In fact, the level of alpha reflects the type error you are willing to make. In other words, if you had to make an error, would you rather reject a true Ho or not? For example, in a study of the effect of a drug on curing cancer, the experimenter would not want to accept the Ho of no effect if there was any chance the drug worked. Thus, the experimenter might set alpha at .30 even though the odds of making a Type I error would be inflated. The experimeter is making sure that the drug has every opportunity to show its effectiveness. On the other hand, setting alpha at .001 decreases the odds of sending other researchers on a "wild goose chase," or it reduces the odds of making a Type I error.

We cannot tell you where to set alpha; however, we can say that the levels .05 or .01 are widely accepted in the scientific community. If it is to be moved up or down, then justify the reason. Regardless, set alpha prior to the research and compare your values to the established level. If borderline findings are to be reported, clearly label them as borderline.

While the magnitude of Type I error is specified by alpha, you may also make a Type II error, the magnitude of which is determined by beta (β). By looking at Figure 5.6, you can see the overlap of the score distribution on the dependent variable for X (the sampling distribution if the Ho is true) and Y (the sampling distribution if the Ho is false). By specifying α, you indicate that the *M* of Y (given a certain distribution) must be a specified distance away before the Ho is rejected. However, if the *M* of Y falls anywhere between the *M* of X and the specified Y, you could be making a Type II error (β). That is, you do not reject the Ho when, in fact, there is a true difference. Although we will not go into

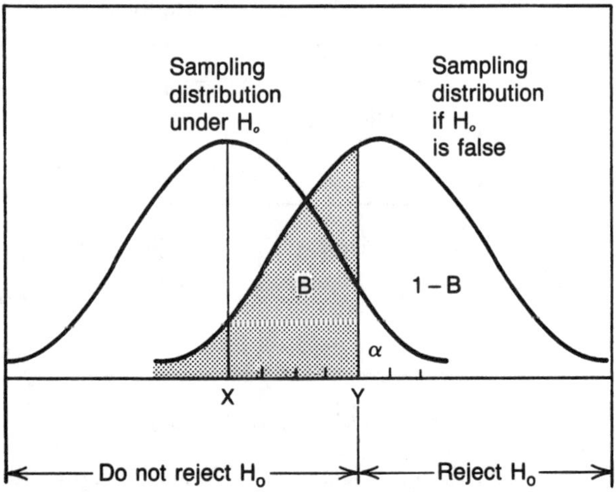

Figure 5.6 Regions under the normal curve corresponding to probabilities of making Type I and Type II errors. From *Experimental design: Procedures for the behavioral sciences* (p. 30) by R.E. Kirk, 1968, Belmont, CA: Brooks/Cole Publishing. Reprinted with permission.

the formulas here, β can be calculated (Kirk, 1968; Winer, 1971). As you can see, there is a relationship between α and β, for example, as α is set increasingly smaller, β becomes larger.

Once β is determined, then power $(1 - \beta)$ can be determined. Power is the probability of rejecting the Ho when the Ho is false, for example, $1 - \beta$ or the chances of making a correct decision. Having "power" in the statistical analysis is important because it increases the odds of rejecting a false Ho. Once β is determined along with certain other parameters, the necessary sample size needed for any level of power can be calculated. As Kirk (1968, p. 9) has indicated, five factors are necessary to estimate the sample size required to test a statistical hypothesis:

1. Minimum treatment effects an experimenter is interested in detecting,
2. Number of treatment levels,
3. Population error variance,
4. Probability of making a Type I error, and
5. Probability of making a Type II error.

Of course, all the necessary information may not be available in all experiments. However, the formulas for estimating some of the above parameters as well as power and sample size can be found in Kirk (1968) and Winer (1971). This will be discussed further in Chapter 7 although our approach is more *post hoc*, as it involves reporting the variance accounted for in significant findings and interpreting whether this is a meaningful effect. The procedures described above and calculated *a priori* are more desirable, but they are not always applicable.

PROBLEMS

Two groups ($n = 7$ in each group) of 7-year-old children are led on a 35 m jog down a 50 m string placed on the ground. They are then asked to reproduce the distance by jogging 35 m on a second 50 m string placed at a right angle to the first string. The experimental group is told before they begin that the best way to remember the distance jogged is to count steps. The control group is told to remember as best they can. Below is the error in m each subject made when asked to estimate the distance jogged.

Experimental Group	Control Group
2.55	7.68
3.62	6.80
3.42	5.68
2.86	3.97
2.00	7.23
1.08	5.48
1.16	6.03

1. Using formula 5.1, calculate the mean for each group.
2. Using formula 5.2, calculate the standard deviation for each group.
3. Use formula 5.3 to calculate the standard deviations to see if the answer is the same as 5.2.
4. Make a list of 50 names. Using the table of random numbers (A.1 in Appendix A), randomly select 24 subjects and then randomly assign the 24 subjects to two groups of 12 each.

Chapter 6

Relationships Among Variables

Correlation is a statistical technique used to determine the relationship between two or more variables. This chapter will briefly discuss several types of correlation, the reliability and meaningfulness of correlation coefficients, and the use of correlation for predictions.

THE PURPOSE OF CORRELATION

Oftentimes a researcher is interested in the degree of relationship between performances, such as the relationship between performances on a distance run and a step test as measures of cardiovascular fitness. Sometimes an investigator wishes to establish the relationship between traits and behavior, such as how personality characteristics relate to participation in high-risk recreational activities. Still other correlational research problems might involve relationships between anthropometric measurements, such as skinfold thicknesses and percent fat as determined by underwater weighing. Here, the researcher may wish to predict percent fat from the skinfold measurements.

Correlation may involve two variables such as the relationship between height and weight, or more than two variables as when one investigates the relationship between a criterion (dependent variable) such as cardiovascular fitness and two or more predictor variables (independent variables) such as body weight, percent fat, speed, muscular endurance, and so on. This is multiple correlation. There is also a technique (canonical correlation) to study the relationships between two or more dependent variables and two or more independent variables. These types of correlation will be discussed in more detail later in the chapter.

THE NATURE OF CORRELATION

The coefficient of correlation is a quantitative value of the relationship between two or more variables. The correlation coefficient can range from 0.00 to 1.00 in either a positive or negative direction. Hence, perfect correlation is 1.00 (either +1.00 or −1.00) and no relationship is 0.00.

Positive correlation is when a small amount of one variable is associated with a small amount of another variable, and a large amount of one variable is associated with a large amount of the other. Strength and body weight are positively correlated in that heavier persons are generally stronger than lighter persons. (However, some lighter people are stronger than some heavier people and weaker than some who weigh even less.)

In Figure 6.1 is a graphic illustration of a perfect positive correlation. Notice that Tom's body weight is one standard deviation above the mean, for he weighs 110, and the mean is 90. Thus, he is 20 pounds heavier than the mean, which is one standard deviation ($s = 20$). His strength score is 250 pounds, which is 50 pounds higher than the mean of 200. Since the standard deviation is 50, this means he is one standard deviation above the mean on strength just as he was on body weight. The second boy, Bill, is one standard deviation below the mean on weight and one s below on strength. The third boy is exactly at the mean on both variables (he weighs 90 lbs and has a strength score of 200). Joe is one-half standard deviation above and Dick is one-half standard deviation below the means for weight and strength.

Hence, when the scores are plotted, they form a perfectly straight, diagonal line. This is perfect correlation ($r = 1.00$). The relative positions of the boys' pairs of scores are identical in the two distributions. In other words, each boy

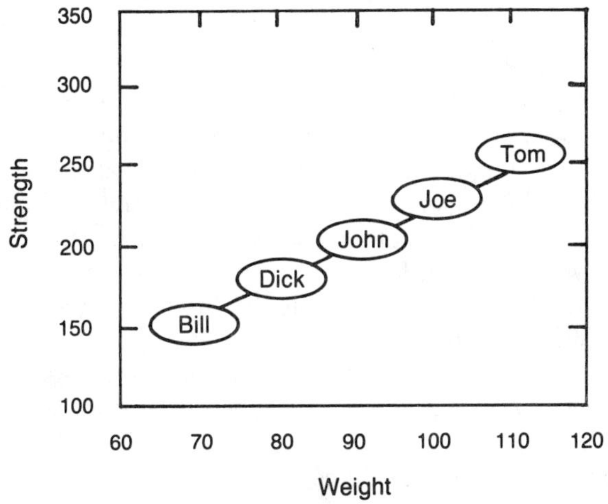

Figure 6.1. Perfect positive correlation.

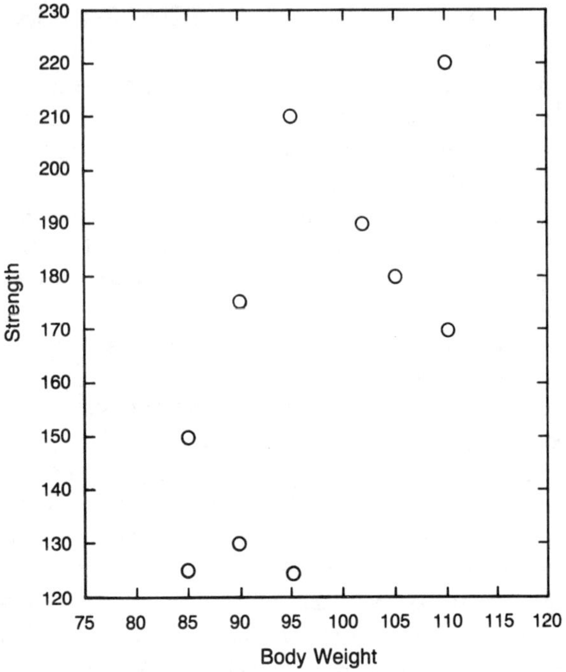

Figure 6.2 A more realistic correlation between body weight and strength (r = .67).

is the same relative distance from the mean of each set of scores. Common sense tells us that perfect correlation does not exist in human traits, abilities, and performances because of "people variability" and other influences.

Figure 6.2 illustrates a more realistic relationship between body weight and strength (r = .67). (Fictional examples have been used for purposes of presentation in this and other chapters. These examples do *not* represent actual data.)

When these 10 sets of body weights and strength scores are plotted, they no longer constitute a straight line, but they still form a diagonal plot in the same lower left to upper right pattern as the previous example in Figure 6.1.

Next, in Figure 6.3, let us plot the body weights and pull-up scores for the same 10 boys. A pull-up is performed by hoisting one's body weight from a hanging position until the chin is above the bar. For this test, body weight is somewhat of a liability, often indicating that heavier persons tend to do fewer pull-ups than lighter persons. As a result, a small number of pull-ups is associated with larger body weights, and, conversely, greater numbers of pull-ups are associated with lesser body weights: This is a negative correlation. A perfect negative correlation would be a straight diagonal line in exactly the opposite direction as that of the perfect positive correlation. Figure 6.3 depicts a negative correlation but of a rather low degree (r = −.54). However, an upper left to lower right pattern is still apparent.

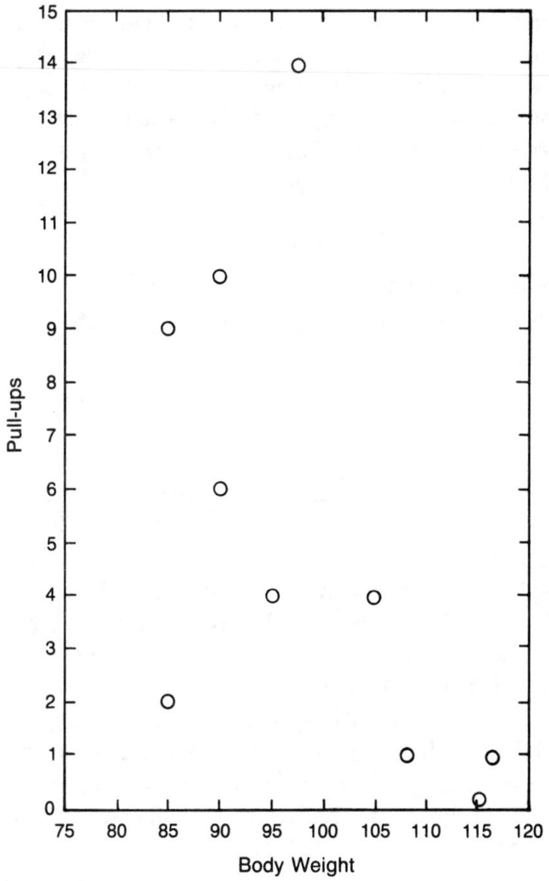

Figure 6.3 Negative correlation between body weight and pull-ups ($r = -.54$).

When there is virtually no relationship between variables the correlation is 0.00. This denotes independence between sets of scores. The plotted scores exhibit no discernible pattern at all. The interpretation of correlations as to their reliability and meaningfulness will be explained later.

PEARSON PRODUCT MOMENT CORRELATION

Several times in the preceding discussion we have used the symbol r. This symbol denotes the Pearson product moment coefficient of correlation. In this type of correlation, there is one criterion (or dependent) variable and one predictor (or independent) variable. Thus, every subject has two scores, such as body weight and strength.

The computation of the correlation coefficient involves the relative distances of the scores from the two means of the distributions. The computations can be accomplished with a number of different formulas; we will just present one. This formula is sometimes called the computer method because it involves similar operations as performed by a computer. The formula appears large and imposing, but actually it only consists of three operations:

1. Summing each set of scores,
2. Squaring and summing each set of scores, and
3. Multiplying each pair of scores and obtaining the cumulative sum of these products.

The formula is

$$r = \frac{N\Sigma XY - (\Sigma X)(\Sigma Y)}{\sqrt{N\Sigma X^2 - (\Sigma X)^2}\ \sqrt{N\Sigma Y^2 - (\Sigma Y)^2}} \qquad \textbf{(6.1)}$$

To illustrate the calculations involved, we will use the body weight and pull-up scores from Figure 6.3 and designate the body weights as the X variable. In a correlation problem to just determine the relationship between two variables, it doesn't matter which one is X and which is Y. If the investigator wants to predict one score from the other, then Y designates the criterion (dependent) variable—that which is being predicted—and X is the predictor or independent variable. In this example, strength performance would be predicted from body weight as it would not make much sense to predict body weight from strength scores. Prediction equations are discussed later in this section.

The computations for the correlation between body weight and pull-ups are shown in Table 6.1. Note that N refers to the number of *paired* scores, not the total number of scores.

The ΣX^2 and ΣY^2 columns are the raw scores squared and summed. For the $(\Sigma X)^2$ and the $(\Sigma Y)^2$ values, the *sums* of the raw scores for X and Y are then squared. Notice that these values are not the same as the ΣX^2 and ΣY^2 values. The ΣXY—the sum of the cross products of the X and Y scores—determines the direction of the correlation as to whether it is positive or negative. In this example, a negative correlation was obtained because the first half of the numerator ($N\Sigma XY$) was smaller than the second half, $(\Sigma X)(\Sigma Y)$.

The negative correlation between body weight and pull-ups means that as body weight increased, pull-up performance decreased. Sometimes a negative correlation coefficient results when the relationship is really positive. Confusing? The following examples should clarify the meaning. Suppose we were to correlate scores on the vertical jump and the 40-yard dash. Both performances are heavily loaded with power. Thus, persons who score well on the vertical jump should also do well on the 40-yard dash because the two tests are measuring much the same thing; hence, the relationship between performances is positive. However,

TABLE 6.1
CALCULATING *r*

X (Body Wt)	*Y* (Pull-ups)	X^2	Y^2	*XY*
104	4	10816	16	416
86	2	7396	4	172
92	6	8464	36	552
112	1	12544	1	112
96	4	9216	16	384
98	13	9604	169	1274
110	0	12100	0	0
86	9	7396	81	774
105	1	11025	1	105
91	10	8281	100	910
980	50	96842	424	4699

$$r = \frac{N\Sigma XY - (\Sigma X)(\Sigma Y)}{\sqrt{N\Sigma X^2 - (\Sigma X)^2}\ \sqrt{N\Sigma Y^2 - (\Sigma Y)^2}}$$

$$r = \frac{(10)4699 - (980)(50)}{\sqrt{10(96842) - (980)^2}\ \sqrt{10(424) - (50)^2}}$$

$$r = \frac{46990 - 49000}{\sqrt{968420 - 960400}\ \sqrt{4240 - 2500}}$$

$$r = \frac{-2010}{\sqrt{8020}\ \sqrt{1740}}$$

$$r = \frac{-2010}{(89.6)(41.7)} = \frac{-2010}{3736.3} = -.54$$

the vertical jump is scored in inches (or centimeters) where a high score is good; and the 40-yard dash is scored in seconds where a low number (fewer seconds) is good. Therefore, the correlation coefficient would be negative.

The correlation between the distance a person could run in 12 minutes and heart rate after exercise would also be negative. This is because a greater distance covered is good, and a lower rate after exercise is good. A person who has good cardiovascular endurance would have a high score on the one test (the run) and a low score on the other.

THE INTERPRETATION OF *r*

So far we have been dealing with the nature of correlation as to direction (positive or negative) and the calculation of *r*. An obvious question that arises is, What does a coefficient of correlation mean in terms of being high or low, satisfactory or unsatisfactory? This seemingly simple question is not so simple to answer.

First, there are several ways of interpreting r. One criterion is its *reliability* or *significance*. Is it a real correlation? That is, if the study were repeated, what is the probability of getting a similar relationship? For this statistical criterion of significance, simply consult a table. In using the table, select the desired level of significance, such as the .05 level, and then enter the table in accordance with the appropriate degrees of freedom, which is equal to $N - 2$. Table A.2 (Appendix A) contains the necessary correlation coefficients for significance at the .05 and .01 levels. Refer back to the example of the correlation between body weight and pull-ups ($r = -.54$). The degrees of freedom arc $N - 2 = 10 - 2 = 8$ (remember, the N in correlation refers to the number of pairs of scores). When entering the table at 8 degrees of freedom (*df*), we see that an r of .632 is necessary for significance at the .05 level (and .765 at the .01 level). Therefore, we would have to conclude that our correlation of $-.54$ is not significant.

A lingering glance at Table A.2 reveals a couple obvious facts. One, the correlation needed for significance decreases with increased numbers of subjects—degrees of freedom. In our example, we only had 10 subjects (or pairs of scores). However, if four more boys had been in the sample ($N = 14$), then the *df* would be 12, and the r required for significance at the .05 level for 12 *df*, is .532, and our r of $-.54$ meets that test of significance. But notice that very low correlation coefficients can be significant if you have a large sample of subjects. At the .05 level, an r of .38 is significant with 25 *df*; $r = .27$ is significant at 50 *df*; and .195 is significant with 100 *df*. In fact, with 1000 *df*, an r of .08 is significant at the .01 level.

The second observation noted from the table is that a higher r is required for significance at the .01 level than at the .05. This should make sense. Remember, Chapter 5 stated that the .05 level means that if 100 experiments were conducted, the null hypothesis (that there is no relationship) would be rejected incorrectly—just by chance—on 5 of the 100 occasions. At the .01 level, we would expect a relationship of this magnitude less than 1 time in 100 due to chance. Therefore, the test of significance at the .01 level is more stringent than at the .05 level, and so a higher r is required for significance at the .01 level.

The interpretation of a correlation for statistical significance is important, but because of the vast influence of sample size, this criterion is not always meaningful. As Chapter 5 explained, statistics can tell two things about data: Are the effects reliable? and Are they meaningful?

The most commonly used criterion for interpreting r as to meaningfulness is the *coefficient of determination* (r^2). In this method, the portion of common association of the factors which influence the two variables is determined. In other words, r^2 indicates the portion of the total variance in one measure which can be explained, or accounted for, by the variance in the other measure.

For example, the standing long jump and the vertical jump are common tests of explosive power. The tests are so commonly used that we tend to think of them as interchangeable—that is, as measuring the same thing. Yet correlations between the two tests usually range between .70 and .80. The coefficients of determination (r^2) range from .49 ($.70^2$) to .64 ($.80^2$). Usually the coefficient of determination is multiplied by 100 and then expressed as *percent of variation*. Thus, $.70^2 = .49 \times 100 = 49\%$, and $.80^2 = .64 \times 100 = 64\%$.

For a correlation of .70 between the standing long jump and vertical jump, only about half (49%) of the variance (or influences) in one test is associated with the other. Both tests involve explosive force of the legs with some flexing-extending of the trunk and swinging of the arms; both are influenced by body weight in that the subject must propel his or her body through space; both involve the ability to get psychologically and physiologically ready to generate an explosive exertion of force; and both involve relative strength, and so on. These are factors held in common in the two tests. If the $r = .80$, then 64% of the performance in one test is associated with, or explained by the factors involved in the performance of the other test.

But what about the *unexplained* variance—$(1.0 - r^2)$ 100? With an r of .70, there is 49% common or explained variance and 51% $(1.00 - .70^2)$ 100 unexplained or error variance. What are some unique factors to each test? We cannot explain this fully, of course, but some of the factors could be (a) the standing long jump requires that the body be propelled forward and upward, whereas the vertical jump is only upward; (b) the scoring of the vertical jump neutralizes one's height because standing reach is subtracted from jumping reach, but in the standing long jump perhaps the taller person has some advantage; and (c) perhaps more skill (coordination) is involved in the vertical jump because the person has to jump and turn and touch the wall.

The foregoing is not intended to be any sort of mechanical analysis of the two tests. These are simply suggestions of what might be some factors of common association, or explained variance, and some factors that might be unexplained or unique to each test of power.

When using r^2 to interpret correlation coefficients, it becomes apparent that it takes a rather substantial relationship to account for a great amount of common variance. It takes a correlation of .71 to account for just half of the variance in the other test, and an r of .90 accounts for just 81%. In some of the standardized tests used to predict success in college and graduate school, the correlations between the tests and success are generally quite low, usually somewhere around .40. You can see by r^2 that an r of .40 accounts for only 16% of the factors contributing to academic success, and, therefore, there is a great deal of unexplained variance. Still, these measures are often used very rigorously as *the* criterion for admission. Of course, the use of multiple predictors can greatly improve the estimate for success. The comparative sizes of correlations by means of the coefficient of determination can also be observed. A correlation of .90 is not just three times larger than an r of .30; it is nine times larger ($.30^2 = .09$ or 9% and $.90^2 = .81$ or 81%).

Interpreting r is further complicated by the fact that it depends on the purpose of the correlation with regard to whether the r is "good" or "inadequate." For example, if we are looking at reliability (the repeatability) of a test, a much higher correlation is needed than if we are just determining whether there is a relationship between two variables. A correlation of .60 would not be acceptable for the relationship between the odd- and even-numbered questions on a health knowledge test, but an r of .60 between health knowledge and health behavior would be quite noteworthy.

PREDICTION EQUATIONS

As stated several times, one of the purposes of correlation may be prediction. College entrance examinations are used to predict success. Sometimes, we try to predict some criterion such as percent fat by the use of skinfold measurements, or maximal oxygen consumption by a distance run. In studies of this type, the predictor variables such as skinfold measurements are less time-consuming, less expensive, and more feasible for mass testing than the criterion variable, and so a *prediction* or *regression equation* is developed.

Prediction is based on correlation. The higher the relationship between two variables, the more accurately you can predict one from the other. If the correlation were perfect, you could predict with complete accuracy.

Of course, we do not encounter perfect relationships in the "real world," but in introducing the concept of prediction (regression) equations, it is often advantageous to begin with a hypothetical example of a perfect relationship.

Verducci (1980) provided one of the best examples in introducing the regression equation concerning monthly salary and annual income. If there are no other sources of income, we can predict with complete accuracy the annual income of, for example, teachers by simply multiplying their monthly salaries by 12. Figure 6.4 illustrates this perfect relationship. By simply plotting the monthly salary (the X variable—the predictor variable), the annual income (the Y variable—the criterion variable) can be obtained. Hence, if we know that another teacher, Ms. Brooks, earns a monthly salary of $1750, we can easily plot this on the graph where $1750 on the horizontal ($X$) axis, called the *abscissa*, intercepts the vertical (Y) axis, called the *ordinate*, at $21,000.

The equation for prediction Y', predicted annual income, is thus $Y' = 12X$. In the above example Ms. Brooks' monthly salary (X) is inserted in the formula: $Y' = 12(1750) = \$21,000$.

Next, suppose that all teachers got an annual supplement of $1000 for coaching or supervising cheerleaders or some other extracurricular activity. Now, the formula becomes

$$Y' = 1000 + 12X.$$

Ms. Brooks' annual income is predicted as follows: $Y' = 1000 + 12(1750) = \$22,000$. All teachers' annual incomes could be predicted in the same manner. This formula is the general formula for a straight line and is expressed as follows:

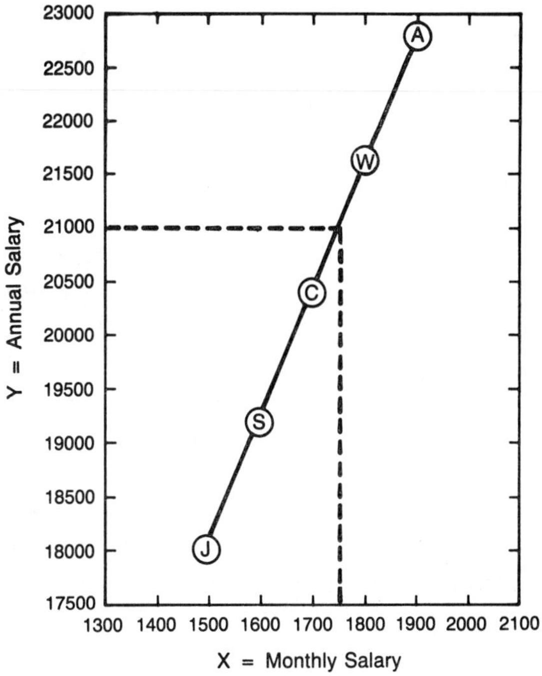

Figure 6.4 Plotting of monthly and annual salaries with perfect *r*.

$$Y' = a + bX \qquad \textbf{(6.2)}$$

in which Y' = predicted score or criterion, a = intercept, b = slope of the regression line, and X = predictor.

In the example we have been using, the b factor was ascertained by common sense because we know that there are 12 months in a year. The slope of the line (b) signifies the amount of change in Y that accompanies a change of one unit of X. Therefore, any X unit (monthly salary) is multiplied by 12 to obtain the Y value.

In actual regression problems, we won't intuitively know what b is, so we have to calculate it by this formula:

$$b = r(s_y/s_x) \qquad \textbf{(6.3)}$$

in which r = the correlation between X and Y, s_y = standard deviation of Y, and s_x = standard deviation of X.

In our previous example, application of formula 6.3 uses these data:

X = (monthly salary)	Y (annual income)
$M_x = 1700$	$M_y = 21400$ (1000 added Figure 6.4)
$s_x = 141.42$	$s_y = 1697.06$

$r = 1.00$

Therefore, the computation of b is

$$b = 1.00 \left(\frac{1697.06}{141.42}\right) = 12$$

The a in the regression formula indicates the intercept of the regression line on the Y axis. Another way of saying this is that it is the value of Y when X is zero. On a graph, if you extend the regression line sufficiently you can see where the regression line intercepts Y. The a is a constant in that it is added to each of the calculated bX values. Once again, in our example we know this constant is \$1000. But to calculate the a value, b first has to be calculated. Then use the following formula:

$$a = M_y - bM_x \qquad \textbf{(6.4)}$$

in which a = the constant (or intercept), M_y = mean of the Y scores, b = slope of the regression line, M_x = mean of the X scores. In our example, $a = 21400 - 12(1700) = 1000$. Then the final regression equation is

$$Y' = a + bX$$
$$Y' = 1000 + 12X.$$

Next, let us use a more practical example in which the r is not 1.00. We can use the data which were used in Figure 6.2 where the correlation between body weight and dynamometer strength was $r = .67$. The means and standard deviations are as follows:

X (Body weight)	Y (strength)
$M_x = 98.00$	$M_y = 167.00$
$s_x = 9.44$	$s_y = 33.52$

$$r = .67$$

First, we calculate b as follows from formula 6.3:

$$b = r(s_y/s_x) = .67(33.52/9.44) = 2.38$$

Then, a is calculated as follows from formula 6.4:

$$a = M_y - b(M_x) = 167 - 2.38(98) = -66.24$$

The regression equation (formula 6.2) becomes

$$Y' = a + bX =$$
$$Y' = -66.24 + (2.38)X$$

For any body weight, we can calculate the predicted strength score. For example, a boy weighing 100 lbs (X) would have a predicted strength score (Y') of

$$Y' = -66.24 + (2.38)100 = 171.8 \text{ lbs.}$$

The big difference between this example and the example of monthly and annual salary is that there was no error of prediction in the latter because r was 1.00. In predicting strength from body weight, however, the r is less than 1.00, so there is an error of prediction.

Provided in Appendix B is a computer program for the Apple II that will calculate Pearson r and compute the regression equation. In addition, this program provides a predicted Y' for any X variable entered. A sample on this program using the data from Figure 6.2 is included.

Before presenting the formula for calculating error of prediction, let us return to the derivation of the prediction formula. Figure 6.2 shows that there was no straight line connecting the weight and strength scores as there was in the hypothetical example in Figure 6.1. Consequently, we calculate a line of "best fit" in order to predict Y from the X scores. To do this, we take a high X score (body weight) such as 110 and a low body weight, such as 91, and apply the prediction formula.

For a body weight of 110 we predict

$$Y' = -66.24 + (2.38)110 = 195.6$$

For a body weight of 91, we predict

$$Y' = -66.24 + (2.38)91 = 150.3$$

Then we plot these two predicted values and connect them with a straight line. This line will pass through the intersection of the X and Y means. Figure 6.5 shows this line of best fit. The 10 actual body weight and strength scores are also plotted. You can readily see that the scores do not fall on the straight line as they did with perfect correlation.

In constructing this best fit line, we selected a high body weight (110) and a low body weight (91) and predicted their Y' values. When we examine their actual Y values, we see there is some error in prediction. The predicted strength score for the 110 lb boy was 195.6, yet the boy actually only scored 170 lbs, a difference of -25.6 lbs. The 91 lb boy was predicted to score 150.3 lbs on the dynamometer, yet he scored 175 lbs, a difference of $+24.7$ lbs. These differences between predicted and actual Y scores represent the errors of prediction and are called residual scores.

If we computed all of the residual scores, the mean would be zero and the standard deviation would be the *standard error of prediction or standard error of estimate*.

A simpler way of obtaining the standard error of estimate is to use the formula

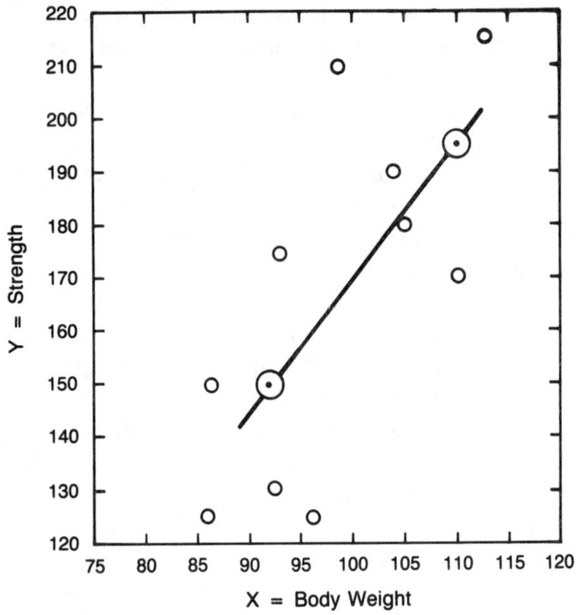

Figure 6.5 Regression line of best fit between body weight and predicted strength scores.

$$
\begin{aligned}
s_{y \cdot x} &= s_y \sqrt{1 - r^2} \\
s_{y \cdot x} &= 33.5 \sqrt{1 - .67^2} \\
s_{y \cdot x} &= 24.9
\end{aligned} \qquad (6.5)
$$

The standard error of estimate is interpreted the same way as standard deviation. In other words, the predicted value (strength) of a boy in our example, plus or minus the standard error of estimate, will occur approximately 68 times out of 100. Thus, we predict a 104 lb boy will score 181.3 ± 24.9. To express it another way, the "prediction range" will be 156.4 to 206.2 lbs, 68 times out of 100 (or, the chances are 2 in 3).

The larger the r, the less the error of prediction. Also, the smaller the standard deviation of the criterion, the smaller the error. In the previous problem, if we had an r of .85, for example, the standard error of estimate would be only

$$s_{y \cdot x} = 33.5 \sqrt{1 - .85^2} = 17.6.$$

The line of "best fit" is sometimes called the *least squares* method. This means that the calculated regression line is one about which the sum of squares of the perpendicular distances of points from the line is minimum. We will not develop this point here. Sum of squares will be discussed in the next chapter.

PARTIAL CORRELATION

The correlation between two variables is sometimes misleading and may be erroneous when there is little or no correlation between the variables *other* than that brought about by their common dependence on a third (or several other) variables.

For example, there are many attributes that increase regularly with age from 6 to 18 such as height, weight, strength, mental performance, vocabulary, reading skills, and so on. Over a wide age range, the r between any two of these traits will almost certainly be positive and probably high, due to the common maturity factor with which they are highly correlated.

In fact, the r may drop to zero if the variability caused by age differences is eliminated. We can control *this* factor of age in two ways: (a) We can select only children of the same age, or (b) we can partial out the effects of age statistically by holding it constant.

The symbol for partial correlation is $r_{12 \cdot 3}$ which means the correlation between variables 1 and 2, with variable 3 held constant (could partial out any number of variables, e.g., $r_{12 \cdot 345}$).

The calculation of partial correlation among three variables is quite simple. Let us refer back to the correlation of shoe size and achievement in mathematics. This is a good example of *spurious* correlation, which means that the correlation between the two variables is due entirely to the common influence of age or maturing. When the effect of the third variable (age) is removed, the correlation between shoe size and achievement in mathematics diminishes or vanishes completely.

We will label the three variables as follows: 1 = math achievement, 2 = shoe size, 3 = age. Then, $r_{12 \cdot 3}$ is the partial correlation between variables 1 and 2 with 3 held constant.

We will make up some correlation coefficients between the three variables, as follows:

$$r_{12} = .80;\ r_{13} = .90;\ r_{23} = .88.$$

The formula for $r_{12 \cdot 3}$ is

$$r_{12 \cdot 3} = \frac{r_{12} - r_{13}r_{23}}{\sqrt{1 - r_{13}^2}\ \sqrt{1 - r_{23}^2}} \qquad \textbf{(6.6)}$$

$$\frac{.80 - (.90 \times .88)}{\sqrt{1 - .90^2}\ \sqrt{1 - .88^2}}$$

$$\frac{.80 - .792}{\sqrt{1 - .81}\ \sqrt{1 - .77}}$$

$$r_{12 \cdot 3} = .038$$

Thus, we see that the correlation between math achievement and shoe size drops to about zero when age is partialed out.

The primary value of partial correlation is that it is used in the process of the development of a multiple regression equation with two or more predictor variables. In the selection process, when a new variable is "stepped in," its correlation with the criterion is determined with the effects of the preceding variable(s) partialed out. The size and the sign of a partial correlation may be different from the zero order (two variables) correlation between the same variables.

SEMIPARTIAL CORRELATION

In the previous section on partial correlation, the effects of a third variable on the relationship between two others were partialed out. In other words, in $r_{12 \cdot 3}$, the relationship of variable 3 to the correlation of variable 1 and variable 2 is partialed out. In some situations, the investigator may wish to partial out a variable from only one of the variables being correlated. This is *semipartial correlation*. The symbol is $r_{1(2 \cdot 3)}$, which indicates that the relationship between variables 1 and 2 is determined after the influence of variable 3 on variable 2 has been partialed out.

Suppose for example, that a researcher is studying the relationship between perceived exertion (i.e., one's feelings of how hard he or she is working) and heart rate (HR) and workload (WL). Obviously, WL is going to be correlated with HR. The researcher wants to investigate the relationship between perceived exertion (PE) and HR while controlling for WL. Regular partial correlation will show this relationship. However, regular partial correlation will partial out the effects of WL on the relationship between PE and HR. But the researcher does not want to remove the effects of WL on the relationship of PE and HR, he or she only wants to remove the effects of WL on HR. In other words, the main interest is in the net effect of HR on PE—after the influence of WL has been removed. Thus, in semipartial correlation, WL is partialed out from HR but not from PE. The uses of semipartial correlation will be discussed further in Chapter 7.

MULTIPLE REGRESSION

Multiple regression consists of one dependent variable, usually a criterion of some sort, and two or more predictor variables (independent variables). The use of more than one predictor variable almost always increases the accuracy of prediction. This should be self-evident. If you wished to predict basketball playing ability, you would expect to get a more accurate prediction using several basketball skills tests rather than just one.

Some years ago, it was rather common practice to construct a motor fitness test by the use of multiple regression. The typical methodology was to define the components of fitness, such as cardiovascular endurance, strength and muscular endurance, power, speed, and so on. Then a number of test items were chosen which purportedly measured each of the components. Thus, there may be 20 or more test items selected and administered to a sample of subjects. The scores (usually standard scores) of all the tests were then added. The resulting total score was used as the criterion of fitness.

The motor fitness test battery was established by a multiple correlation technique called the Wherry-Doolittle Test Selection Method. We will not go into the statistical steps. The process involves the calculation of zero-order (two variable) correlation coefficients among the independent variables and between the independent variables and the criterion. Then the process selects the independent variables in order of their importance, insofar as relating highly with the criterion and poorly with the other independent variables (items which relate highly with one another are probably measuring the same thing). The result of the Wherry-Doolittle Test Selection Method is a battery of the fewest items which contribute the most to the criterion. It is based on the premise that when there are a number of predictor variables, there is usually much overlap, which means that the prediction is probably just as good with a few variables as with many.

The Wherry-Doolittle method is a stepwise method in that multiple correlation (R) is calculated, cumulatively, after the selection of each variable until the size of the R no longer increases to any extent. When this happens, the battery is established. Believe it or not, the Wherry-Doolittle method used to be performed by hand, even before the days of the pocket calculator.

Now the computer does all of the multiple prediction (regression) calculations in seconds. There are several programs, or approaches, to accomplish the selection of the independent variables which best predict the criterion. Brief descriptions of some of these approaches follow:

FORWARD SELECTION MULTIPLE REGRESSION

In this method, a new predictor variable is added at each step. The first variable selected is the one which has the highest correlation with the criterion. Then, at each subsequent step, a variable is added which, with the one(s) already chosen, results in the best prediction. (It is difficult to explain these methods without using terms with which you are probably not yet familiar.) The variables selected cumulatively produce the least *residual sum of squares*. What that basically means is that the residual sum of squares constitute error. If you recall from our discussion of linear regression with two variables, the differences between predicted and actual scores are termed residuals.

Sometimes, the researcher will set a probability level for entry, such as the .05 or .01. In this way, variables are stepped in until they no longer *significantly* increase the prediction of the criterion. Remember the concept of "overlap" in that oftentimes some predictor variables are measuring about the same thing, and, thus, if we have two such variables, the inclusion of both is no better than the use of just one.

Another important concept is that after the first step, the selection of additional variables is determined by the "combined effect," not just the additive effect. In other words, the process takes into account the interrelationship among the *X* variables. If there were no relationships among the *X* variables, prediction could simply be made in an additive fashion, but, of course, this is never the case. After each *X* variable is stepped in, the remaining correlations between the criterion and *X* variables are recomputed with the selected variables partialed out.

Thus, in forward selection multiple regression, variables are stepped in as to their importance and the process stops when there is no further significant contribution to the prediction. In essence, this is similar to the Wherry-Doolittle Test Selection Method.

BACKWARD SELECTION MULTIPLE REGRESSION

In this procedure, the independent variables (*X* variables) are eliminated in respect to their unimportance. Consequently, you begin with all of the independent variables, and you drop out those variables which do not significantly contribute to the prediction of the criterion. Once again, you usually set a significance level, and those variables which do not meet this level, insofar as their inclusion in the linear composite of predictor variables, are dropped.

In most instances (but not always), you will end up with the same battery of important predictor variables with the backward selection method as the forward method.

MAXIMUM *R*-SQUARED METHOD

In the Maximum R^2 method, the "best" of all possible one-variable models is selected, the best two-variable model, the best three-variable model, and so on. The term "best" relates to the size of the R^2 value.

As explained in an earlier discussion of the coefficient of determination, squaring the r (in this case, R) can estimate the degree of meaningfulness in terms of the amount of common association (or amount of variance held in common) between the dependent and independent variables.

The maximum R^2 method will continue until the full model is included. However, the researcher usually sets some criterion as to when to stop. It may be a level of significance or a measure of meaningfulness such as the amount of variance accounted for (see Chapter 7 for discussion of this). Usually, it is a combination of significance and meaningfulness. The researcher also may incorporate some practical criteria in the selection process such as amount of time and effort involved in obtaining the measurements for the different size models as in test batteries.

STEPWISE REGRESSION PROCEDURE

The Stepwise Regression method is a variation of the forward technique except that each time a new predictor variable is "stepped in," the new relationship between the criterion and predictor variables is reevaluated; that is, to see if the predictor variable(s) already selected still significantly contributes when later variables are added. It is possible, then, that a predictor entered earlier may be dropped out later when new predictors are brought into the equation. In most instances, however, the Stepwise method is identical to the Forward Selection method.

MULTIPLE REGRESSION PREDICTION EQUATIONS

The prediction formula resulting from multiple regression is basically that of the two-variable regression model, $Y' = a + bX$. The difference is merely that there is more than one X variable, thus the equation is

$$Y' = a + b_1X_1 + b_2X_2 + \ldots b_iX_i.$$

We will not delve into the formula for the calculation of a and the bs for the selected variables. As we have indicated before, a researcher will undoubtedly use a computer in a multiple regression problem. An example of what a multiple prediction formula might look like is given below. In this equation, a man's lean body weight (LBW) is being predicted from several anthropometric measures including skinfold thicknesses, circumferences, and diameters. The following formula, developed by Behnke and Wilmore (1974), has an R of .958 and a standard error of estimate of 2.358, which is interpreted just the same as we discussed in the regression equation with only one predictor variable.

$$\begin{aligned}\text{LBW} = 10.138 &+ 0.9259\ (\text{Wt.}) - 0.1881\ (\text{thigh skinfold}) \\ &+ 0.637\ (\text{bi-iliac diameter}) + 0.4888\ (\text{neck circumference}) \\ &- 0.5951\ (\text{abdominal circumference})\end{aligned}$$

SOME PROBLEMS ASSOCIATED WITH MULTIPLE REGRESSION

The basic determiner in multiple regression is the same as regression with only two variables—the size of the correlation. The higher the R, the more accurate the prediction. However, there are some other factors that should be mentioned.

One limitation of prediction is in regard to generalizability. Regression equations that were developed with a particular sample often lose considerable accuracy when applied to others. This is called *population specificity*. This, along with ways of improving generalizability through cross-validation, will be discussed more in Chapter 13. Recognize that the more accuracy is sought through selection procedures (forward, backward, stepwise, max R^2) which capitalize on specific characteristics of the sample, the harder it is to generalize to other populations. Thus, the researcher should select the sample carefully with regard to the population for which the results are to be generalized.

Obviously, in prediction studies the number of subjects in the sample should be sufficiently large. For one thing, usually the larger the sample, the more likely it is that the sample will represent the population from which it is drawn. However, another problem with small samples in multiple regression studies is that the R may be spuriously high. A direct relationship exists between the R and the ratio between the number of subjects and number of variables. In fact, if there are the same number of variables as subjects, R will be 1.00. A ratio of number of subjects to number of variables of 10 to 1 (or greater) is the ideal.

CANONICAL CORRELATION

So far, we have discussed correlation where we have one dependent variable and one independent (predictor) variable (zero-order correlation, r) and correlation where we have one dependent variable and two or more independent variables (multiple R). There is also a correlational technique which can determine the relationship when there are two or more dependent variables and two or more independent variables. This technique is called *canonical* correlation.

The computations involved in canonical analyses with a number of variables are so complex that we will not even attempt to treat them here. We will let the computer "worry" about the calculations, and we will merely look at the basic concepts of canonical correlation.

In essence, there are two linear combinations, one of Y variables and one of X variables. These composites are weighted in such a way that the maximum possible correlation is achieved. This is the canonical correlation (R_c), and R_c^2 is the estimated amount of common association (shared variance) between the two *linear composites* of these variables. This is different from multiple regression where only the X variables were weighted in terms of their linear combination effects.

Canonical correlation is sometimes used in an exploratory manner in order to find out which variable(s) might best be manipulated for use as the independent variable(s), and which will best show results as dependent variables. For example, suppose we have several physical characteristics for a group of athletes such as height, weight, percent fat, as well as several performance measures of power, speed, endurance, and aerobic capacity. We may wish to find which among the physical characteristics are best suited to act as predictor variables and which of the performance variables are most appropriate to serve as a criterion. Canonical correlation will identify the best solution and then multiple R is used to "follow up" for interpretation and prediction purposes.

Canonical analysis is actually the most general of all the statistical analysis techniques. It encompasses all of the correlation techniques covered in this chapter, and the t test, analysis of variance, factorial analysis of variance, discriminant analysis, and multivariate analysis discussed in the next chapter. All of these statistical techniques are simply part of canonical analysis, because if you have only one dependent variable and more than one independent variable, you have multiple R; if you have more than one dependent variable and one independent variable, you have discriminant analysis, and so on. Canonical analyses can be considered as an "omnibus" technique for determining the most predictive and important variables to use in interpreting the results of a study.

SUMMARY

We have explored some statistical techniques for determining relationships among variables. Although a number of nonparametric correlational techniques exist, this chapter has dealt only with parametric correlational techniques. Remember, Chapter 5 stated that nonparametric statistics do not have to meet the assumptions of normal distribution and equal variances.

The simplest type of correlation is the zero-order correlation which establishes the relationship between two variables. We introduced linear regression which can be used to predict one variable from another (or others). Correlation is interpreted for significance (reliability) and meaningfulness (r^2) which indicates the portion of the total variance in one measure which can be explained by or accounted for by the other measure.

Partial correlation is a procedure where a correlation between two variables is obtained while the influence of one or more other variables is partialed out. Semipartial correlation partials out the influence of a third variable on only one of the two variables being correlated. Partial correlation (or semipartial correlation) is used in multiple correlation and in developing multiple regression formulas.

In multiple regression, two or more independent variables are used to predict the criterion variable. The most efficient weighted linear composite of independent variables for prediction of the dependent variable is determined through such techniques as forward selection, backward selection, stepwise selection, and maximum R^2.

Canonical correlation is the most complete and general of all statistical techniques. In canonical correlation, the relationship between two or more independent and two or more dependent variables is determined. A set of weights for the linear composites of both the X and Y variables that will maximize the correlation coefficient is obtained.

PROBLEMS

1. What is the correlation (r) between fat deposits on two different body sites? Variable X is the triceps skinfold measure and variable Y is the suprailiac skinfold measure.

X (triceps)	Y (suprailiac)
16	9
17	12
17	10
15	8
14	8
11	6
11	5
12	5
13	6
14	5
4	1
7	4
12	7
7	1
10	3

2. (a) Using Table A.2 determine whether the r obtained in problem 1 is significant at the .01 level. What size r would be necessary for significance at the .01 level if we had 30 subjects? (b) What is the percent of common variance between the two skinfold measurements in problem 1?
3. Compute the regression equation (Formula 6.2) for predicting maximal oxygen consumption (max $\dot{V}O_2$) from scores on the 12-minute run. The information you will need is:

X (12 min run)	Y (max $\dot{V}O_2$)
$M_x = 3120$ yds	$M_y = 52.6$ ml•kg•min
$s_x = 334$	$s_y = 6.3$ ml•kg•min

$$r = .79$$

4. Using the prediction formula developed in problem 3, what is the predicted max $\dot{V}O_2$ for a subject who ran 3230 yds in 12 minutes? For a subject who ran 2940 yds in 12 minutes?
5. What is the standard error of estimate (Formula 6.5) for the prediction equation in problem 3? How would you interpret the predicted max $\dot{V}O_2$ for the subjects in problem 4?

Chapter 7

Differences Among Groups

Statistical techniques for determining differences among groups are most frequently used for data analysis in experimental and quasi-experimental research. These techniques enable us to evaluate the effects of an independent (cause) or categorical (gender, age, race, etc.) variable upon a dependent variable (effect). Remember, however, the use of the techniques described in this chapter does not establish cause-effect; they only evaluate the influence of the independent variable. Cause-effect is not established by statistics, but by the total nature of the research.

In experimental research, the *levels* of the independent variable are established by the experimenter. For example, the experiment might involve the investigation of the effects of intensity of training on cardiorespiratory endurance. Thus, intensity of training is the independent variable or *treatment factor* while a measure of cardiorespiratory endurance is the dependent variable. Intensity of training could have any number of levels. If intensity of training is evaluated as a percentage of maximal oxygen consumption ($\dot{V}O_2$ max), then it could be 30%, 40%, 50%, and so forth. The investigator would choose the number and intensity of levels. In a simple experiment, the independent variable might be two levels of intensity of training, 40% and 70% of $\dot{V}O_2$ max. The length of each session (30 minutes), frequency (3 times per week) and number of weeks (12) of training are all controlled (equal for both groups). The dependent variable is the distance a person runs in 12 minutes.

The purpose of the statistical test is to evaluate the null hypothesis (*Ho*) at a specific level of probability ($p < .05$). In other words, do the two levels of treatment differ significantly ($p < .05$) so that these differences would not be attributable to a chance occurrence more than 5 times in 100? The statistical test is always of the null hypothesis. All that statistics can do is *reject* or *fail to reject* the null hypothesis. Statistics cannot accept the research hypothesis. Only logical reasoning, good experimental design, and appropriate theorizing can do so. Statistics can only determine *if* the groups are different, not *why* they are different.

In the use of statistics which test differences among groups, you want to establish not only if the groups are significantly different, but the strength of the association between the independent and dependent variables. The t and F ratios will be used throughout this chapter to determine if groups are significantly different. Omega squared (w^2) will be used to estimate the degree of association (called *percent variance accounted for*) between the independent and dependent variables. To some extent w^2 is similar to r^2 for the correlations presented in Chapter 6; both represent the same idea, which is percent variance accounted for.

In addition to the assumptions for parametric statistics presented in Chapter 5, the use of the t and F distributions as presented in the chapter have four assumptions (Kirk, 1968, p. 43).

1. Observations are drawn from normally distributed populations.
2. Observations represent random samples from populations.
3. Variances of populations are equal.
4. Numerator and denominator of F (or t) ratios are independent.

While t and F tests are robust (only slightly influenced) to violations of these assumptions, the assumptions, nevertheless, are not trivial. The researcher should be sensitive to their presence and that violations affect the probability levels that may be obtained in connection with t and F ratios.

t TESTS

The t tests are of three types. First, we may want to know if a sample of subjects differs from a larger population. For example, suppose we know that for a standardized knowledge test in personal health, the $M = 76$ for a large population of college freshmen. When tested, a personal health class ($N = 32$) that you are teaching has a $M = 81$, $s = 9$. Is your class significantly better than the typical college freshman class?

The t test is a test of the null hypothesis which states that there is no difference between the sample mean (M) and the population mean (M) or $M - \mathrm{M} = 0$. Formula 7.1 is the t test between a sample and a population mean.

$$t = \frac{M - \mathrm{M}}{s_M / \sqrt{n}} \tag{7.1}$$

In Table 7.1 this formula is applied to the means and standard deviation of the example for the standardized personal health knowledge test. Note that the t value

TABLE 7.1
USING A t TEST BETWEEN A SAMPLE AND A POPULATION MEAN

Population (N = 10,000)	Sample Health Class (n = 32)
M = 76	M = 81
σ = 7	s = 9

$$t = \frac{M - \text{M}}{s_M / \sqrt{n}}$$

$$t = \frac{81 - 76}{9/\sqrt{32}} = \frac{5}{1.59} = 3.14$$

$$df = n - 1 = 32 - 1 = 31$$

$t(31) = 3.14, p < .05$

obtained, 3.14, is significant. The number in parenthesis is the degrees of freedom (*df*) for the t test. The degrees of freedom are based upon the number of subjects with a correction for bias as in Formula 7.2.

$$df = N - 1 \tag{7.2}$$

The degrees of freedom are used to enter a t table to determine if the calculated t is as large as or greater than the tabled t value. Look at Table A.3 in the Appendix. Note that across the top of the table are probability levels. Read across to the .05 level. Now read down the left side (*df*) to the number in the t-test from Table 7.1, $df = 31$. Read where the *df* row and the .05 column intersect. Is the calculated value ($t = 3.14$) larger than this value (2.04)? Yes, so the t is significant at $p < .05$. Thus, our sample class is reliably (significantly) different from the population average on the health test.

The above t test, applied to determine if a sample differs from a population, is not used very frequently. The most frequently used t test is to determine if two sample means differ reliably from each other. Suppose we return to our example at the beginning of this chapter—do two groups, training at different levels of intensity, 40% or 70% of $\dot{V}O_2$ max, 30 minutes per day, 3 days per week for 12 weeks, differ from each other on a measure of cardiorespiratory endurance (12-minute run)? Let us further assume that there were 30 subjects who were randomly assigned to form the two groups of 15 each.

Formula 7.3 is the t test formula for two independent samples.

$$t = \frac{M_1 - M_2}{\sqrt{s_1^2/n_1 + s_2^2/n_2}} \tag{7.3}$$

where M_1 = mean for 70% group, M_2 = mean for 40% group, s_1^2 = variance (standard deviation squared) for the 70% group, s_2^2 = variance for the 40% group, n_1 = number of subjects in 70% group, and n_2 = number of subjects in 40% group. The degrees of freedom (*df*) for an independent *t* test are calculated as in formula 7.4.

$$df = (n_1 + n_2) - 2 \qquad \textbf{(7.4)}$$

Formula 7.5 is the version of the *t* test formula most easily used with a calculator.

$$t = \frac{M_1 - M_2}{\sqrt{\dfrac{[\,\Sigma X_1^2 - (\Sigma X_1)^2/n_1 + \Sigma X_2^2 - (\Sigma X_2)^2/n_2\,]}{(n_1 + n_2) - 2} \cdot [1/n_1 + 1/n_2]}} \qquad \textbf{(7.5)}$$

Table 7.2 shows how these formulas would be applied to the intensity of training experiment. Thus, you can see that the 70% intensity of training allowed subjects to run reliably further (M = 3004 m) than did the 40% intensity of training (M = 2456 m). If the 12 minutes run is a valid measure of cardiorespiratory endurance and if all other conditions were controlled, we can say that the cause of this increased level of cardiorespiratory endurance was the fact that the 70% group's training was more intense than the 40% group's.

The question then becomes, How meaningful is this effect? Or stated more simply, is the increase in cardiorespiratory endurance of running an additional

TABLE 7.2
AN INDEPENDENT *t* TEST

Characteristics	70% $\dot{V}O_2$ max	40% $\dot{V}O_2$ max
M	3004 m	2456 m
s	114 m	103 m
n	15	15

$$t = \frac{M_1 - M_2}{\sqrt{\dfrac{s_1^2}{n_1} + \dfrac{s_2^2}{n_2}}}$$

$$t = \frac{3004 - 2456}{\sqrt{\dfrac{(114)^2}{15} + \dfrac{(103)^2}{15}}} = \frac{548}{39.67} = 13.81$$

$$df = (n_1 + n_2) - 2 = (15 + 15) - 2 = 28$$

$$t(28) = 13.81, p < .05$$

$$w^2 = \frac{t^2 - 1}{t^2 + n_1 + n_2 - 1} = \frac{190.72 - 1}{190.72 + 15 + 15 - 1} = \frac{182.72}{219.72} = .86$$

548 m (3004 − 2456) worth the additional work of training at 70% of $\dot{V}O_2$ max as compared to 40% of $\dot{V}O_2$ max? What we really want to know is, given the total variation in running performance of the two groups, How much of this variation is accounted for (associated with) the difference in the two levels of the independent variable (70% vs. 40%)? The best way to estimate this is to calculate Omega squared (w^2) (Tolson, 1980).

$$w^2 = \frac{t^2 - 1}{t^2 + n_1 + n_2 - 1} \tag{7.5}$$

At the bottom of Table 7.2 is the application of this formula to our example. We can conclude that the $w^2 = .86$ means 86% of the variance in the distance run can be accounted for by the difference in the two groups' level of training. The remaining variance, 14% (100% − 86% = 14%), is accounted for by other factors. The question is now, "Is this a meaningful percentage of variance?" No one can answer that but you. Are you willing to increase the intensity of training 30% to produce this effect? There is no statistical answer—only the person(s) involved can answer that. The research has only told you what will happen if you increase the intensity of training from 40% to 70% of $\dot{V}O_2$ max.

DEPENDENT *t* TEST

We have now considered use of the *t* test to evaluate if a sample differs from a population and if two independent samples differ from each other. A third application is called a *dependent t* test. This means the two groups of scores are related in some manner. Usually, the relationship takes one of two forms: Two groups of subjects are matched on some characteristic(s) and thus are no longer independent; or one group of subjects is tested twice on the same variable, and the experimenter is interested in the change between the two tests. For example,[1] 10 dancers are given a jump and reach test (difference between height they can reach and touch on wall and how high they can jump and touch), then 10 weeks of dance activity that involves leaps and jumps, three days per week. The dancers are again given the jump and reach test after the 10 weeks. Our research hypothesis is that the 10 weeks of dance experience will improve jumping skills as reflected by the change in jump and reach scores. The null hypothesis is that the difference between the pre- and posttest of jumping is not significantly different from 0, $Ho = M_{pre} - M_{post} = 0$. The formula for a dependent *t* test is as follows:

$$t = \frac{M_{pre} - M_{post}}{\sqrt{s^2_{pre}/n_{pre} + s^2_{post}/n_{post} - 2r_{pp}s_{pre}s_{post}}} \tag{7.6}$$

[1]This is not proposed to be a real experiment, just a simple example illustrating the statistical technique.

Notice that the top part of this formula is the same as the independent t test formula (7.3). In addition, the bottom (under the square root symbol) is also the same on the left side. However, an amount is subtracted from the bottom (error term) of the t test ($-2r_{pp}s_{pre}s_{post}$). This series of numbers and letters is read as "two times the correlation (r) between the pre- and posttest times the standard deviation for the pretest times the standard deviation for the posttest." The independent t test (7.3) assumes the two groups of subjects are independent. In this case, the subjects are the same people tested twice (pre and post). Thus we adjust downward (make smaller) the error term of the t test by taking into account the relationship (r) between the pre- and posttests adjusted to their standard deviations. The degrees of freedom for the dependent t test is

$$df = N \text{ (number of paired observations)} - 1 \qquad \textbf{(7.7)}$$

Formula 7.6 is rather cumbersome to compute because the correlation (r) between the pre- and posttest has to be calculated. Thus, the raw score formula is much easier to use.

$$t = \frac{\Sigma D}{\sqrt{[N\Sigma D^2 - (\Sigma D)^2]/(N-1)}} \qquad \textbf{(7.8)}$$

where D = pretest − posttest for each subject and N = number of paired observations. Table 7.3 provides an example of formula 7.8 applied to the dance study reported previously. The results indicate that the posttest mean (19.7 cm) was significantly better than the pretest mean (16.5 cm), $t(9) = 4.83$, $p < .05$. The *Ho* can be rejected and if everything else has been properly controlled in the experiment, we can conclude that the dance training produced a reliable increase in the height of jumping performance of 3.2 cm.

A computer program for calculating t tests is included in Appendix B. The first example following this program is for a dependent or correlated t test. The example uses the data from Table 7.3 and, of course, the results are the same. Compare the sample printout to Table 7.3.

A standard formula is not available for calculating w^2 for a dependent t test. But we could estimate the magnitude of the effect by dividing the average gain by the pretest mean and multiplying by 100 as in the bottom of Table 7.3. The gain is 19.4% of the pretest or represents nearly 20% improvement. While this is a rather crude way of estimating the effect, it does suffice.

INTERPRETING *t*

At this point, refer again to Table A.3 in the Appendix—the tabled values of t to which you compare the values calculated. Remember, you decide the probability level (we've been using .05), calculate the degrees of freedom for $t(n-1)$ and read the tabled t value at the column (probability) by row (df) intersection. If your calculated t exceeds the tabled value, it is significant at the specified alpha and

TABLE 7.3
A DEPENDENT *t* TEST

Subjects	Jump and Reach Test **Pre**	**Post**	***D***	***D*²**
1	12 cm	16 cm	4	16
2	15 cm	21 cm	6	36
3	13 cm	15 cm	2	4
4	20 cm	22 cm	2	4
5	21 cm	21 cm	0	0
6	19 cm	23 cm	4	16
7	14 cm	16 cm	2	4
8	17 cm	18 cm	1	1
9	16 cm	22 cm	6	36
10	18 cm	23 cm	5	25
Σ	165	197	32	142
M	16.5	19.7		

$$t = \frac{\Sigma D}{\sqrt{[N\Sigma D^2 - (\Sigma D)^2]/(N - 1)}} = \frac{32}{\sqrt{[10(142) - (32)^2]/(10 - 1)}}$$

$$= \frac{32}{\sqrt{(1420 - 1024)/9}} = \frac{32}{6.63} = 4.83$$

$df = 10 - 1 = 9$

$t(9) = 4.83, p < .05$

$$\text{Magnitude of increase} = \left(\frac{M\ \text{gain}}{M\ \text{pretest}}\right) \times 100 = \left(\frac{3.2}{16.5}\right) \times 100 = 19.4\%$$

df. This table is called a *two-tailed t table*. The reason is that we have assumed the difference between the two means could favor either mean. Sometimes, Group 1 will either be better than Group 2, or at worst no poorer than Group 2. In this instance, the *t* test is a one-tailed one—it can only go one direction. Then when looking at Table A.3, the .05 level is .10, .025 is .05, and .01 is .02. However, generally we are not so sure of our results as to employ the one-tailed *t* table.

Previously, in Chapter 5, *power* was mentioned as the probability of rejecting the null hypothesis when the null hypothesis is false. To obtain power in research is very desirable as the odds of rejecting a false null hypothesis are increased. The independent *t* test will be used to explain the three ways to obtain power. However, the ways apply to all types of experimental research.

Consider the formula for the independent *t* test:

$$t = \frac{M^1 - M_2}{\sqrt{\frac{s_1^2}{n_1} + \frac{s_2^2}{n_2}}} \qquad \begin{matrix} 1 \\ 2 \\ 3 \end{matrix}$$

Note that we have placed numbers (1, 2, 3) beside the three horizontal levels of this formula. These three levels represent what can be manipulated to obtain power.

First, level 1 ($M_1 - M_2$) gives power if we can increase the difference between M_1 and M_2. You should see that if levels 2 and 3 remain the same, a bigger difference between the means increases the size of the *t* ratio, which increases the odds of rejecting the *Ho*, which increases power. How can the difference between the means be increased? The logical answer is, stronger, more concentrated treatments.

The second level is s_1^2, s_2^2,or the variances (standard deviation squared) for each of the two groups. Recall that the standard deviation represents the spread of the scores about the mean. If this spread becomes smaller (scores distributed more closely about the mean), the variance (s^2) is also smaller. Because this term is in the denominator of the *t* test, if levels 1 and 3 remain the same, the *t* ratio will become larger increasing the odds of rejecting the *Ho*, which increases power. How can the standard deviation and thereby the variance be made smaller? The answer is to apply the treatments more consistently. The more consistently the treatments are applied to each subject, the more the subjects will become similar in response on the *dv*, which reduces the standard deviation.

Finally, level 3, n_1, n_2 is the number of subjects in each group. If n_1 and n_2 are increased and levels 1 and 2 remain the same, the denominator will become smaller (note *n* is divided into s^2), the *t* ratio will be larger, increasing the odds of rejecting the *Ho* and obtaining power. Obviously, n_1 and n_2 can be increased by placing additional subjects in each group.

Of course, power may also be influenced by varying alpha (i.e., if alpha is set at .10 as opposed to .05, increased power is attained). But in doing this, the risk of rejecting a true *Ho* is increased.

In summary, power is desirable to obtain because it increases the odds of rejecting a false *Ho*. Power may be obtained by using strong treatments, administering those treatments consistently, using as many subjects as feasible, or by varying alpha. But remember, there is always a second question even in the most powerful experiments. After the *Ho* is rejected, the strength (meaningfulness) of the effects must be evaluated.

The *t* ratio has a numerator and denominator. From a theoretical point of view, the numerator is regarded as true variance, or the real difference between the means. The denominator is considered error variance or variation about the mean. Thus, the *t* ratio is

$$t = \frac{\text{True variance}}{\text{Error variance}}$$

where True = $M_1 - M_2$ and Error = $\sqrt{s_1^2/n_1 + s_2^2/n_2}$. If no real differences exist between the groups, True Variance = Error Variance, or the ratio between them is True/Error = 1. When a significant *t* ratio is found, we are really saying that true variance exceeds error variance to a certain degree. The degree needed for significance is dependent upon the number of subjects (*df*) and the alpha level established.

The estimate of the strength of the relationship (w^2) between the independent and dependent variables is represented by the ratio of True Variance to Total Variance.

$$w^2 = \frac{\text{True variance}}{\text{Total variance}}$$

Thus, w^2 represents the proportion of the total variance that is due to the treatments (True variance).

RELATIONSHIP OF *t* AND *r*

As we mentioned previously, our separation of statistical techniques into the two categories of *relationships among variables* (Chapter 6) and *differences among groups* (this chapter) is an artificial one because both sets of techniques are based upon the general linear model. A brief demonstration with *t* and *r* should make the point. However, the concept can be extended into the more sophisticated techniques discussed in Chapter 6 and later in this chapter.

In Table 7.4, we have provided an example of the relationship between *t* and *r*. Note that Group 1 has a set of scores (dependent variable) for 5 subjects as does Group 2. We have calculated the *M* and *s* of each group by the previously provided formulas and then we have done an independent *t* test. The two groups are significantly different, $t\ (8) = 5.00$.[2] We have then assigned each subject a dummy code (either 1 or 0) which stands for their group. If we treat the dummy coded variable as *X* and the dependent variable as *Y* and ignore group membership (10 subjects with two variables), then the correlation formula (*r*) used earlier can be applied to the data. When we solve for the *r*, it is .87. By applying a *t* test to the *r*, the *t* is 5.0, the same as the *t* test done on the group means. The point is *r* represents the relationship between the independent and dependent variables (in fact, r^2 is a biased estimator of w^2) and the test of *r*, i.e., the *t* test, evaluates the reliability (significance) of the relationship.

We are *not* trying to confuse you. The point is that there are three sources of variance (True variance + Error variance = Total variance). The *t* test is the ratio of True to Error while the *r* is the square root of the proportion of Total accounted for by True. To get *t* from *r* only means manipulating the variance components in a slightly different way. This is because all parametric correlational and differences-among-groups techniques are based upon the general linear model. This result can easily be shown to exist in the more advanced statistical techniques (for a thorough treatment of this topic, see Pedhazur, 1982). You need to understand this basic concept because it is becoming increasingly common for

[2]In Appendix B an example of an independent *t* test using the data from Table 7.4 is provided. The same program with a different option does either dependent or independent *t*.

TABLE 7.4
COMPARISON OF t AND r

	Group 1		Group 2	
	Dummy Code	Dependent Variable	Dummy Code	Dependent Variable
	1	1	0	6
	1	2	0	7
	1	3	0	8
	1	4	0	9
	1	5	0	10
Σ	5	15	0	40
M		3		8
s		1.58		1.58

$$t = \frac{M_1 - M_2}{\sqrt{\frac{s_1^2}{n_1} + \frac{s_2^2}{n_2}}} = \frac{3 - 8}{\sqrt{\frac{1.58^2}{5} + \frac{1.58^2}{5}}} = 5.0$$

$$df = (n_1 + n_2) - 2 = 8$$

$$t(8) = 5.0,\ p < .05$$

$$r = \frac{N\Sigma XY - (\Sigma X)(\Sigma Y)}{\sqrt{N\Sigma X^2 - (\Sigma X)^2}\ \sqrt{N\Sigma Y^2 - (\Sigma Y)^2}} = \frac{10(15) - (5)(55)}{\sqrt{10(5) - 25}\ \sqrt{10(385) - 3025}}$$

$$= \frac{12.5}{14.4} = .87$$

$$t = \sqrt{\frac{r^2}{(1 - r^2)/(N - 2)}} = \sqrt{\frac{.87^2}{(1 - .87^2)/(10 - 2)}} = \sqrt{\frac{.757}{.030}} = 5.0$$

researchers to use regression techniques to analyze what has been traditionally termed experimental data. These data have usually been analyzed by techniques discussed in this chapter. We have, however, just demonstrated that what is traditional is not required. What is important is, if the data have been appropriately analyzed to answer the following two basic questions: Are the groups significantly different? and Does the independent variable account for a meaningful proportion of the variance in the dependent variable? Significance is always evaluated as the ratio of True variance divided by Error variance while percent variance accounted for is always the ratio of True variance divided by Total variance.

ANALYSIS OF VARIANCE

SIMPLE ANALYSIS OF VARIANCE (ANOVA)

The concept of simple (sometimes called one-way, but seldom considered simple by graduate students) ANOVA is an extension of the independent t test. In fact, t is just a special case of simple ANOVA in which there are two groups. Simple

ANOVA allows the evaluation of the *Ho* among two or more group means with the restriction that the two or more groups are levels of the same independent variable. In an earlier example, we suggested a *t* test was appropriate to test between the means of two groups who trained at 40% and 70% of $\dot{V}O_2$ max. This represents two levels (40% and 70%) of one independent variable (intensity of training). In fact, simple ANOVA and its statistic symbol, the *F* ratio, could just as easily have been used. But what would happen if there were more than two levels of the independent variable, for example, 40%, 60%, and 80% of $\dot{V}O_2$ max? Simple ANOVA could be used in this situation to test the *Ho* that $M_1 = M_2 = M_3 = 0$, or that the difference among the three group means is not significant.

Why not do a *t* test between the 40% and 60% groups, a second *t* test between the 40% and 80% groups, and a third *t* test between the 60% and 80% groups? The reason is because this would violate an assumption relative to the established alpha level (let it be $p < .05$). The .05 level means 1 chance in 20 of a chance difference, assuming that the subjects on which the statistical test are made are from independent random samples. In our case, this is not true—each group has been used in two comparisons (e.g., 40% vs. 60%, and 40% vs. 80%) rather than only one. Thus, we have increased the chances of making a Type I error (i.e., alpha is no longer at .05). Making this type of comparison in which the same group's mean is used more than once is called increasing the *experiment-wise error rate*. Simple ANOVA allows all three group means to be compared simultaneously, thus keeping alpha at the designated level of .05.

Table 7.5 provides the formulas for calculating simple ANOVA and the *F* ratio. This method, called the ABC method, is rather simple and is as follows:

- $A = \Sigma X^2$—This means to square each subject's score, sum up these squared scores (regardless of which group the subject is in), and set the total equal to A.
- $B = (\Sigma X)^2/N$—For this value, we sum each subject's score (regardless of group), square the sum, divide by the total number of subjects, and set the answer equal to B.
- $C = (\Sigma X_1)^2/n_1 + (\Sigma X_2)^2/n_2 + \ldots + (\Sigma X_i)^2/n_i$—This requires that we sum each subject's score in Group 1, square the sum, divide by the number of subjects in Group 1; do the same for the scores in Group 2; and so on for however many groups (i) there are; and set the answer to C.

Then fill in the "Summary Table for ANOVA" using A, B, and C. Thus, the Between groups (True variance) *sum of squares* (*SS*) is equal to C − B; the *degrees of freedom* (*df*) for Between groups is the number of groups minus 1 ($k - 1$); the *variance or mean square* (*MS*) for Between is the *SS* for Between divided by the *df* for Between. The same follows for Within (Error variance) and then Total. The *F* ratio is the MS_B/MS_W.

Table 7.6 provides an example for which the formulas in Table 7.5 are used. The scores from Groups 1, 2, and 3 are the sums of two judges' skill ratings

TABLE 7.5

FORMULAS FOR CALCULATING SIMPLE ANOVA

$$A = \Sigma X^2$$

$$B = \frac{(\Sigma X)^2}{N}$$

$$C = \frac{(\Sigma X_1)^2}{n_1} + \frac{(\Sigma X_2)^2}{n_2} + \ldots + \frac{(\Sigma X_i)^2}{n_i}$$

Summary Table for ANOVA

Source	***SS***	***df***	***MS***	***F***
Between (True)	C − B	$k - 1$	(C − B)/(k − 1)	MS_B/MS_W
Within (Error)	A − C	$N - k$	(A − C)/(N − k)	
Total	A − B	$N - 1$		

where X = a subject's score
N = total number of subjects
n = number of subjects in a group
k = number of groups

SS = sum of squares
df = degrees of freedom
MS = mean square

for a particular series of dance movements. The groups are randomly formed from 15 junior high school students. Group 1 was taught with videotaping and used individual corrections by the teacher while the student viewed the videotape. Group 2 was taught with videotaping but only general group corrections were made while viewing the tape. Group 3 was taught by the teacher without the benefit of videotape equipment. From looking at the formulas in Table 7.5, you should be able to see how each number in Table 7.6 was calculated.

Your first interest in Table 7.6, after you make sure you understand how the numbers were obtained, is in the F ratio of 10.00. Table A.4 in the Appendix contains tabled F values for the .05 and .01 levels of significance. Even though the numbers in this table are obtained the same way as the t table, you use the table in a slightly different way. Note in Table 7.6, the F ratio is obtained by dividing the MS Between by the MS Within. The MS_B has 2 df associated with it (numerator) while the MS_W has 12 df associated with it (denominator). Notice also that the F Table (Table A.4) has df across the top (numerator) and down the left hand column (denominator). For our F of 10.00, read down the 2 df column to the 12 df row; there are two numbers where the row and column intersect. The top number (3.88) in light print is the tabled F for the .05 level while the bottom number (6.93) in dark print is the tabled F for the .01 level. If our alpha had been established as .05, then you can see that our F value of 10.00 is larger than the tabled value of .05 (actually, it is also larger than .01), so our F is significant and could be written in the text of an article as $F\,(2,12) = 10.00, p < .05$

TABLE 7.6
A SIMPLE ANOVA

	Group 1		Group 2		Group 3	
	X	X^2	X	X^2	X	X^2
	12	144	9	81	6	36
	10	100	7	49	7	49
	11	121	6	36	2	4
	7	49	9	81	3	9
	10	100	4	16	2	4
Σ	50	514	35	263	20	102
M	10		7		4	

$A = \Sigma X^2 = 514 + 263 + 102 = 879$

$B = (\Sigma X)^2/N = (50 + 35 + 20)^2/15 = (105)^2/15 = 11025/15 = 735$

$C = (\Sigma X_1)^2/n_1 + (\Sigma X_2)^2/n_2 + (\Sigma X_3)^2/n_3 = (50)^2/5 + (35)^2/5 + (20)^2/5$
$= 2500/5 + 1225/5 + 400/5 = 825$

Summary Table for ANOVA

Source	SS	df	MS	F
Between	90	2	45.0	10.00*
Within	54	12	4.5	
Total	144	14		

*$p < .05$

(read F with 2 and 10 df is equal to 10.00 and is significant at less than the .05 level).

A computer program to calculate simple (one-way) ANOVA is provided in Appendix B. Following the listing of this program is a sample printout using the data from Table 7.6.

We now know that significant differences exist among the three group means (Group 1 $M = 10$, Group 2 $M = 7$, and Group 3 $M = 4$). But we do not know if all three groups differ, if 1 and 2 differ from 3 but not each other, or what. Thus, we next perform a follow-up test. One way to do follow-up tests is to do t tests between 1 and 2, 1 and 3, and 2 and 3. However, the same problem that we discussed earlier still exists with alpha. There are several follow-up tests that protect the experimentwise error rate. These methods include Scheffé, Newman-Keuls, Duncan's, and several others. Each of the tests is calculated in slightly different ways; however, they all are conceptually similar to the t test in that they identify which groups differ from each other. The Scheffé method is the most conservative, which means it identifies fewer significant differences. Duncan's is the most liberal with more significant differences. Newman-Keuls falls between the other two.

For our purposes, one example will suffice so we will demonstrate the use of the Newman-Keuls method of making multiple comparisons among means. In Table 7.7 the means are arranged from highest (10) to lowest (4). (The means could also be arranged from lowest to highest.) By following steps 1-8, you can observe that all three groups differ from each other, $p < .05$. We could conclude that the techniques used in Group 1 were better than those used in Group 2 and 3; and also, the techniques used in Group 2 were better than those used in Group 3.

Look more carefully at Table A.5 in the Appendix. Note that as the means are further apart in terms of size, a greater difference is required for significance. This is what protects alpha in a technique of this type. You should plan for the type of multiple range test to be used if significant differences are obtained in the ANOVA. These are called *post-hoc* comparisons which means you do them after finding a significant F ratio. Some people refer to this as *data snooping* (you snoop around to see which groups differ).

In addition to data snooping, the researcher may use *planned comparisons* to test for differences among groups. Planned comparisons are *a priori* in nature; that is, they are "planned" prior to the experiment. Thus, an experimenter might

TABLE 7.7

NEWMAN-KEULS TEST APPLIED TO DATA FROM TABLE 7.6

Group	*M*	2	3
1	10	3.16*	6.32*
2	7	—	3.16*
3	4	—	—

Step 1. Calculate error term: $E = \sqrt{MS_w/n} = \sqrt{4.5/5} = .95$.

Step 2 Order the means from highest to lowest: 10, 7, 4.

Step 3. Calculate the differences between the means: 3, 6, 3.

Step 4. Divide the difference by E and enter in above table: 3/.95 = 3.16, 6/.95 = 6.32, 3/.95 = 3.16.

Step 5. Calculate the steps between means; this is the number of means in the ordered set—Group 1 to 2 is 2 steps, Group 1 to 3 is 3 steps, Group 2 to 3 is 2 steps. The number of steps is called k.

Step 6. The *df* for Error is 12 (see Table 7.6).

Step 7. Enter the Studentized range table (Table A.5 in Appendix) with k and 12 *df* depending on which groups are being compared—Group 1 and 2 would be 2 and 12 *df*, Group 1 and 3 would be 3 and 12 *df*, and Group 2 and 3 would be 2 and 12 *df*.

Step 8. Compare value calculated for above table with value in Table A.5 at alpha (.05 for this example) and * the differences that are larger than the tabled value.

$^*p < .05$

postulate a test between two of the groups prior to the experiment because "in theory" this particular comparison is important and should be significant. However, the number of planned comparisons in an experiment should be small relative to the total number of possible comparisons.

Now that we know the F is significant and have followed it up to see which groups differ, we should answer our second question: What percent variance is accounted for by our treatments, or how meaningful are our results? One way to get a quick idea is to look back at Table 7.6 and to put True variance over Total variance, $SS_{True}/SS_{Total} = 90/144 = .625$ or 62.5% of the variance is accounted for by the treatments. Although this is sufficient for a quick estimate, it is biased. The more accurate way is to use Formula 7.9 from Tolson (1980):

$$w^2 = \frac{[F \cdot (k - 1)] - (k - 1)}{[F \cdot (k - 1)] + (N - k) + 1} \qquad \textbf{(7.9)}$$

where $F = F$ ratio, $k =$ number of groups, and $N =$ total number of subjects. If we do that with the data from Table 7.6, then we have

$$w^2 = \frac{[10.00 \cdot (3 - 1)] - (3 - 1)}{[10.00 \cdot (3 - 1)] + (15 - 3) + 1} = \frac{18}{33} = .545$$

Thus, w^2 indicates that 54.5% of the total variance is accounted for by the treatments.

Appendix B contains a computer program to calculate Omega squared (w^2) when the variance components from simple ANOVA are available. By entering the requested sums of squares (*SS*), mean squares (*MS*), and degrees of freedom (*df*), this program will calculate w^2. The sample following this program uses the information from Table 7.6.

Putting our statistics altogether, we could say that the treatments were significant, $F(2,12) = 10.00$, $p < .05$, and accounted for a meaningful proportion of the variance ($w^2 = 54.5\%$). In addition, a follow-up Newman-Keuls test indicated all three groups were different ($p < .05$) with Group 1 showing the best performance and Group 3 the poorest.

One final point to recall before leaving simple ANOVA is that t was a special case of F when there were only two levels of the independent variable (two groups). In fact, this relationship is exact, $t^2 = F$. Table 7.8 provides a specific example (within rounding error). In other words, there is very little need for t since F will handle two or more groups. However, t remains in use because it was developed first being the simplest case of F.

FACTORIAL ANOVA

Up to this point, examples of two levels (t) or two or more levels (simple ANOVA) of one independent variable (IV) have been discussed. In fact, what has occurred is that all other IVs have been controlled except the single IV to be manipulated

TABLE 7.8
COMPARISON OF t AND F

	Experimental Group			Control Group		
	X	$(X - M)^2$	X^2	X	$(X - M)^2$	X^2
	2	.09	4	8	4	64
	4	2.89	16	7	1	49
	3	.49	9	5	1	25
	3	.49	9	4	4	16
	2	.09	4	7	1	49
	1	1.69	1	5	1	25
	1	1.69	1	6	0	36
Σ	16	7.43	44	42	12	264
M	2.3			6.0		
s	1.11			1.41		

$$t = \frac{M_1 - M_2}{\sqrt{(s_1^2/n_1) + (s_2^2/n_2}} = \frac{2.3 - 6}{\sqrt{(1.11^2/7) + (1.41^2/7)}} = \frac{3.7}{.68} = 5.44$$

$$A = \Sigma X^2 = 44 + 264 = 308$$

$$B = (\Sigma X)^2/N = (58)^2/14 = 240.29$$

$$C = (\Sigma X_1)^2/n_1 + (\Sigma X_2)^2/n_2 = (16)^2/7 + (42)^2/7 = 36.57 + 252 = 288.57$$

Summary Table for ANOVA

Source	SS	df	MS	F
Between	48.28	1	48.28	29.80
Within	19.43	12	1.62	
Total	67.71	13		

$t^2 = F$, $(5.44)^2 = 29.8$, $29.6 = 29.8$ (within rounding error)

to evaluate its effect upon a dependent variable (dv). This is called the "Law of the independent variable." But, in fact, we can manipulate more than one IV and statistically evaluate the effects on a dv. This procedure is called *factorial ANOVA*, meaning that there is more than one factor or IV. Theoretically, a factorial ANOVA may have any number of factors (two or more) and any number of levels within a factor (two or more). However, we seldom encounter ANOVAs with more than three or four factors. This is another good place to apply the KISS principle (Keep It Simple, Stupid).

For our purpose we will only consider a two-way factorial ANOVA meaning the use of only two IVs. There would be two *main effects* and one *interaction*. Main effects are tests of each IV when the other IV is held constant. Look at Table 7.9 and note the first IV (IV_1) has three levels labeled A_1, A_2, and A_3.

TABLE 7.9
FACTORIAL (3 × 2) ANOVA MODEL

		IV_2		
Cell Means		B_1	B_2	Row Means
	A_1	$M_{A_1B_1}$	$M_{A_1B_2}$	M_{A_1}
IV_1	A_2	$M_{A_2B_1}$	$M_{A_2B_2}$	M_{A_2}
	A_3	$M_{A_3B_1}$	$M_{A_3B_2}$	M_{A_3}
Column Means		M_{B_1}	M_{B_2}	

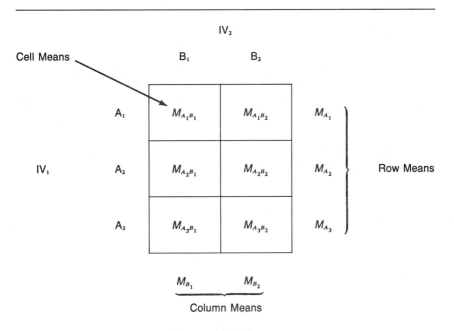

IV_1—Main effect is the test of the Row Means by F_A
IV_2—Main effect is the test of the Column Means by F_B
The Interactions is the test of the six Cell Means by F_{AB}

F_A = (True variance due to A)/(Error variance)
F_B = (True variance due to B)/(Error variance)
F_{AB} = (True variance due to A × B)/(Error variance)

Assume that these three levels represent the intensity of training, 40%, 60%, and 80% of $\dot{V}O_2$ max for 20 minutes a day for a 12 week period. The second IV (IV_2) represents frequency of training, 2 days per week (B_1) versus 3 days per week (B_2). We can test IV_1 by comparing the Row Means (M_{A1}, M_{A2}, M_{A3}) because IV_2 (B_1 and B_2) are equally represented at each level of A. That is, for each level of A, two groups—one training 2 days and one 3 days per week—are included. Thus, frequency of training is held constant to allow the test of intensity of training by the F_A ratio.

The same thing holds true for IV_2, frequency of training. By looking at the Column Means (M_{B1} and M_{B2}), you can see that the three levels of A(IV_1), intensity of training, are equally represented in the two levels of B. Therefore, the main effect of frequency of training can be tested by the F_B ratio.

In a study of this type, the main interest usually lies in the interaction. We want to know if the effect of the levels of A depends on or changes across the levels of B, or, if the effect of intensity of training depends on (interacts with) the frequency of training. This effect is tested by the F_{AB} ratio which evaluates the six cell means: M_{A1B1}, M_{A1B2}, M_{A2B1}, M_{A2B2}, M_{A3B1}, M_{A3B2}. Unless some special circumstance exists, interest in the testing of main effects is usually limited by the presence of a significant interaction. A significant interaction means that what happens in one IV depends upon the level of the other IV. Thus, normally it makes little sense to evaluate main effects when the interaction is significant.

This particular factorial ANOVA is labeled as a 3 (intensity of training) × 2 (frequency of training) ANOVA—read 3 by 2 ANOVA. As the bottom of Table 7.9 indicates, the True variance can be divided into three parts: True variance due to A (intensity of training); True variance due to B (frequency of training); and True variance due to interaction of A and B. Each of these True variance components is tested against (divided by) Error variance to form the three *F* ratios for this ANOVA. Each of these *F*s will have its own set of *df* so it can be checked for significance in the *F* table in Appendix A.4.

Table 7.10 gives the ABC method for calculating a two-way factorial ANOVA. Then, Table 7.11 provides an example using intensity of training and frequency of training as the IVs and distance covered on the 12-minute run as the dv. There are 30 subjects who are randomly assigned to one of the six groups (*n* per group = 5). Thus, this is a 3 × 2 ANOVA. The test for intensity is signifi-

TABLE 7.10

THE ABC METHOD FOR CALCULATING A TWO-WAY FACTORIAL ANOVA

$A = \Sigma X^2$

$B = (\Sigma X)^2/N$

$C\ (\text{rows}) = (\Sigma X_{r_1})^2 + (\Sigma X_{r_2})^2 + \ldots + (\Sigma X_{r_i})^2/n_{r_1}$

$D\ (\text{columns}) = (\Sigma X_{c_1})^2 + (\Sigma X_{c_2})^2 + \ldots + (\Sigma X_{c_j})^2/n_{c_1}$

$E(r \times c) = (\Sigma X_{cell_1})^2 + (\Sigma X_{cell_2})^2 + \ldots + (\Sigma X_{cell_k})^2/n_{cell_1}$

Summary Table for ANOVA

Source	*SS*	*df*	*MS*	*F*
Rows (IV_1)	C − B	r − 1	SS_R/df_R	MS_R/MS_E
Columns (IV_2)	D − B	c − 1	SS_c/df_c	MS_c/MS_E
R × C	(E − B) − (C − B) − (D − B)	(r − 1)(c − 1)	SS_{Rc}/df_{Rc}	MS_{Rc}/MS_E
Error	(A − B) − (E − B)	(*N* − 1) − (r − 1) − (c − 1) + (r − 1)(c − 1)	SS_E/df_E	
Total	A − B	*N* − 1		

where r = number of rows or levels of IV_1
c = number of columns of levels of IV_2

TABLE 7.11
AN EXAMPLE OF A TWO-WAY FACTORIAL ANOVA

		IV_2—Frequency of Exercise				
		2 days/wk		3 days/wk		
		X	X^2	X	X^2	
		2940	8643600	2980	8880400	
		3070	9424900	3160	9985600	
	40%	3100	9610000	3025	9150625	$\Sigma X_{r_1} = 30285$
		2925	8555625	3045	9272025	
		3050	9302500	2990	8940100	
		X	X^2	X	X^2	
IV_1		3150	9922500	3720	13838400	
Intensity		3020	9120400	3630	13176900	
of	60%	2990	8940100	3570	12744900	$\Sigma X_{r_2} = 33510$
Exercise		3050	9302500	3690	13616100	
		2980	8880400	3710	13764100	
		X	X^2	X	X^2	
		3170	10048900	3920	15366400	
		3120	9734400	4040	16321600	
	80%	3050	9302500	4110	16892100	$\Sigma X_{r_3} = 35620$
		3110	9672100	4005	16040025	
		3105	9641025	3990	15920100	
		$\Sigma X_{c_1} = 45830$		$\Sigma X_{c_2} = 53585$		

$$A = \Sigma X^2 = 8643600 + 9424900 + \ldots + 15920100 = 334010825$$

$$B = (\Sigma X)^2/N = (2940 + 3070 + 3100 + \ldots + 3990)^2/30 = 329444741$$

$$C = [(\Sigma X_{r_1})^2 + (\Sigma X_{r_2})^2 + (\Sigma X_{r_3})^2]/n_{r_1} = [(30285)^2 + (33510) + (35620)^2]/10 = 330888573$$

$$D = [(\Sigma X_{c_1})^2 + (\Sigma X_{c_2})^2]/n_{c_1} = \{(45830)^2 + (53585)^2]/15 = 331449408$$

$$E = [(\Sigma X_{cell_1})^2 + (\Sigma X_{cell_2})^2 + \ldots + (\Sigma X_{cell_i})^2]/n_{cell_1}$$
$$= [(15085)^2 + (15200)^2 + (15190)^2 + (18320)^2 + (15555)^2 + (20065)^2/5 = 333903595$$

Summary Table for ANOVA

Source	***SS***	***df***	***MS***	***F***
Rows (A)	1443832	2	721916	161.57*
Columns (B)	2004667	1	2004667	448.68*
A × B	1010355	2	505177	113.07*
Error	107230	24	4468	
Total	4566084	29		

*$p < .05$

cant, F (2,24) = 161.57, $p < .05$. This F is then followed-up with a Newman-Keuls test, and we see that the 80% intensity group performed significantly better than both the 60% and 40% group (Table 7.12), while the 60% group was significantly better than the 40% group.

The test for frequency of training is also significant, F (1,24) = 448.00, $p < .05$. However, no follow-up is required for this IV because there are only two levels (thus $t^2 = F$). All that is necessary is to note that the 3 day per week condition (M = 3772.3) produces significantly better performance than the 2 day per week condition (M = 3055.3).

Finally, the test for the A × B interaction is significant, F (2,24) = 113.07, $p < .05$. Thus, what happens with intensity of training depends upon the frequency of the training. Figure 7.1 is a plot of this interaction. You can see that the three intensities of training are very similar in their effect upon the 12-minute run when training is 2 days per week. However, the 80% level is clearly the best at 3 days per week, and the 60% level is better than the 40% level. The 40% level is very similar to all three intensities at the 2 days per week training frequency. In looking at this interaction, we might conclude that training 2 days per week or at 40% of max is not very effective. However, if the frequency of training is at least 3 days per week and at intensities of 60% of max or higher, significant cardiorespiratory benefits (as measured by the 12-minute run) occur.

As you can see, all we have done to follow-up the significant interaction is to verbally describe the plot in Figure 7.1. Considerable disagreement exists among researchers about how to follow-up significant interactions. Some researchers use a multiple comparison of means test (such as Newman-Keuls) to contrast the interaction cell means. However, these multiple comparison tests were developed for contrasting levels within an IV, and not for cell means across two or more IVs; thus, their use may be inappropriate. Other researchers use a follow-up called

TABLE 7.12

NEWMAN-KEULS FOLLOW-UP TO SIGNIFICANT MAIN EFFECT *F* FROM TABLE 7.11

Group	*M*	2	3
1 40%	3028.5	15.26*	25.24*
2 60%	3351.0	—	9.98*
3 80%	3562.0		—

$E = \sqrt{MS_E/n} = \sqrt{4468/10} = 21.14$

$t_{12} = (3028.5 - 3351)/21.14 = 322.5/21.14 = 15.26$

$t_{13} = (3028.5 - 3526)/21.14 = 533.5/21.14 = 25.24$

$t_{23} = (3351 - 3562)/21.14 = 211/21.14 = 9.98$

*$p < .05$

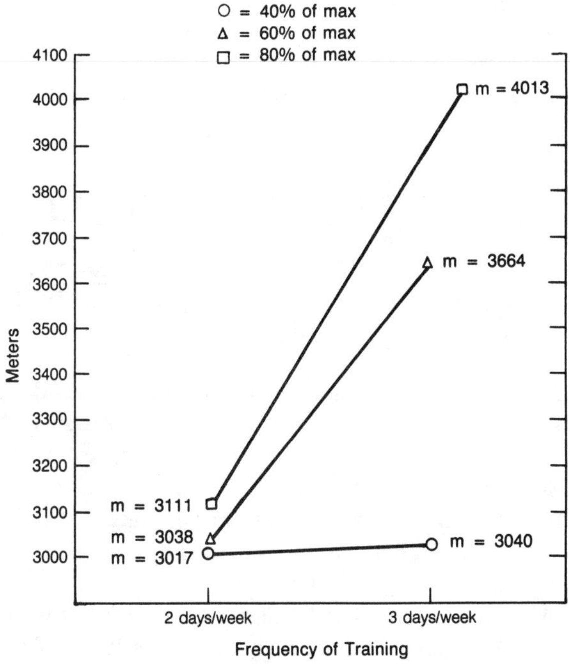

Figure 7.1. The plot of the interaction for a two-way factorial ANOVA.

a test of *simple main effects*. In our example, this indicates that a multiple comparison test should be applied to the three cell means within the levels of the IV of B. That is, the three levels of intensity are tested against each other at the 2 day per week training and then at the 3 day per week training. If the interaction is to be followed up with a statistical test, simple main effects would be the preferred technique.

Our preference for testing an interaction is to do as we have done—plot the interaction and describe it. This takes into account the true nature of an interaction: What happens in one IV depends upon the other IV. However, you are likely to encounter all of these ways (and probably some others) of testing interactions as you read the research literature. Just remember that the researcher is trying to show you how the two or more IVs interact. Also, remember that follow-ups on main effects are usually unnecessary when the interaction is significant. While we have done the follow-ups in this example (in order to help you understand the procedures better), the follow-ups would be of limited interest in the presence of a significant and meaningful interaction.

In Appendix B a computer program to calculate a two-way factorial ANOVA is provided. Following the listing of this program is a sample printout using the data from Table 7.11.

We have now answered the first statistical question about a factorial ANOVA—What are the significant effects? As in previous examples, we now turn to the meaningfulness of the effects, or what percent of the variance in the dv is accounted for by the IVs and their interaction? The three formulas below (from Tolson, 1980) provide the w^2 test for each component of the ANOVA:

$$w_A^2 = \frac{(p-1)F_A - (p-1)}{(p-1)F_A + (q-1)F_B + (p-1)(q-1)F_{AB} + (N-pq) + 1}$$

$$w_B^2 = \frac{(q-1)F_B - (q-1)}{(p-1)F_A + (q-1)F_B + (p-1)(q-1)F_{AB} + (N-pq) + 1}$$

$$w_{AB}^2 = \frac{(p-1)(q-1)F_{AB} - (p-1)(q-1)}{(p-1)F_A + (q-1)F_B + (p-1)(q-1)F_{AB} + (N-pq) + 1} \quad \textbf{(7.10)}$$

where p = number of levels of A and q = number of levels of B. These formulas all involve the proportion of True variance over Total variance. Note that once you calculate Total variance it remains the same for the test of all three proportions. In Table 7.13 we have applied the formula 7.10 to the Fs calculated in Table 7.12. Each w^2 represents the percent variance accounted for by that component of the ANOVA model. The w^2 can be summed to estimate the percent of the Total variance that is True variance.

Our discussion of simple and factorial ANOVA has dealt with studies where the levels of the IV(s) have the subjects randomly assigned. This is not always the case. Frequently levels of the IV may be categorical (also called classification) in nature. For example, we could do a simple ANOVA where the levels (or groups) of the IV involve beginning, intermediate, and advanced modern dance performers. Or in the previously presented factorial ANOVA, we could look at the effects of intensity of training (40%, 60%, and 80% of max) 3 days per week,

TABLE 7.13

THE CALCULATION OF w^2 FOR THE F RATIOS FROM TABLE 7.11

$$w_A^2 = \frac{(3-1)161.57 - (3-1)}{(3-1)161.57 + (2-1)448.00 + (3-1)(2-1)113.07 + (30-6) + 1}$$

$$= \frac{2(161.57) - 2}{(2)161.57 + (1)448.00 + (2)(1)113.07 + 24 + 1}$$

$$= \frac{321.14}{323.14 + 448.00 + 226.14 + 25} = \frac{447}{1022.28} = .31$$

$$w_B^2 = \frac{(2-1)448.00 - (2-1)}{1022.28} = \frac{447}{1022.28} = .44$$

$$w_{AB}^2 = \frac{(3-1)(2-1)113.07 - (3-1)(2-1)}{1022.28} = \frac{226.14 - 2}{1022.28} = \frac{224.14}{1022.28} = .22$$

Thus, the IV of intensity accounts for 31% of the True variance; the IV of frequency accounts for 44% of the True variance; the interaction accounts for 22% of the True variance; the Total True variance is 97%.

20 minutes per day for 12 weeks as one IV (3 levels) and have the other IV as a categorical one, gender. That is, we would be interested in whether intensity of training affected males and females differently. The levels of the first IV have subjects randomly assigned while subjects cannot be randomly assigned to the categorical variable—you are either male or female. Another common use of categorical variables is age levels. A study might look at the effects of the levels of a treatment or IV (where subjects are randomly assigned) on 6-, 9-, and 12-year-old females. Clearly, the interest in this type of factorial ANOVA is the interaction—Does the effectiveness of treatment differ according to the age of the child?

REPEATED MEASURES ANOVAS

Much of the research in HPERD (particularly physical education) involves studies that measure the same dv more than one time. For example, a study in sport psychology might investigate whether athletes' state anxiety (how nervous they feel at the time) changes from before to after the game. Thus, a state-anxiety inventory would be given just preceding and immediately following the game. The question of interest is, Does state anxiety change significantly from before to after the game? A dependent *t* test could be used to see if significant changes occurred. This is the simplest case of repeated measures.

Another study might have subjects measured on the dv on several occasions. Suppose we wanted to know if children (between 6 and 8 years of age) would increase the distance they threw a ball using an overhand throwing pattern. We decide to measure the children's distance throw every 3 months during the 2 years of the study. Thus, each of the children was assessed eight times on how far each could throw. We now have eight repeated measures on the same children. We would use a simple ANOVA with repeated measures on the one factor. Basically, the repeated measures is used as eight levels of the IV which is time (24 months). This analysis may also be referred to as a split-plot or subject × trials ANOVA. They all mean the same thing.

The most frequent use of repeated measures involves a factorial ANOVA in which one or more of the factors (IVs) is repeated measures. An example is an investigation of the effects of knowledge of results (KR) on skilled motor performance. There are three groups of subjects (three levels of IV_1) who receive varying types of KR (no KR, short or long of the target, and number of cm short or long of the target). The task is to position a handle that slides back and forth on a trackway (called a linear slide) as close to the target as possible. But the subjects are blindfolded, so they can't see the target. They only have verbal KR to correct their estimate of where the target is located along the trackway.

In this type of study, subjects are usually given multiple trials (assume 30 trials in this example) so the effects of the precision of KR can be judged. The score on each trial is error from the target in cm. This type of study is frequently analyzed as a two-way factorial ANOVA with repeated measures on the second factor. Thus a 3 (levels of KR) × 30 (trials) ANOVA with error as the dv is used to analyze the data. The first IV (levels of KR) is a true IV (three groups are randomly formed). The second IV (30 trials) is repeated measures. Sometimes this ANOVA is also called a two-way factorial ANOVA with one between subjects' factor (levels of KR) and one within subjects' factor (30 repeated trials). While an F ratio is calculated for each IV, the major focus is usually on the interaction; for example, Do the groups change at different rates across the trials?

Repeated measures designs have three advantages (Pedhazur, 1982).

1. They provide the experimenter the opportunity to control for individual differences among subjects, probably the largest source of variation in most studies. In between subject designs (completely randomized), the variation among subjects goes into the error term. Of course, this tends to reduce the F ratio unless it is offset by a large number of subjects. Remember the error term of the F ratio consists of dividing the variation among subjects by the *df* (which is based on the number of subjects). In repeated measures designs, individual difference variation can be identified and separated from the error term, thereby reducing it and increasing power.
2. As can be deduced from the first advantage, repeated measures designs are more economical in that fewer subjects are required.
3. Finally, repeated measures designs allow the study of a phenomenon across time. This is particularly important in studies of change—learning, fatigue, forgetting, performance, and aging.

However, several problems adversely affect repeated measures designs including (a) carry-over effects—treatments given earlier influence those given later; (b) practice effects—subjects get better at the task (dependent variable) as a result of repeated trials in addition to the treatment (also called the testing effect); (c) fatigue—subjects' performance is adversely influenced by fatigue (or boredom); and (d) sensitization—subjects' awareness of the treatment is heightened because of repeated exposure. Note that some of the "problems" may be the variables of interest in repeated measures designs. In learning studies, carry-over effects are what interest the researcher. Or increased fatigue over trials may be of major interest to an exercise physiologist.

The tricky part of repeated measures designs involves how to statistically analyze the data. We have already mentioned ANOVA models with repeated measures as one way to analyze the data. Unfortunately, these repeated measures ANOVAs have assumptions in addition to the ones we have given for all techniques. The major one is called *compound symmetry* which means that all the variables within a group have equal variances; that all the correlations among variables are equal; and that the covariance matrices of all groups are equal. In repeated measures studies, particularly within physical education, these assumptions are seldom met (Stamm & Safrit, 1975). The failure to meet them results in an increase in Type I error; that is, the alpha level may be considerably larger than the researcher intended. Greenhouse and Geisser (1959) have proposed the use of conservative F tests while others (Davidson, 1972; Harris, 1975; Morrow & Frankiewicz, 1979) have suggested the use of multivariate techniques as the more appropriate means of analysis. However, two additional points are important (Pedhazur, 1982): (a) when the assumptions are met, the ANOVA with repeated measures is more powerful than the multivariate tests; and (b) if the number of subjects is small, only the ANOVA repeated measures test can be used.

If you are contemplating a study using a repeated measures design, then several additional sources of reading should be helpful to you. Stamm and Safrit (1975) provide an informative discussion of when to use the regular F test, the conservative F test, or the multivariate F test for repeated measures designs. A more complete overview of design and statistical issues in repeated measures designs can be obtained by reading a series of papers by Morrow, Morris, and Looney reported in *AAHPERD Research Consortium Symposium Papers* (Cox & Serfass, 1981).

In Table 7.14 the formulas (ABC method) used to calculate a one-way ANOVA with repeated measures have been provided. This analysis may also be called a subject × trials ANOVA or a two-way ANOVA with one subject per cell.

An example of these calculations is provided in Table 7.15. In this example, 5 subjects were given three trials on the same task. The scores represent the number of hits each subject made in 10 throws at a target. As you can see from the Ms, the subjects improve on the average number of hits from Trial 1 (M = 4.6) to Trial 2 (M = 6.0) to Trial 3 (M = 7.2). This increase across the three trials is significant, $F(2,8) = 15.14$, $p < .05$.

TABLE 7.14

THE ABC METHOD FOR CALCULATING ONE-WAY REPEATED MEASURES ANOVA

A = ΣX^2

B = $(\Sigma X)^2/N$

C (subjects) = $[(\Sigma X_{r1})^2 + (\Sigma X_{r2})^2 + \ldots + (\Sigma X_{ri})^2]/n_{r1}$

D (trials) = $[(\Sigma X_{c1})^2 + (\Sigma X_{c2})^2 + \ldots + (\Sigma X_{cj})^2]/n_{c1}$

Summary Table for ANOVA

Source	***SS***	***df***	***MS***	***F***
Subjects	C − B	r − 1	SS_S/df_S	MS_S/MS_R
Trials	D − B	c − 1	SS_T/df_T	MS_T/MS_R
Residual	(A − B) − (C − B) + (D − B)	(r − 1)(c − 1)	SS_R/df_R	
Total	A − B	N − 1		

where r = number of subjects
c = number of trials
N = total number of scores (# subjects × # trials)

TABLE 7.15
REPEATED MEASURES ANOVA

Subjects	X	X^2	X	X^2	X	X^2
1	5	25	7	49	9	81
2	3	9	4	16	4	16
3	4	16	6	36	7	49
4	5	25	5	25	7	49
5	6	36	8	64	9	81
Σ	23	111	30	190	36	276
M	4.6		6.0		7.2	

A = 111 + 190 + 276 = 577

B = $(23 + 30 + 36)^2/15$ = 528.07

C = $[(5 + 7 + 9)^2 + (3 + 4 + 4)^2 + (4 + 6 + 7)^2 + (5 + 5 + 7)^2 + (6 + 8 + 9)^2]/3$
$[(21)^2 + (11)^2 + (17)^2 + (17)^2 + (23)^2]/3$ = 1669/3 = 556.33

D = $[(23)^2 + (30)^2 + (36)^2]/5$ = 545

Summary Table for ANOVA

Source	*SS*	*df*	*MS*	*F*
Subjects	28.27	4	7.07	
Trials	16.93	2	8.47	15.14*
Residual	3.73	8	0.46	
Total	48.93	14		

*$p < .05$

In this analysis, the variance between subjects (*SS* = 28.27) has been removed. While it could be tested, the fact that the variance among several subjects is significant is to be expected. This analysis has all of the strengths and weaknesses previously discussed. If we were going to actually use this technique, we would probably want to use the conservative *F* test as recommended by Stamm and Safrit (1975) and follow their suggestions. This conservative test involves this formula

$$\theta = 1/(k - 1) \tag{7.11}$$

where k = number of repeated measures. Then the degrees of freedom for trials are multiplied by this value, $\theta(k - 1)$, as well as the degrees of freedom for error, $\theta(n - 1)(k - 1)$. These adjusted degrees of freedom (to the nearest whole *df*) are used to look up the *F* ratio in the *F* Table. If the *F* ratio is significant under the conservative test, then the effect is likely a real one. The problem is encountered when the F is significant under the regular test but not the conservative test. Then either a decision must be made between them or the data must be analyzed in a multivariate model.

ANALYSIS OF COVARIANCE (ANCOVA)

ANCOVA is a combination of regression and ANOVA. The technique is used to adjust the dv for some distractor variable (called the covariate). Suppose we want to evaluate the effects of a training program to develop leg power on the time required to run 50 yards. However, we know that reaction time (RT) will influence the 50-yard dash time because those who begin more quickly after the start signal have an advantage. We form two groups, measure RT in each group, train one with our power development program while the other serves as a control group, and measure each subject's time for running 50 yards. This is a study where ANCOVA might be used to analyze the data. There is an IV with two levels (power training and control), a dv (50 yard dash) and an important distractor variable or covariate (RT).

ANCOVA is actually a two-step process where first an adjustment is made for the 50-yard dash score of each subject according to his or her RT. A correlation (r) is calculated between RT and time in the 50-yard dash. The resulting prediction equation (50-yard dash time $= a + (b)$RT, same as $Y' = a + bX$) is used to calculate each subject's predicted 50-yard dash time (Y'). The difference between the actual 50-yard dash time (Y) and the predicted time (Y') is called the residual ($Y - Y'$). A simple ANOVA is then calculated using each subject's residual score as the dv[3] (1 df for within sums of squares is lost because of the correlation). This allows an evaluation of 50-yard dash speed with RT controlled.

ANCOVA can be used in factorial situations and with more than one covariate. The results are evaluated just like an ANOVA except one or more distractor variables have been controlled. ANCOVA is also frequently used in situations where a pretest is given, some treatment applied, and then a posttest given. The pretest is used as the covariate in this type analysis. Note in the preceding section (repeated measures), we indicated this same situation could be analyzed by repeated measures. In addition, ANCOVA is used when comparing intact groups because the groups' performances (dv) can be adjusted for distractor variables (covariates) on which they differ.

While ANCOVA may seem to be the answer to many problems, its use does have limitations. In particular, its use to adjust final performance for initial differences can result in misleading interpretations (Lord, 1969). In addition, if the correlations between the covariate and the dependent variable are not equal across the treatment groups, standard ANCOVA (there are nonstandard ANCOVA techniques) is inappropriate.

[3]Actually, the procedure is slightly different, but the concept is the same.

EXPERIMENTWISE ERROR RATE

Sometimes several comparisons are made on different dependent variables but using the same subjects. In most instances, use of a multivariate technique (discussed next) is the appropriate solution. However, when dependent variables are combinations of other dependent variables (e.g., cardiac output is heart rate × stroke volume), a multivariate model using all three dependent variables is inappropriate.[4] Thus, an ANOVA among three groups might be calculated separately for each dependent measure (i.e., three ANOVAs). The problem is that this procedure results in increasing the alpha that has been established for the experiment. One of two solutions is appropriate for adjusting experimentwise alpha (α_{EW}). The first is called the ***Bonferroni technique*** and simply divides the alpha level by the number of comparisons to be made:

$$\alpha_{EW} = \alpha/c \qquad \textbf{(7.12)}$$

where c = number of comparisons. In our example, if $\alpha = .05$ and $c = 3$, then the α for each comparison is $\alpha = .05/3 = .017$. This means that the F ratio would have to reach an alpha of .017 to be declared significant.

The second option is to leave the overall $\alpha = .05$ but calculate the upper limit that the alpha might be

$$\alpha_{EW} = 1 - (1 - \alpha)^k \qquad \textbf{(7.13)}$$

where α = alpha and k = number of groups. Again, using our example, $\alpha_{EW} = 1 - (1 - .05)^3 = .14$. Thus, the hypotheses are really being tested somewhere between an alpha of .05 if the dependent variables are perfectly correlated, and .14 if they are independent.

MULTIVARIATE TECHNIQUES

Up to this point we have discussed research examples in which there were one or more IVs but only one dv. Multivariate cases have one or more IVs and two or more dvs. It seems much more likely that when IVs are manipulated, they influence more than one thing. The multivariate case allows for more than one dv. To use techniques which allow only one dv (called univariate techniques) repeatedly when there are several dvs increases the *experimentwise* error rate in the same way as doing multiple t tests instead of simple ANOVA when there are more than two groups.

---

[4]This book is not the appropriate place to explain why. For more detail, see Thomas (1977).

DISCRIMINANT ANALYSIS

This technique is used when there is one IV (two or more levels) and two or more dvs. The technique is a combination of multiple regression and simple ANOVA. In effect, discriminant analysis uses a combination of the dv to predict the IV, which in this instance is group membership. In the discussion of multiple regression in Chapter 6, several predictor variables were used in a linear combination to predict a criterion variable. In essence, discriminant analysis does the same thing except several dvs are used in a linear combination to predict group membership. This prediction of group membership is the equivalent of discriminating among the groups (recall how t could be calculated by r). The same methods used in multiple regression to identify the important predictors are used in discriminant analysis. These include forward, backward, and stepwise selection techniques.

As mentioned previously, the forward selection technique enters the dvs in the order of their importance: That is, the dv that contributes the most to separation of the groups (discriminates among or predicts group membership the best) is entered first. By correlation techniques, the effect of the first dv on all other dvs is removed, and the dv that contributes the next greatest amount to separation of the groups is entered at Step 2. This procedure continues until all dvs have been entered or some criterion for stopping the process (established by the researcher) is met.

The backward selection procedure is similar except all the dvs are entered and the one contributing the least to group separation is removed. This continues until the only variables remaining are those that contribute significantly to the separation of the groups. The stepwise technique is similar to the forward selection except at each step all the dvs are evaluated to see if each still contributes to group separation. If one dv does not it is stepped out (removed) from the linear combination.

Table 7.16 provides an example of the use of discriminant analysis with a forward selection technique for choosing significant dvs. In this study (Tew & Wood, 1980) varsity football players were classified into three groups: offensive and defensive backs, offensive and defensive linemen, and linebackers and receivers. Data were collected for 28 athletes in each group (N = 84) on 7 variables: 40-yard dash, 12-minute run, shuttle run, vertical jump, standing long jump, bench press, and squat. Discriminant analysis was applied to determine how many of the 7 dvs were needed to separate (predict) the three groups of football players. At the top of Table 7.16 are the 7 original variables with the R^2s (estimate of percent variance accounted for) and the Fs for each variable. This F is only a simple ANOVA on this variable for the three groups. As you can see, the three groups are significantly ($p < .05$) different on all 7 variables. The question not answered is, ''What is the relationship among these 7 variables for the 84 athletes?'' For example, the shuttle run (which requires speed) would be expected to relate highly to the 40-yard dash.

TABLE 7.16

EXAMPLE OF THE USE OF DISCRIMINANT ANALYSIS (FORWARD SELECTION TECHNIQUE)

Original Variables ($df = 2, 81$)

Variable	R^2	F	Probability
40-yd dash	.36	23.11	.0001
12-min run	.08	3.65	.03
Shuttle run	.21	10.48	.0001
Vertical jump	.30	17.25	.0001
Standing long jump	.27	14.85	.0001
Bench press	.39	25.90	.0001
Squat	.13	5.87	.004

Forward Selection Summary

Step	Variable Entered	F to Enter	Probability of F	Average Squared Canonical Correlation
1	Bench press	25.90	.0001	.20
2	40-yd dash	28.22	.0001	.34
3	Vertical jump	3.21	.05	.35

$F(6, 158) = 19.46, p < .0001$

Variables not in the Equation ($df = 2, 78$)

Variables	R^2	F	Probability
12-min run	.03	1.19	.31
Shuttle run	.00	0.05	.95
Standing long jump	.02	0.94	.40
Squat	.06	2.42	.10

In applying discriminant analysis we set two criteria for the statistical computer program: to include the variable at each step with the largest F ratio; and to *stop* when no remaining variable has an F significant at $p < .05$. By looking at the "Original Variables," you can see which one will be entered at Step 1. The bench press is entered because it has the biggest F (25.90). The program then uses a semipartial correlation procedure to remove the effects of the bench press from the remaining 6 dv. Note that the 40-yard dash is included next at Step 2. If you looked at the computer printout (not provided here), you would see that the 40-yard dash has the largest F (28.22) at Step 2. (You should now be looking at Forward Selection Summary in the middle of Table 7.16.) At Step

3 the vertical jump is entered ($F = 3.21, p < .05$) because it has the largest F among the remaining 5 dv when they are adjusted for the bench press and the 40-yard dash. At this point, none of the 4 remaining dv variables had significant Fs, so the program provides the overall test of the composite of dvs' (bench press, 40-yard dash, and vertical jump) ability to separate the three groupings of players, $F(6,158) = 19.46, p < .0001$. On the right of the Forward Selection Summary is the Averaged Squared Canonical Correlation which is cumulative at each step. This is an estimation of the percent variance accounted for (20% with first variable, 34% with the first and second variables, and 35% with all three). At the bottom of Table 7.16 are the dvs not included in the discriminant analysis equation. Note that none of the remaining 4 dv are significant in their ability to separate the three groups when the effects of the bench press, 40-yard dash, and vertical jump are removed from them. This means that the characteristics underlying performance in the three dv variables included are the same characteristics underlying performance in the 4 dv not included. This seems to be a reasonably good explanation except for the 12-minute run. But note it did not discriminate very effectively among the groups to begin with ($F = 3.65, p < .03$, 8% variance accounted for). This really addresses the issue of why the 12-minute run would be expected to discriminate among football players since none of their training regimens is designed to develop cardiovascular endurance.

We might want to follow-up the discriminant analysis with univariate techniques to determine which groups actually differed from each other on each of the three dvs included. There are several ways to approach this follow-up, but for simplicity, consider the fact that you could perform the Newman-Keuls test among the three groups on the first dv. Then ANCOVA could be done among the three groups on the second dv using the first dv as a covariate. This would provide adjusted means (means of second dv corrected for the first dv) on the second dv. A Newman-Keuls test could be done among the adjusted means using the adjusted mean square for error. This procedure is continued through each dv using the previously stepped in dvs as covariates and is called a step-down F technique. There are also other ways to follow up discriminant analysis.

As you can see, we have used discriminant analysis in a situation where the three groups were intact (i.e., not randomly formed). This is a very common application of discriminant analysis. However, discriminant analysis does not overcome the need to randomly form the groups if determination of cause-effect is the purpose of the research.

Discriminant analysis can also be used to actually place people into groups. We could write a prediction equation, $Y' = a +$ bench press(B_1) + 40-yard dash(B_2) + vertical jump(B_3), that could be used to classify players as backs, linemen, and linebackers and receivers. However, given that only 35% of the variance is accounted for in this model, the usefulness of this prediction equation could be questioned. Of course, football coaches would love to find a valid and reliable equation of this type; then the tests could be given to high school athletes in order to predict those that might be succesful at the various positions on college teams.

MULTIVARIATE ANALYSIS OF VARIANCE (MANOVA)

From an intuitive point of view, MANOVA is a rather straightforward extension of ANOVA. The only difference being that the *F* tests of the IVs and interactions are based on a linear composite of several dvs. There is no need to consider simple MANOVA as this is discriminant analysis (one IV with two or more levels and two or more dvs).

The mathematics are rather complex for factorial MANOVA, but the idea is relatively simple. A combination (linear composite) of the dvs is made that will maximally separate (predict) the levels of the first IV. Then a combination of the dvs is made that will maximally separate the levels of the second IV and so on. Note that the combination to separate the second IV may be different from the combination to separate the first IV. However, certain statistical computer programs offer the option of using the same linear combination for all IVs and interactions. Finally, the combination of dvs that maximizes the interaction(s) is calculated. Each of the test of IVs and interaction(s) has an associated *F* with *df* which is interpreted as *F* for ANOVA. There are several ways to obtain this *F* in MANOVA, Wilks' lambda, greatest characteristic root, Roa's *F* approximation, and others. We point this out only because authors sometimes identify how the MANOVA *F*s were obtained. For your purposes, these distinctions are not important—just consider the MANOVA *F* ratios similar to ANOVA *F* ratios.

Once MANOVA has been used, a significant linear composite of dvs is identified as separating the levels of the IV. Then, the question of importance is usually "which of the dvs contributes significantly to this separation?" One of many ways to answer this question is to use discriminant analysis and the step-down *F* procedures discussed in the previous section as follow-up techniques. This works well for the IVs but not so well for interactions. MANOVA interactions are most frequently handled by calculating factorial ANOVA for each dv although this procedure fails to take the relationships among the dvs into account.

SUMMARY

This chapter has presented techniques used in situations where differences among groups are the focus of attention. Basically, these techniques are categorized into three groups:

1. *t* test is used to determine how a group differs from a population, how two groups differ, how one group changes from one occasion to the next, and how several means differ (the multiple range tests).
2. ANOVA shows differences among the levels of one IV (simple ANOVA), of two or more IVs (factorial ANOVA), and among levels of IVs when there is a distractor variable or covariate (ANCOVA).

TABLE 7.17

COMPARISON OF STATISTICAL TECHNIQUES FROM CHAPTERS 6 AND 7

Description	Differences Among Groups	Relationships Among Variables
1 IV (2 levels)→1 dv	Independent *t* test	
1 predictor→1 criterion		Pearson *r*
1 IV (2 or more levels)→1 dv	Simple ANOVA	
2 or more IVs→1 dv	Factorial ANOVA	
2 or more predictors→1 criterion		Multiple regression
1 IV (2 or more levels)→2 or more dv	Discriminant analysis	
2 or more IVs→2 or more dv	MANOVA	
2 or more predictors→2 or more criteria		Canonical correlation

3. Multivariate techniques show differences among levels of one IV given two or more dvs (discriminant analysis) and differences among two or more IVs given two or more dvs (MANOVA).

Table 7.17 provides an overall look at the techniques of this chapter and Chapter 6 (relationships among variables) with regard to their appropriate use. Note that there are techniques for relationships among variables that parallel each of the techniques for differences among groups. In fact, the relationship between *t* and *r* that was demonstrated earlier in this chapter holds for each of these parametric techniques. ANOVA techniques are the equivalent of multiple regression and discriminant analysis and MANOVA is the equivalent of canonical correlation. Each of the techniques evaluates our two basic questions: Is the effect or relationship significant? and Is the effect or relationship meaningful?

Some of the ideas presented here are complex and may not be easily understood in one reading. We have provided some suggested additional readings and problems at the end of the chapter that should be helpful. If you do not feel confident in your understanding of this material, reread the chapter, do the problems, and read some of the suggested readings. This is important because information in Sections III and IV will assume that you understand Section II.

PROBLEMS

1. *t* test
   a. Critique the statistical part of a study that uses an independent *t* test.
   b. Calculate w^2 for the *t* in this study.

c. Find a study that uses a multiple range test (Newman-Keuls, Duncan's, Scheffé) as a follow-up to ANOVA, and critique the use of this test.

d. Table 7.18 provides a problem and data set for a *t* test. Answer the questions at the bottom of the table.

2. ANOVA

a. Critique the statistical part of a study that uses simple ANOVA. Calculate w^2 for the *F*.

b. Critique the statistical part of a study that uses a two-way factorial ANOVA. Calculate the w^2 for each factor and the interaction.

c. Critique a repeated measures study that uses ANOVA.

TABLE 7.18

EXAMPLE FOR PROBLEM 1d

Differences Between Groups

Two groups of 7-year-old children are asked to jog 35 m down a string placed on the ground. Then they are asked to reproduce the distance jogged on a second string placed at a right angle to the first. One group (Experimental) is cued before they begin that the best way to remember the distance is to count the number of steps. The control is just told to remember as best they can. Below is the error in meters each subject made when they estimated the 35 m distance jogged on the second trial.

Experimental Group		Control Group	
S_1	2.55	S_8	7.68
S_2	3.62	S_9	6.80
S_3	3.42	S_{10}	5.68
S_4	2.86	S_{11}	3.97
S_5	2.00	S_{12}	7.23
S_6	1.08	S_{13}	5.48
S_7	1.16	S_{14}	6.03

Questions

1. Are the two groups significantly different (alpha = .05)?
2. What percent variance is accounted for by the treatment?
3. Place the following statistics into a table: *M* and *s* for each group; *t*; *df*; w^2.
4. Did the use of a counting strategy produce a reliable and meaningful performance difference for the experimental group when compared to the control group? Justify your answer.

3. Critique a study using MANOVA. How are significant MANOVA effects followed-up?

SUGGESTED READINGS

Sometimes graduate students are interested in additional information on some of the statistical techniques; therefore, we have listed the following suggested readings:

GENERAL

Ferguson, G.A. (1971). *Statistical analysis in psychology & education* (3rd ed.). New York: McGraw-Hill.

Harris, R.J. (1975). *A primer of multivariate statistics*. New York: Academic Press.

Pedhazur, E.J. (1982). *Multiple regression in behavioral research*. New York: Holt, Rinehart and Winston.

Winer, B.J. (1971). *Statistical principles in experimental design*. New York: McGraw-Hill.

REPEATED MEASURES

Analysis of repeated measures. In R.H. Cox & R.C. Serfass. *AAHPERD Research Consortium Papers, (1981)*. Reston, VA: AAHPERD, 1981, pp. 5-60.

Morrow, J.R., & Frankiewicz, R.G. (1979). Strategies for the analysis of repeated and multiple measures designs. *Research Quarterly*, **50**, 297-304.

Stamm, C.L., & Safrit, M.J. (1975). Comparison of significance tests for repeated measures ANOVA designs. *Research Quarterly*, **46**, 403-409.

MANOVA FOLLOW-UPS

Bray, J.H., & Maxwell, S.E. (1982). Analyzing and interpreting significant MANOVAs. *Review of Educational Research*, **52**, 340-367.

Section III

TYPES OF RESEARCH

Research may be divided into four basic categories: *analytical, descriptive, experimental,* and *creative.* These headings best represent the nature of the types of research which are included. Chapter 8, "Historical Research," is a type of analytical research which answers questions through the use of past knowledge and events. Chapter 9, "Meta-Analysis," is another type of analytical research which focuses on the shortcomings of the typical literature analysis. Meta-analysis is a more useful solution in analyzing a large body of literature. While several other types of research are considered analytical, historical research and meta-analysis are the most common and useful in HPERD.

Chapter 10, "Descriptive Research," focuses upon the present and shows the relationship among people, events, performances, and so on, as they now exist. Included as descriptive research are surveys, case studies, correlational studies, developmental studies, and observational studies.

Chapter 11, "Experimental Research," deals with future events or the establishment of cause-effect. What independent variables can be manipulated to create change in the future in a certain dependent variable(s)? After a discussion of how difficult cause-effect is to establish, the chapter is divided according to the strengths of various designs: preexperimental, true experimental, and quasi-experimental. Our purpose is to illustrate which designs and principles are best suited to controlling for the various sources of invalidity that threaten experimental research.

Finally, Chapter 12, "Creative Research," provides something unique to a research book: With much assistance from a member of our dance faculty, the chapter presents a treatment of the processes used in planning a specific type of creative research—dance choreography. The chapter is divided into four parts which include (a) development of the choreographic problem, (b) planning and teaching the choreography, (c) evaluating the choreography, and (d) presenting and recording the choreographic work. While this chapter may be of limited functional value to most people (other than dancers) in HPERD, understanding the processes is important to anyone who wants or needs a broad knowledge of research techniques.

To be either a producer or consumer of research in HPERD, an understanding of accepted techniques for systematically solving problems is essential. The following four chapters attempt to provide the basic underpinnings of research planning. Many of the research types reported here are closely associated with appropriate statistical analyses (presented in the previous section). Frequent references to the appropriate statistics will be made as the many types of research are discussed. Use the knowledge gained from the previous section to understand this application. An understanding of the relationship between the correct type of design and the appropriate statistical analysis is one you should begin acquiring as soon as possible.

Chapter 8

Historical Research

Helen Fant*

HISTORY

WHAT IS HISTORY?

In one sense everything that has happened is history. But in research it is helpful to think of history as a written account of significant events, actions, or thoughts set in the context of the time. To write such a narrative requires a search for *all* the truth. History is not a newspaper story or the minutes of a professional organization or the records of marathoners as reported in Olympic yearbooks. These may or may not be facts, but it is not historical research. There has not been a search for all the truth nor have the data been synthesized or interpreted in relation to the period in which the events occurred.[1,2]

Written history can be organized in a number of ways. It can be expressed in the lives of significant people; and it can be written as the development of social practices, customs, ideas, and beliefs. For instance, the history of the sports concerns in Title IX of the Educational Amendments Act would be incomplete without tracing the changes in ideas about gender roles and abilities. The determination of how ideas and beliefs evolve is one of the most demanding and yet exciting types of historical research. In physical education and sport, philosophical beliefs about mind/body relationships as expressed in asceticism or humanism

---

*We thank Dr. Helen Fant, professor of Physical Education at Louisiana State University, for writing the Historical Research chapter. This chapter is written in the format prescribed by *A Manual of Style* (Chicago: The University of Chicago Press, 1982). We asked Dr. Fant to write the chapter in this style because this is the accepted writing style for historical research.

Although historical research is appropriate and is needed in all areas of HPERD, most of the studies have been in the areas of physical education and sport. Consequently, the examples in this chapter pertain to these areas.

can be examined in a historical setting. These are ways to extend historical writing beyond listing dates and leaders.

WHY IS HISTORY IMPORTANT?

A search into the past where we cannot go has fascinated men and women since storytellers sat around campfires. Then they spoke or sang of what had been and some painted or scratched pictures of hunts or battle onto stone. Brave deeds, cataclysmic happenings, and humdrum everyday events were recalled. They wanted to remember for pleasure, to warn of repeating mistakes, and to tell their children how things had been. We do the same today, still seeking to find meaning in our own lives by understanding the present in terms of the past. We do not live in a vacuum, but are a part of a great parade of persons in the past, present, and future. In a practical sense, a study of history can suggest courses of action in light of what has been successful. In the 1960s, physical education, in order to retain its status on some university campuses, was a profession searching for identity as an academic discipline. One generally accepted criterion of a discipline is that it has a history or tradition.[3] Studying the history of a profession or an ethnic group or country can instill a sense of pride and a determination to perpetuate and to improve the institution. The past can give direction to the future.

THE STATUS OF HISTORICAL RESEARCH IN PHYSICAL EDUCATION AND SPORT

Sport studies have virtually replaced physical education as an area for historical research. Even history theses and dissertations written by graduate students in physical education are dominated by sport with a 3 to 1 ratio.[4] Within the past decade (the 1970s), sport has become a favorite topic not only for historians but for psychologists, sociologists, philosophers, and physiologists.[5] The field of sport history has been promoted by physical educators in universities rather than by departments of history. Seward Staley, former Chairman of Physical Education at the University of Illinois, was a leader in developing sport history as an area for research in the 1950s.[6] His efforts were a forerunner to the Big Ten Body of Knowledge Project in which eight subdisciplines, including history, were identified as making up the discipline of physical education. The North American Society for Sport History (NASSH) was established in 1972 "to promote, stimulate, and encourage study and research and writing of the history of sport. . . ."[7] While biographical studies of physical educators and histories of departments and organizations may interest physical educators, the avenue of publication for these "special" studies is narrow.[8,9] A sport topic such as the history of basketball can be narrow too, but sport is and has been such a pervasive factor in society that it is usually the preferred area of research for the serious historian. Because there is a need for the development of physical education to be examined in relation to legal, political, medical, and social phenomena, the researcher should consider these factors in choosing a topic.

TYPES OF HISTORICAL RESEARCH IN PHYSICAL EDUCATION AND SPORT

In the section above, special and general histories were identified. Jable discusses some other approaches to historical research, namely descriptive, interpretive, quantitative, oral, and psychohistory.[10] *Descriptive* history simply describes events or persons, telling when, where, who, and what. Some excellent examples of descriptive history can be found in the detailed work of Ellen Gerber as she writes of leaders such as Edward Hitchcock, and schools such as the Boston Normal School of Gymnastics.[11] *Interpretive* history goes beyond the descriptive to analysis and explanation. It tells *why* events happened.

Psychohistory is a form of interpretive history in which specialized researchers attempt to explain the behavior of individuals. An interesting thesis might come from a psychohistory of John McEnroe, Jack Lambert, Bear Bryant, or Reggie Jackson. Studies based on *quantitative data* have been made immensely easier through the use of computers which locate and analyze vast quantities of data, for example, as in demographic studies. Hardy, in his study of Boston parks, collected data on voting patterns of wards, taxation, annexation, and from minutes of various committees and councils.[12] Mormino used census and immigration data to study Italian immigrants and sport in St. Louis.[13] Other studies on recreational patterns and in public health make extensive use of population density and status data.

Oral history, greatly facilitated by the use of a tape recorder, is a valuable source of information. It is the use of carefully designed questions addressed to an individual or group. This was the technique used in the popular *Foxfire* series describing the life of the eastern United States mountaineers.

SOURCES OF DATA

PRIMARY SOURCES

Historians classify data as being from primary or secondary sources. *Primary* sources are data which are derived from reliable witnesses who saw and heard the event and recorded it soon after. The writer might have been an eyewitness, or the information was obtained from another reliable source. Most sources are records that were specifically intended to preserve information for posterity; and public records of governments, businesses, and institutions account for almost all information about these units.[14,15] Table 8.1 shows the variety of records available.

Official records can be an invaluable source of information and they are usually available (by law). Local and state school board minutes and budgets can

TABLE 8.1
SOURCES OF PRIMARY DATA

Official Records
Legislative, judicial, or executive documents prepared by federal, state, or local governments, such as constitutions, laws, charters, court proceedings and decisions, tax lists, and vital statistics; the data preserved by churches, such as baptismal, marriage, financial, and board meeting records; the information compiled by federal and state education departments, special commissions, professional organizations, school boards, or administrative authorities, such as the minutes of meetings, reports of committees, administrative orders or directives, school surveys, annual reports, budgets, courses of study, class schedules, salary lists, attendance records, health records, safety and accident reports, and athletic records

Personal Records
Diaries, autobiographies, letters, wills, deeds, contracts, lecture notes, and original drafts of speeches, articles, and books

Oral Traditions
Myths, folk tales, family stories, dances, games, ceremonies, reminiscences by eyewitnesses to events, and recordings

Pictorial Records
Photographs, movies, microfilms, drawings, paintings, and sculpture

Published Materials
Newspaper, pamphlet, and periodical articles; literary and philosophical works that convey information about education

Mechanical Records
Tape recordings of interviews and meetings, phonograph records of pupils' speech or reading efforts

Note. From *Understanding Educational Research* (p. 180) by D.B. Van Dalen, 1962, New York: McGraw-Hill. Reprinted with permission.

be used to determine the status of support for physical education or athletics over a period of time.

A study of state and federal laws shows the development of required physical education or health instruction or sports programs. Jable's study on Quaker suppression of sport and Riess' work on Sunday baseball are other studies based on legal data.[16]

Other primary sources biographers rely upon are personal records, interviews, pictures, tape recordings, articles, and letters written by the person studied. The paintings of George Catlin are a prime source of information about games of American Indians. Newspaper accounts are important in finding out about one or more of the modern Olympic games. Thompson employed a variety of techniques in collecting data for a study of national tournaments for black high schools. He used newspaper archives, personal and telephone interviews, tournament programs, pictures from individuals and newspapers, official college athletic department records (Hampton and Tuskegee Institutes), and minutes of high school sports governing bodies.[17]

The terms *remains* and *relics* are used to describe physical evidence that was not intended to be a formal record and yet is a primary source. Archaeologists excavating the ancient Pan-Hellenic Nemean game site in the hills of southern Greece have discovered foundations of training centers, a stadium under acres of dirt with a tunneled entrance for athletes, and a sanctuary dedicated to the worship of Zeus. These and coins, pottery, strigils (metal instruments athletes used to scrape off dirt), and other remains are used to piece together the drama of the games.[18] Gymnasium costumes or baseball uniforms from the 19th century are another type of relic to be used in historical research.

Primary data are much preferred over secondary sources because of the increasing chance for error when the researcher must rely on second- or third-hand information. But sometimes original documents cannot be located or they are housed in Houston or Tibet, and it is too late for legitimate eyewitnesses to the event to come forward.

SECONDARY

Secondary sources are those in which there is greater distance between the writer and the event than one observer or commentator. They are written by one who was not there at an event or who lived in another time. Their main value is to show the work already done and to furnish a bibliography of primary sources.[19] Newspaper accounts can be either primary or secondary. The minutes of an NCAA meeting are a primary source, but an editorial comment based on the minutes is a secondary source.[20] Text books and encyclopedias are secondary sources. Beginning researchers should make every effort to locate primary data; to use all secondary sources may result in a good literature review, but it is not usually publishable research. Cantor suggests that the best way to use secondary sources is to say that so-and-so's interpretation is being followed.[21]

EVALUATION OF SOURCES OF DATA

Unlike experimental researchers, the historian does not create data—or, at least, is not supposed to! The key to competent historical research lies not only in locating records and relics left by others, but the integrity of historical research depends on the ability of the writer to evaluate all sources of information critically and objectively. There are errors lying in wait for the lazy or naive researcher of history. The parameters of experimental research limit procedures and choices in a controlled laboratory setting but in endeavoring to develop good habits, "each student of history is left to go to hell in his own way."[22] Every piece of data, whether a primary or secondary source, is to be judged on the basis of authenticity, accuracy, and completeness. Statements should not be confused with facts just because they appear in print. There are special terms for evaluating historical evidence.

EXTERNAL CRITICISM

First the writer looks at the whole document from the "outside," in a sense, to find out as much as possible about it. He or she may ask "Is the document or relic original, genuine, and complete? Did the purported author really write it? Are the date, time, and place given for the writing correct? External criticism is often referred to as determining *authenticity*.

The identity of the author may appear obvious as most letters, articles, books, minutes, and speeches are signed. But there are times when a piece is anonymous as in newspapers, or ghost written for a political speech or "autobiography" of someone famous, or the authorship of ancient literature may be in doubt. In 1983 an elaborate hoax resulted in the purchase by the *Sunday Times* of London of 62 volumes purported to be Hitler's diary. Their authenticity was attested to by Lord Dacre, an eminent historian and national director of the *Times*, as well as by West Germany's *Stern* magazine. When German federal archivists uncovered the hoax within two days, Lord Dacre's credentials as a historian were shattered and two chief editors of *Stern* were fired.[23]

In this case, and in other instances of doubtful or unknown authorship, the writing was subjected to a rigorous study of its tone, style, and use of idioms. Whole sentences, complete with errors, were found to have been lifted from a compilation written in 1964 of Hitler's speeches. Further, chemical analysis of the binding revealed synthetics not available while Hitler lived; furthermore, analysis of the paper showed it to be manufactured after 1955, 10 years after Hitler's death.[24] A classic example of establishing authorship is the work of Bible scholars who claim that the book of Isaiah was written, not by one, but by at least two authors. The process of determining that a "Second" Isaiah actually lived over 200 years after the "First" Isaiah required years of work. The determination of the succession of kings and the chronology of other historic events in several ancient kingdoms—and a knowledge of archaic languages—were needed to date the writings in time.[25] The time for "First" Isaiah has been set at about 700 B.C., but through the carbon-14 technique, the earliest existing document was written down at the beginning of the Christian era. Seven hundred years passed from the life of the prophet until the existing document was written. Errors and omissions may have occurred in the copyings.

One of the earliest accounts, and an exciting and dramatic one, of athletic contests is that of the funeral games described in Homer's *Iliad*. The games were held during the 10-year war between Troy and Sparta. Richard Lattimore, a renowned classical scholar, fixes the best date for the fall of Troy at 1184 B.C.[26] But all evidence about Homer suggests that he lived about 400 years later. He knew about events that did not occur until centuries after the Trojan wars. He wrote (if he could write) or composed his verse from the oral tradition and selected parts from it to present a story.[27] Therefore, the *Iliad* is a story of events occurring about 1200 B.C., composed 350-400 years later and with the oldest text dated 200 years after the composing. External criticism of this poem helps the reader understand its limitations as a source of information. These examples of external criticism are intended to show the researcher the care that historians use in evaluating data. The authenticity of more modern sources is not so difficult to evaluate. Educational data are not as likely to be forged as political records.

INTERNAL CRITICISM

Once the document has been judged to be authentic and original, and when the author and the time and place of writing are known, then the researcher turns to a different sort of analysis. Internal criticism is the evaluation of the accuracy and trustworthiness of each statement. After all, untrue statements may be found in completely genuine documents.[28] Criticism of each statement means to determine the real meaning (sometimes in doubt in older writings) as well as to question the author's bias or accuracy. Greek writers assumed their audience knew the event and did not describe it in detail. Jumpers carried weights in their hands throughout the jump and distances of 52 and 55 feet are recorded, well beyond the current world record.[29] Were the Greeks twice as good as modern athletes? Were their measurements different? or Is there a problem in translation? Harris, a noted classics scholar, believed that the event was a double jump based on one statement that the jump was an example of a discontinuous motion and another reference to the ''first'' jump.[30]

Consider the problem of a sport historian of the year 2200 who has only scraps of information with which to reconstruct the game of football.

> Chris Bahr boots blast to boost Raiders by Bills.[31]
>
> Cowboys make turkeys of Cardinals; coast to 35-17 victory.

and

> The Dallas Cowboys had little room for their Thanksgiving dinner Thursday because they spoiled their appetite with a healthy serving of Cardinal. . . . with running back Tony Dorsett and quarterback Danny White both passing milestones . . ., the Cowboys roasted St. Louis.[32]

At least, the historian might say, they roasted them before eating them.

Besides determining the real meaning of a statement, internal criticism also means to determine the *purpose* of the author, his or her bias, and the extent of his or her information. Was he or she trying to present him/herself, a situation, or another person in a favorable light? Was his or her memory reliable? A firsthand account of the Round Hill School was written by George Ellis, a student there in the 1820s. His description is a detailed and delightful account, but examination of the dates shows that it was written in 1891, 70 years after he was there.[33]

Interviews with sports figures or other notables and not-so-notables may produce biased information. Persons tend to place themselves in a favorable light.

Writers of history, too, may be tempted to fill in information that *could* be true in order to present a complete story; or they may sacrifice accuracy for an entertaining style. Sometimes the researcher relies on legend or on "common knowledge" without sufficient critical analysis. As Bennett admonishes sport historians, "let us finally stamp out once and for all the myth that Abner Doubleday invented baseball."[34] The work of Paul indicates that it was not Senda Berenson who first published basketball rules for women (modified from Naismith's), but Clara Baer, director of physical education for women at Sophie Newcomb College of Tulane University.[35]

The researcher must also consider *word meanings*. The "football" (soccer, rugby) terms are an example of possible misunderstandings as are "athletics" (track and field or athletics in general) and "gymnastics" which were to the Greeks and Germans much broader than to Americans. The reader should evaluate sources in the context of the times in which they were written and not in terms of contemporary times.[36]

Examining evidence requires a patient, detailed, and open-minded approach. The integrity of the research report depends on it.

THE HISTORICAL RESEARCH REPORT

STATEMENT OF THE PROBLEM

The problem statement is discussed in detail in Chapter 3. The key is to know exactly what it is that is to be investigated and to be realistic in the choice of a topic. Unlike experimental research, the historian does not have to rely on the cooperation of subjects, but rather on the availability of data. Two publications should be of great help in selecting a problem: The special review issue of the *Journal of Sport History* and the aforementioned monograph, *Getting Started in the History of Sport and Physical Education.*[37]

HYPOTHESIS

Hypotheses are especially important in experimental research. They are tentative theories, opinions, and explanations based on available evidence and on intelligent speculation. They serve to focus the purpose of the study, to make the researcher aware of key concepts, and to organize the data.[38] It is not always necessary to have a hypothesis in historical research. The purpose of a study may be to find out about and accurately record a particular event. If, however, the study is an examination of present events in the light of past occurrences, or seeks to identify trends, a hypothesis serves a valuable purpose. Often hypotheses come only after earlier researchers have established a large data base. *Data collection* was explained in the previous section.

RESULTS

Once the data have been collected, the easy part remains—writing the results. To write a historical paper requires the same kind of care and analysis that experimental research requires. Using the style of experimental research is awkward in history, but the same attention to the spirit of the scientific process is essential. The exact style of the thesis or dissertation will vary according to the requirements of your university or college. An approach some physical education thesis writers have used is to discuss limitations, delimitations, definitions, and sources of data (including evaluation of the data) in a preface. The body of the thesis can begin with Chapter 1. This style requires much less rewriting when the work is to be submitted for publication.

PROBLEMS AND ERRORS IN PHYSICAL EDUCATION HISTORICAL RESEARCH

The problems of historical research in physical education are related to the problems of other research in physical education. As graduate study has become specialized, the research techniques of not only history but physiology, psychology, sociology, and other related areas have become essential.[39] Historians in physical education, until the last decade, have typically earned graduate degrees in general programs with a professional orientation. Such training did not produce first-rate historians.

One other point deserves repeating. Physical education research has not been set in the context of the time and place because researchers have not had the necessary broad background of other aspects of the society being studied. The research often is a catalogue of facts isolated from the cultural mainstream and not placed within a significant pattern.[40] In order to be recognized as legitimate historical scholars, physical educators must apply the methodology developed by historians. This requires a blending of sport history and history similar to that occurring between physiologist and exercise physiologist, psychologist and motor behaviorist, and research on teaching and research on teaching physical education.

NOTES

1. Norman F. Cantor and Richard I. Schneider, *How to Study History* (New York: Thomas Y. Crowell Company, 1967), p. 19.

2. Carter V. Good, *Introduction to Educational Research* (New York: Appleton-Century-Crofts, 2nd edition, 1963), p. 181.

3. Sherwin S. Shermis, "On Becoming an Intellectual Discipline," *The Phi Delta Kappan*, 44 (November, 1962), 82-86.

4. See Recent Dissertation listings in the *Journal of Sport History (JSH)*, 6.3 (Winter, 1979), 88-93; *JSH*, 7.3 (Winter, 1980), 136-161; *JSH*, 9.3 (Winter, 1981), 91-96.

5. Melvin L. Adelman, "Academicians and American Athletics: A Decade of Progress," *JSH*, 10.1 (Spring, 1983), 80. Adelman (p. 83) discusses several kinds of studies including sport and social control, sport and the city, and sport and demographic groups.

6. "Editorial," *JSH*, 1.1 (May, 1974), 1.

7. Ibid., p. iv.

8. Special histories examine "cultural products" of society such as education, art, medicine, and are usually written by someone within the field. Special histories may be less valuable for examining the past than are general histories because they typically do not take into account the social, economic, or political setting of the times. See Maurice Mandlebaum, *The Anatomy of Historical Knowledge* (Baltimore: The Johns Hopkins University Press, 1977), p. 12.

9. *JOPERD, The Physical Educator* and state journals accept special physical education topics.

10. J. Thomas Jable, "The Types of Historical Research for Studying Sport," *Getting Started in the History of Sport and Physical Education*, ed. by William H. Freeman (unpublished manuscript of History of Sport and Physical Education Academy, 1980), 13-20.

11. Ellen W. Gerber, *Innovators and Institutions* (Philadelphia: Lea and Febiger, 1971).

12. Stephen Hardy, "Parks for the People: Reforming the Boston Park System, 1870-1915." *JSH*, 7.3 (Winter, 1980), 5-24.

13. Gary Ross Mormino, "The Playing Fields of St. Louis: Italian Immigrants and Sports, 1925-1941," *JSH*, 9.2 (Summer, 1982), 5-19.

14. Deobold B. Van Dalen, *Understanding Educational Research* (New York: McGraw Hill, 1962), p. 180.

15. Cantor and Schneider, p. 64.

16. Steven Riess, "Professional Sunday Baseball: A Study in Social Reform, 1892-1934," *The Maryland Historian*, 4.2 (Fall, 1973), 95-108; J. Thomas Jable, "Pennsylvania's Early Blue Laws: A Quaker Experiment in the Suppression of Sport and Amusements," *JSH*, 1.2 (Nov., 1974), 107-121.

17. Charles Herbert Thompson, "The History of the National Tournaments for Black High Schools," (unpublished dissertation, Louisiana State University, 1980).

18. "Berkeley archeologists uncovering missing links in Greek history," *The Hellenic Journal* (December 16, 1976), p. 4.

19. David H. Clarke and H. Harrison Clarke, *Research Processes in Physical Education, Recreation and Health* (Englewood Cliffs: Prentice Hall, 1970), p. 69.

20. Good, 194-195.

21. Cantor and Schneider, p. 92.

22. Ibid., p. 15.

23. "The Hitler Diaries Hoax," *MacLeans Magazine* (May 16, 1983), 20-21.

24. Ibid.

25. *The Interpreter's Dictionary of the Bible*, Vol. 2 (Nashville, TN: Abingdon Press), pp. 737-738.

26. Richard Lattimore. *The Iliad of Homer* (Chicago: University of Chicago Press, 1951), p. 18.

27. Ibid.

28. Carter V. Good, A.S. Barr, and Donald E. Scates, *The Methodology of Educational Research* (New York: Appleton-Century-Crofts, 1941), p. 262.

29. H.A. Harris, *Greek Athletes and Athletics* (Indiana University Press, 1967) pp. 81-82.

30. Ibid.

31. *Morning Advocate*, Baton Rouge, LA, Nov. 21, 1983.

32. Ibid., Nov. 25, 1983.

33. George Ellis, "Recollections of Round Hill School," *Educational Review*, 1 (Apr. 1891), 337-344.

34. Bruce L. Bennett, "My Eight Point Platform for Sport Historians," *Getting Started in the History of Sport and Physical Education*, History of Sport and Physical Education Academy, 1980, p. 31.

35. Joan Paul, "Clara Gregory Baer: An Early Role Model for Southern Women in Physical Education" (paper delivered at the NASPE History Academy, AAHPERD Convention, Minneapolis, MN, April 8, 1983).

36. David H. Clarke and H. Harrison Clarke, p. 71.

37. *JSH*, 10.1 (Spring, 1983), William Freeman, Ed., *Getting Started.*

38. Good, Barr, and Scates, pp. 185-187.

39. Roberta Park, *Research Quarterly for Exercise and Sport*, 54.2 (June, 1983), 93.

40. Ibid., 95; Cantor and Schneider, 19.

Chapter 9

Meta-Analysis

LITERATURE ANALYSIS

An analysis of the literature is a part of all types of research. The scholar is always aware of past events and how they influence current research. However, sometimes the literature review stands by itself as a research paper—a paper which involves the analysis, evaluation, and integration of the published literature. As mentioned in Chapter 1, a number of journals consist entirely of literature review papers while nearly all research journals publish review papers occasionally.

All of the procedures discussed in detail in Chapter 2 apply to the literature analysis. The difference is that the purpose here is to use the literature for empirical and theoretical conclusions rather than to document the need for a particular research problem. A good literature analysis will result in several tangible conclusions and should spark interest in future directions for research. Sometimes a literature analysis will lead to a revision or to the proposal of a theory. The point is, a literature analysis is not just a summary of the related literature; it is a logical type of research which leads to valid conclusions, hypothesis evaluations, and the revision and proposal of theory.

The approach to a literature analysis is like any other type of research. The researcher must clearly specify the procedures that are to be followed. Unfortunately, the literature review paper seldom specifies the procedures the author used. Thus, the basis for the many decisions made about individual papers is usually unknown to the reader. Of course, this makes the objective evaluation of a literature review nearly impossible. Questions that are important yet usually unanswered in the typical review of literature include the following:

1. How thorough was the literature search? Did it include a computer search and hand search? In a computer search, what were the descriptors used? Which

journals were searched? Were theses and dissertations searched and included?

2. On what basis were studies included or excluded from the written review? Were thesis and dissertations arbitrarily excluded? Did the author make decisions about inclusion or exclusions based on the perceived internal validity of the research? Or on sample size? Or on research design? Or on appropriate statistical analysis?

3. How did the author arrive at a particular conclusion? Was it based on the number of studies supporting or refuting the conclusion (called *vote counting*)? Were these studies weighted differentially according to sample size, meaningfulness of the results, quality of the journal, internal validity of the study?

Many more questions could be asked about the decisions made in the typical literature review paper, for good research involves a systematic method of problem solving. However, in most literature reviews, the author's systematic method remains unknown to the reader, thus prohibiting an objective evaluation of these decisions.

PURPOSE OF META-ANALYSIS

In recent years, several attempts have been made to solve the problems associated with literature reviews. The most notable was proposed in a paper by Glass (1976) and followed up with a book (Glass, McGraw, & Smith, 1981). This technique is called *meta-analysis*. Meta-analysis involves two procedures lacking in previous literature reviews: First, a definitive methodology is reported concerning the decisions in a literature analysis; and second, the results of various studies are quantified to a standard metric which allows the use of statistical techniques as a means of analysis. Here are the steps in a meta-analysis:

1. Identification of a problem
2. A literature search by specified means
3. A review of identified studies to determine inclusion or exclusion
4. Identification and coding of important study characteristics;
5. Calculation of effect size (ES)
6. Application of appropriate statistical techniques
7. Reporting of all the above steps and the outcomes in a review paper

Of course, one of the major problems in a literature review paper is the number of studies which must be considered. To some extent, analyzing all these studies is like trying to make sense of all the data points in a single study. However, within a study statistical techniques are used to reduce the data in order to understand it. The procedures of meta-analysis are very similar. The findings within individual studies are considered data points for use in a statistical analysis across the findings of many studies.

How, then, can findings based upon *different* designs, data collection techniques, dependent variables, and statistical analysis be compared? Glass has addressed this issue by using an estimate he calls Effect Size (ES or the symbol Δ). ES is determined by the following formula:

$$\Delta = \frac{M_E - M_c}{s_c} \tag{9.1}$$

where M_E = mean of experimental group, M_c = mean of control group, and s_c = standard deviation of control group. Note that this formula places the difference between the experimental and control group in control group standard deviation units. For example, if $M_E = 15$, $M_c = 12$, $s_c = 5$, then $\Delta = (15 - 12)/5 = .60$. The experimental group's performance exceeded the control group's performance by .60 of a standard deviation. If this were done across several studies addressing a common problem, the findings of the studies would be in a common metric, ES(Δ), which could be compared. The mean and standard deviations of the ES could be calculated from several studies. This would allow a statement about the average ES of a particular type of treatment.

Suppose we wanted to know if a particular treatment affects males and females differently. In searching the literature, we find 15 studies on males comparing the treatment effects and 12 studies on females. We could calculate an ES for each of the 27 studies, calculate the mean (and standard deviation) of the ES for males ($n = 15$) and for females ($n = 12$). Then an independent t test could be used to see if the average ES differed for males and females. If the t value was significant and the average ES for the females was greater, we could conclude that the treatment had more effect on females than males.

Glass et al. (1981) provide considerable detail on the methods of meta-analysis. These details include literature search strategies, how to calculate ES from the statistics reported in various studies, suggestions for how and what to code from studies, and examples of the use of meta-analysis.

Certainly meta-analysis is not the answer to all the problems associated with literature reviews. But Glass has provided an objective way to evaluate the literature. Recent advances (Hedges, 1981, 1982a, 1982b, Hedges & Olkin, 1980, 1983, 1985) in studying the statistical properties of ES have contributed considerably to the appropriate use of meta-analysis.

Of course, meta-analysis has been criticized—in particular, that it is like comparing apples and oranges. However, meta-analysis provides the means of objectively analyzing what was previously handled in a subjective way, thus justifying its use and further development.

EXAMPLES OF META-ANALYSIS

Since Glass's (1976) original proposal of the meta-analysis technique, several meta-analyses have been published, including a few in physical education. A brief overview of some of these studies should identify the value of meta-analysis.

Gender differences in cognitive performance are widely reported in the psychological literature. In a frequently quoted review, Maccoby and Jacklin (1974) said that gender differences in three areas were "well-established." They reported that boys were superior to girls in mathematical and visual-spatial abilities while girls exceeded boys in verbal abilities. Hyde (1981) reported the results of a meta-analysis using findings from the studies reviewed by Maccoby and Jacklin (1974). She calculated the ES differences for each study and also reported the percent variance accounted for (Omega squared, w^2, review Chapter 7 if necessary to refresh your memory on this statistic) according to gender. She found that gender differences were actually very small and accounted for little variance. For example, the median ES for verbal ability was .24, or the girls' performance exceeded the boys' by one-quarter of a standard deviation unit. The median w^2 was .01, or this gender difference accounted for only 1% of the variance. For quantitative ability, boys' performance exceeded girls' by .43 (median ES), and this effect accounted for about 1% of the variance. For visual-spatial ability, the median ES was .45 favoring the boys with only 4% of the variance accounted for.

These "well-established" differences between males and females are, in fact, so small (and account for so little variance) they appear to be meaningless. This indicates that gender is a poor predictor of these abilities and should not be used as a basis for directing students into high school or university courses or vocational choices. Results such as these occur because of a problem identified in Chapter 5: Researchers have a tendency to report the significance (or reliability) of the effect but not its meaningfulness (percent variance accounted for).

When the overlap in the data distributions of males and females on studies like these are evaluated, we should probably be discussing the amazing nature of "gender sameness" rather than "gender differences." These results also help us understand why theories to explain sex differences such as brain lateralization produce conflicting findings (Sherman, 1978).

As a second example of meta-analysis, social facilitation, the effects of the presence of others on performance, has been studied since Triplett's (1898) first investigation. Zajonc (1965) provided a classic explanation within "Drive theory" that said the presence of others increases the probability of the subject emitting the dominant response. Cottrell (1972) argued that the mere presence of others was insufficient to increase drive; the other had to be perceived as evaluating the performance. This phenomenon has also received considerable attention in the physical education literature.

Bond and Titus (1983) reported a social facilitation meta-analysis of 241 studies involving nearly 24,000 subjects. The presence of others accounted for 0.3% to 3% of the variance, a very small effect. Bond and Titus (p. 265) thus summarized social facilitation effects:

> (a) the presence of others heightens an individual's physiological arousal only if the individual is performing a complex task; (b) the presence of others increases the speed of simple task performance and decreases the speed of complex task performance; (c) the presence of others impairs

complex performance accuracy and slightly facilitates simple performance accuracy, though the facilitation is vulnerable to the "file drawer problem" of unreported null results; and (d) social facilitation effects are surprisingly unrelated to the performer's evaluation apprehension.

Given the size of these effects, we question whether social facilitation really influences performance in real-world settings, particularly in sport settings where the skills are complex and well-learned. Also, we question the general title "social facilitation." Perhaps "social defacilitation" is a more appropriate term.

A few meta-analyses have been done in physical education. In a meta-analysis on the effects of perceptual-motor training for improving academic, cognitive, or perceptual-motor performance, Kavale and Mattson (1983) reported a distinct lack of success for perceptual-motor training in the 180 studies included. The largest ES they found was .198, and it was associated with the 83 studies rated low in internal validity. In fact, in studies with high-internal validity, the "trained" subjects did worse. Thus, perceptual-motor training does not appear useful for any type outcome (academic, cognitive, perceptual-motor) for any type of subject (normal, educable mentally retarded, trainable mentally retarded, slow learner, culturally disadvantaged, learning disabled, reading disabled, or motor disabled) at any age level (preschool, kindergarten, primary grades, middle grades, junior high school, or high school).

Sparling (1980) reported a meta-analysis of ES differences between males and females for maximal oxygen uptake. One of the most interesting findings was that when averaged across studies, ES was reduced when corrections were made for the differing body compositions of males and females. When maximal oxygen uptake was expressed as liters/min, 66% of the variance was explained by knowing the subject's gender. But when maximal oxygen uptake was expressed as ml/min • kg BW, the explained variance was reduced to 49%; and when expressed as ml/min • kg FFW, the explained variance was reduced to 35%. Thus, the advantage of males over females in maximal oxygen uptake is reduced when corrected for body weight (BW) and is reduced even more when corrected for fat-free weight (FFW).

In a meta-analysis on the effects of exercise on blood lipids and lipoproteins, Tran, Weltman, Glass, and Mood (1983) reported an analysis of 66 training studies involving a total of 2,925 subjects. They found significant relationships between training and beneficial changes in blood lipids and lipoproteins. However, ". . . initial levels, age, length of training, intensity, $\dot{V}0_2$ max, body weight, and percent fat have been shown . . . to interact with exercise and serum lipids and lipoprotein changes" (Tran et al., 1983).

As a final example from physical education, Feltz and Landers (1983) reported a meta-analysis of the effects of mental practice on motor-skill learning and performance. From 60 studies, they calculated an average ES of .48, less than one-half of a standard deviation unit. They concluded that mentally practicing a motor skill is slightly better than no practice at all.

These examples have been used to illustrate the value of the meta-analysis approach. In two of the studies (gender differences in cognitive performance and social facilitation), results consistently reported in the literature were shown to be so small as to be meaningless in a practical sense. In the perceptual-motor meta-analysis, the controversial issue of the value of this type of training appears resolved—no benefit. In the meta-analysis of gender differences in maximal oxygen uptake, these large differences appear to be accounted for in large part by differences in body composition rather than any differences in underlying mechanisms. Also, exercise appears to have a positive effect on cholesterol and its components. And finally, mental practice is better than no practice, but not by much.

Meta-analysis, when applied appropriately and interpreted carefully, offers a means of reducing large quantities of studies to underlying principles. These principles can become the bases for program development, future research, and theory testing as well as various practical applications like practice and training.

METHODOLOGICAL CONSIDERATIONS

The following important issues arise when doing a meta-analysis:

1. Selecting the sample
2. Coding appropriate characteristics from the sample
3. Determining effect size and percent variance accounted for
4. Selecting appropriate statistical analyses

SELECTING THE SAMPLE

When planning a meta-analysis, the sample of studies to be used must be defined. Of course, the statement of the problem delimits this somewhat, but a number of considerations remain. How should the literature be searched? A standard starting point would be a computer search by key words through the appropriate indices; however, this is not sufficient. In many cases, the titles and key words will not identify some studies because the authors fail to title and identify the studies adequately. Chapter 3 discussed the importance of appropriately selecting the title and key words. A more effective search method is to compile a list of key journals and to search these journals by hand.

Dissertations and theses will need to be included which can be searched partially by computer, but much of this search will also need to be completed by hand. The question soon becomes, "Where do you stop?" For example, what about abstracts of studies reported at various conferences? To include these abstracts requires writing the authors and requesting a complete copy of the paper, which is frequently unavailable if it has not been published. Include as much as possible, but set a reasonable limit; however, do not include only published studies because they are biased toward reporting significant differences. Therefore, to attempt to include both published and unpublished conference abstracts is often not feasible.

Some studies will lack the necessary information required for conducting a meta-analysis. Some of the data can be obtained by writing to the first author and asking for the necessary data. Hyde (1981), in her meta-analysis of gender differences in cognitive performance, reported that 18 of the 53 studies (31%) provided insufficient data for a meta-analysis. After writing to the authors of the 18 studies, 7 responded, but only 2 could provide the information requested (*M*, *s*, *t*, or *F*). Nevertheless, both included and excluded studies should be listed as part of the reporting procedures for meta-analysis.

Glass et al. (1981) suggest that studies should not be included or excluded based upon the perceived quality of the research. However, this perceived quality should be coded as a characteristic of the study and related to the ES. Kavale and Mattson (1983) did this when they rated the internal validity of the 180 perceptual-motor training studies. They rated 83 (46%) as low, 62 (35%) as medium, and 35 (19%) as high in internal validity. Results show an effect size of about 2% favoring training for the studies rated low and average with an ES actually favoring the controls and significantly different from the other two levels of validity for the studies with high-internal validity.

CODING APPROPRIATE CHARACTERISTICS FROM THE SAMPLE

To some extent, the characteristics to be coded from individual studies will vary according to the purpose of the meta-analysis. Table 9.1 provides some examples of characteristics coded from three of the previously cited meta-analyses.

Once the characteristics to be coded are determined and all studies to be used identified, the task becomes one of reading each study and extracting and coding the selected characteristics. The researcher should be aware of the total number of studies and characteristics to be coded as this can become a monumental task if 10-20 characteristics are used for several hundred studies. The following two considerations are important: First, make sure you have uses for all characteristics that are coded; and second, in a large meta-analysis if more than one coder is used, an estimate of consistency among coders is needed. This may be obtained by overlapping a percentage of the studies coded and calculating a reliability estimate.

DETERMINING EFFECT SIZES AND PERCENT VARIANCE ACCOUNTED FOR

Earlier in the chapter, the basic formula for calculating ES or Δ (see Formula 9.1) was provided. Sometimes the question may arise as to the appropriate *s* to use in the ES estimate. When the ES is to be determined from an experimental versus a control group, the *s* of the control group is appropriate. This places any

TABLE 9.1
CHARACTERISTICS CODED FROM THREE META-ANALYSES

Study	Characteristics Coded
Bond & Titus (1983)	Date of study, publication status (published or unpublished), number of subjects, experimental design (between/within), control condition validity (low, high, or unknown), mean subject age, proportion of male subjects, number of others, proportion of male others, role, observer status, familiarity, visibility of others, visibility of subjects, evaluation potential,, subject anxiety, task complexity, dependent measure
Feltz & Landers (1983)	Subject characteristics—sex, age, previous experience with task Type task—motor, strength, cognitive, self-paced, reactive Design characteristics—attentional control, simple control, pre/post only design, immediate posttest, delayed posttest, number of practice sessions, length of mental practice Published or unpublished
Tran, Weltman, Glass, & Mood (1983)	Repeated measures, controls, treatment (exercise only, exercise and diet), source (journal, nonjournal), design (control group, no controls), sex (male, female), type subject (normal, nonnormal)

change in standard deviation units beyond what is "normal" (the control group). But what about studies that compare groups where no control group exists—males versus females, 7-year-old children versus 9-year-old children, high skilled versus low skilled? In this instance, which standard deviation should be used? There seems to be no good answer to this question. A frequent solution is to average the two s's. While Glass et al. (1981) do not recommend averaging, Hedges (1981) does believe a pooled estimate of the variance is best (assuming the groups have equal population variances). This appears to be the best solution; a pooled estimate weighted for sample size can be obtained by the following formula.

$$s_p = \sqrt{\frac{s_1^2\,(n_1 - 1) + s_2^2\,(n_2 - 1)}{n_1 + n_2 - 2}} \qquad \textbf{(9.2)}$$

where s_p = pooled standard deviation, s_1^2 = variance (standard deviation squared) for Gp 1, s_2^2 = variance (standard deviation squared) for Gp 2, n_1 = number of subjects in the Gp 1, and n_2 = number of subjects in the Gp 2.

Hedges (1979) has reported that ES is biased and needs correction, especially in small samples. He provided a formula for correcting this bias.

$$E(\Delta) = \Delta[K(n_2 - 1)] \qquad \textbf{(9.3)}$$

TABLE 9.2

VALUES OF $K(n_2 - 1)$ FOR CONTROL GROUP TO BE USED IN CORRECTING ES (Δ) FOR BIAS

$n_2 - 1$	K	$n_2 - 1$	K	$n_2 - 1$	K
2	0.56419	21	0.96378	40	0.98111
3	0.72360	22	0.96545	41	0.98158
4	0.79788	23	0.96697	42	0.98202
5	0.84075	24	0.96837	43	0.98244
6	0.86863	25	0.96965	44	0.98284
7	0.88820	26	0.97083	45	0.98322
8	0.90270	27	0.97192	46	0.98359
9	0.91387	28	0.97293	47	0.98394
10	0.92275	29	0.97387	48	0.98428
11	0.92996	30	0.97475	49	0.98460
12	0.93594	31	0.97558	50	0.98491
13	0.94098	32	0.97635		
14	0.94529	33	0.97707		
15	0.94901	34	0.97775		
16	0.95225	35	0.97839		
17	0.95511	36	0.97900		
18	0.95765	37	0.97957		
19	0.95991	38	0.98011		
20	0.96194	39	0.98062		

Note. From *Meta-analysis in social research* (p. 113) by G.V. Glass, B. McGraw, & M.L. Smith, 1981, Beverly Hills, CA: Sage. Reprinted with permission.

where $E(\Delta)$ = unbiased estimate of ES or Δ and $n_2 - 1$ = control group sample size minus 1 and K is the tabled value. Table 9.2 is a reproduction of a slightly modified version of Hedges' (1979) table by Glass et al. (1981). Once ES (Δ) is calculated, Table 9.2 is entered for the $n_2 - 1$ value and the unbiased estimator is obtained by multiplying ES times K. Thus, if the ES were calculated as .82 and the control group had 30 subjects, $n_2 - 1 = 29$, and the K for this is .97387. Thus, the unbiased estimator of ES is $E(\Delta) = .82(.97387) = .80$. As you can see from looking at Table 9.2, the adjustments in ES are increasingly smaller as the sample size of the control group increases.

In some instances, the means and standard deviations needed for calculating effect sizes will not be provided. This is relatively common in research journals where conservation of space is important. While we believe means and standard deviations for all variables is a basic minumum for any quantitative study to report, not everyone agrees. What should you do if the means and standard deviations are not in the paper? If the sample size for each group, the t ratio, and which group had the larger mean is provided, the following formula (Glass, 1977, p. 368) can be used to calculate ES (Δ).

$$ES = t\sqrt{1/n_E + 1/n_c} \qquad \textbf{(9.4)}$$

The ES can also be estimated if the sample size for each group, probability level, and which group mean is larger is provided. For example, suppose two groups ($n = 15$ for each group) are declared significantly different at $p = .05$, and the experimental group was better than the control. By looking at Table A.3, the t value may be determined because the $df = n_E + n_c - 2 = 28$ and $p = .05$. Read down the df column to 28 and across the levels of significance for two-tailed tests to .05. The t is 2.048. By substituting this value in Formula 9.3, Δ can be estimated as .75. Glass et al. (1981) and Hedges and Olkin (1985) provide formulas for estimating Δ from other statistics.

In addition to estimating effect sizes for studies in meta-analysis, we recommend that some estimate of percent variance accounted for be provided for each finding, preferably Omega squared (w^2), the statistic in Chapter 7. The formulas for calculating w^2 from t and F were given in Chapter 7 and can be applied to studies reporting these statistics.

The reason for reporting w^2 in addition to Δ is that Δ is subject to the influence of sample size. Formula 9.1 shows that Δ is calculated by dividing the difference between the experimental and control groups means by the control group standard deviation. Recall from Chapter 5 that the size of the standard deviation is sensitive to the sample size. Generally, the bigger N gets, the smaller the standard deviation becomes. A smaller standard deviation results in a bigger ES; that is, if the difference between the means stays the same but the standard deviation becomes smaller, the ES becomes larger. Thus, both ES and w^2 are useful to report because one places the difference in standard deviation units (ES) while the other provides an unbiased estimate of the percent variance accounted for (w^2).

Sometimes the report of a study will say no significant difference, but the effect is of interest for a meta-analysis. This creates no problem if the means and standard deviations are given or if the information to use Formula 9.4 is provided. But often in a research report in a journal, the only statement made is that the effect is not significant. In studies involving gender and age differences, the design may be collapsed across these factors if they are not significant. If these are the factors of interest, what should be done if the necessary information to conduct the meta-analysis is not reported? Of course, one unsatisfactory answer is to omit the study from the meta-analysis. We recommend that an ES of zero be entered in this case. No significant difference actually means that the difference between the two groups is not reliably different from zero. If entering a zero biases the results, at least they are biased toward not rejecting a true null hypothesis.

SELECTING APPROPRIATE STATISTICAL ANALYSES

Meta-analysis presents many of the same problems for statistical analysis as any other study. The major question is "Does the data meet the assumptions for the statistical model to be used?" Some frequent issues in meta-analysis include the following:

1. Are the findings included independent? For example, suppose several variables are reported for a single set of subjects—are males and females different on running speed, jumping for distance, and throwing velocity? In a meta-analysis on gender differences in motor performance, should the ES for each finding be included? If so, the ES are not independent because they are based on the same subjects. If not, substantial amounts of data are being discarded.
2. Should statistical tests be applied repeatedly? For example, a *t* test is to be done on ES of studies of training. ES are calculated for males (difference between experimental and controls) and for females (difference between experimental and controls). A *t* test is then done under several conditions: with all ES included; on ES of published papers only; and on ES without zero scores for nonsignificant findings. The experiment-wise error rate is now an issue (see Chapter 7) and should probably be calculated and reported.
3. What if effect sizes are not normally distributed? In fact, it would probably be strange indeed if the ES across a number on studies were normally distributed. Especially since the studies had different lengths of treatment, different intensities of treatments, subjects from different populations, dependent variables which measure the effect of interest to varying degrees, and many other differences. To some extent, coding the study characteristics addresses this problem. That is, variables of this type can be identified and coded so that data are sorted and stratified for analysis by these factors. Hedges (1982a and 1982b) has developed techniques for testing the assumption of whether a pool of ES comes from a single population. If this test of homogeneity of ES is used and indicates that the ES are from one population, then the appropriate statistical test can be used. If the ES are not from one population, then the researcher can begin to look for patterns of variations of ES on which to group the data.

Numerous other issues exist but the previous examples highlight some of the important ones. More detailed treatment of these and other issues can be obtained by reading Glass et al. (1981), Hedges (1982a and 1982b), and Hedges and Olkin (1985).

We believe meta-analysis has much to offer for research synthesis in HPERD. The application of this technique is likely to yield a number of "principles" on which programs can be based. Graduate students should become familar with this technique as its use is likely to become increasingly popular. In fact, we would predict that in the near future, the traditional literature analysis, whether it is narrative or uses a vote-counting technique, will become unacceptable as a sound scientific technique. However, in making this prediction about the value of meta-analysis as a solution to the problem of the literature analysis, always keep in mind Smith's Law—*no real problem has a solution.*

PROBLEM

Select an experimental problem. Find 10 studies which compare an experimental and control group on this problem (make sure the M and s for each group is reported). Calculate the ES or Δ for each of the studies. Calculate the M and s of Δ . Describe what the M and s of Δ imply about the particular treatment you selected.

Chapter 10

Descriptive Research

Descriptive research is a study of status which is widely used in education and in the behavioral sciences. Its value is based on the premise that problems can be solved and practices can be improved through objective and thorough observation, analysis, and description. Several techniques or methods of problem solving fall in the category of descriptive research.

The most common descriptive research method is the survey, which includes questionnaires, interviews, and normative surveys. Developmental research is also descriptive. Through cross-sectional and longitudinal studies, researchers investigate the interaction of growth and maturation and of learning and performance variables. The case study is descriptive research that is widely used in a number of fields. A type of case study is the job analysis. Observational research and correlational studies constitute other forms of descriptive research: observational research is a method of obtaining quantitative and qualitative data about people and situations; correlational studies determine and analyze relationships. Predictions are also generated from correlational research.

This chapter will discuss some of the characteristics and basic procedures of the various types of descriptive research.

THE SURVEY

The survey is generally broad in scope. The researcher usually seeks to determine present practices (or opinions) of a specified population. The survey is a widely used research tool in education. The questionnaire, the interview, and the normative survey are the three main types of surveys.

THE QUESTIONNAIRE

The questionnaire and the interview are the same except for the method of questioning. The procedures for developing questionnaire and interview items are similar. Consequently, much of the discussion regarding the steps in the construction of the questionnaire also pertains to the interview.

The questionnaire is used to obtain information by asking subjects to respond to questions rather than by observing their behavior. The very obvious limitation to the questionnaire is that the results are simply what people say they do or what they say they believe or like or dislike. However, certain information can only be obtained in this manner, and, thus, it is imperative that the questionnaire is planned and prepared carefully to ensure the most valid results.

The several steps in the survey research process include

1. Determining the objectives;
2. Delimiting the sample of respondents;
3. Constructing the questionnaire;
4. Conducting a pilot study;
5. Writing the cover letter;
6. Sending the questionnaire;
7. Sending out the follow-up(s);
8. Analyzing the results; and
9. Preparing the research report.

Determining the Objectives. This step may seem too obvious to mention, yet countless questionnaires have been prepared without clearly defined objectives. In fact, this may primarily account for the low esteem in which survey research is sometimes held. The investigator must have a clear understanding as to what information is needed and how each item is going to be analyzed. As with any research, the analysis is determined in the planning phase of the study, not after the data have been gathered.

The researcher must decide upon the questionnaire's specific purposes. In other words, what information is wanted? Moreover, how will the responses be analyzed? Will they merely be described by listing what percentage of the subjects responded in a certain way, or will the responses of one group be compared with those of another?

Thus, one of the most common mistakes made in constructing a questionnaire is not specifying the variables to be analyzed. In some instances, when the investigator fails to list the variables, questions unrelated to the objectives are asked. In other cases, the investigator forgets to ask pertinent questions. For example, in a survey of curricular offerings in health education, if one of the objectives is to compare the offerings on the basis of how health education is scheduled, the respondent has to be asked about the scheduling. If male teachers are to be compared with female teachers, then gender must be indicated, and so on. What is to be analyzed must be made clear.

Delimiting the Sample. Most researchers who use questionnaires have a specific population in mind which is to be sampled. Obviously, the subjects selected must be the ones who have the answers to the questions. In other words, the investigator has to be knowledgeable about who can supply what information. If information about policy decisions is desired, the subjects should be those involved in making such decisions.

Sometimes the source used in selecting the sample is inadequate. For example, some professional associations are made up of teachers, administrators, professors, and other allied professional workers. Thus, this association's membership is not a good choice as subjects for a study geared only for public school teachers. Unless there is some screening mechanism as to place of employment, many incomplete questionnaires will be returned because the questions were not applicable.

The representativeness of the sample is an important consideration. Stratified random sampling, as discussed in Chapter 5, is sometimes used. In a questionnaire surveying the recreational preferences of a university student body, the sample should reflect the proportion of students at the different class levels. Thus, if 35% of the students are freshmen, 30% are sophomores, 20% are juniors, and 15% are seniors, then the sample should be selected according to those percentages. Similarly, if a researcher is studying school program offerings, and 60% of the schools in the state have less than 200 enrollment, then 60% of the sample should be from such schools.

The selection of the sample is going to be based on the variables specified to be studied. Certainly, this affects the generalizability of the results. If an investigator specifies that the study deals with just one sex or one educational level or one institution, and so on, then the population is narrowly defined, and it may be easy to select a representative sample of that specific population. However, the generalizations that can be made from the results are also restricted to that specific population. On the other hand, if the researcher is aiming the questionnaire at all of a specific population, such as "all recreation directors" or "all dance teachers," then the generalizability is enhanced, but the sampling procedures are made more difficult, and a larger sample size is required.

Sample size is important from two standpoints: (a) for adequacy in representing a population, and (b) for practical considerations of time and cost. There are formulas which can be used to determine adequacy of sample size (Tuckman, 1978, p. 232). The formulas involve probability levels and amount of sampling error deemed acceptable. The practical considerations of time and cost need attention within the planning phase of the study. Surprisingly, students often ignore these considerations until they are forced to sit down with a calculator and tabulate the costs of printing, initial mailing along with self-addressed stamped return envelopes, follow-ups, scoring, and data analysis. Sometimes the costs are so substantial that some sponsoring agency or grant must be found to subsidize the study, or the project must be narrowed or abandoned altogether. The time factor is also important with regard to variability of subjects, possible seasonal influences, and various deadlines.

Constructing the Questionnaire. The notion that constructing a questionnaire is easy is a fallacy. Questions are not just "thought up." Anyone who prepares a questionnaire and asks someone to read it soon discovers that it is not such an easy task after all. Those questions which were so clear and concise to the writer are often met with misinterpretation, perplexed frowns, and sometimes even raucous laughter.

Continually asking yourself, "What specific objective is this question measuring?" is one of the most valuable guidelines for writing questions. Then ask, "How am I going to analyze the response?" While you are writing questions, a good suggestion is to prepare a table. The table will have the categories of responses, comparisons, and other breakdowns of data analysis so that you can readily determine just how each item will be handled and how each will contribute to the objectives of the study.

Next, you must decide on the format for the questions. Open-ended, closed, fill-in, scaled, rankings, checklist, and categorically are several of a variety of ways to ask questions.

Open form questions, such as "How do you like your job?" or "What aspects of your job do you like?" may be the easiest for the investigator to write. Such questions allow the respondent considerable latitude to express feelings and to expand on ideas. However, the several drawbacks to open questions usually make them less desirable than closed questions. For example, most respondents do not like open questions. For that matter, most people do not like questionnaires. They feel questionnaires are encroachments on their time, and open questions require more time to answer than closed questions. Another drawback is the limited control as to the nature of the response allowing the respondent to ramble and stray from the question. Also, open question responses are difficult to synthesize and to group into categories.

Sometimes open questions are used to construct closed questions. Student evaluations, or questionnaires, are often developed by having students list all the things they like and dislike about a course(s). From such lists, closed questions are constructed by categorizing the open question responses.

Closed questions come in a variety of forms. (Some of the measurement scales will be covered in more detail in Chapter 15.) A few of the more commonly used closed questions are rankings, scaled items, and categorical responses.

Rankings force the subject to place responses in a rank order according to some criterion. As a result, value judgments are made, and the rankings can be summed and analyzed quantitatively. An example of a rank order response question is as follows.

Rank the following activities with regard to how you like to spend leisure time. (Use numbers 1 through 5, with 1 being the most preferred and 5 the least preferred.)

______ Reading

______ Watching television

______ Arts and crafts

______ Vigorous sports such as tennis, racquetball

______ Mild exercise activity such as walking

Scaled items are one of the most commonly used closed questions. Subjects are asked to indicate the strength of their agreement or disagreement with some statement or the relative frequency of some behavior as in the following example:

Indicate the frequency with which you are involved in committee meetings and assignments during the academic year.

Rarely	Sometimes	Often	Frequently

The Likert scale is a 5-point scale like the following in which there is an assumption of equal intervals between responses:

In a required physical education program, students should be required to take at least one dance class.

Strongly agree	Agree	Undecided	Disagree	Strongly disagree

The difference between "strongly agree" and "agree" is considered equivalent to the difference between "disagree" and "strongly disagree," and so on. Different response words can be used in scaled responses, such as "excellent," "good," "fair," "poor," "very poor," "very important," "important," "not very important," "of no importance," and many others.

Categorical responses offer the subject only two choices. Usually, the responses are "yes" or "no" or "true" or "false." An obvious limitation of categorical responses is the lack of other options such as "sometimes" or "it depends." Categorical responses do not require as much time to administer as scaled responses, but they also do not provide as much information as to the subject's degree of agreement or frequency of behavior.

Sometimes questions in questionnaires are keyed to the responses of other items. For example, a question might ask whether the respondent's institution offered a doctor's degree. If the subject answered "yes," then he or she would be directed to answer subsequent questions about the doctoral program. If the answer were "no," the subject would be directed to either stop or to move on to the next section.

Borg and Gall (1983) offer the following rules for constructing questionnaire items:

1. The items must be clearly worded so that the items mean the same to all respondents. Avoid words that have no precise meaning, such as "usually," "most," and "generally."
2. Use short questions rather than long questions because they are easier to understand.
3. Do not use items that have two or more separate ideas in the same question. For example, "Although everyone should learn how to swim, passing a swimming test should not be a requirement for graduation from college." This item cannot really be answered because a person might agree with the first part of the sentence but not the last, or vice versa. Another example is, "Does your department require an entrance examination for master's and doctoral students?" This is confusing because the department may have such an examination for doctoral students but not master's students, or vice versa. If the response choices are only "yes" or "no," a "no" response would indicate no examination for either program, and a "yes" would mean exams for both. This should be a two-part question.
4. Avoid using negative items such as "Health education should not be taught by physical education teachers." Negative items are often confusing and the negative word is sometimes overlooked, causing the individual to answer in exactly the opposite way.
5. Avoid technical language and jargon. Attempt to achieve clarity and the same meaning for everyone.
6. Be careful that you do not bias the answer or lead the respondent to answer in a certain way. Sometimes questions can be stated in such a way that the person knows what is the "right" response. The same applies to the problem of threatening questions. If the respondent perceives certain items to be threatening, he or she will probably not return the questionnaire. A questionnaire on grading practices, for example, may be viewed as threatening because poor grading practices would indicate that the teachers are not doing a good job. Hence, a teacher who feels threatened may either not return it or may give responses that seem to be "right answers."

Finally, the entire appearance and format of the questionnaire can have a significant bearing on the return rate. Questionnaires which appear to be poorly organized and prepared are likely to be "filed" in the wastebasket. Remember, many people have negative attitudes toward questionnaires, so anything that the researcher can do to overcome this negative attitude will enhance the likelihood of the questionnaire being answered. Some of the suggestions in this regard are merely cosmetic, such as the use of colored paper or an artistic design. Even little things, such as having dotted lines from the questionnaire item to the response options or grouping related items together, may pay big dividends.

The questionnaire should provide the name and address of the investigator. It is especially important that the instructions for answering the questions are clear and complete, and that examples are provided for any items that are anticipated as being difficult to understand.

The first few questions should be easy to answer; the respondent is more likely to start answering easy questions and is also more apt to complete the questionnaire once he or she is committed. A poor strategy is to begin with questions that require considerable thought or time to gather information. In that regard, every effort should be made to make difficult questions as convenient to answer as possible. For example, questions that ask for enrollment figures, size of faculty, number of graduate assistants, and so on, can often be asked as ranges, for example, 1-10, 11-20, 21-30. In the first place, you will probably group the responses for analysis purposes anyway. Second, the respondent can often answer "range" questions without having to consult the records, or at least can supply the answers more quickly. An even more basic question to ask yourself is "Do I really need that information?" "Does it pertain to my objectives?" Unfortunately, some investigators just ask for information off the top of their heads with no consideration as to the time required to supply the answer or as to whether the information is relevant.

A general rule is that short questionnaires are more effective than long ones. According to Borg and Gall (1983), an analysis of 98 questionnaire studies showed that, on the average, each page added to a questionnaire reduced the number of returns by about .5%. Because many people are prejudiced toward questionnaires, the cover letter (which will be discussed later) and the size and appearance of the questionnaire are crucial. A lengthy questionnaire requiring voluminous information will very likely be put aside until later—if not discarded immediately.

The Pilot Study. A pilot study is recommended for any type research, but it is imperative with a survey. Actually, the designer of a questionnaire may be well advised to do two pilot studies. The first trial run simply consists of asking a few colleagues or acquaintances to read over the questionnaire. These people can provide valuable critiques about the questionnaire format, content, the expression and importance of the items, and whether questions should be added or deleted.

After revising the questionnaire in accordance with the criticisms obtained in the first trial run, a sample of respondents are selected who are a part of the intended population for the second pilot study. The questionnaire is administered and the results are subjected to item analysis (which will be discussed in Chapter 15). In some questionnaires, correlations may be run between scores on each item and the whole test to see whether the items are measuring what they are intended to measure. In all cases, responses are examined to determine whether the items seem clear and appropriate. First, questions which are answered the same by all of the sample need to be evaluated. This probably means that the items lack discrimination. Those responses which are quite unexpected may indicate that the questions are poorly worded. Some rewording and other changes might also be necessary if the subjects, who might be sensitive to some questions, do not respond to them. Furthermore, the pilot study will determine if the instructions are adequate.

A trial run of the analysis of results should always be accomplished in the pilot study. The researcher can see whether the items can be analyzed in a meaningful way and ascertain if some changes may be warranted for easier analysis. This is one of the most profitable outcomes of the pilot study. Of course, if substantial changes are mandated by the results of the pilot study, another pilot study is recommended to determine whether the questionnaire is ready for initial mailing.

The Cover Letter. Unquestionably, the success of the initial mailing depends largely on the effectiveness of the letter that accompanies the questionnaire. Although it has several purposes, a good cover letter should still be brief and to the point.

The cover letter should explain the purposes and importance of the survey. In other words, it should convince the respondent of the worth of the study. If the purposes are explained in a succinct and professional manner, (and if indeed the purposes are worthy of study), the respondent will likely become interested in the problem and will be inclined to cooperate.

An effective cover letter should also indicate a brief and tactful assurance of confidentiality, specifying how the respondents' privacy and anonymity will be maintained. In this regard, if anonymity is to be stressed, then the respondent's name should not be typed on the cover letter because this might create doubt about the sincerity of the pledge of confidentiality. A code number is a much better method of identification.

Furthermore, the cover letter should make an appeal to the importance of the respondent's cooperation. Some use of subtle flattery may be desirable with reference to the respondent's professional status and the importance of his or her response. This must be done tactfully, however, and used only when appropriate. In this situation, the person's name and address should appear on the cover letter. Preferably, if a word processor is available, the letters should look as if they were individually typed. It is insulting to try to convince persons that they have been handpicked for their expertise and valued opinions when the letters are addressed "Dear Occupant."

If the survey is endorsed by recognized agencies, associations, or institutions, specify this in the cover letter. If possible, use the organization's or institution's letterhead stationery. Respondents will be much more cooperative if some respected person(s) or organization is supporting the study. Also acknowledge if financial support is being given and by whom. Identify yourself by name and position. If the study is part of your thesis or dissertation, give your advisor's name. Sometimes it is advantageous if the department chair or dean of the college signs the letter. Then, in order to increase the response rate, contact subjects by letter, card, or phone call asking for their participation in the survey. Provided the purposes of the study are worthwhile, it is usually effective at this time to offer the respondent a summary of the results. However, be sure that you follow through with your promise.

Because a questionnaire is an imposition on a person's time, strategies involving rewards and incentives are sometimes used in an effort to amuse or involve the respondent. Some questionnaires have enclosed money such as a dollar as a token of appreciation. This may appeal to a person's integrity and evoke cooperation. Then again, you may just be out a dollar. The disadvantage of this is that inflation plays havoc with the effects of such rewards. A quarter may have been effective years ago, whereas 1, 2, or more dollars may be required to elicit the same "sense of guilt" for not responding.

The cover letter should request that the questionnaire be returned by a certain date. (This same information should be specified on the questionnaire, also.) When establishing the date of the return data, consider such things as the respondent's schedule of responsibilities, vacations, and so forth. Be reasonable in allowing the person ample time to respond; although with questionnaires, it is advisable not to give the respondents too much time because of the tendency to put it aside and later forget it. Allowing a week is ample time for the respondent to answer (in addition to the mailing time).

The appearance of the cover letter is just as important as the appearance of the questionnaire. Grammatical errors, misspelled words, sloppy erasures, and improper spacing and format give the respondent the impression that the author does not attach much importance to details, and that the study will probably be poorly done.

A number of subtle and tactful approaches have been tried to establish rapport with the respondent: Some have tried a very solemn appeal to the monumental importance of the survey; some have attempted a casual humor; and others have tried a homespun, folksy approach. Obviously, the success of any approach depends on the skill of the writer and the receptiveness of the reader. Any of these attempts can backfire.

A number of years ago, one of the authors (Nelson) received from the head of his department a note to which this letter was attached:

> Dear Dr. ______________________
>
> It has been said: "There are two kinds of information, knowing it or knowing where to find it." I asked three men you know, Doctors Eeney, Meeney and Moe, a certain question and each said: "Sorry, I don't know his name." But they came back with the helpful suggestion—to write to you.

Now for the question: What is the name of the person in your department or school who is in charge of your graduate program in physical education? etc etc etc.

Cordially yours,

Harry Homespun

The department head answered the letter; then shortly thereafter, this letter arrived:

Dear Dr. Nelson:

Your good work in administering a graduate program is well known throughout our profession. Even though there are many knotty problems, everyone wants to upgrade the resources for graduate studies. But how? Because of your scholarly approach, my associates, Doctors Eeney, Meeney and Moe suggested that I write to you.

Knowledgeable leaders, like you, tell us of the ever present struggle between physical education and the cultural lag, etc etc.

It has been said: "If you want to get something important done, ask a busy person." My associates tell me you are busier than a bird dog in tall grass. They also say that you have a high regard for excellence. . . . If you could find it convenient to return your checked copy on or before May 1, you might help reduce the cultural lag, etc.

Cordially yours,

Harry Homespun

About a month later, another letter arrived:

Dear Dr. Nelson:

You're a great help. Your prompt reply was like a major league catcher, brilliantly fielded and efficiently returned. Many thanks.

Professional people in your position represent a storehouse of knowledge. Consequently, there is additional information which only you can supply. Please go over the enclosed check sheet, etc etc.

. . . Your timely help is appreciated. Your good work has preceeded (sic) our correspondence. etc etc.

Keep up the good work.

Cordially yours,

Harry Homespun

We have, of course, omitted the main parts of the letters concerning what was being studied and what the instructions specified. This was generally done well.

About a year later another questionnaire arrived with the following cover letter:

> Dear Dr. Nelson:
>
> Your excellent leadership in administering graduate programs is well known throughout the profession. Because of your genuine interest in upgrading our mutual field of endeavor, my advisors, Doctors Eeney, Meeney and Moe suggested that I correspond directly with you.
>
> Scholarly graduate administrators and advisors like you often come in contact with the problems of standards. Your considered judgment is solicited in this study to arrive at some common criteria for evaluating graduate programs, etc. etc.
>
> Cordially yours,
>
> Fred Folksy

Then came another letter:

> Dear Dr. Nelson:
>
> Your prompt return of the checked statements is greatly appreciated. My advisors, Doctors Eeney, Meeney and Moe were certainly correct when they indicated you would gladly cooperate in this survey.
>
> It has been said: "If you want to get something important done, ask a busy person." My associates tell me that you are busier than a bird dog in tall grass. etc etc.
>
> If you could find it convenient to return your checked copy . . . you would help us reduce the cultural lag in our profession. etc.
>
> Cordially yours,
>
> Fred Folksy

It is safe to assume that these two graduate students had the same research methods course at the same institution. Most likely, in the discussion of the survey method, some examples of cover letters were given with different approaches. Professors Eeney, Meeney, and Moe would undoubtedly be embarrassed if they knew that the two students had written such identical letters.

In most respects, the cover letters contained the essential information and the topics were worthwhile. The authors were simply too heavy-handed in their attempts at a "downhome" approach, and their efforts to flatter the respondent regarding the respondent's expertise were rather obviously lacking in subtlety. The remarkable thing was that a bird dog helped reduce cultural lag.

Table 10.1 is an example of a cover letter for a questionnaire that dealt with a potentially threatening topic. The letter effectively explains to the respondent how confidentiality will be assured.

Table 10.2 is a cover letter which focuses on the importance of the topic and on the agencies endorsing the study. It also tactfully appeals to the respondent's ego.

TABLE 10.1

SAMPLE COVER LETTER

Dear ______________________

Your participation in a national survey of perceived leader behavior in physical education is needed. As a doctoral student in physical education at the University of Georgia, I am conducting this study to compare and contrast male and female faculty members' perceptions of their male and female department heads' leader behavior. This institution was randomly selected to take part in this research project. Your department head has already been contacted and expressed willingness to take part in the study. I am now asking randomly selected faculty members from your institution to become involved. Your name was one of those selected to ask to participate by answering the enclosed questionnaires.

Participation will require approximately 15 minutes of your time to answer both questionnaires that will be used and to fill out an information sheet. The questionnaires and instructions as to how they are to be completed have been included with this letter in the hopes you will agree to be a participant. There is no evaluation intended or implied with this study. The instruments used describe the perceived leader behavior of the administrator. The analysis of the data will be utilized in group mean scores. Following the completion of the survey and the statistical analysis of the data, I will gladly send you a summary of the findings. All data will be dealt with confidentially and no institution or individual taking part in the study will be identified.

Hopefully, you will find time in your busy schedule to participate in this study. Thank you for your time and participation. I look forward to your early response.

Sincerely,

Kay A. Johnson

Clifford G. Lewis
Major Professor

Enclosures: 5

Reprinted with permission from C.G. Lewis.

TABLE 10.2

SAMPLE COVER LETTER

Dear ______________________

The responsibilities that I have in providing leadership in physical education for a large school district have caused me to give consideration to the approach needed to achieve acceptable objectives of physical fitness in the secondary boys' physical education program.

Through the cooperation of the San Diego Unified School District, the School of Education and the Physical Education Department of the University of California, Los Angeles, and the Bureau of Health Education, Physical Education and Recreation of the California State Department of Education, I am undertaking a study in the area of physical fitness. Representatives of the President's Council on Physical Fitness have said this information would be most valuable for them also. The purpose of the study is to establish criteria that can be utilized in planning activities in physical education classes for secondary aged boys (12-18) to develop and maintain selected aspects of physical fitness. The selected aspects to be considered are those commonly referred to as cardiorespiratory endurance (stamina), muscular strength and endurance, and flexibility. The information gained will be used in program planning by helping to answer such questions as these: What part of the physical education lesson should be spent on specific fitness activities (such as calisthenics, interval running, weight training, etc.) and what part of the lesson should be spent on sports and games of our culture (such as basketball, volleyball, softball, track, tennis, gymnastics, dance instruction, etc.)? What guidelines should be established in planning the specifics of physical fitness work? What physical fitness activities should be used?

A committee of exercise physiologists nominated you as a person who is qualified to comment on this topic because of your recognized position as a leader and your research in the area of physical fitness. It would be most appreciated if you would answer the enclosed questions and return them in the envelope provided at your earliest convenience. A summary of the answers will be returned to you.

Sincerely yours,

Asahel E. Hayes
Physical Education Specialist

AEH:sh
Encs.

Reprinted with permission of Curriculum Services Division, San Diego City Schools.

Sending the Questionnaire. The investigator needs to carefully consider when is the best time for the initial mailing. Such considerations include holidays, vacations, and especially busy times of the year. A self-addressed stamped envelope should be included. It is almost an insult to ask the respondent to answer the questionnaire, then to address an envelope and to furnish a stamp to mail it back.

Other matters regarding the mailing of the questionnaire such as establishing the date to be returned have been covered in previous sections. The initial mailing represents a substantial cost to the sender. Securing a sponsor to underwrite or defray expenses and using bulk mailing are important considerations.

Follow-up Procedures. This should not come as a big shock, but it is unlikely that you will get 100% return on the initial mailing. A follow-up letter is nearly always needed, and this can be done in many different ways. One approach is to wait several days after the expected return date and then to send another letter along with another copy of the questionnaire and another self-addressed, stamped envelope to those who have not responded. (This is expensive, of course.) An alternative is to simply send a postcard reminding the subjects that the completed questionnaire has not been received. Then after a few weeks, send another letter, questionnaire, and self-addressed envelope.

Follow-ups are effective. In a number of instances, the person has forgotten to respond, and a mere reminder will prompt a return. Other nonrespondents who had not planned to return the questionnaire may be influenced by the researcher's efforts in reiterating the significance of the study and the importance of his or her input.

The follow-up letter should be tactful. The person should not be chastised for not responding. The best approach is to write as though the person would have responded had it not been for some oversight or mistake on the part of the investigator. See Table 10.3 for a sample of a follow-up letter.

Follow-ups increase the percentage of returns. Tuckman (1978) reports that ordinarily about one- to two-thirds of the questionnaires are returned during the

TABLE 10.3
SAMPLE FOLLOW-UP LETTER

Dear ______________________

I sent a questionnaire regarding criteria for planning physical fitness work in physical education classes to you a few weeks ago and have not heard from you. As you can appreciate, it is important that we obtain response from everyone possible inasmuch as only a few select individuals were contacted. Our school district is planning an immediate study and updating of its physical education program based on the results of this study so it is of vital concern.

The questionnaire was sent during the summer when you may have been away from your office. I have included another copy, however, and it would be most helpful if you could take from 30-45 minutes to give your opinions on the information requested.

Thank you so much for your cooperation.

Sincerely yours,

Asahel E. Hayes
Physical Education Specialist

AEH:ew
Encs.

Reprinted with permission of Curriculum Services Division, San Diego City Schools.

first month. After this, about 10% to 25% can be obtained through follow-up techniques. Most studies aim for at least a 75% to 90% return rate.

Sometimes a second follow-up is carried out, usually via a postcard. Occasionally, telephone calls are made to nonrespondents. If a significant number (e.g., over 20%) of persons do not return the questionnaire, this poses a serious threat to the validity of the results. The overriding concern is that these nonrespondents may represent a different "population" than the respondents. This is especially likely when the questionnaire deals with some sensitive area. For example, surveys about program offerings and grading practices are often not returned by schools with inadequate programs and poor grading practices. Thus, the obtained responses are apt to be biased in favor of the better programs and better teachers.

In instances where over 20% of the questionnaires are not returned, it is recommended that a sample of the nonrespondents be surveyed. Of course, this isn't easy. If people have ignored the initial mailing and one or two follow-ups, the chances are not good that they will respond to another request. However, it is worth a try. The preferred technique is to randomly select a small number (e.g., 5-10%) of the nonrespondents by using the table of random numbers. (The technique is sometimes called "double-dipping.") Then contact is made either by telephone or by a special cover letter. After the responses have been obtained, comparisons are made between the way the nonrespondents answered the various items and the answers of the subjects who responded initially. If the responses are similar, you can assume that the nonrespondents are not different from those who replied. If there are differences, then you need to either try to get a greater percentage of the nonrespondents, or be sure that these differences are noted and discussed in the research report.

Analyzing the Results and Preparing the Report. These last steps will not be discussed here but rather in Chapter 17 which deals with Results and Discussion. The main consideration here is that the analysis must be decided in the planning phase of the study. Many surveys are "analyzed" by merely tallying the responses to the various items and reporting the percentage of the subjects who answered one way and the percentage that answered another. Oftentimes, not much in the way of meaningful interpretation can be gained. For example, when the researcher states simply that 18% of the respondents strongly agreed to some statement, 29% agreed, 26% disagreed, 17% strongly disagreed and 10% had no opinion, the reader's reaction is, "So what?" Surveys must be designed and analyzed with the same care and scientific insight as experimental studies.

THE DELPHI METHOD

The Delphi survey method uses questionnaires, but in a different manner than the typical questionnaire survey. The Delphi technique uses a series of questionnaires in such a way that the respondents finally reach a consensus about the subject. It is basically a method of using expert opinion to help make decisions about practices, needs, and goals.

The procedures include the selection of the "experts," the informed persons who are to respond to the series of questionnaires. A set of statements or questions is prepared for consideration. The first stage in the Delphi technique, called a *round*, is mostly exploratory. The respondents are asked their opinions and evaluations on various issues, goals, and so on. There may be open-ended questions included which allow the subjects to express their views and opinions.

The questionnaire is then revised as a result of the first round and sent to the respondents, asking them to reconsider their answers in light of the analysis of all respondents to the first questionnaire. Subsequent rounds are carried out, and the "panel of experts" are given summaries of previous results and asked to revise their responses if appropriate. The groups' consensus about the issue is finally achieved through the series of rounds of analysis and subsequent considered judgments. Anonymity is a prominent feature of the Delphi method, and the consensus of recognized experts in the field provides a viable means of arriving at decisions concerning important issues.

THE INTERVIEW

As mentioned earlier, the steps for the interview and the questionnaire are basically the same. The focus here will be only on the differences.

The most obvious difference between the questionnaire and the interview is in the gathering of the data. In this respect, the interview is more valid because the responses are apt to be more reliable; also there is a much greater percentage of "returns."

The selection of subjects should be done in the same manner as the questionnaire in terms of sampling techniques. Generally speaking, the interview uses smaller samples, especially when a graduate student is doing the survey. Cooperation must be secured by contacting the subjects selected for interviewing. If subjects refuse to be interviewed, the researcher must consider possible bias to the results, the same as with nonrespondents in a questionnaire study.

To effectively conduct an interview takes a great deal of preparation. Graduate students sometimes have the impression that anyone can do it. The same procedures as with the questionnaire are followed in preparing the items, with which the interviewer must be very familiar. The researcher has to carefully rehearse the interview techniques. One of the sources of invalidity is that the interviewer tends to improve with experience, and, thus, the results of earlier interviews may differ from interviews conducted later in the study.

Training is required in making initial contact and presenting the verbal "cover letter" by phone. At the meeting, the interviewer has to establish rapport and to make the person feel at ease. If a tape recorder is to be used, permission must be obtained. If a tape recorder is not going to be used, then the interviewer must have an efficient system of coding the responses without consuming much time and appearing to be "taking dictation." The interviewer must not inject his or her own bias into the conversation and certainly should not argue with the respondent. Although there are many advantages of the interview over the questionnaire with regard to the flexibility of the questioning, there is also the danger of straying from the questions and getting off the subject. The interviewer has to *tactfully* keep the respondent from rambling, and this requires skill.

The interview has the following advantages over the questionnaire:

1. The interview is more adaptable. Questions can be rephrased and further questions can be asked.
2. The interview is more versatile with regard to the personality and receptiveness of the respondent.
3. The interviewer can observe *how* the person responds and can thus achieve greater insight as to the sensitivity of the topic and the intensity of feelings from the respondent. This can add considerably to the validity of the results, for this is one of the greatest threats to validity in questionnaire studies.
4. Because each person is contacted prior to the interview, interviews have a greater rate of return. Moreover, people tend to be more willing to talk than to fill out a questionnaire. A certain amount of ego is involved because a person feels more flattered to be interviewed than just being sent a questionnaire.

THE TELEPHONE INTERVIEW

Interviewing by telephone is becoming more and more prevalent. Some of the advantages of telephone interviewing over face-to-face interviewing are as follows:

1. Telephone interviewing is less expensive. The use of WATS lines and other reduced-cost plans greatly lessens the costs of conducting an interview study. One study reported that telephone interviews cost about one-half as much as personal interviews (Graves & Kahn, 1979).
2. The interviewer(s) can work from a central location which facilitates the monitoring and quality control of the interviews and provides better opportunity for computer-assisted interviewing techniques (Borg & Gall, 1983).
3. Many people are more easily reached by telephone than personal visitation.
4. The telephone interview enables the researcher to reach a wide geographical area, which is a limitation of the personal interview. This advantage also can increase the validity of the sampling.

5. There is some evidence that persons will respond more candidly to sensitive questions over the telephone than in personal interviews where the presence of the interviewer may inhibit some responses.

The use of the microcomputer in telephone interviewing provides an excellent means of data collection and analysis. There are several ways by which microcomputers can be used in the data-gathering process. For example, the microcomputer displays the questions for the interviewer to ask, and the interviewer then types the subject's responses. Each response triggers the next question, which eliminates the turning of many pages and the likelihood of asking inappropriate questions. This is most helpful when some responses are linked to further questions which may be on another page of the actual questionnaire. In addition, the responses are stored for analysis, reducing scoring errors, plus the stored responses can then be called out for the statistical analysis.

An obvious limitation of telephone interviewing is that some people do not have telephones. While this needs to be considered, especially in sampling the poor, the percentage of adults who do not have telephones is actually quite small. The problem of unlisted numbers can be mostly overcome by using a table of random numbers to select the four numbers after the three-number exchange. You can reach both listed and unlisted numbers by this method. Dillman (1978) provides a comprehensive discussion of the relative advantages and disadvantages of the telephone survey.

THE NORMATIVE SURVEY

The normative survey is not described in most research methods textbooks. As is implied in the name, this method involves establishing norms for abilities, performances, beliefs, and attitudes. A cross-sectional approach is used in that samples of people of different ages, gender, and other classifications are selected and measured.

The steps in the normative survey are generally the same as in the questionnaire. The basic difference is the manner in which the data are collected. The researcher selects the most appropriate tests to measure the desired performances or abilities, such as the components of physical fitness.

The AAHPERD has sponsored several normative surveys. Probably the most notable was the Youth Fitness test (1958) which was conducted in response to the furor caused by the results of the Kraus-Weber test (Kraus & Hirschland, 1954), which had revealed that American children were inferior to European children in minimum muscular fitness. The Youth Fitness test was originally given to 8500 boys and girls in a nationwide sample. Follow-up testing was done, and the norms were updated in 1965 and 1975.

In the AAHPERD normative survey, a seven-item motor fitness test battery was determined by a committee. The University of Michigan Survey Research

Center selected a representative sampling of boys and girls in grades 5 through 12. Initial contact was made requesting each school's cooperation. Directions for giving the test items were prepared and physical education teachers in various parts of the country were selected and trained to administer and to supervise the testing. In any normative survey, it is important that the testing be administered in a rigidly standardized manner. If there are deviations in the way in which the measurements are taken, the results are meaningless.

The data from the survey are collected and analyzed by some norming method such as percentiles, T-scores, or stanines. Norms are constructed for the different categories of age, sex, and so on.

AAHPERD has also conducted a sport skills testing project which has established norms for skills of boys and girls of different ages in a number of sports. The AAHPERD recently developed and constructed norms for a health related physical fitness test (1980). The test battery includes measures of cardiovascular condition (distance run), body composition (triceps and subscapular skinfolds), strength and endurance of the abdominal muscles (sit-ups), and flexibility of the muscles of the posterior thigh and lower back (sit-and-reach).

Sometimes comparisons are made between the norms of different populations. In other studies, the major purpose is simply to establish norms. The primary drawbacks to any normative survey are (a) the selection of tests to measure the behavior in question; and (b) the standardization of testing procedures in the gathering of the data. The problem with the selection of the testing instrument is the danger of generalizing on the basis of specific tests. For example, if one test item (such as pull-ups) is used to measure a particular component (strength), too much importance may be placed on the score. In other words, pull-ups are decidedly influenced (adversely) by body weight and primarily involve the arm and shoulder muscle groups. Strength in other parts of the body is not being assessed, and the assumption cannot be made that a person who does well (or poorly) in pull-ups would perform the same way in other strength tests. This question of test selection is, of course, important in any type of research. The standardization of testing procedures is essential for establishing norms. However, when a normative survey involves a number of different testers from different parts of the country, this becomes a source of possible measurement error. Published test descriptions simply cannot address all the aspects of test administration and ways of handling the many problems of interpretation of procedures that arise. Extensive training of testers is the answer, but this is often impossible from a logistic standpoint.

DEVELOPMENTAL RESEARCH

Developmental research implies the study of changes in behavior across the life span. While much of the developmental research has focused on infancy, childhood, and adolescence, research on senior citizens and even across the total human life span is increasingly common.

The focus of developmental research involves cross-age comparisons. For example, children at ages 6, 8, and 10 years could be compared on how far they can jump. Or adults at 45, 55, and 65 could be compared on their knowledge of the effects of obesity on life expectancy. These are both developmental studies. One of the major characteristics of developmental studies is whether the same subjects are followed across the years (*longitudinal* design) or if different subjects are selected at each age level (*cross-sectional* designs).

Longitudinal designs are powerful ones because the changes in behavior across the time span of interest are within the same subjects. However, longitudinal designs are time consuming. A longitudinal study of children's jumping performance at 6, 8, and 10 years of age obviously requires 4 years to complete. That is probably not a very wise choice of designs for a master's thesis. Longitudinal designs have additional problems besides the time required to complete them. First, over the several years of the study, some of the subjects are likely to move away when parents change jobs; or school districts will rezone attendance causing the subjects to be spread out over several schools. In longitudinal studies of senior citizens, some will die over the years of the study. The problem with this loss of subjects is whether the sample characteristics remain the same when subjects are lost. For example, when children are lost from the sample because of parents changing jobs, is the sample then composed of lower socioeconomic level children because the more affluent parents move? Furthermore, if obesity *is* related to longevity, then are older citizens more likely to be less obese and consequently have increased knowledge because the more obese subjects with less knowledge have died? Thus, knowledge about obesity may not be changing from 45 to 65 years of age; the sample is what is changing.

The second problem with longitudinal designs is that subjects become increasingly familiar with the test items, and the items may cause changes in behavior. The knowledge inventory on obesity may prompt subjects to seek information about obesity. This may change their knowledge, attitudes, and behaviors. Thus, the next time they complete the knowledge inventory, they have gained knowledge. However, this gain of knowledge is the result of having been exposed to the test earlier and might not have occurred without that exposure.

Cross-sectional studies are usually less time consuming to carry out. Cross-sectional studies involve testing several age groups (e.g., 6, 8, and 10 years) at the same point in time. While cross-sectional studies are more time efficient than longitudinal studies, a problem called *cohorts* exist. This means, Are all the age groups really from the same population (group of cohorts)? Said another way, Are environmental circumstances that affect jumping performance the same today for 6-year-olds as when the 10-year-olds were 6? As an illustration, Have physical education programs improved over this 4-year span so that 6-year-olds receive more instruction and practice in jumping than the 10 year olds did when they were 6? If this is true, then we are not looking at the development of jumping performance, but rather at some uninterpretable interaction between "normal" development and the effects of instruction. The cohorts problem exists in all cross-sectional studies.

For a recent example of a longitudinal developmental study, read Halverson, Roberton, and Langendorfer (1982), who follow the same children from early elementary school through junior high school to study throwing velocity of the overarm throw. Thomas et al. (1983) provide an example of a cross-sectional developmental study. They look at the development of memory for distance information by selecting different age groups. Then they compare the effects of a practiced strategy for remembering distance at each age level to show that appropriate use of strategy reduces age differences in remembering distance. Each of these studies suffers from the specific defects associated with the type of developmental design. Halverson, Roberton, and Langendorfer (1982) had a loss of subjects over the several years of the study while Thomas et al. cannot establish that their younger subjects are not more familiar with memory strategies than the older subjects were when they were younger.

While both longitudinal and cross-sectional designs have some problems, they are the only means available to study development. Thus, both are needed and are important parts of the research process. These two types of designs are listed under descriptive research. However, either may fall under experimental research (Chapter 11); that is, an independent variable may be manipulated within an age level. In the Thomas et al. study, the use of strategy was manipulated within each of the three age levels. Thus, age was a categorical variable while strategy was a true independent variable. This point is addressed here because developmental research will not be covered in Chapter 11 (Experimental Research).

Whether the developmental research is longitudinal or cross-sectional, a number of methodological problems exist (for a more detailed discussion, see Thomas, 1984). One of the most common problems is an unrepresentative score. These scores, called *outliers*, occur in all research but are particular problems at the extremes of developmental research (children and senior citizens). Outliers frequently result from shorter attention spans, distraction, and lack of motivation to do the task. The best way to handle these unrepresentative scores is to

1. Plan the testing situation within a reasonable time limit that accounts for attention span;
2. Set up the testing situation where distractions cannot occur; and
3. Be aware of what an unrepresentative score is and retest when one occurs.

The last thing a researcher wants to do is use unrepresentative scores. Therefore, outliers not detected at testing should be found when the distribution of the data is studied. There are several ways to test for these extreme and unrepresentative scores (for example, see Barnett & Lewis, 1978). The most important fact is that the developmental researcher should expect and plan for handling outliers in the data set.

A second problem in developmental research involves semantics. Selecting the words to use in explaining the task to various age groups of children is a formidable one. If the researcher is not careful, older children will perform better than younger children only because they grasp the idea of what to do more quickly. While the standard rule in good research is to give exactly the same instructions to all the subjects, this rule must be bent for developmental studies with children. The researcher must explain the testing situation in a way the subject can understand. In addition, tangible evidence must be obtained that the various age subjects did understand before being tested. This frequently involves having the subject demonstrate the activity to some criterion level of performance prior to data collection.

A good example of this problem involved a group of early elementary school children taking a computer course through continuing education at a local college. The children were doing fine until the teacher (a college instructor of computer science) began to write instructions on the blackboard. Then everyone stopped working. Finally, one of the children whispered to the teacher, "Some of us can't read cursive." After the teacher printed the instructions in block letters, all the children happily returned to their work computing (*Chronicle of Higher Education*, 1983).

A third developmental research problem involves the lack of reliability in younger children's performances. When a performance score is obtained for children, it should be a reliable one—that is, if the child is tested again, the performance score should be about the same. Obtaining reliable performance is frequently a problem with younger children for many of the same reasons that outliers occur. Of course, making sure the child understands the task must be first. Then maintaining motivation is a second consideration. A task which can be made fun and enjoyable is more likely to elicit a consistent performance. This can be done by the use of cartoon figures, encouragement, and rewards. For some ideas on how cartoon figures can be used to improve motivation on many gross motor tasks, see Herkowitz (1984).The developmental researcher should maintain frequent reliability checks (for appropriate techniques, see Chapter 13) during testing sessions.

The final developmental problem to mention is a statistical one. A frequent means of making across-age comparisons is to use ANOVA. One of the assumptions of ANOVA (see Chapter 7) is that the groups being compared have equal variances (spread of scores about the mean). This assumption may often be violated in making across-age comparisons. Depending on the nature of the task, older children may have considerably larger or smaller variances than younger children. A developmental researcher should be aware of this potential issue and some of the solutions. In particular, pilot work using the task(s) of interest in the research should provide insight into this problem.

The protection of human subjects in research was discussed in Chapter 4. Of course, this protection is also extended to children. Parents' or guardians' permission is required for minors to participate in research. This permission should be obtained in the same way as for an adult subject except that the explanation and consent forms are given to the parents or guardians. When minors are old enough to understand the methodology, their consent should also be obtained. This means explaining the purpose of the research in terms the child can understand. Most public and private schools have their own requirements concerning approval of research studies.

The normal sequence of events involves planning the research; acquiring approval of the university's committee for protection of human subjects; locating and getting the approval of the school system, the school involved, and the teachers; and then getting parents and, when appropriate, students' approval. You can see that a good deal of paperwork is required. Thus, beginning the process well in advance of the time you plan to begin data collection is necessary.

In summary, developmental research is an important type of study which generally involves either longitudinal or cross-sectional designs. Each design has some flaws but also has strengths that the other lacks. In particular, the researcher must be aware of several methodological problems existing in developmental studies. While developmental studies have been presented in the chapter on descriptive research, they frequently may be experimental or quasi-experimental in nature. Finally, the reseacher must be especially careful in protecting the rights of children as subjects in developmental research.

THE CASE STUDY

In the case study, the researcher strives for an in-depth understanding of a single situation or phenomenon. This technique is used in many fields such as clinical psychology, sociology, medicine, speech pathology, and in various educational areas such as disciplinary problems and reading difficulties. It has been used considerably in the health sciences and to some extent in physical education.

The case study is a form of descriptive research. Although it consists of a rigorous, detailed examination of a single case, the underlying assumption is that this case is an example of many other such cases. Consequently, by in-depth study of a single case, a greater understanding about other similar cases is achieved. This is not to say, however, that the purpose of case studies is to make generalizations. Quite the contrary, for drawing general conclusions from a case study is not justifiable. On the other hand, the findings of a number of case studies may play a part in the inductive reasoning that is involved in the development of hypotheses.

The case study is not confined to the study of an individual. The case study technique can be used in research involving programs, institutions, organizations, political structures, communities, and situations.

The case study involves the collection and analysis of many sources of information. In some respects, the case study has some of the same features as historical research. Although it consists of intensive study of a single unit, it may be that the ultimate worth is an insight and knowledge of a general nature and improved practices. The case study approach is most frequently used in trying to understand why something has gone wrong.

The case study is very flexible as to the amount and type of data that are gathered, as well as the procedures used in gathering the data. Hence, the steps in the methodology are not distinct or uniform with all case studies. The following steps are suggested by Helmstadter (1970). One of the first steps is to define and describe the present situation. In other words, what precisely is the problem? In what areas does the problem appear to be most serious? and Is the problem of a sudden nature, or has it been gradually growing?

Background information is then required in the effort to better understand the present situation and perhaps to shed light on some possible causes. This step can be compared to medicine in that it is a search for symptoms. This step involves a diligent examination of as many sources of information as seems relevant. For example, in a case study involving a child, data from medical examinations, physical performance tests, achievement tests, grades, interest inventories, scholastic aptitude tests, teacher anecdotal records, autobiographies, and various other sources of information might be examined. From these "symptoms," hypotheses may evolve as to the origin and causes of the problem.

As with any type of research, once hypotheses have been formulated, they should be tested. This step may involve the elimination of some possible causes, reexaminations in certain areas, and new evaluations in other areas, as suggested by the analysis of the background information.

The final step is to verify one or more of the hypotheses. In accomplishing this step, some remedial action is usually prescribed, and then the consequences of such action are later checked to determine its effectiveness in bringing about favorable changes.

Several case studies in physical education were directed by H. Harrison Clarke at the University of Oregon (Clarke & Clarke, 1970). The studies dealt with persons of low (and high) fitness levels. Most of the studies sought to discover factors which may contribute to low fitness or the substrength individual. A remarkable example of the case study approach and effective follow-up was seen in a demonstration project undertaken by Frederick Rand Roger and Fred E. Palmer (Clarke, 1967-1968). Twenty junior high school boys with the lowest physical fitness scores were studied as to the cause of low fitness, using information such as somatotype, IQ, academic scholarship, medical history, and status. A follow-up project involved individual attention and special class meetings through exercises, improved health habits, medical referrals, and counseling. Vast improvements were reported in fitness, scholarship, and behavior.

One of the principal advantages of the case study approach is that it can be fruitful in formulating new ideas and hypotheses about problem areas, especially areas in which there is no clear cut structure or model. On the other hand, a primary weakness of case studies is the temptation to generalize from just one situation or subject. Other weaknesses include the failure to utilize the appropriate sources of information and subsequently concluding that the problem stems from a source which is not really relevant. There is also the danger of relying too heavily on memory. Nevertheless, the case study can yield valuable information in certain problem areas.

JOB ANALYSIS

A job analysis may be considered as a type of case study. It is a technique designed to determine the nature of a particular job and the types of training, preparation, skills, and attitudes necessary for success in the job.

Job analyses are regularly done in fields such as counseling and vocational training. There have been a few such studies in HPERD dealing with administrative positions, intramural duties, and coaching and teaching responsibilities.

The procedures vary in conducting a job analysis. The objective is to obtain as much relevant information about the job and the job requirements as possible. One method is to observe someone in the particular occupation. Of course, this is time consuming and probably bothersome for the person in the job. Nevertheless, the procedure is recommended because the researcher can acquire a kind of vicarious on-the-job experience and can gain valuable insight into the whole atmosphere connected with the occupation. A limitation to this method is the lack of sufficient time in order to observe all facets of the job, particularly seasonal duties and responsibilities.

Questionnaires and interviews are effective job analysis techniques which elicit a person's responses to the kinds of duties performed, the types and degree of preparation required or recommended for accomplishing the tasks, and the perceived advantages and disadvantages of the job.

The limitations of the job analysis as a research technique include the fallibility of memory and self-reports. There may be a tendency to accent either the positive or negative aspects of the job depending upon the time, circumstances, and the subject. Also, there is the danger that the approach can be too mechanical, thus neglecting some of the more abstract aspects of the job and its requirements.

OBSERVATIONAL RESEARCH

Observation, used in a variety of research endeavors, is a means of collecting data, and is a descriptive method of researching certain problems. In the questionnaire and interview techniques, the researcher relies on self-reports as to how the subject behaves or believes. A weakness of self-reports is that persons may not be candid as to what they really do or feel and may give what they perceive as the socially desirable responses. An alternative descriptive research technique is for the researcher to observe subjects' behavior and use qualitative or quantitative analysis of the observations. Some educators claim that this yields more accurate data. There are, of course, several limitations to observational research.

Basic considerations in observational research include:

1. What behavior(s) is to be observed?
2. Who is to be observed?
3. Where are the observations to be conducted?
4. How many observations are to be made?
5. When are the observations to be done?
6. How are the observations to be scored and evaluated?

Many other considerations are connected to these basic ones. Depending upon the problem and the setting, each individual investigation has its own unique procedures. Therefore, only the basic considerations can be discussed in rather general terms.

WHAT BEHAVIOR(S) IS TO BE OBSERVED?

This consideration relates to the statement of the problem and to the operational definitions. For example, a study on teacher effectiveness must have clearly defined observational measures of teacher effectiveness. Definite behaviors must be observed, for example, the extent to which the teacher asks students questions. Some other aspects of teacher effectiveness include giving individual attention, demonstrating skills, dressing up for activities, and starting class on time. In determining what behaviors are to be observed, the researcher must also limit the scope of the observations to make the study manageable.

WHO IS TO BE OBSERVED?

As with any study, the population from which samples will be drawn must be determined. Is the study going to focus just on elementary school teachers? What grades? Is the study going to include only physical education specialists, or also classroom teachers who teach physical education? Besides these basic decisions, there is the question about the number of teachers to be observed. Is the study going to include observations of students in addition to teachers? In other words, the researcher must describe precisely who the subjects of the study are to be.

WHERE ARE THE OBSERVATIONS GOING TO BE CONDUCTED?

In addition to the basic considerations regarding the size of the sample and the geographical area, the setting for the observations must also be considered. Is the setting going to be unnatural or natural? An unnatural setting means bringing the subject to a laboratory or room or other locale for the observations.

There are some advantages to an unnatural setting in terms of control and of freedom from distractions. For example, a one-way glass is advantageous for observation, thus removing the influence of the observer on the behavior of the subject. That behavior is affected by the presence of an observer is also shown in a classroom situation. When the observer first arrives, the students (and perhaps the teacher) are curious about the observer's presence. Consequently, they may behave differently than if the observer were not there. The teacher may also act differently, possibly by perceiving the observer as a threat, or by being aware of the purpose of the observations. In any case, the researcher should not make observations on the initial visit. Allowing the subjects to become gradually accustomed to the observer's presence is best.

Whether the subject is to be observed alone or in a group is also related to the setting. In a natural setting such as the playground or classroom, the subject may behave more typically, but there are also likely to be more extraneous influences on behavior.

HOW MANY OBSERVATIONS ARE TO BE MADE?

As with most measurements, because of the increased reliability with increased number of trials, or observations, the more observations, the better. However, there are obvious practical considerations with respect to feasibility; therefore, the researcher has to decide on just how many observations may realistically be made.

Many factors determine the decision on the number of observations to be made. Certainly, one is the operationally defined behavior(s) in question, along with the time constraints of the study itself. For example, if a person is studying the amount of actual activity or participation of students in a physical education class, several considerations must be taken. First of all, the type of activity unit and the number of units encompassed in the study have to be decided upon in the planning phase of the study. The number of observations for each activity is dependent upon the particular stage of learning in the unit, whether in the introductory phase, the practice stage, the playing stage, and so on. This has to be specified in the operational definitions, of course, but the length of the unit and subsequent length of each stage within each unit play a major role in determining the number of observations that are feasible.

Another factor to consider is the number of observers. If only one person is doing the observations, either the number of students (subjects) being observed or the number of observations per subject (or both) will be restricted. To attempt to generalize from observing a few subjects on a few occasions as to their "typical" behavior is hazardous.

Some types of behavior may not be manifested very frequently. Sportsmanship, aggression, leadership, and other traits (as operationally defined) are not readily observable because of the lack of opportunity to display such traits, among other things. The occasion must present itself and the elements of the situation must materialize in a way that the student has the opportunity to react. Consequently, the number of observations are bound to be extremely limited if left to chance occurrence. On the other hand, situations which are contrived to provoke certain behavior are often unsuccessful because of their artificiality.

We cannot say how many observations are necessary, but can only warn against too few observations and recommend a combination of feasibility and measurement considerations. This question will be readdressed in the discussion on recording and scoring observations.

WHEN ARE THE OBSERVATIONS TO BE DONE?

You can easily observe that all of the basic considerations being discussed are related and overlap with one another. The "when" includes decisions about time of day, day of the week, phase in the learning experience, season, and other time factors.

In reference to our previous example of observing the amount of actual student activity in a physical education course, different results would be expected if the observations were made at the beginning of the unit than at the end. Also allowing the subjects to get used to the situation so that the observational procedures do not interfere with normal activity is another "when" consideration. In observing student teachers, for example, differences would certainly be expected if some were observed at the beginning of their student teaching experience and others at the end of the semester.

Graduate students encounter major problems with regard to time and observational research. They find it difficult to spend the time necessary to make a sufficient number of observations to provide reliable results. Furthermore, graduate students usually have to gather the data by themselves, making it much more time consuming than if other observers were available.

HOW ARE THE OBSERVATIONS TO BE SCORED AND EVALUATED?

A number of techniques are employed for recording observational data. Great strides have been made in recent years in this respect. The use of microcomputers and other computer-assisted event recording methods have alleviated many of the technical problems that plagued observational research in the past. Significant advancements will undoubtedly be made in the speed and accuracy in entering and analyzing data in the future.

Some of the more commonly used procedures for recording observational data include (a) narrative or continual recording, (b) tallying or frequency counting, (c) interval, and (d) duration methods.

The *narrative or continual recording* technique is where the researcher records in a series of sentences the occurrences as they happen. This is the slowest and least efficient method of recording. The observer must be able to select the most important information to record because everything that occurs in a given situation cannot possibly be recorded. Probably the best use of this technique is in developing more efficient recording instruments. The researcher first uses the continuous method and then develops categories for future recording from the narrative.

The *tallying or frequency counting* method is recording each time a certain behavior occurs. The behavior must be clearly defined. The frequency counts are made within a certain time frame, such as the number of occurrences in 10 minutes or 30 minutes per session.

The *interval* method is used when the researcher wishes to record whether the behavior in question occurs in a certain interval of time. This method is useful when it is difficult to count individual occurrences. One of the leading standardized systems for interval recording is the Flanders' Interaction Analysis System (Flanders, 1970) in which the observer records the behavior of the subject according to 10 specific behavior classifications within each timed interval. All classroom behavior can be classified into one of the 10 categories. In the simplest interval system, the observer merely records whether or not the subject exhibits the prescribed behavior in a given interval of time.

Sometimes the time intervals are selected randomly or on some fixed basis rather than on continuous observation. Hence, a form of *time sampling* can be employed.

The Academic Learning Time in Physical Education (ALT-PE) is an observational instrument developed by Siedentop, Trousignant, and Parker (1982) for use in physical education. It entails time sampling in which a child is observed for a specified period of time, and the child's activities during that time period are coded. The recording system encompasses (a) the setting or learning environment established by the teacher; (b) the content of the instruction, such as skills, practice, knowledge, and game playing; (c) the responses of the learner whether engaged or not engaged in the content of the lesson; and (d) the difficulty of the responses when the learner is engaged in the activity.

The Cheffers Adaptation of the Flanders' Interaction Analysis System (CAFIAS) was developed by Cheffers (1972) to allow systematic observation of physical education classes as well as classroom situations. The CAFIAS provides a device for coding nonverbal behavior through a double category system so that any behavior can be categorized as verbal, nonverbal, or both verbal and nonverbal. The CAFIAS permits the coding of the class as a whole where the entire class is functioning as one unit, or where the class is divided into small groups, or where the students are working individually or independently with no teacher influence.

The *duration* method involves some timed behavior. The researcher uses a stopwatch or other timing device to record how much time a subject spends engaged in a particular behavior. A number of studies have used this method in observing student time on-task and time off-task. In the previous example about the amount of activity in a physical education class, a researcher could simply record the amount of time a student(s) spent in actual participation and/or the amount of time spent standing in line or waiting to perform. The researcher usually observes a subject for a given unit of time, such as a class period, starting and stopping a stopwatch as the behavior starts and stops so that a cumulative time-on-task (or off-task) is recorded.

VIDEOTAPE

A potentially invaluable instrument for observational research is the videotape. Its greatest advantage is that the researcher does not have to worry about recording observations at the time the behavior is occurring. Furthermore, it is possible for a number of persons to be observed at one time. For example, both teacher and student(s) can be observed simultaneously, which is difficult in normal observational techniques. In addition, the videotape can be replayed as often as needed to evaluate the behavior, and a permanent record can be retained.

The use of videotape does have some disadvantages: It is expensive, the filming requires a significant degree of technical competence for lighting and positioning, and it may be cumbersome at times in "following the action." The presence of a camera may also alter behavior to the extent that the subjects do not behave normally. However, if the disadvantages can be resolved, videotaping can be an effective process for observational research.

WEAKNESSES IN OBSERVATIONAL RESEARCH

Problems and limitations of observational research include the following:

1. A primary danger in observational research lies in the operational definitions of the study. The behaviors have to be carefully defined in order to be observable, and in doing this, the actions may be so restricted that they do not really depict the critical behavior. For example, teacher effectiveness encompasses many behaviors, and to observe only the number of times the teacher asked questions or gave individual attention may be inadequate samples of effectiveness.
2. Using observation forms effectively requires much practice. Inadequate training, therefore, represents a major pitfall in this form of research. In conjunction with this are the difficulties encountered in trying to observe too many things. Oftentimes, the observation form is too ambitious for one person to use.
3. Certain behaviors cannot be evaluated as finely as some of the observation forms dictate. A common mistake is to ask the observer to make discriminations which are too precise, thus reducing the reliability of the ratings.
4. The presence of the observer almost always affects the behavior of the subjects. The researcher must be aware of this and try to reduce the amount of disturbance.

5. Generally, observational research is greatly expedited by having more than one observer. Failure to use more than one observer results in decreased efficiency and objectivity.
6. As with other forms of descriptive research, there must be sufficient numbers of subjects and observations per subject to have adequate internal and external validity. A study with only a handful of subjects on which a small number of observations are made before and after some treatment intervention contributes little to the body of knowledge concerning teacher-student behavior analysis.

OTHER UNOBTRUSIVE RESEARCH MEASURES

There are multiple methods of gathering information about people besides questionnaires, case studies, and observation. Webb, Campbell, Schwartz, and Sechrest (1966) discuss different approaches which they term *unobtrusive* measures. Some samples mentioned include the replacement rate for floor tiles around museum exhibits as a measure of relative popularity of exhibits. The degree of fear caused by telling ghost stories to children has been assessed by observing the shrinking diameter of the circle of the seated children. Eye pupil dilation has been used as an index of fear and interest. Boredom has been measured by the amount of fidgeting movements in the audience. The rate of library withdrawals of fiction and nonfiction books has been studied to determine the impact of television in communities. Children's interest in Christmas has been demonstrated by the size of their drawings of Santa Claus and the amount of distortion in the figures.

In some of the methods such as those just mentioned, the experimenter is not present when the data are being produced. There are conditions, however, when the researcher is present but still acts in a nonreactive manner. In other words, the subjects are not aware that the researcher is gathering data. For example, a researcher in psychology measured the degree of acceptance of strangers among delinquent boys by measuring the distance maintained between a delinquent boy and a new boy who the researcher introduced to the delinquent subjects. Sometimes, the researcher actually intervenes to "speed up the action" or force the data, but in a manner that does not attract attention to the method. In studying the cathartic effect of activity on aggression, Ryan (1970) had an accomplice behave in an obnoxious manner and then measured the amount of electric shock the subjects administered to that accomplice and to "innocent" bystanders. Other researchers have intervened by causing subjects to fail or succeed in order to observe their responses to winning and losing competitive situations.

Unobtrusive measures also include a multitude of records such as birth certificates, political and judicial records, actuarial records, magazines, newspapers, archives, and inscriptions on tombstones. An interesting use of city records (Webb et al., 1966) was the analysis of city water pressure as an index of television viewing interest: Immediately after a television show, the water pressure drops as drinks are obtained and toilets flushed. Mabley (1963) presented data on Chicago's water pressure on a day of an exciting Rose Bowl game which showed a drastic drop in pressure at the time of the game's end.

The issue of ethics arises in some forms of unobtrusive measures with regard to the invasion of privacy. Informed consent compliance has placed considerable restraints on certain research practices such as those which involve entrapment, and experiments which aim to induce heightened anxiety.

CORRELATIONAL RESEARCH

Correlational research is descriptive in that it explores relationships that exist among variables. Sometimes predictions are made based on the relationships, but correlation cannot determine cause and effect. The basic difference between experimental research and correlational research is that the latter does not cause something to happen. There is no manipulation of variables or experimental treatments administered. The basic design of correlational research is to collect data on two or more variables on the same subjects and to determine the relationship among the variables. But of course the researcher should have a sound rationale for exploring the relationships.

Different correlational techniques were discussed in Chapter 6 with examples of situations which lend themselves to correlational research. The two main purposes in doing a correlational study are for analyzing the relationships among variables and for prediction.

STEPS IN CORRELATIONAL RESEARCH

The steps in a correlational study are similar to those used in other research methods. First, the problem is defined and delimited. The selection of the variables to be correlated is of critical importance. Many studies have failed in this regard. Regardless of how sophisticated the statistical analysis may be, the statistical technique can only deal with the variables that are entered—hence the saying, "Garbage in, garbage out." The validity of a study that seeks to identify basic components or factors of fitness hinges on the identification of the variables to be analyzed. A researcher who wishes to discriminate between starters and substitutes in a sport is faced with the crucial task of determining what physiological or psychological variables are the important determinants of success. The researcher must lean heavily on past research in defining and delimiting the problem.

Subjects are selected from the pertinent population using recommended sampling procedure. The magnitude and even direction of a correlation coefficient can vary greatly depending upon the sample used. Remember that correlations only show the degree of relationship between variables, not the cause of the relationship. Consequently, due to other contributing factors, one might obtain a correlation of .90 between two variables in a sample of young children and .10 between the same variables in adults, or vice versa. Chapter 6 used examples of how factors such as age can influence certain relationships. Another aspect of correlation is that the size of the correlation coefficient depends to a considerable extent on the spread of the scores.

A sample that is fairly homogeneous in certain traits seldom will yield a high correlation between variables associated with those traits. For example, the correlation between a distance run and maximal oxygen consumption with a sample of elite track athletes will almost invariably be low because the athletes are so similar. Because the scores on the two measurements are too uniform, there is not enough variability to permit a high correlation. If some lesser trained subjects were included in the sample, the size of the correlation coefficient would increase dramatically.

In prediction studies, the subjects *must* be representative of the population for whom the study is directed. One of the major drawbacks to prediction studies is that the prediction formulas are often population specific, which means that a formula's accuracy is greatest (or maybe only acceptable) when applied to the particular sample on whom it was developed. Chapter 13 will discuss this *shrinkage* phenomenon as well as *cross-validation* which is used to counteract shrinkage.

The collection of data requires the same careful attention to detail and standardization as in all research designs. A variety of methods for collecting data may be used, such as physical performance tests, anthropometric measurements, paper and pencil inventories, questionnaires, and observational techniques. The scores have to be quantified, however, to be correlated.

Analysis of the data can be performed by a number of statistical techniques. Sometimes the researcher wishes to use simple correlation or partial correlation to study how variables, either by themselves or in a linear composite of variables, are associated with some criterion performance or behavior. *Factor analysis* is a "data reduction" method which is employed to see whether relationships among a number of variables can be reduced to smaller combinations of factors or common components. *Path analysis* is a technique used to test some theoretical model about causal relationships between three or more variables.

Prediction studies usually employ multiple regression, because the accuracy of predicting some criterion behavior is nearly always improved by using more than one predictor variable. *Discriminant analysis* is a technique used to predict group membership, and canonical correlation is a method for predicting a combination of several criterion variables from several predictor variables.

Limitations of correlational research include both planning and analysis factors. We have already pointed out the importance of the identification of pertinent variables and the selection of proper tests to measure those variables. There should be hypotheses based on previous research and theoretical considerations, rather than just correlating a set of measurements to see what happens. The selection of an inadequate measure to use as a criterion in a prediction study is a common weakness. For example, a criterion of success in some endeavor is often difficult to operationally define.

A basic mistake in correlational research is to assume cause and effect rather than just association. In prediction studies, researchers sometimes fail to use proper cross-validation procedures. As stated in Chapter 6, a researcher can rely too much on statistical significance and not enough on the meaningfulness of the size of correlation coefficients.

PROBLEMS

1. Locate a thesis (or dissertation) which uses a questionnaire to gather data. Briefly summarize the methodology such as the procedures used in constructing and administering the questionnaire, the selection of the subjects, any follow-up techniques, and so on.
2. Locate two developmental studies, one cross-sectional and one longitudinal, and answer the following questions about each:
   a. Is the study descriptive or experimental?
   b. What age levels are studied?
   c. What are the independent and dependent variables?
   d. What statistics are used to make across-age comparisons?
   e. Do the variances (standard deviations squared) of the dependent variables appear to differ across age levels? Have the authors considered this? How?
   f. Does the study try to justify loss of subjects (longitudinal) or the cohort problem (cross-sectional)? How?
3. Write a brief abstract of a case study found in the literature. Indicate the problem, the sources of information used and the findings.
4. Find an observational study in the literature and write a critique of the article, concentrating on the methodology.
5. Locate and write a brief abstract of three correlational research studies as follows:
   a. a study which focuses on relationships among variables
   b. a study which develops a prediction equation
   c. a study which uses factor analysis or discriminant analysis.

Chapter 11

Experimental Research

Experimental research attempts to establish cause-effect relationships. That is, an independent variable(s) is manipulated in order to judge its effect(s) upon a dependent(s) variable. However, the process of establishing cause-effect is a difficult one. We have already discussed the fact that just because two variables are correlated does not mean one causes the other. But cause-effect cannot exist unless two variables are correlated. Because of this, correlational research is frequently used prior to experimental research. We may do an investigation to see if two variables are related prior to trying to manipulate one in order to change the other.

Also, remember that cause-effect is not established by statistics. All statistical techniques can do is reject the null hypothesis (establish that groups are significantly different) and identify the percent variance in the dependent variable accounted for by the independent variable. Neither of these procedures establishes cause-effect. Cause-effect can only be established by the application of logical thinking to well-designed experiments. This logical process establishes that there is no other reasonable explanation for the changes in the dependent variable except the manipulation done as the independent variable. The application of this logic is made possible by the selection of a good theoretical framework; the application of an appropriate experimental design; the use of the correct statistical model and analyses; proper selection and control of the independent variable; appropriate selection and measurement of the dependent variable; and finally, correct interpretation of the results.

TYPES OF VARIABLES

Chapter 3 identified five types of variables. While it may be slightly redundant, a review of these variables seems appropriate at this point:

Independent variable(s)—the cause, the treatment, the factor to be manipulated

Dependent variable(s)—the effect, the outcome, the response that is measured

Categorical variable(s)—a classification variable which is analyzed, for example, gender, race, skill level

Control variable(s)—a characteristic that is restricted, for example, use of only males, use of only blacks, use of only dance majors

Extraneous variable(s)—a factor outside the bounds of the experiment that is uncontrolled.

SOURCES OF INVALIDITY

The various types of designs we will discuss all have strengths and weaknesses. These strengths and weaknesses are identified as threats to the validity of the research design, as stated so well by Campbell and Stanley (1963, p. 5):

> Fundamental... is a distinction between *internal validity* and *external validity*. *Internal validity* is the basic minimum without which any experiment is uninterpretable: Did in fact the experimental treatments make a difference in this specific experimental instance? *External validity* asks the question of *generalizability*: To what populations, settings, or treatment variables can this effect be generalized?

Both internal and external validity are important in experiments. However, they are frequently at odds in the planning and designing of research. To gain internal validity, everything must be controlled so the researcher can eliminate all rival hypotheses as explanations for the outcomes observed. Yet in controlling and constraining the research setting to gain internal validity, the generalization (external validity) of the findings are placed in jeopardy. In studies with strong internal validity, the answer to the question—to whom, what, or where can the findings be generalized?—is very uncertain. This is because in "real world settings" everything is not controlled and may not operate in the same way as in the controlled, laboratory context. Thus, the researcher is left on the "horns of a dilemma": Is it more important to be certain that the manipulation of the independent variable caused the observed changes in the dependent variable, or is it to be able to generalize the results to other populations, settings, and so on? We cannot provide an easy answer to that question, which is often debated at scientific meetings and in the literature (for example, see Martens, 1979; Siedentop, 1980; Thomas, 1980).

To expect any single experiment to meet all research design considerations is unreasonable. A more realistic approach is to identify the specific goals and limitations of the research effort. Given the question to be answered, is internal validity or external validity the more important issue? Once that is decided, then the researcher can plan the research with one type of validity as the major focus while maintaining as much of the other type of validity as possible. Another recourse is to plan a series of experiments where the first would have strong internal validity even at the expense of external validity. If the first experiment identified that changes in the dependent measure are the result of manipulating the independent variable, subsequent experiments could be designed with increasing external validity even at the expense of internal validity. This would allow evaluation of the treatment in more "real-world" settings.

INTERNAL VALIDITY

Campbell and Stanley (1963) identify eight threats to the internal validity of experiments. If these threats are uncontrolled, the change in the dependent variable may be difficult to attribute to the manipulation of the independent variable. Table 11.1 includes definitions of these eight threats to internal validity.

History means that some unintended event occurred during the treatment period. If a study was evaluating the effects of a semester of physical education on the physical fitness of fifth graders, the fact that 60% of the children participated in a recreational soccer program would constitute a history threat to internal validity. The soccer program is also likely to produce benefits to physical fitness, which would be difficult to separate from the benefits of the physical education program.

Maturation as a threat to internal validity is most often associated with aging. This threat occurs frequently in designs in which one group is tested on several

TABLE 11.1

EIGHT THREATS TO INTERNAL VALIDITY

1. *History*—events occurring during the experiment that are not part of the treatment
2. *Maturation*—processes within the subjects that operate as a result of time passing, for example aging, fatigue, hunger
3. *Testing*—the effects of one test upon subsequent administrations of the same test
4. *Instrumentation*—changes in an instruments calibration including lack of agreement within and between observers
5. *Statistical regression*—the fact that groups selected on the basis of extreme scores are not as extreme on a subsequent testing
6. *Selection biases*—identification of comparison groups in other than a random manner.
7. *Experimental mortality*—loss of subjects from comparison groups due to nonrandom reasons
8. *Selection-maturation interaction*—specific to nonequivalent group designs where the passage of time might effect one groups but not the other

Note. Paraphrased from *Experimental and quasi-experimental designs for research*, by D.T. Campbell and J.C. Stanley, 1963, Chicago: Rand McNally. Reprinted with permission.

occasions over a long period of time. Elementary physical education teachers frequently encounter this source of invalidity when they give a physical fitness test in the early fall and again in the late spring. The children nearly always do better in the spring. The teacher would like to claim that the physical education program was the cause. Unfortunately, maturation is a plausible rival hypothesis for the observed increase. That is, the children have grown larger and stronger and thus probably run faster, jump higher, and throw further.

Testing is the effect that taking a test once has upon taking it again. If a health class was administered a 50-item multiple choice test on drugs today and again two days later, the class would do better the second time even though no treatment intervened. Taking the test once helps in taking it again. The same effect is present in physical performance test, especially if the subjects are not allowed to practice the test a few times. If a class of beginners in tennis hits 20 forehand shots delivered to them from a ball machine today and again 3 days later, the subjects will, in general, do better the second time. They learned something from performing the test the first time.

Instrumentation is a problem frequently faced in HPERD research. Suppose the researcher uses a spring-loaded device to measure strength. Unless the spring is calibrated regularly, it decreases in tension with use. Thus, the same amount of applied force will produce increased readings of strength. Instrumentation also applies to research using observers. Unless training and regular checks occur, the same observer may systematically vary his or her ratings across time (or subjects), or different observers may not rate the same performance in the same way.

Statistical regression may occur when groups are not randomly formed but are selected based upon an extreme score on some measure. For example, if a group of children have their behavior on a playground recorded on an activity scale (very active to very inactive), and two groups are formed—one of very active children and one of very inactive children—statistical regression is likely to occur when the children are next observed on the playground. The children who were very active will be less active (although still active), and the very inactive children will be more active. In other words, both groups will regress (move) toward the overall average. This phenomenon only reflects the fact that a subject's true score tends to vary about the mean. If we use extreme scores, the subject is observed on the high (or low) side of a typical performance. The next performance is usually not as extreme and, thus, when averaged across groups, the high group on the particular attribute appears to get worse while the low group appears to get better. Statistical regression is a particular problem in studies which attempt to compare highly skilled with lower skilled subjects, highly anxious versus low anxious, and so on.

Selection bias occurs when groups are formed on some basis besides random assignment. Thus, when treatments are administered, the rival hypothesis that the differences are due to initial selection biases is always present; that is, the groups were different to begin with rather than as a result of the treatments. Showing that the groups were not different at the beginning on the dependent variable does not overcome this shortcoming. Any number of other unmeasured variables on which the groups differ might explain the treatment effect.

Experimental mortality refers to loss of subjects from the treatment groups. Even when groups are randomly formed, this threat to internal validity may occur. Subjects may remain in an experimental group receiving a fitness program because it is fun, while subjects in the control group become bored, lose interest, and drop out of the study.

Finally, a *selection-maturation interaction* only occurs in specific types of designs. In these designs, one group is identified because of some specific characteristic while the other group lacks this characteristic. An example might be subjects with a psychological illness compared to a "normal" sample. Many psychological illnesses tend to improve just due to the passage of time. Thus, the effects of treatment are hard to assess when the comparison group is "normal" subjects.

Any of these eight threats to internal validity may reduce the researcher's ability to claim that the manipulation of the independent variable produced the changes in the dependent variable. The various experimental designs and how they control (or fail to control) the threats to internal validity will be discussed later in this chapter.

One additional threat to internal validity not mentioned by Campbell and Stanley has been identified. *Expectancy* (Rosenthal, 1966), refers to experimenters or testers anticipating that certain subjects will perform better. This effect, although usually unconscious on the part of the experimenter, occurs where subjects or experimental conditions are clearly labeled. For example, testers will rate "smart" subjects better than "dumb" subjects regardless of treatment. This effect is also evident in observational studies where the observers will rate posttest better than pretest performance because they expect change. Or if the experimental and control groups are identified, observers will rate the experimental group better than the control without any treatment occurring.

EXTERNAL VALIDITY

Campbell and Stanley (1963) identify four threats to external validity or the ability to generalize results to other subjects, settings, measures, and so on. These four threats are defined in Table 11.2.

Reactive or interactive effects of testing may be a problem in any design with a pretest. Suppose a fitness program is to be the experimental treatment. If a physical fitness test is administered to the sample first, the subjects in the experimental group might realize their low level of fitness and be particularly motivated to follow the prescribed program closely. However, in an unpretested population, the program might not be as effective because the subjects would be unaware of their low level of physical fitness.

The *interaction of selection biases and the experimental treatment* may prohibit the generalization of the results to subjects lacking the particular characteristics (bias). For example, a drug education program might be quite ef-

TABLE 11.2

FOUR THREATS TO EXTERNAL VALIDITY

1. *Reactive or interactive effects of testing*—the fact that the pretest may make the subject more aware of or sensitive to the upcoming treatment. This results in the treatment not being as effective without the pretest.
2. *Interaction of selection biases and the experimental treatment*—when a group is selected on some characteristic, the treatment may work only on groups possessing that characteristic.
3. *Reactive effects of experimental arrangements*—the fact that treatments which are effective in very constrained situations (e.g., laboratories) may not be effective in less constrained (more real-world) settings.
4. *Multiple-treatment interference*—when subjects receive more than one treatment, the effects of previous treatments may influence subsequent ones.

Note. Paraphrased from *Experimental and quasi-experimental designs for research*, by D.T. Campbell and J.C. Stanley, 1963, Chicago: Rand McNally. Reprinted with permission.

fective in changing the attitude toward drug use of college freshmen. This same program would probably lack effectiveness for third-year medical students.

Reactive effects of experimental arrangements is a persistant problem for laboratory-based research (e.g., exercise physiology, biomechanics, motor control and learning). In these situations, is the researcher investigating an effect, process, or outcome that is specific to the laboratory and cannot be generalized to other settings? We have referred to this earlier as ecological validity. For example, in a study employing high-speed cinematography, the skill to be filmed must be performed in a certain place with joints marked for later analysis. Is the skill performed in the same way during participation in a sport? One specific type of reactive behavior has been labeled the Hawthorne effect (Brown, 1954). This refers to the fact that subjects' performances change when attention is paid to them. This may be a threat to both internal and external validity as it is likely to produce better treatment effects as well as reducing the ability to generalize the results.

Multiple-treatment interference is most frequently a problem when the same subjects are exposed to more than one level of the treatment. Suppose subjects are going to learn to move to the hitting position in volleyball using a lead step or a cross-over step. We want to know which gets the subjects in a good hitting position most quickly. If the subjects all attempt both types of steps, the learning of one might interfere (or enhance) learning the other. Thus, the researcher's ability to generalize the findings may be confounded by use of multiple treatments. A better design might have been to have two separate groups, each of which learns one of the techniques.

The ability to generalize findings from research to other subjects or situations, is a question of random sampling more than any other. Do, in fact, the subjects, treatments, tests, and situations represent any larger populations? While a few of the experimental designs to be discussed next control certain threats to external validity, in general, the researcher controls these threats by the way the sample, treatments, situations, and tests are selected.

CONTROLLING THREATS TO VALIDITY

INTERNAL VALIDITY

Many of the threats to internal validity are controlled by equating the subjects in the experimental and control groups. This is most often done by random assignment of subjects to groups. As mentioned in Chapter 5, this allows the assumption that the groups do not differ at the beginning of the experiment. The randomization process controls for *history* up to the point of the experiment. That is, the researcher can assume that past events are equally distributed among groups. It does not control for history effects during the experiment if experimental and control subjects are treated at different times or places. Only the researcher can make sure that no events, beside the treatment, occur in one group and not the other.

Randomization also controls for *maturation* as the passage of time would be equivalent in all groups. *Statistical regression* is controlled as it only operates when groups are not randomly formed. Both *selection biases* and *selection-maturation interaction* are controlled because these threats only occur when groups are not randomly formed.

Sometimes ways other than random assignment of subjects to groups are used to attempt to control threats to internal validity. The matched-pair technique equates pairs of subjects on some characteristic and then randomly assigns the pairs to groups. The researcher might want very tight control on previous dance experience. Thus subjects would be matched on this characteristic and then randomly assigned to the experimental and control groups.

A matched-group technique may also be used. This involves assigning subjects to experimental and control groups so that the group means are equivalent on some variable. This is generally regarded as an unacceptable procedure because the groups may not be equivalent on other unmeasured variables which could effect the outcome of the research.

In within subjects designs, the subjects are used as their own control. This means each subject receives both the experimental and control treatment. In this type design, the order of treatments should be counterbalanced. That is, half the subjects should receive the experimental treatment first and then the control. The other half should receive the control first and then the experimental. If there are three levels of the independent variable (1 = control, 2 = experimental A, 3 = experimental B) then the six possible combinations should be identified (1-2-3, 1-3-2, 2-1-3, 2-3-1, 3-2-1, 3-1-2) and subjects should be randomly assigned to order.

Three of the threats to internal validity remain uncontrolled by the randomization process. *Testing* can only be controlled by elimination of the pretest. However, it can be evaluated by two of the designs (randomized groups pretest, posttest, and Solomon four group) to be discussed later in this chapter.

Instrumentation cannot be controlled or evaluated in any design. Only the experimenter can control this threat to internal validity. Section IV (Measurement) goes into some detail on techniques for controlling instrumentation. Of particular significance is test reliability. Whether the measurement is obtained from a laboratory device (oxygen analyzer), motor performance test (standing long jump), attitude-rating scale (feelings about drug use), observer (coding percentage of time a child is active), knowledge test (history of dance), or survey (available recreational facilities), the answer must be a consistent one. This frequently involves the assessment of test reliability across situations, between and within testers or observers, and within subjects. The validity of the instrument (does it measure what it was intended to measure?) must also be established to control for instrumentation. The total process of establishing appropriate instrumentation for research is called *psychometrics*. One final point about instrumentation is called the "halo effect." This occurs in ratings of several skills on the same individual. Raters seeing a skilled performance on one task are likely to rate the subject higher on subsequent tasks regardless of the level of skill displayed. In effect, the skilled behavior has rubbed off (created a halo) on later performance.

Experimental mortality is not controlled by any type experimental design. Only the experimenter, by seeing that subjects are not lost (at all, if possible) from groups, can control this. Many of these problems can be handled in advance of the research by carefully explaining the research to the subjects and the need for them to follow through with the project. (During the experiment itself, begging, pleading and crying sometimes work.)

Other ways of controlling threats to internal validity include *placebos* and *blind* and *double blind* set-ups. A placebo is used to evaluate if the treatment effect is real or due to some psychological effect. A blind study is where the subject does not know if he or she is receiving the experimental or control treatment. In a double blind study, neither the subject nor tester knows which treatment the subject is receiving. These are useful in controlling Hawthorne, expectancy, and halo effects as well as what we call the *Avis* effect (also called the *John Henry* effect)—the fact that subjects in the control group may try harder just because they are in the control group.

A good example of the use of these techniques for controlling psychological effects is the use of steroids to build strength. Many athletes have become convinced that steroids aid strength development. A number of studies were done to evaluate the effects of steroids. To combat the fact that athletes may get stronger because they think they should when using steroids, a placebo (another pill that looks just like the steroid) is used. The athletes are blind as to whether they receive the placebo or not. In a double blind, the athlete, the person dispensing the steroids (or placebo), and the testers would all be blind to which group received the steroids.

Unfortunately, until recently, these procedures had not worked very well in this specific type of study because taking large quantities of steroids made the athlete's urine smell badly. Thus, the athlete knew whether or not he or she was receiving the steroid or placebo.

Placebos are also useful in studies other than drug-related studies. When comparing treatments which require individual attention, the treatment and individual attention effects may be confounded. This is especially true when outcomes are compared to groups receiving neither the treatment nor the individual attention. Many of the significant academic benefits of perceptual-motor programs on mildly mentally retarded children and slow learners are probably due to the individual attention these children receive, rather than the perceptual-motor program. A placebo group which received the individual attention but not the perceptual-motor program could be used to evaluate this hypothesis.

EXTERNAL VALIDITY

External validity is generally controlled by selecting the subjects, treatments, experimental situation, and tests to be representative of some larger population. Of course, random selection is the key to controlling most of the threats to external validity. Remember, more than the subjects may be randomly selected: For example, the levels of treatment can be randomly selected from the possible levels; and experimental situations can be selected from possible situations.

Reactive or interactive effects of testing can be evaluated by the Solomon four group design (discussed later in this chapter). *Interaction of selection biases and the experimental treatment* is controlled by random selection of subjects. *Reactive effects of experimental arrangements* can be controlled only by the researcher. If the results are to be generalizable to "real-world" settings, the subjects must perceive the experimental arrangements as "real-world." Otherwise, the researcher is unsure whether or not the results will generalize. *Multiple-treatment interference* may be partially controlled by counterbalancing treatments across subjects. But only the researcher can control whether or not the treatments will still interfere. That decision is based upon knowledge about the treatment rather than the type of experimental design.

TYPES OF DESIGNS*

This section is divided into three categories, preexperimental designs, true experimental designs, and quasi-experimental designs. We will use the following notation:

R— random assignment of subjects to groups.

---

*Much of this section is taken from *Experimental and quasi-experimental designs for research* by D.T. Campbell and J.C. Stanley, 1963. Chicago: Rand McNally.

O— An observation or test (subscripts refer to the order of testing, that is, O_1 is the first time a test is given, while O_2 is the second test administration.

T— means a treatment is applied (subscripts T_1, T_2 on different lines refer to different treatments; subscripts on the same line mean the treatment is administered more than once); a blank space means the group is a control.

---|— a dotted line between groups means the groups are used intact rather than being randomly formed.

PREEXPERIMENTAL DESIGNS

These three designs are called preexperimental designs because they control very few of the sources of invalidity. None of the designs have random assignment of subjects to groups.

1. *One shot study*: In this design a group of subjects receives a treatment followed by a test to evaluate the treatment.

T O

This design fails all the tests of good research. All that can be said is that at a certain point in time this group of subjects performed at a certain level. In no way can the level of performance (O) be attributed to the treatment (T).

2. *One group pretest-posttest design*: This design, while very weak is better than design 1. At least we can observe if any change in performance has occurred.

O_1 T O_2

If O_2 is better than O_1, we can say that the subjects improved. Unfortunately, this design does not allow us to say *why* the subjects improved. Certainly it could be due to the treatment but it could also be due to *history*. Some event other than the treatment (T) may have occurred between the pretest (O_1) and the posttest (O_2). *Maturation* is a rival hypothesis. The subjects may have gotten better (or worse) due to the passage of time. *Testing* is a rival hypothesis—the increase at O_2 may be only as a result of experience with the test at O_1. If the group being tested is selected for some specific reason, then any of the treatments involving selection biases could occur. This design is most frequently analyzed by the dependent *t* test to evaluate if significant change occurred between O_1 and O_2.

3. *Static group comparison*. This design compares two groups, one which receives the treatment while the other does not.

T O_1
- - - - - - -
O_2

However, the dotted line between the groups indicates that the groups were not equivalent when the study began. Most frequently, this means that the groups were selected intact rather than being randomly formed. This leaves one in the position of being unable to determine if any differences between O_1 and O_2 are caused by T since O_1 and O_2 might have been different only because the groups differed initially. This design is subject to invalidity due to selection biases and the *selection-maturation interaction*. A *t* test for independent groups is used to evaluate if O_1 and O_2 differ significantly. But even if they do, the difference cannot be attributed to T.

Designs, 1, 2, and 3 are not a valid means of answering research questions. They do not represent experiments because the change in the dependent variable cannot be attributed to manipulation of the independent variable. Generally, you will not encounter these preexperimental designs in research journals, and we hope you will not find (or produce) theses or dissertations using these designs. Basically, designs 1,2, and 3 represent much wasted effort because little or nothing can be concluded from the findings.

TABLE 11.3

PREEXPERIMENTAL DESIGNS AND THEIR CONTROL OF THE THREATS TO VALIDITY

Validity Threats	One-Shot Study	One Group Pretest Posttest	Static Group
Internal			
History	–	–	+
Maturation	–	–	?
Testing		–	+
Instrumentation		–	+
Statistical regression		?	+
Selection	–	+	–
Experimental mortality	–	+	–
Selection × maturation		–	–
Expectancy	?	?	?
External			
Testing × treatment		–	
Selection biases × treatment	–	–	–
Experimental arrangements		?	
Multiple treatments			

+ = strength, – = weakness, = not relevant, ? = questionable

Adapted from Campbell and Stanley (1963).

TRUE EXPERIMENTAL DESIGNS

These are called true experimental designs because the groups are randomly formed. This allows the assumption that they were equivalent at the beginning of the research. This controls for past (but not present) *history, maturation* (should occur equally in the groups), *testing*, and all sources of invalidity that are based on nonequivalency of groups (*statistical regression, selection biases,* and *selection-maturation interaction*). However, only the experimenter can make sure that nothing happens to one group (besides the treatment) and not the other (present *history*); that scores on the dependent measure do not vary as a result of *instrumentation* problems; and that the loss of subjects is not different between the groups (*experimental mortality*).

4. *Randomized groups design*: Note that this design is very similar to design 3 except that the groups are randomly formed.

R T O_1

R $\quad$ O_2

If the researcher controls the threats to internal validity not controlled by randomization, then this design allows the conclusion that significant differences between O_1 and O_2 are due to T. An independent *t* test is used to analyze the difference between O_1 and O_2.

This design as depicted represents two levels of one independent variable. It may be extended to any number of levels of an independent variable (see example of three levels below).

R T_1 O_1

R T_2 O_2

R $\quad$ O_3

In this case three levels of the independent variable exist where one is the control and T_1 and T_2 represent two levels of treatment. This design can be analyzed by simple ANOVA which contrasts the dependent variable (O_1, O_2, O_3) as measured in the three groups. Using an example from a previous chapter, T_1 is training at 70% of $\dot{V}O_2$ max, T_2 is training at 40% of $\dot{V}O_2$ max, while the control is not training. O_1, O_2, and O_3 are the measures of cardiorespiratory fitness (12-minute run) in each group taken at the end of the training.

This design may also be extended into a *factorial* design: That is, more than one independent variable could be considered. Table 11.4 provides an example of a factorial design. Independent variable 1 has three levels (A_1, A_2, A_3) and independent variable 2 has two levels (B_1, B_2). This results in six cells (A_1B_1, A_1B_2, A_2B_1, A_2B_2, A_3B_1, A_3B_2) to which subjects are randomly assigned. At the end of the treatments, each cell is tested on the dependent variable (O_1, O_2, O_3,

TABLE 11.4

EXTENSION OF DESIGN 4 INTO A FACTORIAL DESIGN

		IV_2	
		B_1	B_2
	A_1	A_1B_1	A_1B_2
IV_1	A_2	A_2B_1	A_2B_2
	A_3	A_3B_1	A_3B_2

R	A_1B_1	O_1
R	A_1B_2	O_2
R	A_2B_1	O_3
R	A_2B_2	O_4
R	A_3B_1	O_5
R	A_3B_2	O_6

Analyzed in a 3 × 2 Factorial ANOVA

F_A = main effect of A
F_B = main effect of B
F_{AB} = interaction of A and B

O_4, O_5, O_6). This design is analyzed by a 3 × 2 factorial ANOVA which tests the effects of independent variable 1 (F_A), independent variable 2 (F_B), and their interaction (F_{AB}).

This design may also be extended to an increased number of independent variables (three, four, or more) and retain all the controls for internal validity previously discussed. Sometimes this design is used with a categorical independent variable. Looking again at Table 11.4, suppose independent variable 2 (B_1, B_2) represented two age levels. Clearly, the levels of B could not be randomly formed. The design would appear as below:

	R	A_1	O_1
B_1	R	A_2	O_2
	R	A_3	O_3
	R	A_1	O_4
B_2	R	A_2	O_5
	R	A_3	O_6

The levels of A are randomly formed within B, but the levels of B cannot be randomly formed. This no longer qualifies as a completely true experimental design but is frequently used in HPERD. This design is analyzed in a 3 × 2 ANOVA, but interpretation of results must be done more conservatively.

Any of the versions of design 4 may also have more than one dependent variable. While the consideration of the design remains the same, the statistical analysis becomes multivariate in nature. Where two or more levels of one independent variable exist but several dependent variables are present, discriminant analysis is the appropriate multivariate statistic. In the factorial versions of this design (two or more independent variables), if multiple dependent variables are used, then MANOVA is the appropriate analysis.

5. *Pretest-posttest randomized groups design.* In this design the groups are randomly formed but both groups are given a pretest as well as a posttest. This design is labeled as:

R O_1 T O_2
R O_3 O_4

The major purpose of this type design is to determine the amount of change produced by the treatment: That is, Does the experimental group change more than the control group? This design has the threat to internal validity of testing. But this threat is controlled as the O_3 to O_4 comparison in the control group includes the testing effect as well as the O_1 to O_2 comparison in the experimental group. Thus, while the testing effect cannot be evaluated in this design, it is controlled.

This design is used frequently in HPERD, but its analysis is rather complex. There are at least three common ways used to do a statistical analysis of this design. First, a factorial repeated measures ANOVA can be used. One factor (between subjects) is the treatment versus no treatment, while the second factor is pretest versus posttest (within subjects or repeated measures). A second analysis is to use simple analysis of covariance (ANCOVA) with the pretest for each group (O_1 and O_3) used to adjust the posttest (O_2 and O_4). Finally, the experimenter could subtract each subject's pretest value from the posttest value (called a gain score) and perform a simple ANOVA (or with only two groups an independent *t* test) using each subject's gain score as the dependent variable. Each of these techniques has strengths and weaknesses, but you will find all three used in the literature.

In this design the important question is, "Does one group change more than the other group?" While this issue is frequently called the analysis of *gain scores*, a more appropriate label is the *assessment of change*. Clearly, in a learning study the change is expected to be gain. But in an exercise physiology study, the change might be decreased performance caused by fatigue. Regardless, the issues are the same. How can this change be assessed appropriately?

The easiest answer is to obtain a change score by subtracting the pretest from the posttest. While this is intuitively attractive, it does have some problems. First, these change scores tend to be unreliable. Second, the subjects who begin low in performance can improve more easily than those who begin with a high score. Thus, initial score is negatively correlated with the change score. How would you like your tennis performance evaluated on change if your initial score was high (e.g., 5 successful forehand drives out of 10 trials), compared with a friend who began with a low score initially (e.g., 1 out of 10 successful hits). If you improved to 7 out of 10 on the final test, and your friend improved to 5 out of 10 (the level of your initial score), your friend has improved twice as much as you (a gain of 4 versus 2 successful hits).

The issues involved in the proper measurement of change are complex ones. We cannot treat these issues here. However, much has been written on this topic. We suggest you read Schmidt (1982, Chapter 11) about this problem in motor learning and performance, or for more complete coverage, see Harris (1963).

This design may also be extended into more complex forms. First, more than two (pretest and posttest) repeated measures can be used. This is very frequent in the motor learning and control area of physical education. Two randomly formed groups of subjects might be measured 20, 30, 40 or more times as they learn a task. The two groups might differ in the information they are given after each trial. Thus, if 30 trials were given, the design is a 2 (groups) × 30 (trials) and a 2 × 30 ANOVA with repeated measures on the second factor (trials) might be the statistical analysis. (There are other choices).

Sometimes the design is extended in other ways. For example, we could take the design in Table 11.4 (a 2 × 3 factorial) and add a third factor of a pre- and posttest. This would result in a three-way factorial with repeated measures on the third factor.

All of the versions of this design are subject to the first threat to external validity—*reactive or interactive effects of testing*. The pretest may make the subject more sensitive to the treatment and thus reduce the ability to generalize the findings to an unpretested population.

6. *Solomon four group design*: This design is the only true design to specifically evaluate one of the threats to external validity, *reactive or interactive effects of testing*. The design is depicted as:

R	O_1	T	O_2
R	O_3		O_4
R		T	O_5
R			O_6

As you can judge, it is a combination of designs 4 and 5. The purpose is explicitly to determine if the pretest results in increased sensitivity of the subjects to the treatment. This design allows a replication of the treatment effect (is $O_2 > O_4$ and is $O_5 > O_6$), an assessment of the amount of change due to the treatment [is $(O_2 - O_1) > (O_4 - O_3)$], an evaluation *testing* effect (is $O_4 > O_6$), and finally does the pretest interact with the treatment is $(O_2 > O_5)$? Thus, this is a very powerful experimental design.

Unfortunately, it is also an inefficient design. Obviously, twice as many subjects are required in this design. This results in very limited use, especially among graduate students doing theses and dissertations. In addition, no good way exists to statistically analyze this design. The best alternative (and this does not use all the data) is a 2 × 2 ANOVA set up as:

	No T	T
Pretested	O_4	O_2
Unpretested	O_6	O_5

Thus, independent variable 1 has two levels (pretested and unpretested), and independent variable 2 has two levels (no treatment and treatment). In the ANOVA, the *F* ratio for IV_1 establishes the effects of pretesting; the *F* for IV_2 establishes the effects of the treatment; and the *F* for interaction evaluates the external validity threat of interaction of the pretest with the treatment.

TABLE 11.5

TRUE EXPERIMENTAL DESIGNS AND THEIR CONTROL OF THE THREATS TO VALIDITY

Validity Threats	Randomized Groups	Pretest Posttest Rand. Gps.	Solomon Four Group
Internal			
History	+	+	+
Maturation	+	+	+
Testing	+	+	+
Instrumentation	+	+	+
Statistical regression	+	+	+
Selection	+	+	+
Experimental mortality	+	+	+
Selection × maturation	+	+	+
Expectancy	?	?	?
External			
Testing × treatment	−	+	+
Selection biases × treatment	?	?	?
Experimental arrangements	?	?	?
Multiple treatments			

+ = strength, − = weakness, = not relevant, ? = questionable

Adapted from Campbell and Stanley (1963).

QUASI-EXPERIMENTAL DESIGNS

Not all research in which an independent variable is manipulated fits clearly into one of the true experimental designs. As researchers attempt to increase external and ecological validity, the careful and complete control of the true designs becomes increasingly difficult, if not impossible. The purpose of quasi-designs is to fit the design to more "real-world" settings while still controlling as many of the threats to internal validity as possible. The use of these types of designs in HPERD and the field of education has increased considerably in recent years. The most authoritative text on quasi-experimental designs is probably Cook and Campbell's (1979) *Quasi-experimention: Design and analysis issues for field settings*.

7. *Time series designs*: This design has only one group but attempts to show that the change which occurs when the treatment is interjected differs from the times when it is not. This design may be depicted as:

$$O_1 \quad O_2 \quad O_3 \quad O_4 \quad T \quad O_5 \quad O_6 \quad O_7 \quad O_8$$

The basis for claiming that the treatment causes the effect is that a constant rate of change can be established from O_1 to O_4 and from O_5 to O_8, but that this rate of changes varies between O_4 and O_5. For example, in Figure 11.1, the lines (A, B, C) on the left graph suggest that the insertion of the treatment (T) results in a visible change across observations while the lines (D, E, F, G) on the right of the figure indicate the treatment has no reliable effect.

The typical statistical analyses previously discussed do not fit time series designs very well. For example, a repeated measure ANOVA with appropriate follow-ups applied to line C (Figure 11.1) might indicate that all observations (O_1 to

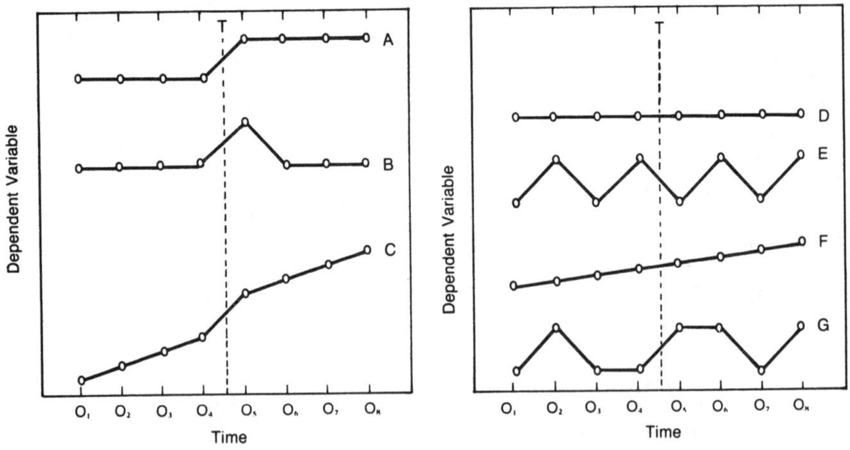

Figure 11.1 Examples of times series changes. Adapted from *Experimental and quasi-experimental designs for research* (p. 38) by D. Campbell and J. Stanley, 1963, The American Educational Research Association, Boston, MA: The Houghton-Mifflin Company. Reprinted with permission.

O_8) differ significantly even though we can see that the rate of increase changes between O_4 and O_5. We are not going to present the details, but statistical techniques are available to test both the slopes and intercepts in time series designs.

This type design appears to control for a number of the threats to internal validity. For example, *maturation* would appear to be constant between observations. *Testing* effects can also be evaluated though they could be difficult to separate from maturation. *Selection biases* also appear to be controlled because the same subjects are used at each observation. Of course, *history, instrumentation,* and *mortality* are, as always, only controlled to the extent the researcher controls them.

8. *Reversal design:* This type design is increasingly used in school settings and is depicted as:

$$O_1 \quad O_2 \quad T_1 \quad O_3 \quad O_4 \quad T_2 \quad O_5 \quad O_6$$

Like the time series, the purpose is to determine a baseline measure (O_1 to O_2), evaluate the treatment (O_2 to O_3), return to baseline (O_3 to O_4), evaluate the treatment (O_4 to O_5), and finally return to baseline (O_5 to O_6).

In Figure 11.2, lines A, B, and C on the left suggest the insertion of the treatment is effective while lines D, E, and F on the right do not support a treatment effect. Statistical analyses for reversal designs also need to be tests of the slope and intercept of the lines among various observation.

One final point is applicable to designs 7 and 8: We have discussed these designs as if one group is measured repeatedly over time; however, the format of these two designs is also used in single-subject research. Instead of one group being followed across all the time periods, a single subject is followed. But many more observations (data points) are needed when these designs are used for single-subject research. However, single-subject designs do not lend themselves to statistical analysis.

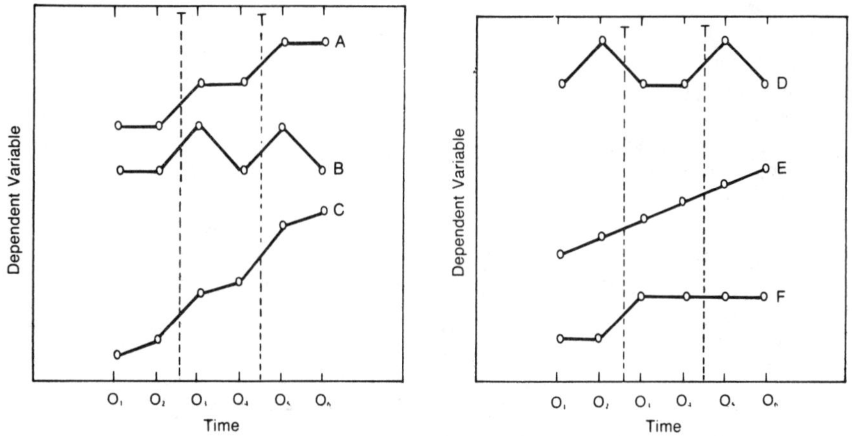

Figure 11.2 Examples of changes across time in reversal designs.

9. *Nonequivalent control group*: This design is frequently used in "real-world" settings because groups cannot be randomly formed. The design is as follows:

$$\frac{O_1 \quad T \quad O_2}{O_3 \qquad\quad O_4}$$

You will recognize this as design 5 without randomization. Frequently, researchers will compare O_1 to O_3 and declare the groups equivalent if this comparison is not significant. Unfortunately, because the groups do not differ on the pretest does not mean they are not different on any number of unmeasured characteristics which could affect the outcome of the research.

If the groups differ when compared (O_1 versus O_3), ANCOVA is usually employed to adjust O_2 and O_4 for initial differences. While this design is frequently used, we believe designs 7 and 8 are much stronger quasi-experimental designs for investigating intact situations.

TABLE 11.6

QUASI-EXPERIMENTAL DESIGNS AND THEIR CONTROL OF THE THREATS TO VALIDITY

Validity Threats	Time Series	Nonequiv. Control	Reversal	Ex Post Facto
Internal				
History	–	–	–	?
Maturation	+	+	+	?
Testing	+	+	+	
Instrumentation	?	+	?	
Statistical regression	+	?	+	
Selection	+	+	+	–
Experimental mortality	+	+	+	
Selection × maturation	+	–	+	–
Expectancy	?	?	?	?
External				
Testing × treatment	–	–	?	–
Selection biases × treatment	?	?	?	?
Experimental arrangements	?	?	?	?
Multiple treatments			?	

+ = strength, – = weakness, = not relevant, ? = questionable

Adapted from Campbell and Stanley (1963).

10. *Ex post facto design*: In its simplest instance, this is design 3 in which the treatment is not under the control of the experimenter. For example, we frequently compared the characteristic of athletes versus nonathletes, skilled players versus unskilled players, and expert dancers versus novice dancers. In effect, we are searching for variables that discriminate among these groups. Our interest usually resides in questions like "Did these variables influence the way these groups became different?" Of course, this design cannot answer this question, but it may provide interesting characteristics for manipulation in other experimental designs.

There are other quasi-experiment designs, but these cover the frequently used types. Of course, quasi-designs never quite control internal validity as well as true designs; but they do allow us to investigate areas when either true designs cannot be used or the use of a true design significantly reduces external validity.

Chapters 8, 9, 10, and 11 have provided an overview of most types of research in HPERD. Based upon these chapters, you should now understand the uses of various types of research to solve problems. The following chapter presents a special type of investigation process, creative research and its specific application to dance choreography.

PROBLEMS

Locate two research papers in refereed journals in your area of interest. One paper should have a true experimental design and the other, a quasi-experimental design. Answer the following questions about each:

1. Describe the type of design. Draw a picture of it using the notations from this chapter. How many independent variables are there? How many levels of each? What are they? How many dependent variables? What are they?
2. What type of statistical analysis was used? Explain how it fits the design.
3. Identify the threats to internal validity that are controlled and uncontrolled? Explain each.
4. Identify the controlled and uncontrolled threats to external validity? Explain each.

Chapter 12

Creative Research*

Terry Worthy

NATURE OF CREATIVE RESEARCH

In one sense all research endeavors are creative; however, creative research is a specific type of investigation generally associated with the arts. It is research of a slightly different order than the analytical, descriptive, or experimental research which seek to produce factual data. The aim of creative research is the actual creation of an art product possessing aesthetic quality (Van Tuyl, 1968). An art product possessing aesthetic quality is one judged to have value or some claim to aesthetic merit. The art product may emerge from any of the various art forms, including visual, performing, and literary. Some examples might be the creation of a collection of poetry, a contemporary opera, a liturgical dance composition, or a sculpture series in metal.

There is no difference in producing art and producing creative research except that in the latter, the problem is stated specifically, the product is achieved through a systematic process, and the results are presented for public sharing. Some would argue that the restraints imposed by the systematic process of research would stifle or inhibit the spontaneity of creative work. However, there are many benefits derived from an investigation that is carefully designed to scrutinize the creative process and to examine the perceptual qualities and intrinsic values of the finished art product. Sharing the product includes not only the performance or exhibition, but in many cases, may also include a written account of the procedures involved in the actual creation of the work. The written manuscript pro-

*We believe this chapter adds a rather unique contribution. The process of choreographic research is not well documented in either the research methods or dance literature. We would like to thank Dr. Terry Worthy, Coordinator of Dance, Louisiana State University, for preparing this chapter as an important contribution in this area of research methods in HPERD.

vides valuable information regarding the qualities of the work and insight into the creative process itself.

The art product must have some claim to originality. The product may not be an entirely new idea, but should represent a new point of view or different approach to the idea. The original endeavor must also make a contribution of value to existing knowledge in terms of artistic content or treatment.

CHOREOGRAPHIC RESEARCH

Creative research in this text is limited to the art of dance and involves the creation of an original dance composition. Sometimes called choreographic research, this investigation focuses on the choreographic solution to a problem. The choreographic problem may spring from almost any source of motivation as long as the selected problem lends itself to expression through the medium of movement.

After identifying the problem to be solved, a subsequent investigation into the literature and related art work is undertaken. A decision must then be made regarding the most appropriate dance idiom and the format best suited to solving the choreographic problem. Evaluative criteria must be carefully chosen in terms of the choreographer's stated problem or intent. These criteria are then used in preliminary showings of the work in progress for the purpose of guidance. The revised choreography is then presented publicly, and a final choreographic evaluation is conducted. Finally, a written manuscript is completed which includes a statement of the problem, procedural developments, and conclusions in terms of a retrospective view of the choreography.

Before describing choreographic research procedures in detail, it should be understood that an important prerequisite to creative research is a fundamental knowledge of choreographic principles and previous experience in the craft of dance composition. The choreographer must be highly perceptive and sensitive to the medium of movement as an art form. Those undertaking creative research may prepare themselves through formal choreography and dance theory course work and through familiarization with the literature. Additional preparation may include exposure to the art of choreography by viewing dance concerts and films and through further study of aesthetic principles as they relate to dance and to other art forms.

SELECTION OF THE CHOREOGRAPHIC PROBLEM

There are several important considerations in the initial phase of selecting the choreographic problem. The problem should be of sufficient breadth to stimulate choreographic exploration, but should not be of such complexity that it goes beyond the choreographer's ability. A problem too large in scope may result in an incomplete exploration of the thematic materials or in a naive choreographic treatment of those materials. For example, a problem which attempts to depict the creation of the world is obviously too cosmic in nature and too broad in scope to be a practical choice. Literary works with highly philosophical content may also be poor choices because the content has little inherent action or movement potential. Certain literary themes and ideational sources have been the inspiration for so many different artists and mediums that a fresh approach or new treatment of the material would be a difficult choreographic problem.

The types of problems suited to choreographic research are numerous and may evolve from ideas, events, sensory and emotional perceptions both real and imagined. Further, the problem itself may be one of unusual choreographic treatment, such as caricature or satire. Possible choreographic problems may also be derived from various choreographic approaches such as improvisation and chance, as well as the integration of movement and other media. It would be futile to attempt a complete listing of possibilities; however, the following choreographic theses, the essence of which are implied in their titles, illustrate the range and diversity of potential choreographic topics: *Rhapsody in blue: A celebration of American music and dance* (Bailey, 1976), *A farewell to Lincoln Square: A choreographic thesis based on the paintings of Rafael Soyer* (Loring, 1977), *A choreographic problem: Application of the philosophies of De Stijl, Cubism, and Surrealism in the creation of three dances* (Parris, 1978), and *Computerized choreography* (Sidrow, 1978). Oftentimes a problem emerges which has implications for use in formal educational settings. An example of this is Raabe's (1981) thesis, in which the choreographic problem was to explain the nature of dance to children by choreographing a lecture demonstration. This problem involves not only synthesizing an enormous amount of material, but also translating the material into movement and improvisational structures elucidating the choreographer's meaning in a manner that a simple narration or lecture would not. Many times the research topic will require an integration of art forms, such as the multi-media choreographic thesis entitled *Parabola* (Gottfried, 1980), which incorporated dance, music, and film. An example of a thesis employing electronic manipulation created by De Freitas (1975) is entitled *Space toys—an event for dancers and audience in an electronically modifiable sound and light environment.*

Of course, practical matters need to be considered in the selection of the problem. The demands of producing the choreographic endeavor must be in balance with available resources. The choreographer must think in terms of number and skill level of available dancers as well as the cost of sets, costumes, accompaniment, and other production elements. The presentation site, whether it be a theatre, museum, or particular environmental setting, must also be considered before the problem is finalized.

REVIEW OF LITERATURE

The procedures involved in the review of literature are determined by the intrinsic nature of the choreographic problem. The problem may require an extensive search for published and unpublished literature. For example, a choreographic work based on a particular character in history or one using a mythological theme would require in-depth background readings in order to prepare the choreographer for projecting these motifs through dance adequately. In Novak's (1982) liturgical choreographic thesis, performed in a church setting and based on *A ceremony of carols* by Benjamin Britten, the following areas were reviewed: a brief history of the development of dance in the Christian church; the evolution of the carol from the medieval dance form; and a description of Benjamin Britten's musical composition in terms of style and form.

Another type of choreographic problem might necessitate an inquiry into related art. For example, if the problem is an attempt to reflect or elaborate on a painter's style through movement, the choreographer would then review the available paintings produced by the artist as well as any written material. Problems originating from a musical source might require concert attendance in order to hear a particular artist's interpretation of a musical composition.

In nonliteral dance where choreography is based not on a specific idea, but solely on communication through movement and motion, the literature review may be less extensive. It should, however, help prepare the choreographer for the choreographic exploration and development of kinetic properties, and should facilitate the best possible selection of accompaniment and other production elements. Wall (1981), in her nonliteral choreographic thesis entitled *Lumen proprium*, briefly reviewed materials related to presentational choreography, effective use of production elements, and the properties of refraction and reflection which were used initially as motivation for movement.

It is unwise to predetermine the precise extent of the literature review. The search for background literature should be an ongoing process to locate all information that would further equip the choreographer for solving the selected problem. The process of reviewing the literature for a choreographic thesis is not unlike that used in the conventional forms of research; therefore, the choreographer may follow essentially the same procedures as those outlined in Chapter 2.

CHOREOGRAPHIC REQUIREMENTS

Specific requirements must be delineated before the choreography is developed. An initial task is the selection of the idiom which best suits the choreographic problem. The idioms of modern dance, ballet, and ethnic dance are generally accepted as the kinds of dance having the greatest potential for development in terms of aesthetic merit. However, there are certain problems such as the choreography of musicals or dramatic productions in which tap or jazz might be entirely appropriate forms of dance. The specific nature of the selected problem will ultimately be the determining factor regarding the selection of the idiom.

Other factors determined by the nature of the chosen problem will be the scope and format. In this instance, scope refers to the actual length of the choreographic presentation and not the breadth of the problem itself. If the choreographic project is thesis research used in partial fulfillment of degree requirements, there may be a minimum length specification. Authorities in dance research agree that approximately 20 minutes should be the minimum length for a choreographic thesis (Worthy, 1977, p.47). In nonthesis research, the requirements may be less stringent and a specific length may not be predetermined.

The choreographic problem dictates the exact format and will generally fall into one of the following categories: a single dance or a continuous piece such as a dance drama, a selected number of individual dances, a suite of related dances, an integral part of a musical or dramatic production, a concert or an entire program of dance, and a lecture demonstration. Specific formats may be stipulated in thesis research, but under other circumstances, the format is a decision of the choreographer based on the structural form arising from the specific problem.

Requirements involving the performance site and production design must also be established. It is to the choreographer's advantage to know exactly where the choreographic endeavor will be presented publicly, because the character and actual physical dimensions of the performance site may influence the choreography itself. The site may limit or enhance choreographic possibilities. Prior knowledge of the size and shape of the performance area, as well as the type of flooring, possible seating arrangements, and technical facilities, will greatly benefit the choreographer in terms of determining the type of movement, number of dancers, the floor patterns, the entrances and exits, and, in particular, the use of production elements.

If the production elements are to be an integral part of the choreographic process, the total design must be considered from the outset. Production elements include accompaniment, costume, lighting and set designs, properties, program notes, and publicity. They are employed to enhance and sustain the choreographic idea. The choreographer may or may not be responsible for production design. If the choreographic endeavor is a thesis research project and if the choreographer is qualified, designing the production elements will probably be an integral part of the choreographic requirement. The choreographer, with practically no exception, will be responsible for selecting the accompaniment, if accompaniment is used. Requirements regarding the choreographer's responsibility in designing the other production elements will vary but should be determined as early as possible in the development of the research project.

At this point, the choreographic problem has been defined and thought must be given to establishing evaluative criteria as a guideline in the actual shaping of the choreography and as a standard in the eventual decision regarding aesthetic merit. Assigning value or aesthetic merit to a choreographic work and determining common qualities or properties of artful works are topics aestheticians have been battling for centuries, and the definitive solution will not be attempted in this chapter. However, some agreement exists on the means to a successful solution of choreographic problems and on the effective use of compositional principles, which will serve as the basic criteria for judging the creative effort. These criteria, if carefully chosen, will assist the choreographer in furthering the purpose, the direction, and the clarification of the work in progress. Detailed information on evaluative criteria appears later in this chapter.

CHOREOGRAPHIC DEVELOPMENT

The next step, which is the essence of choreographic research and likened to the gathering of data, is the actual selection and organization of movement. The choreographer, never straying too far from the problem to be solved, must utilize the power of imagination coupled with knowledge of the choreographic craft to begin the movement structure. The compositional materials require manipulation and rearticulation until the movement materials convey the choreographic intent. A description by Virginia Moomaw (1968, p.134), clearly summarizes this challenging process:

> A successful dance means that much material—ideas, information, movement with its psychological and kinetic properties—has been examined in terms of the idea of the dance. Much has been discarded in the search for the most effective and economical phrase, the one best design of the bodies, the best use for all of the elements used to shape this dance.

During this creative phase, any choreographic approach or improvisational structure may be employed in order to produce initial movement themes which are eventually developed into well-articulated sequences to effectively communicate the dance idea.

Before the choreographer begins to teach and rehearse movement, auditions should be held to select the dancers best suited to the style of the particular work. As the composition is taught, changes and adaptations may occur in the planned sequences and spatial patterns and relationships. It is very important for the choreographer to visually perceive the actual movement patterns and spatial relationships as they develop; therefore, the choreographer should not dance in the piece. If for some reason the choreographer must perform, an understudy should be employed until the choreography is complete.

The choreographer should maintain a diary or log throughout the research. Entries will note movement and production possibilities, potential spatial designs as well as personal reactions to technical problems in movement. The diary should prove useful in the actual development of the choreography and later in the retrospective view of the choreographer, which may be required in the written work.

Because the choreographer may have difficulty being objective about the work, outside guidance is beneficial. The research director or person(s) selected to evaluate the dance should do so as the choreography develops in what is known as *preliminary showings*. These are informal evaluations in which the choreography is presented as a work in progress for the purpose of guidance. At this point, even though the choreography may not be complete or technically perfect, the implementation of certain criteria may assist the choreographer. The preliminary showing should allow the choreographer and those evaluating the work to answer the following questions: (1) Is the selected theme suitable for development through dance? (2) Is the work developing with clarity, and is it free of extraneous movements, elements, and development? (3) Is the dance style appropriate to the choreographic intent? (4) Are the movement themes inventive and thoroughly developed? (5) Does the work demonstrate effective use of space patterns and relationships, rhythmic organizations, and movement dynamics? and (6) Does the work evidence an inventive approach to the dance idea and its treatment? These questions represent important criteria, and if the work is lacking in any of these areas the choreographer should be made aware so revisions can be attempted. This procedure is actually a time-saving device in that any choreographic element needing further development is noted early in the research process.

The number of preliminary showings will depend on the strength of the first showing and on the choreographer's ability to incorporate suggestions to enhance the work. The showing may involve the use of a formal written instrument, such as the one presented in Table 12.1, whereby the evaluators check the presence or absence of those criteria listed in the preceeding paragraph; or the evaluation may simply involve a verbal exchange of ideas and opinions. The preliminary showings also provide the choreographer an opportunity to use the evaluators as a sounding board in discussing the potential design of production elements.

PRESENTATION AND EVALUATION

After all choreographic revisions have been made, the choreographer finalizes plans for producing the work. Assuming the choreography is complete and the dances are technically ready for performance, the choreographer moves from the studio to the presentation site for technical and dress rehearsals. Almost always, last-minute changes arise from unexpected problems when costumes, lights, sets, or live music are added; and always difficulties arise from the work when it is placed into a new space. Therefore, the choreographer must not be inflexible to change and must be cognizant of how each change affects the overall production.

The final evaluation generally occurs at the time of dress rehearsal or the public presentation of the work. All previously selected criteria are now under consideration, including those regarding production elements. In addition to the criteria used in the preliminary showings, several other items should also be considered. The first item in the final evaluation concerns whether or not the researcher has choreographed an effective solution to the stated problem. In most cases, the response to this will be positive unless, of course, the choreographer strayed in some way from the original intent. Another criterion, one considered essential to successful composition, is whether or not the work demonstrated an effective handling of the movement materials, thereby producing organic form. Organic form is derived from the structure and internal relationships of all components which give the composition its unique character and a sense of wholeness and order. Organic form is more than structural form; it is a means of demonstrating the work as an entity in which every component is interrelated and indispensable.

A criterion which applies only to choreographic problems which are narrative or otherwise literal in nature addresses the use of abstraction and symbolic

TABLE 12.1
PRELIMINARY CHOREOGRAPHIC EVALUATION

Choreographer ______________________ Composition Title ______________________

The Choreographic Work:	YES	NO	REMARKS
Demonstrates that the selected theme was suitable for development through the dance medium	___	___	
Communicates the dance intent with clarity and is free in extraneous movement, elements, and development	___	___	
Employs movements and dance styles appropriate to the choreographic intent	___	___	
Demonstrates thorough development of movement themes and inventive movement relationships	___	___	
Demonstrates an inventive approach to the thematic source and its treatment	___	___	
Demonstrates effective use of space patterns and relationships in order to further the intent and create visual or psychological interest	___	___	
Demonstrates effective rhythmic pattern and rhythmic organization in accordance with the dance idea	___	___	
Demonstrates effective manipulation of movement qualities to convey intent and avoid monotony in dynamics	___	___	

Note. Revised from *The creative thesis: Criteria for procedural development and evaluation*. Unpublished dissertation, by T. Worthy, 1977, Texas Woman's University, Texas.

movements. The completed compositional endeavor should allude to ideas and suggest images through abstraction and stylization of movement. The idea to be articulated can certainly be conveyed through abstracted movement and a literal reproduction of the dance idea should be avoided.

Production elements should be considered in terms of their general contributions to the work as a whole. Together they should support and enhance the dance idea. The following questions should be asked when considering specific elements:

1. Was the accompaniment appropriate in scope and character to the dance idea and movement style?
2. Were the costumes appropriate in style and color to the dance idea without restricting or prohibiting effective execution of the dance movement?
3. Did the lighting design create an appropriate atmosphere and enhance the dancer's movement?
4. Were the set designs and properties both visually and functionally effective?

The last items concern the degree to which the dance achieved and maintained interest. First, did the finished product employ sufficient repetition and variety of movement? Repetition of movement is necessary to explicate significant sections, and adequate variety of movement is equally important in maintaining interest. Second, were transitions used effectively in the evolution of the dance from its initial phase to its conclusion, giving the work continuity and a sense of ongoingness? Finally, was the dance performed with vitality and sufficient technical proficiency to maintain interest in order for the choreographic intent to be clearly communicated?

The manner in which the evaluation is conducted and the importance placed upon that evaluation will depend on whether or not the researcher is using the project in partial fulfillment of degree requirements or as an independent work for personal growth. In independent or nonthesis research, these criteria may be implemented informally and may require only a verbal critique or discussion of the work in terms of its choreographic strengths and weaknesses. Oftentimes, however, in thesis research, a more formal evaluation is staged in order to accept or reject the work as a valid study. A lack of consensus among reviewers may occur when determining the artistic significance of the dance product; therefore, a written instrument may be used as an evaluative tool in the implementation of criteria. A final evaluative instrument is shown in Table 12.2 and is offered as a guide in analyzing the qualitative aspects of the choreographic work.

Both the preliminary and final evaluative instruments may be adapted to meet the particular needs of the individual work. Certain other criterion items may need to be added while some, if nonapplicable, should be deleted. The criteria listed are of a general nature and would perhaps be more useful if reworded in order to make them more specific to the choreographic work. Certain items lend

TABLE 12.2

FINAL CHOREOGRAPHIC EVALUATION RATING SCALE

Choreographer ______________________ Composition Title ______________________

The Choreographic Work:	Circle Response				
Demonstrates an effective solution to the choreographer's stated problem	1	2	3	4	5★★
Demonstrates the selected theme was suitable for development through the dance medium	1	2	3	4	5
Demonstrates effective selection and development of materials producing organic form	1	2	3	4	5
Communicates the dance intent with clairty and is free of extraneous movement, elements, and development	1	2	3	4	5
Employs movements and dance styles appropriate to the choreographic intent	1	2	3	4	5
Demonstrates thorough development of movement themes and inventive movement relationships	1	2	3	4	5
Demonstrates an inventive approach which creates images and alludes to ideas, thus avoiding a literal reproduction	1	2	3	4	5
Demonstrates sufficient and effective variety to maintain interest	1	2	3	4	5
Develops from the initial phase to conclusion with effective and subtle transition	1	2	3	4	5
Demonstrates effective use of space patterns and relationships in order to further the intent and create visual or psychological interest	1	2	3	4	5
Demonstrates effective rhythmic pattern and rhythmic organization in accordance with the dance idea	1	2	3	4	5

TABLE 12.2 Cont.

The Choreographic Work:	Circle Response				
Employs production elements (lights, costumes, set design, properties, and accompaniment) effectively to enhance the choreographic work	1	2	3	4	5
Employs accompaniment appropriate in scope and character to the dance idea and movement style	1	2	3	4	5
Employs lighting design which creates an appropriate atmosphere and enhances the dancer's movement	1	2	3	4	5
Employs costumes appropriate in style and color to the dance idea without restricting or prohibiting effective execution of the dance movement	1	2	3	4	5
Employs set designs and properties which are both visually and functionally effective	1	2	3	4	5
Is performed with vitality and sufficient technical proficiency	1	2	3	4	5
Is of sufficient interest to capture and maintain audience attention	1	2	3	4	5
Demonstrates effective use of repetition in order to explicate dominant or significant passages	1	2	3	4	5
Demonstrates effective manipulation of movement qualities to convey intent and avoid monotony in dynamics	1	2	3	4	5

★★5 represents the rating of highest merit

Note. Revised from *The creative thesis: Criteria for procedural development and evaluation* unpublished dissertation, by T. Worthy, 1977, Texas Woman's University, Texas.

themselves to dichotomous measurement while others tend to be more easily implemented using a rating scale, showing the extent to which criterion items are demonstrated in the choreographic work. Therefore, another method of adapting the instrument is to combine the checklist and rating scale methods into a single instrument. If certain criteria are considered more important to successful dance compositions, then the instrument can be further adapted by weighing the criteria. Weighing can be achieved by placing criteria into categories such as essential, important, and desirable, and assigning numerical values to the categories according to their relative importance to effective choreography. Regardless of the form the instrument takes, it is imperative to establish *a priori* a minimum point total for interpreting the results. The point total becomes the minimal standard for accepting the choreographic research as having significant artistic merit.

RECORD OF THE CHOREOGRAPHIC RESEARCH

In many cases, a written record or manuscript of the research will be required of the choreographer. In order to preserve and to further share the research, a film, videotape, or notated score of the choreography may also be stipulated. There are those who may prefer videotape to film or perhaps Laban notation to other notation systems, but it is generally agreed that there should be both a written and filmed account of the project.

The exact form of the written record is not standard but will vary with each choreographic problem. Certain items are imperative if the account is to represent the research thoroughly and accurately and if the written account is to be of any real value to other readers. Items generally comprising the written document are listed in the following paragraphs.

Obviously, the first item for inclusion, a *statement of the choreographer's intent*, should be worded clearly and succinctly. The *review of related literature and art* with accompanying bibliography may or may not be included in the final document depending on its relevance to the reader's comprehension of the problem. A *list of procedures* and, if necessary, an explanation of the methods used to produce the research should be clearly delineated.

A DESCRIPTION OF THE CHOREOGRAPHY

A description of the choreography should be included and may appear in various forms. A formally notated score offers the most thorough record of the choreography and may be required if the choreographer possesses adequate facility in the acceptable notation system. Another method of describing the work is simply a general summary of the types and qualities of movement and the characteristic style of the dance written in the choreographer's own style. Important movement themes and symbolic actions may also be explained in this manner. An additional device which may be employed is a diagrammatic account of the spatial designs.

This is especially useful in clarifying floor patterns and specific usage of stage directions and areas. Sketches and photographs may prove beneficial in conveying choreographic details as well.

A DESCRIPTION OF THE SPECIFIC USE OF PRODUCTION ELEMENTS

The accompaniment should be documented giving appropriate credit to composers and performers. Many times the choreographer will supply a justification for the selection of a certain piece of music or type of accompaniment and explain the particular integration of choreography and accompaniment. A light plot, description of any special effects, techniques, or instrumentation, as well as a general summary of the function of the lighting plan, will also be included in this section of the written document. Next, the costume selection and construction should be discussed as it relates to the choreographic intent. Sketches and photographs are helpful as references in this description. More than helpful, sketches and photographs are almost essential to the description of set designs and properties. If the set is fully integrated into the choreography becoming more than mere stage decor, an explanation of this achievement would be necessary. Finally, program notes, if used, will be included along with any further material which will help describe production aspects of the choreographic research.

After describing production elements, the choreographer then documents his or her subjective thoughts about the choreographic project in a section that can be appropriately titled, *Retrospective View of the Choreography*. The choreographer writes a summary of the process in terms of problems encountered, insights gained, and other information related to creative aspects of the experience. The diary, which provides a chronological record of thoughts and occurrences during the creative phase, is then discussed in terms of strengths and weaknesses. The choreographer gives a personal evaluation of the composition and relates retrospectively how and why choreographic decisions were made, and how they might have been different. If a formal evaluation were performed, the results would be described along with the choreographer's personal reaction to opinions expressed in the evaluation.

If the choreographic project is thesis research, all the preceding information should be compiled in accordance with an acceptable editorial style. In order to share the research, a bound copy of the manuscript should be placed in the library and an abstract of the choreographic project should be reported to appropriate sources as completed research.

The film or videotape provides another record of the choreographic project. Depending on when it is made, the filmed record may be of assistance in the evaluation of the dance composition and may be helpful to the choreographer in writing the retrospective account. The film or tape should be produced in such a way that the choreography is shown as clearly and completely as possible. This record should not be subject to special filming techniques or editing. The major benefit of this additional record is, of course, to share the work further and to serve in the reconstruction of the choreography, if desired.

A precaution should perhaps be inserted here to those interested or involved in choreographic research. The precaution addresses the idea that dance and choreographic design flourish in diversity; therefore, no holy commandments (standard procedures) can apply. The methods of developing, presenting, and evaluating choreographic research presented in this chapter are guidelines and should be discerningly implemented. Without compromising the basic tenents of research, the selected problem should reflect the individuality and interests of the choreographer, and the exact method and requirements of procedural development should be derived intrinsically from the unique nature of the choreographic endeavor. The flexibility inherent in designing choreographic research allows research standards to be maintained without inhibiting or infringing on the creative act of choreography.

Section IV

MEASUREMENT

A basic step in the scientific method of problem solving is collection of the data; therefore, an understanding of measurement theory is necessary. Although measurement is discussed here as a research tool, measurement is in itself an area of research. The measurement specialist in physical education, for example, is concerned with test reliability theory and the analysis of the measurement process regardless of what aspect of psychomotor performance is being measured. In this section, three chapters are devoted to measurement as it applies to the types of research commonly performed in the fields within HPERD.

Chapter 13 explains the fundamental criteria for judging the quality of measures used in collecting research data: validity and reliability. Validity is the degree to which a test or instrument measures what it purports to measure. The different forms of validity—logical, content, criterion, and construct— are described. Ways by which the different types of validity may be established are also explained. Reliability refers to the consistency and dependability of a measure. A test must be reliable in order to be valid. Several techniques are discussed by which coefficients of reliability may be calculated for different types of measures.

Chapters 14 and 15 are devoted to the two main categories of measures used in research in HPERD: physical, or movement, and written responses. Chapter 14 summarizes some of the dependent variables used in research on movement and the various problems associated with such measures. This chapter makes no attempt to deal with the meaningful research questions about movement, only to present some of the measurements used as dependent variables. No two people (not even Thomas and Nelson) can adequately represent the research questions from the various specialties within physical education. This book is concerned with *research methods* (in this instance, methods used in measuring movement), not the content or knowledge base of movement. Thus, the focus here is not to suggest research questions about movement, but rather the ways movement has frequently been measured. Psychophysiological measurements include physical fitness assessment and the measurement of psychomotor parameters. Motor behavior measurements include the evaluation of basic movement patterns, sport skills and motor learning, and performance laboratory measures. Biomechanical measurements such as cinematography and electromyography are briefly discussed as are the characteristics and problems associated with observational measurement techniques.

Many studies in HPERD use written responses to gather research data. In Chapter 15, measurement of affective behaviors such as attitude, personality traits, anxiety, self-concept, and sportsmanship are addressed. The types of responses used in affective behavior measurement and rating scales in general are discussed as to their strengths and weaknesses. Finally, attention is given to the measurement of knowledge and techniques for evaluating test items as to difficulty and discrimination.

Chapter 13

Validity and Reliability

The validity of an experiment has been discussed on numerous occasions. Various sources of invalidity such as history, instrumentation, testing, and maturation were explained in Chapter 11. Validity, in this sense, refers to whether the results can be attributed to the experimental variables rather than to some extraneous variables (internal validity) and, also, whether the results can be generalized beyond the particular experiment (external validity).

In gathering the data on which the results are based, we are also greatly concerned with the validity of the measurements we are using. If, for example, a study seeks to compare training methods for producing strength gains, the researcher must have a valid measure of strength in order to be able to evaluate the effects of the training methods. *Validity* of measurement, then, indicates the degree to which the test, or instrument, measures what it is supposed to measure. Thus, validity refers to the soundness of the interpretation of a test. This is the most important consideration in measurement.

An integral part of validity is *reliability*. Reliability pertains to the consistency or repeatability of a measure. A test cannot be considered valid if it is not reliable. In other words, if the test is not consistent, if you cannot depend on successive trials to yield the same results, then the test cannot be trusted. Of course, a test could be reliable but not valid, but never valid if not reliable.

VALIDITY OF MEASUREMENT IN RESEARCH

There are different purposes for using certain measures. Consequently, there are different kinds of validity. According to the American Psychology Association (APA) and the American Educational Research Association (AERA), the four basic types of validity are *logical, content, criterion*, and *construct*. Logical validity is often cited as a separate type of validity; however, the APA and AERA consider logical validity as a special case of content validity. Because our main concern in this text is measurement for research purposes, logical validity, content validity, criterion validity, and construct validity will only be briefly discussed. A more comprehensive discussion would be necessary if we were directing our attention to the evaluation of educational objectives.

LOGICAL VALIDITY

Logical validity is sometimes referred to as face validity, although some measurement experts eschew the term face validity. Logical validity is claimed when the measure obviously involves the performance being measured. In other words, it means that the test is valid by definition. A static balance test that consists of balancing on one foot has logical validity. A speed of movement test in which the person is timed in running a specified distance has to be considered to have logical validity. Occasionally, logical validity is used in research studies, but a researcher would prefer to have more objective evidence as to the validity of measurement.

CONTENT VALIDITY

Content validity pertains almost exclusively to learning in educational settings. A test has content validity if it adequately samples what was covered in the course. As with logical validity, there is no statistical evidence that can be supplied for content validity. The teacher should prepare a table of specifications (sometimes called a test blueprint) prior to making out the test. The topics and course objectives and relative degree of emphasis that were accorded each can then be keyed to a corresponding number of questions pertaining to each area.

CRITERION VALIDITY

Measurements used in research studies frequently are validated against some criterion. Actually, criterion validity is used in two main contexts: concurrent validity and predictive validity.

Concurrent validity is when a measuring instrument is correlated with some criterion which is administered at about the same time, that is, concurrently. Many physical performance measures are validated in this manner. Several criterion measures that are popularly used include an already validated or accepted measure; judges' ratings and tournament results; or some other observable performance criterion. Usually, concurrent validity is employed when the researcher wishes to substitute a shorter, more easily administered test for a criterion which is more difficult to measure.

To illustrate, maximal oxygen consumption is regarded as the most valid measure of cardiorespiratory fitness. However, it requires a laboratory, expensive equipment, and considerable time for testing; furthermore, only one person can be tested at a time. Let us assume a researcher, Douglas Bag, wishes to screen subjects as to their fitness level prior to assigning them to experimental treatments. Rather than using such an elaborate test as maximal oxygen consumption, it would be advantageous to give a shorter, more easily administered measure. Douglas would like to use a stair-walking test he had devised. To determine whether it is a valid measure of cardiorespiratory fitness, he could administer both the maximal oxygen consumption test and the stair-walking test to a group of subjects (from the same population as will be used in the study) and correlate the results of the two tests. If there is a satisfactory relationship, Douglas can conclude that his stair-walking test is valid.

Written tests may also be validated in the same manner. For example, a researcher might wish to use a more practical group intelligence test than one like the lengthy Stanford-Binet which has to be administered individually.

Judges' ratings serve as criterion measures for some tests. Sport skills are sometimes validated this way. Securing competent judges, providing for practice in the use of the rating scale, testing for agreement among judges, arranging for the subjects to be viewed a sufficient number of trials, and other details require a great amount of time and effort. Consequently, judges' ratings cannot be used routinely to evaluate performances. The use of some skills tests would be more economical. Furthermore, the skills tests usually provide knowledge of results and measures of progress for the students. The skills tests could be initially validated, however, by giving the tests and having judges rate the subjects on those skills. A validity coefficient can be obtained by correlating the scores on the skills tests with the judges' ratings.

Choice of the criterion is, of course, critical in the concurrent validity method. All the correlation can tell you is the degree of relationship between a measure and the criterion. If the criterion is not adequate, then the concurrent validity coefficient is of little consequence.

Predictive validity involves the use of a criterion to be predicted. In many cases, the criterion is some later behavior, such as where entrance examinations attempt to predict later success. Suppose a dance faculty wished to develop a test which could be given in beginning dance classes to predict success in advanced classes. The test would be administered to students while they were in beginner courses. At the end of the advanced course, those test results would be correlated with the criterion of success (grades, ratings, etc.).

In trying to predict a certain behavior, one should try to ascertain whether there is a known *base rate* for that behavior. For instance, a health educator might attempt to construct a test which would predict girls who would develop bulemia at that university. Suppose that the incidence of bulemia is 10% of the female population at the school. Knowing that, one could predict that none in a sample will be bulemic and be correct 90% of the time. If the base rate is very low or very high, a predictive measure may have little practical value because the increase in predictability will be negligible.

In Chapters 6 and 10 aspects of prediction in correlational research were discussed. Multiple regression is often used since several predictors are likely to have a greater validity coefficient than the correlation between any one test and the criterion. Previously, we used the example of the prediction of percent fat from skinfold measurements. The criterion, percent fat, is measured by the underwater (hydrostatic) weighing technique. A number of skinfold measures are taken and multiple regression is used to determine the best prediction equation. The researcher hopes to be able to use the skinfold measures in the future if the prediction formula demonstrates an acceptable validity coefficient.

One of the limitations of such studies is that the validity tends to decrease when the prediction formula is used with a new sample. This tendency is called *shrinkage*. Common sense tells us that shrinkage is more likely when we use a small sample in the original study and particularly when the number of predictors is large. As a matter of fact, if enough predictor variables (equal to the number of subjects) are added to the multiple regression equation, one can achieve perfect prediction. The problem is that the correlations are unique to the sample, and when the results are applied to another sample (even similar to the first one), the relationship does not hold. Consequently, the validity coefficient decreases substantially (i.e., shrinkage).

A technique that is recommended to help estimate shrinkage is cross validation. In this technique, the same tests are given to a new sample from the same population to check whether the formula is accurate. For example, a researcher might administer the criterion measure and predictor tests to a sample of 200 subjects. Using 100 of the subjects, multiple regression is calculated to develop a prediction formula. Then this formula is applied to the other 100 subjects to see how accurately it predicts the criterion for these subjects. Since the researcher has the actual criterion measures on these subjects, the amount of shrinkage can be ascertained by correlating (Pearson r) the predicted scores with the actual scores. A comparison of the R^2 from the multiple prediction with the r^2 between the actual and predicted criterion yields an estimate of shrinkage.

CONSTRUCT VALIDITY

Many human characteristics are not directly observable. Rather, they are hypothetical constructs which carry a number of associated meanings concerning how a person who possesses the trait(s) to a high degree would behave differently from someone who possesses a low degree of the trait(s). Anxiety, intelligence, sportsmanship, creativity, and attitude are but a few of such hypothetical constructs. Because these traits are not directly observable, measurement poses a problem.

Construct validity is the degree to which a test measures a hypothetical construct, usually established by relating the test results to some behavior. A number of behaviors may be expected by someone with a high degree of sportsmanship. For example, a person with a high degree of sportsmanship might be expected to compliment the opponent on shots made during a tennis match. As an indication of construct validity, a test maker could compare the number of times persons scoring high on a test of sportsmanship complimented the opponent with persons scoring lower.

The known group difference method is sometimes used in establishing construct validity. For example, construct validity of a test of anaerobic power could be demonstrated by comparing test scores of sprinters and jumpers with distance runners. Sprinting and jumping require anaerobic power to a great extent while distance running does not. Therefore, the tester could determine whether the test differentiates between the two kinds of track performers. If the sprinters and jumpers score significantly higher than the distance runners, this would provide some evidence that the test measures anaerobic power.

An experimental approach is occasionally used in demonstrating construct validity. For example, a test of cardiovascular fitness might be assumed to have construct validity if it reflected gains in fitness following a conditioning program. Similarly, the originator of a motor skills test could demonstrate construct validity with regard to its sensitivity in differentiating between groups of instructed versus noninstructed children.

Correlation can also be used in establishing construct validity. Hypothesized structures or dimensions of the trait being tested are sometimes formulated and verified with factor analysis. Correlation is also used when the tester wishes to examine relationships between constructs, for example, when it is hypothesized that someone with high scores on the test being developed, such as cardiovascular fitness, should also do well on some total physical fitness scale; conversely, persons with low scores on the cardiovascular test would do poorly on the fitness test.

RELIABILITY OF MEASUREMENT IN RESEARCH

A measure which does not yield consistent results is not valid because you cannot depend on the results. The degree of consistency of a test is reliability. Test reliability is sometimes discussed in terms of *observed score*, *true score*, and *error score*.

When we obtain a test score on an individual, that is the observed score. We do not know whether this is a true assessment of this person's ability or performance. There may well be measurement error involved, pertaining to the test directions, the instrumentation, and the scoring or the emotional-physical state of the subject. Thus, an observed score theoretically consists of the person's true score and error. Expressed in terms of score variance, the observed score variance consists of true score variance plus error variance. The goal of the tester is to try to remove error in order to yield the true score. The coefficient of reliability is the ratio of true score variance/observed score variance. Because true score variance is never known, it is estimated by subtracting error variance from observed score variance. Thus, the reliability coefficient reflects the degree to which the measure is free of error variance.

Measurement error can come from four sources: the subject, testing, scoring, and instrumentation. Measurement error associated with the subject includes many factors such as mood, motivation, fatigue, health, fluctuations in memory (and performance), previous practice, specific knowledge, and familiarity with the test items.

Errors connected with testing are those that can arise due to the lack of clarity or completeness in the directions, to whether the instructions are rigidly followed, to whether supplementary directions or motivation is applied, and so forth.

Errors in scoring relate to the competence, experience, and dedication of the scorers as well as the nature of the scoring itself. The extent to which the scorer is familiar with the behavior being tested and the test items can greatly affect the accuracy of the scoring. Carelessness and inattention to detail produce measurement error.

Measurement error due to instrumentation includes the obvious causes such as inaccuracy and lack of calibration of mechanical and electronic equipment. It also refers to the inadequacy of tests in discriminating between abilities and the difficulty in scoring of some tests.

The degree of reliability is expressed by a correlation coefficient, ranging from .00 to 1.00. The closer the coefficient is to 1.00, the less error variance it reflects, and the more the true score is assessed. Reliability is established in several ways and those will be summarized in the next section.

The type of correlation technique used in computing the reliability coefficient differs from that used in establishing validity. Pearson r is often referred to as *interclass correlation*. This is used in correlating two different variables (bivariate statistic), such as in determining validity where judges' ratings are correlated with scores on a skill test. In establishing reliability, however, interclass correlation is not appropriate because the same variable is being correlated. When a test is given twice, the scores on the first test administration are correlated with the scores on the second administration to determine the degree of consistency. In this case, the two test scores are for the same variable, thus interclass correlation should not be used. *Intraclass correlation* is the appropriate statistical technique. This method uses analysis of variance in obtaining the reliability coefficient.

The main weaknesses of Pearson r (interclass correlation) for reliability determination include the following:

1. As mentioned above, the Pearson r is a bivariate statistic while reliability involves univariate measures.
2. In Pearson r, the computations are limited to just two scores, X and Y. But many times more than two trials are given, and the tester is concerned with the reliability of multiple trials. For example, if a test specifies three trials, the researcher must either give three more trials and use the average or best score of each set of trials for the correla-

tions, or perhaps correlate the first trial with the second, first with third, and second with third. In the first case, extra trials must be given just for reliability; in the second instance, multiple correlations often lose meaningfulness.

3. The interclass correlation does not provide thorough examination of different sources of variability on multiple trials. For example, changes in means and standard deviations from trial to trial cannot be considered in the Pearson *r* method but can be analyzed with intraclass correlation. Intraclass correlation provides estimates of systematic and error variance. For example, systematic differences among trials can be examined. If the last trials differ significantly from the first trials, it may be that there is a learning phenomenon or fatigue effect (or both). If the tester is aware of this, then perhaps initial (or final) trials can be excluded, or the point where performance levels off can be used as the score. In other words, through analysis of variance, the tester is able to truly examine test performance from trial to trial and decide on the most reliable testing schedule.

An example of intraclass correlation (symbol *R*) is given in Table 13.1. Three trials are in the example. The procedures leading to the calculation of *R* are the same as for the sample ANOVA with repeated measures that was presented in Chapter 7.

Let us refer to Table 7.14 for the formulas for calculating the necessary sums of squares (*SS*) and mean squares (*MS*). Using the formulas in Table 7.14, we calculate the total *SS* to be 27.6. The *SS* for subjects is found to be 14.9. The *SS* for trials is 7.6. We can then calculate the *interaction* (residual) *SS* by subtraction and get 5.1. Next, we compute *MS* values for subjects, trials, and interaction by the formulas in Table 7.14:

$$MS \text{ for subjects} = 3.73$$

$$MS \text{ for trials} = 3.80$$

$$MS \text{ for interaction (error)} = .64$$

We can determine whether we have significant differences among the three trials by calculating the *F* for trials as per Table 7.14. We then enter Table A.4 in Appendix A and read down the 2 *df* column to the 8 *df* row. Our *F* of 5.94 is found to be greater than the tabled *F* of 4.46 for the .05 level of probability. Thus, we have significant differences among trials. (Note: The microcomputer program for this analysis is presented as the second example of one-way repeated measures in Appendix B).

At this point, we need to recognize that there are different opinions as to what should be done with trial differences (Baumgartner & Jackson, 1982; Johnson

TABLE 13.1
SUMMARY OF ANOVA FOR RELIABILITY ESTIMATION (3 trials)

Student	Trial 1	Trial 2	Trial 3
A	3	3	4
B	4	6	6
C	2	3	4
D	1	3	4
E	2	4	2
	M = 2.4	M = 3.8	M = 4.0

Summary of ANOVA

Source	*SS*	*df*	*MS*	*F*
Subjects	14.9	4	3.73	
Trials	7.6	2	3.80	5.94*
Residual	5.1	8	.64	

*$p < .05$

& Nelson, 1979; Safrit, 1976). Some test authorities argue that the test performance should be consistent from one trial to the next, and any trial-to-trial variance should be simply attributed to measurement error. If we should decide to do this, the formula for R is

$$R = (MS_S - MS_E) / MS_S \qquad (13.1)$$

in which $MS_S = MS$ for subjects (from Table 13.1) and $MS_E = MS$ for error which is computed as follows:

$$\frac{SS \text{ for trials} + SS \text{ for interaction}}{df \text{ for trials} + df \text{ for interaction}} = \frac{7.6 + 5.1}{2 + 8} = 1.27$$

The R is thus calculated:

$$R = (3.73 - 1.27) / 3.73 = .66$$

Another way of dealing with significant trial differences is to discard the trial(s) that is noticeably different from the others (Baumgartner & Jackson, 1982). Then a second ANOVA is conducted on the remaining trials and another *F*-test is computed. If the *F* is nonsignificant, the *R* is calculated using Formula 13.1 in which trial variance is considered measurement error. If the *F* is still significant, additional trials are discarded and another ANOVA is conducted. The purpose of this method is to find a measurement schedule that is free of trial differences (nonsignificant *F* which yields the largest possible criterion score and is most reliable. This method is especially appealing when there is an apparent trend in trial differences as when a learning phenomenon (or release of inhibitions) is evident in the initial trial or trials. For example, if five trials on a performance test yielded scores 15, 18, 23, 25, and 24, one might discard the first two trials and compute another analysis on the last three trials. Similarly, a fatigue effect may be evidenced by a decrease in the final trials in some types of tests.

In our example in Table 13.1, we note that Trial 1 is considerably lower than Trials 2 and 3. So, we will discard the first trial and compute another ANOVA on Trials 2 and 3. The results are shown in Table 13.2 (The microcomputer program for this analysis is in Example 3 for one-way repeated measures in Appendix B).

The *F* for trials in Table 13.2 is nonsignificant, so we compute *R* with Formula 13.1:

$$R = (2.85 - .7) / 2.85 = .75$$

Note that we computed the MS_E (.7) by combining the *SS* for trials and interaction and dividing by their respective *df*:

$$(.1 + 3.4)/(1 + 4) = .7$$

TABLE 13.2

SUMMARY OF ANOVA FOR RELIABILITY ESTIMATION (2 trials)

Summary of ANOVA

Source	SS	df	MS	F
Subjects	11.4	4	2.85	
Trials	.1	1	.10	.11
Residual	3.4	4	.85	

We can see that the R is considerably higher when we discarded the first trial.

A third approach is to simply not consider trial-to-trial variance as measurement error and compute R as follows:

$$R = (MS_S - MS_I) / MS_S \qquad (13.2)$$

Using the data in Table 13.1, we calculate R to be:

$$R = (3.73 - .64) / 3.73 = .88$$

In this approach, trial-to-trial variance is not considered as true or error score variance. Consequently, the R is notably higher than the previous approaches since all trial-to-trial variance is removed. Although some measurement authorities advocate this approach, it does not seem to follow the theory that observed score variance equals true score variance plus error score variance, and some other measurement specialists argue that every source of variance not attributable to subjects should be considered error-score variance (Safrit, 1976). While we do not intend to enter into the argument, we do think that it should be of interest to the researcher (tester) to ascertain whether there are trial-to-trial differences. Subsequently, if significant differences are found, the tester can decide whether it seems appropriate to eliminate some trials (as with a learning trend), or whether to just consider trial-to-trial differences as measurement error.

Intertester reliability is determined the same way. Thus, the objectivity of judges or different testers is analyzed with intraclass R with judge-to-judge variance calculated in the same way as trial-to-trial variance. Of course, more complex ANOVA designs can be used in which trial-to-trial,day-to-day,and judge-to-judge sources of variance can all be identified. Safrit (1976) discusses some of the different models which can be used for establishing reliability.

METHODS OF ESTABLISHING RELIABILITY

It is easier to establish reliability than validity. We can first look at three types of coefficients of reliability: *stability, alternate forms,* and *internal consistency.*

The coefficient of stability is determined by the *test-retest method on separate days*. This method is frequently used with fitness and motor performance measures but rarely with paper and pencil tests. This is the most severe test of consistency because the errors associated with measurement are likely to be more pronounced when the two test administrations are separated by a day or more.

In the test-retest method, the test is given one day and then administered exactly as before a day or so later. The time interval may be governed to some extent by how strenuous the test is and whether more than one day's rest is needed. Of course, the time interval cannot be so long that actual changes in ability, maturation, or learning occur between the two test administrations.

Intraclass correlation is used to compute the coefficient of stability of the scores on the two tests. Through the analysis of variance procedures, the tester can determine the amount of variance accounted for by the separate days of testing as well as test trial differences, subject differences, and error variance.

The alternate form method of establishing reliability involves the construction of two tests, both which supposedly sample the same material. This method is sometimes referred to as the parallel form method or the equivalence method.

The two tests are given to the same subjects. Ordinarily, there is some time interval between the two administrations. The scores on the two tests are then correlated to obtain a reliability coefficient. The alternate form method is the most widely used technique with standardized tests such as tests of achievement and scholastic aptitude tests. The method is hardly ever used with physical performance tests, probably because it is more difficult to construct two different sets of good physical test items than it is to write two sets of questions.

Some test experts maintain that theoretically the alternate form method is the preferred method. Any test is but a sample of test items from a "universe" of possible test items. Thus, the degree of relationship between two such samples should yield the best estimate of reliability.

An internal consistency reliability coefficient can be obtained by any of several methods. Some of the commonly used methods are the test-retest on the same day, the *split-half* method, the *Kuder-Richardson* method or rational equivalence, and the *Coefficient Alpha* technique.

The test-retest on the same day is used almost exclusively with physical performance tests. Practice effects and recall tend to produce a spuriously high correlation when this technique is used with written tests. The test-retest on the same day method results in a higher reliability coefficient than a test-retest on separate days. One would certainly expect more consistency of performance within the same time period than on different days. Intraclass correlation is used to analyze trial to trial (internal) consistency.

The split-half technique is the most widely used method of determining internal consistency. This method is commonly used in written tests and occasionally in performance tests that require numerous trials. The test is divided in half, and the two halves are correlated. A test could be divided by first half and second half, but this usually is not deemed satisfactory. Sometimes a person tires near the end of the test, and sometimes easier questions are placed in the first half. Usually, the odd numbered questions are compared with the even-numbered ones. That is, the number of odd-numbered questions a person got correct is correlated with the number of correct answers on the even numbered questions.

Since the correlation is between the two halves of the test, the reliability coefficient represents only half the size of the total test; that is, behavior is sampled only half as thoroughly. Thus, a step-up procedure, the *Spearman-Brown Prophecy Formula*, is used to estimate the reliability for the entire test because the total test is based on twice the sample of behavior (twice the number of items). The formula is as follows:

$$\text{corrected reliability coefficient} = \frac{2 \times \text{reliability for } \tfrac{1}{2} \text{ test}}{1.00 + \text{reliability for } \tfrac{1}{2} \text{ test}}$$

If, for example, the correlation between the even-numbered items and the odd-numbered items was .85, the corrected reliability coefficient would be

$$\frac{2 \times .85}{1.00 + .85} = \frac{1.70}{1.85} = .92$$

The Kuder-Richardson method of rational equivalence can be used for items that are scored dichotomously, for example, right or wrong. Only one administration of the test is required, and no correlation is calculated. Two formulas, known as K-R 20 and K-R 21 are the most widely used. The resulting coefficient represents an average of all possible split-half reliability coefficients.

The K-R 20 is considered by many test experts to be the best for determining reliability. The K-R 21 is a simplified version of K-R 20. It is so easily and quickly computed that it is very applicable to the teacher (or researcher) for "home-made" tests. The K-R 21 formula is shown below:

$$\text{K-R } 21 = 1.00 - \frac{M(n - M)}{ns^2}$$

Where M = mean score for the test, n = number of test items, s^2 = test variance (standard deviation squared). The Kuder-Richardson formulas generally result in lower reliability coefficients than other methods. One can assume, then, that the coefficient represents a minimum reliability estimate.

Coefficient Alpha is a form of the K-R 20 formula which can be used for test items which are not scored dichotomously, but it can be used with ordinal data. The Alpha coefficient, usually referred to as the Cronbach Alpha coefficient (1951), is applicable to multiple trial tests. The coefficient Alpha yields an estimate of reliability that is equivalent to intraclass reliability when interval data are used. Coefficient Alpha gives the proportion of total variance that is associated with, or accounted for, by the trial covariances. It is rather easily calculated by finding the sum of the variances for trials and then computing the variance for the total.

INTERTESTER RELIABILITY (OBJECTIVITY)

A form of reliability that pertains to the testers is called *intertester reliability*, or, often, objectivity. This facet of reliability is the degree to which different testers can achieve the same scores on the same subjects.

In general, most teachers and students prefer objective measures over subjective measures because so much depends on how valid and reliable the measures are. Objective measures are not automatically better than subjective ones; but they do yield quantitative scores which are more "visable" and, which, statistically, can be handled more easily. In most research techniques objective measurements are a must.

The degree of objectivity (intertester reliability) can be established by having more than one tester gather data; then the scores are analyzed with intraclass correlation techniques to obtain an intertester reliability coefficient. It is possible to assess a number of sources of variance in one analysis, such as variance due to testers, trials, days, subjects, and error (for coverage of the calculations involved, see Safrit, 1976).

Intertester reliability is more critical in some areas of measurement than in others. For example, anthropometric measurements such as skinfold measurements, body circumferences, and diameters are subject to considerable intertester variability.

STANDARD ERROR OF MEASUREMENT

Section II touched upon the concept of standard error several times with regard to the *t* and the *F* tests and in interpreting significance levels. The section also gave attention to the standard error of prediction in correlational research.

The standard error of measurement is an important concept in interpreting the results of measurement. Sometimes, we get too carried away with the aura of scientific data collection and fail to realize that there is always the possibility of measurement error. For example, maximal oxygen consumption ($\dot{V}O_2$ max) has been mentioned several times in this text as the most valid measure of cardiorespiratory fitness. Field tests are frequently validated by correlating them with $\dot{V}O_2$ max. We must be careful, however, not to consider $\dot{V}O_2$ max as some kind of "perfect" test with no error associated with it. Every test yields only observed scores, and we can only obtain estimates of a person's true score.

We would be much better off if we thought of test scores as falling within a range which contains the true score. The formula for the standard error of measurement (SEM) is

$$\text{SEM} = s\sqrt{1.00 - r}$$

where s = standard deviation of the scores, and r = reliability coefficient for the test. In the measurement of percent body fat for female adults, let us assume that the standard deviation is 5.6%, and the test-retest correlation is .83. The standard error of measurement would be

$$\text{SEM} = 5.6\sqrt{1.00 - .83} = 2.3\%$$

Let us further assume that a particular woman's measured percent fat is 22.4%. We can use the standard error of measurement to estimate a range within which her true percent fat probably falls.

Standard errors are assumed to be normally distributed and are interpreted in the same way as standard deviations. In other words, about two-thirds (actually 68.26%) of all test scores will fall within plus or minus one standard error of measurement of their true scores. In other words, there is a 68% chance that a person's true score will be found within a range of the obtained score plus and minus the standard error of measurement. In the example of the woman who had an obtained score of 22.4% fat, chances are 2 in 3 that her true percent fat is 22.4% $\pm$ 2.3% (the standard error of measurement), or somewhere between 20.1% and 24.7%.

We can be more confident if we multiply the standard error of measurement by 2, because about 95% (95.44%) of the time, the true score can be expected to be found within a range of the observed score plus and minus two times the standard error of measurement. Thus, in the above example, we can be about 95% sure that the woman's true percent fat will be 22.4% $\pm$ (2.3% $\times$ 2), that is, between 17.8% and 27.0%.

From the formula, we can see that the standard error of measurement is governed by the variability of the test scores and the reliability of the test. If we had a higher reliability coefficient, the error of measurement would obviously decrease. In the example we have been using, if the reliability coefficient was .95, the standard error of measurement would only be 1.3%; or, with the same reliability (.83), but with a smaller standard deviation such as 4%, the standard error of measurement would be 1.7%.

Remember the standard error of measurement concept when you are interpreting test scores. As indicated earlier, people sometimes have absolutely blind faith in some measurements, particularly if the measurement appears quite "scientific." With percent fat estimation from skinfold thicknesses, for example, we need to keep in mind that not only is there error connected with the skinfold measurements, but also with the criterion that these measurements are predicting—that is, the density obtained from underwater weighing and the determination of percent fat from the body density values. Yet we have observed people accepting as "gospel" that they have a certain amount of fat because someone measured a few skinfolds. Newspapers have reported that some athletes have only 1% fat. This would be impossible from a physiological standpoint. Moreover, it is possible to obtain a predicted *negative* percent fat from regression equations. Please do not misunderstand, we are not condemning skinfold measurements, but we are trying to stress that all measurements are susceptible to errors. Common sense coupled with knowledge of the concept of standard error of measurement can help us better understand and interpret the results of measurements.

SCALES OF MEASUREMENT

Several times in the discussion of statistics and measurement, interval scale measures and ordinal data have been mentioned. There are basically four types of scales: nominal, ordinal, interval, and ratio.

NOMINAL

When scores are grouped into categories or classes, it is a nominal scale. In other words, it is a classification by name. Obviously, scores of boys and girls can be assigned to two mutually exclusive groups. No score can fall in more than one classification. Because the nominal scale classification is for identification only, there is no differentiation as to order or magnitude of differences between groups. Examples of nominal scales include such categories as gender, age, race, and grade.

Sometimes a researcher creates groups based on some measurement criterion. For example, on the basis of an anxiety measure, subjects might be categorized as high or low anxious. High, average, and low fitness groupings and highly skilled and poorly skilled classifications are other such examples. In these instances, the classifications are not strictly nominal because there is some kind of order distinction. Such scales could be considered as somewhere between nominal and the next scale—ordinal.

ORDINAL

Ordinal measures are ranks. They provide more information than nominal data. The highest ordinal number is better than the next highest, which is in turn better than the third highest. With an ordinal scale, we do not know how *much* better one score is than another. Therefore, we must use caution in making comparisons. For example, John is 6 inches taller than Joe, and Joe is a half inch taller than Bob. Yet by merely ranking them, we have John first, Joe second, and Bob third, and the ordinal difference between ranks 1 and 2 is the same as between ranks 2 and 3. We cannot assume equal intervals between ranks in terms of their actual raw scores.

Percentiles are ordinal numbers, and, consequently, a teacher should not try to average percentiles or interpolate between two percentile ranks. A score falling between the 60th and 65th percentiles should not be assigned a value of 62.5 because it cannot be assumed that the scores are evenly distributed between those two percentile ranks.

INTERVAL

Interval measures provide not only the order between scores, but also the magnitude of the distance between them. A score of 35 sit-ups is not only higher than a score of 25, it is 10 sit-ups higher. Similarly, a difference between 35 and 25 sit-ups is the same relative difference as between 25 and 15. Interval scoring enables us to interpret performances with standard scores, which will be discussed later in this chapter.

RATIO

Ratio scores have all the properties of the other three scales plus having a true zero value, which represents a complete absence of the characteristic. An interval measure does not have a true zero. An example frequently given to distinguish between the interval and ratio scales is the IQ scale. IQ scores are interval scores because there is no "zero intelligence." We cannot say that an IQ of 160 is twice as high as an IQ of 80 because "0" on the IQ scale is an arbitrary point. We can only say that a score of 160 is 80 points higher than a score of 80.

On the other hand, measures of force, time, and distance are ratio scales because they have true zero points. A force of 50 pounds is twice as high as 25 pounds. A jump of 20 feet is twice as far as one of 10 feet. Actually, although a number of the measures used in physical education are ratio scales, they are treated the same as interval scores. For example, even though distance is a ratio scale, the relative differences between performances may not be equal. The 2-inch difference between high jumps of 7'2" and 7'0" is probably more significant than the 2-inch difference of 5'2" and 5'0."

STANDARD SCORES

Direct comparisons of scores are not possible without having some point of reference. Is a score of 46 cm on the vertical jump as good as a score of 25 push-ups? How can you compare centimeters and repetitions? If we know that the class mean for the vertical jump is 40 cm, and that 20 is the mean for push-ups; we know that the performances of 46 cm and 25 push-ups are better than average, but how much better? Is one performance better than the other?

One way to compare the performances is to convert each score to a *standard score*. A standard score is a score expressed in terms of standard deviations from the mean. Standard scores are interval scores because the standard deviation is a constant interval unit throughout the scale.

The basic standard score is the z-score. The z-scale converts raw scores to a mean of 0 and to a standard deviation of 1.0. The formula is

$$z = (X - M) / s$$

Let us suppose that the means and standard deviations for the vertical jump scores and push-up scores are as follows:

Vertical Jump	Push-ups
$M = 40$	$M = 20$
$s = 6$	$s = 5$

Thus, a score of 46 cm is a z-score of + 1.00

$$z = (46 - 40) / 6 = 6 / 6 = 1.00$$

A score of 25 push-ups is also a z-score of + 1.00

$$z = (25 - 20) / 5 = 5 / 5 = 1.00$$

We see then that the person performed exactly the same on the two tests. Both performances were one standard deviation above the mean. Similarly, scores of different students can be compared on the same test by z-scores. A person jumping 37 cm has a z-score of $-.5$; a student who jumps 44 cm has a z of .67, and so on. All standard scores are based on the z-score. However, because z-scores are expressed in decimals and have positive and negative numbers, they are not as easy to work with as some of the other scales. The T-scale, for example, sets the mean at 50 and the standard deviation at 10 ($10z + 50$). This removes the decimal and makes all scores positive. A score of one standard deviation above the mean ($z = 1.0$) is a T score of 60. A score one standard deviation below the mean ($z = -1.0$) is a T score of 40. Because over 99% (99.73%) of the scores fall between plus and minus 3 standard deviations, it is rare to have T scores of less than 20 ($z = -3.0$) and over 80 ($z = 3.0$).

Some standardized tests which use different transformations of means and standard deviations using the z-score distribution are shown in Table 13.3.

Stanines are another type of standard score. The word stanine is derived from the words standard and nine because there are nine standard score units. The mean of the stanine scale is 5, and the standard deviation is 2. The percentages of the distribution for the nine stanines are as follows:

Stanine	1	2	3	4	5	6	7	8	9
%	4%	7%	12%	17%	20%	17%	12%	7%	4%

The decision as to which standard score to use is dependent upon the nature of the research study and to the extent of interpretation required for the test takers. In essence, then, it is a matter of choice in light of the utilization of the measures.

In conclusion to Chapter 13, we would like to stress the point that the researcher (tester) is instrumental in the ultimate determination of the validity and reliability

TABLE 13.3

STANDARDIZED MEANS AND STANDARD DEVIATION OF WELL-KNOWN TEST

Scale	M	s
Graduate Record Examination	500	100z
Stanford - Binet IQ	100	16z
College Entrance Examination	500	100z
National Teachers Examination	500	100z
Wechsler IQ	100	15z

of the measurements. The researcher cannot speak of "the validity" or "the reliability" of any test. A test may be valid and reliable for one group of subjects, but not for another (e.g., adults but not children). Moreover, a test may be quite valid and reliable when given in a careful and systematic manner, but totally unreliable and, hence, invalid in the hands of an incompetent tester.

Chapter 14

Measuring Movement

As indicated in the introduction to Section IV, this chapter summarizes some of the ways that movement has been measured for use as a dependent variable in research. We are presenting the measures independently of the research questions that might be asked about movement. Any attempt to summarize the appropriate research questions in the various areas of physical education would be impossible. No two people can do that. Thus, this chapter presents some of the ways movement has been measured and methodological difficulties associated with these measurements.

PSYCHOPHYSIOLOGICAL MEASUREMENT

A great deal of evaluation and research in physical education is directed at psychophysiological performance. Physical fitness assessment occupies considerable interest among exercise physiologists and physical education teachers. The measurement of basic motor abilities and motor skills pertaining to athletics and dance are other areas which have prompted much study over the years. We will briefly summarize some of the methodology in measuring various psychophysiological parameters.

MEASUREMENT OF PHYSICAL FITNESS

There is no universal definition of physical fitness. It is, after all, a matter of professional opinion. Recently, the concept of health-related physical fitness has enjoyed widespread acceptance. The components of this type of fitness all supposedly have direct health implications for everyone, not just for athletes or other special populations. Nearly everyone agrees that three of the components of health-related fitness are cardiorespiratory endurance, muscular strength, and muscular endurance. Flexibility and body composition are two other components commonly included. However, there is some disagreement among physical fitness authorities as to whether these two parameters meet all of the criteria for physical fitness components.

We have no intention of entering into the debate or even discussing it. We will simply talk about the measurement of the five areas wherever they belong.

Cardiorespiratory Measures. The measurement of cardiorespiratory fitness can be separated basically into laboratory measures and field measures. However, these two categories can be divided even further into what might be called "poor man's" laboratory measures and "pseudoscientific" field measures.

Maximal oxygen consumption ($\dot{V}O_2$ max) is generally considered to be the most valid measure of cardiovascular fitness, or aerobic capacity. The procedure involves exercising to exhaustion using a standardized workout, usually on a treadmill or cycle ergometer because the speed and resistance of the exercise can be regulated. There are a number of methods, or protocols, for progressively increasing the workload depending upon the person's level of fitness and other considerations. The subject is fitted with a mouthpiece to which a hose is attached, and as he or she exercises, the expired air is measured for volume and analyzed for oxygen and carbon dioxide content. The rate of consuming oxygen increases with increased workload up to a point at which the oxygen consumption rate levels off. This is the person's aerobic capacity. It is usually measured in milliliters of oxygen per kilogram of body weight per minute. Modern instrumentation and computers enable the researcher to instantly obtain a variety of measures, a process that used to take a great deal of time and painstaking calculations. Of course, this instrumentation is very expensive. The expense, the time required, and the inability to test but one person at a time prohibit the measurement of $\dot{V}O_2$ max out in the field. Hence, other methods requiring less expensive equipment, less time, and less effort have been devised.

Many of you have probably been tested on a submaximal test of cardiorespiratory fitness in an exercise physiology or a test and measurement laboratory class. Such tests usually entail riding a cycle ergometer for a specified time. Pulse rate is the only measurement taken. Then a nomogram is consulted or a chart is used to predict your aerobic capacity. These tests are what we referred to as "poor man's" laboratory techniques because they only require a cycle ergometer and a stop watch to time the pulse counting.

The most commonly used field tests are distance runs. The length of the distance run has been a subject of many investigations. It appears that a distance which requires about 5 or more minutes is needed for acceptable validity. The validity of distance runs is usually established by correlating performance on the run with $\dot{V}O_2$ max.

The distance run is appealing as a measure because a number of people can be tested at the same time, and because the test is familiar and does not require much skill (although running definitely requires practice to learn optimal pace).

Years ago, people would not run except in an emergency, and thus the distance run tests were quite short, for example, 300, 440, 600 yards. Research has indicated that these distances are too short and rely too heavily on speed to adequately measure cardiorespiratory fitness. Due to the popularity of jogging and the national interest in aerobics, longer distances such as the 1-mile, 2-mile, 9-minute, and 12-minute runs are now commonly used.

A few years ago, step tests were in vogue. These are considered field measures because they require very little equipment, and they lend themselves to mass testing. We were referring to step tests when we used the term "pseudoscientific" field tests because they involve physiological measurement—that of pulse counting. A number of step tests have been developed, ranging from very vigorous to moderately strenuous exercise. In most of the tests, the pulse is taken after exercise. Step tests, like distance runs have construct validity. However, step tests are measuring only an aspect of cardiorespiratory fitness and high correlations have usually not been found using $\dot{V}O_2$ max as the criterion.

Strength and Endurance Measures. We are combining our discussion of strength and endurance measures simply because they are usually combined in field tests, not because they are the same thing. The relationship between strength and endurance varies greatly depending on several factors such as absolute and relative strength and endurance, body weight, and body composition. For example, strength and endurance have a high positive correlation if we are talking about absolute strength and absolute endurance. Absolute means no consideration is given to body size or maximum strength. To illustrate, suppose everyone in a sample is required to lift a 25-pound weight as many times as possible. The stronger person will find this easier than a weaker person because it represents a lighter load for the strong person. Hence, a high positive correlation would be found between strength and endurance. If, however, we first determine everyone's maximum strength, then assign a weight to lift, as for example, 25% of their maximum strength, the correlation will change drastically. In some cases we find no correlation, and in other studies negative correlations between strength and endurance have been found.

Strength and endurance can be measured precisely and separately in the laboratory. To the lay person, strength and endurance are very "simple" because everyone intuitively knows what they are. However, in actuality, both abilities are complex. With strength, for example, there are different manifestations of strength (and strength training) such as isotonic, isometric, and isokinetic. We have already mentioned absolute strength. Relative strength is the ability to exert maximum force (isotonically, isometrically, or isokinetically) in relation to a person's size. With absolute strength, larger persons *tend* to be stronger than smaller persons. With relative strength, a small person may be as strong or stronger than a larger individual if we measure strength in relation to size.

Various instruments, such as dynamometers and tensiometers, have been used for years to measure strength. Of course, lifting weights is an objective measure of strength. The "1RM" means the maximum amount of weight a person can lift once (1RM = one repetition maximum). Because weight training has become an integral part of the conditioning program in athletics, the availability of weights for physical education programs and measurement has also increased. Several weight training "machines" which can be used to measure strength and endurance are available.

Muscular endurance is the ability to persevere in working against a submaximal resistance. In the laboratory, endurance is usually measured by having a subject exercise a particular muscle group until some criterion of exhaustion is reached. The movement is carefully controlled so only the muscle group under study is allowed to work. The weight or resistance used depends upon whether the task is to be absolute or relative endurance. For example, an experiment might be planned in which the elbow flexors are to be exercised using an ergograph. First, the subject is tested for maximal strength of the elbow flexors; then a proportion of that strength is loaded onto the ergograph. The subject is strapped onto a table in such a way that only the elbow flexors can operate in lifting the weight. The subject raises and lowers the weight at a set cadence, which is controlled by a metronome. The criterion of exhaustion is when the subject cannot maintain the cadence on two successive trials.

Barbells and free weights can also be used for endurance testing, as can some of the weight training machines on the market. Muscular endurance can also be measured isometrically by having a subject hold a weight or exert a given amount of force against a dynamometer or other measuring device for as long as possible.

Fitness tests that have been developed for the armed forces, public schools, colleges, and various organizations have traditionally included items that supposedly combine strength and endurance. Pull-ups, push-ups, the flexed arm hang, and sit-ups are among the more popular test items of this kind. One of the contributing reasons for selecting these items is that field tests strive to choose items which are well known and which require little, if any, equipment. Items such as pull-ups are *relative* strength (and endurance) items because the subject must raise and lower his or her own body weight. One of the main objections to a test item such as pull-ups is that it can not be called a test of both strength and endurance if the person can only do one or two. In this case, it is a strength item because it represents maximal resistance. Remember, the definition of endurance specifies *submaximal* resistance which will allow repeated movements (or sustained force). Consequently, you cannot conclude that a person has no endurance if that individual lacks the strength to do the task more than once. Furthermore, if a boy cannot do a single pull-up, do you conclude he lacks both strength and endurance? A further problem with items such as pull-ups is that most of the scores cluster at the low end of the scale; thus the distribution is skewed rather than normally distributed.

Some field tests include items which are aimed primarily at muscular endurance, such as squat thrusts and squat jumps. One of the difficulties with these tests is deciding upon a time limit. If you do not set a time limit, the task causes a great deal of muscle soreness and increases the risk of injury. If you do set a time limit, then agility enters into the task because it takes skillful movement of the body to perform the exercise repetitively in a certain time span.

The administration of strength and endurance tests is surprisingly difficult. There are so many ways that a person can do them incorrectly. In performing a "simple" sit-up with hands clasped behind the head and knees bent, the tester has to make sure the hands stay clasped because they start to move toward the ears as the test progresses. In attempting to develop a little bounce and momentum, the subject tries to omit touching the elbows to the mat each time. As fatigue enters into the exercise, the knees start to straighten, and the person does not sit up completely to touch the thigh. Furthermore, in a timed event the subject is apt to sacrifice desirable form for speed, resulting in a straight back sit-up instead of the desired curl-up. Thus, it is safe to conclude that these well known "simple" test items of strength and endurance are anything but simple.

Flexibility Measures. Advocates of flexibility as a component of health-related physical fitness point to the importance of flexibility in avoiding injury due to sudden strains or movements. One of the inevitable results of inactivity (and hence aging) is the loss of flexibility which hinders mobility. Athletic coaches and trainers have become acutely aware of the importance of flexibility in their training and conditioning programs to avoid injury and to promote more efficient movement.

How much flexibility is needed? and Is too much flexibility harmful? are still unanswered questions. The one thing known is that flexibility is highly specific. This means that a person who is flexible enough to bend and touch the toes easily may be quite inflexible in another part of the body, such as in the movement of the shoulders. Therefore, the results of a single test of flexibility in a fitness test battery cannot be generalized to indicate total flexibility. However, this is true for a test of any kind of ability, whether it be strength, power, or balance.

Flexibility has been measured in a variety of ways. The bend and reach is probably one of the oldest and best known tests. This item produced the greatest number of failures in the Kraus-Weber test of minimum muscular fitness. Through years of clinical experience Kraus and Weber found that lack of flexibility in the back of the legs and in the back contributed significantly to lower back pain problems. This is one of the reasons for the inclusion of the sit and reach test in the AAHPERD Health Related Physical Fitness Test. Other simple field measures of flexibility include the shoulder elevation test, ankle flexibility test, trunk and neck extension, and arms backward and sideward tests (see Johnson & Nelson, 1979).

The Leighton Flexometer is one of the more scientific measuring instruments for evaluating flexibility, measuring range of motion in degrees. Therapists have used the plastic goniometer for years in measuring the loss and recovery of flexibility in joints due to injury and rehabilitation. The electrogoniometer is another instrument which has been used for research purposes.

Body Composition Measures. The analysis of body composition has become very popular in recent years due to the urging of physicians, who have long recognized the association of obesity with a number of diseases and other health problems.

Body composition measurement refers to the leaness-fatness ratio. Lean body weight is composed of muscle, bone, and all other tissues except fat. Fat weight consists of fat contained subcutaneously and internally. Many laboratory and field methods are available for assessing body composition.

Among the laboratory methods, underwater (hydrostatic) weighing is the most commonly used. Body density is estimated by calculating the body's loss of weight underwater. The resulting body density is then put into a formula to compute percent fat. Formulas for converting density to percent fat are based on the difference in density of fat and lean body tissues. The underwater weighing procedures require a tank of water or a swimming pool, and a method for measuring residual lung volume, body weight in air, and body weight underwater. The temperature of the water must also be measured because the density of water varies with temperature. Density is mass (or weight) per unit volume. The weight is simply the individual's body weight in air, that is, on land. Volume has to be estimated by subtracting the person's weight underwater from the weight on land. This value is divided by the volume of water, corrected for the temperature of the water at the time of weighing. Subtracted from this is the residual lung volume and the estimated volume of air in the gastrointestinal tract.

Other laboratory methods for determining body composition include volume displacement, potassium-40, ultrasound, helium dilution, radiographic analysis, and body water content.

Field methods consist mostly of the measurement of skinfold thickness, body circumferences, and skeletal diameters. Of these three, skinfold measurements are most commonly used. Predictions of percent fat are often made from these measurements, using the results of hydrostatic weighing or some other laboratory technique as the criterion.

Skinfold thicknesses are taken at different body sites by the use of calipers. The accuracy of predicting percent fat from skinfold measures (and other anthropometric measurements) is subject to considerable measurement error. A great deal of practice and exacting care is required for accurate results. Skinfold measurements are included in the AAHPERD Health Related Physical Fitness Test (1980).

MEASUREMENT OF PSYCHOMOTOR PARAMETERS

When introducing physical fitness measurement earlier in the chapter, we spoke of the acknowledged difference between fitness components about which everyone should be concerned (health-related) and certain fitness parameters which are needed primarily for skilled performances, such as in athletics and in dance. These components include power, speed, reaction time, agility, balance, kinesthetic perception, and coordination.

Power Measures. In many sports, power is considered to be the most important physical attribute. However, power is not simply a *combination* of strength and speed. (Many coaches have been disappointed by this misconception.) Power involves the skillful *coordination* of strength and speed. An individual may be tremendously strong and may move quickly but still may lack the explosive power of another individual with less strength and less speed. There is a definite skill involved in being able to exert force with lightning speed.

Power is technically defined as the change in work divided by the change in time or the time rate of change of work. You should recall from your physics classes that work is the product of force times distance. This product divided by time is power.

Most of the tests of power commonly used in the schools, such as the vertical jump and the standing long jump, do not include the three components of force, distance, and time. In fact, distance is the only measure usually obtained. Occasionally, for research purposes, body weight will be included to calculate work performed in order to take into account body weight. A heavy person is generally penalized when a jump is scored only by distance jumped. Yet, a heavier person may have performed more *work* than a lighter person even though the latter had jumped further. Keep in mind that we are speaking primarily about measurement for research purposes. Certainly, in basketball, the maximum height jumped is the most important consideration, not a person's body weight.

Margaria (1966) developed a test which has been used to a considerable extent in research studies. The test involves running up a flight of stairs, taking two steps at a time, as rapidly as possible. The time required to run up 6 or 8 (any number) stairs is recorded. Consequently, all three components of power are measured: The height of each stair times the number of stairs climbed constitutes distance. This is multiplied by the person's body weight to obtain the amount of work performed. The time is divided into work to yield a power score, which is then sometimes converted to horsepower. Construct validity has been established with sprinters, for example, scoring higher than distance runners.

The vertical jump has sometimes been scored in power units. The time factor has been measured in various ways, such as timing the length of time in the air and using the acceleration of free-falling bodies. The vertical jump, regardless of how it is measured, still represents a rough but valid indication of athletic power.

Speed of Movement and Reaction Time Measures. Speed of movement can be measured accurately with the use of an electronic timer. The extent of the movement depends on the nature of the research project. In some studies, total body movement such as running speed is measured. In other studies, speed of movement might entail only a finger movement or an eye blink. Speed of movement is defined as the time elapsed from the point of initiation of the movement to the completion of the movement.

Speed of movement is often studied along with reaction time. Reaction time is the time elapsed from the presentation of the stimulus (such as the flash of a light, a sound, or a touch) until the initiation of the response. In a race such as the 40-yard dash, reaction time would be the time from the stimulus, (e.g., the firing of the starter's pistol), until the runner *started* to move (as in exerting pressure against the starting blocks). Speed of movement begins from the exertion of pressure until the subject reaches the 40-yard mark.

Reaction time has been "fractionated" into premotor time (PMT), the central component, and motor time (MT), the peripheral component. The PMT is the time interval between stimulus presentation until the first action potential in the muscle is manifested, whereas the MT is the interval between the first muscle action potential and the initiation of the movement. Electromyography is used to fractionate PMT and MT. The electrical activity is rather quiet during the PMT interval; then a burst of activity signals the onset of MT. Apparently, a very low relationship exists between PMT and MT.

Agility Measures. Agility has been included in a number of applied research studies in physical education. Agility involves the accuracy and speed of changing direction while moving. Agility does not have to involve running. It also includes movement of the body such as scrambling up and down or jumping or hopping for accuracy. In some tests, agility and power are closely associated, such as when a person has to sprint a short distance then change direction and sprint again. In other agility tasks, power is not involved at all. In some agility tests, fitness components such as endurance can enter into the performance, while in others coordination is the primary factor.

Agility performance is highly specific to the task. Correlations between agility tests are notoriously low. For example, a shuttle run (involving a short sprint, stopping and changing direction), a zig-zag run (dodging around obstacles), and a squat thrust (moving rapidly from a standing position to a squat, then to a push-up position, and back to standing) are all recognized agility tests. The correlations among these tests are so low that there is virtually no generality at all. In other words, a person might be good at one task and poor or average at another. Here again, one must be careful in concluding from one test in a fitness battery as to a person's agility. There is no such thing as "general agility." Research in a specific sport should select (or construct) an agility test that involves the type of movements required for that sport, rather than some so-called "standard" agility test.

Balance Measures. Balancing ability depends upon such things as kinesthetic sensations, visual perception, and the mechanisms in the semicircular canals. Of the different kinds of balance, two major categories are static and dynamic. Static balance refers to the ability to hold a stationary position, whereas dynamic balance is the ability to maintain equilibrium while moving. As with many abilities, balance is highly specific to the task. There is virtually no relationship between static and dynamic balance.

Balance tasks have been used considerably in research, particularly in motor learning and performance studies. The stabilometer and the free-standing ladder climb tests are commonly used tasks. The stabilometer consists of a platform on which the subject attempts to stand, keeping the sides from tilting and touching the floor. The stabilometer is usually scored electronically so that the time is stopped or an error is recorded whenever the sides touch the floor. In the free-standing ladder task, the subject attempts to climb as far as possible before the ladder falls over. There is no cause for alarm, for the ladder is only a few feet high (e.g., 5 ft.). Often the ladder climb is scored electronically; for example, it might register a score when the ladder tilts a certain number of degrees from the vertical position.

Balance beam tests have frequently been used in perceptual motor learning studies and research with mentally retarded and brain-damaged subjects. The height, width, and configuration of the beams can vary greatly depending upon the age and ability level of the subjects. The subject may be asked to move forward, backward, or sideward along the beam; the score is usually the point at which the subject steps off the beam.

Balance tests are rarely used in motor fitness test batteries. Simple field tests sometimes used in the schools are the diver's stance, the stork stand, the Bass stick tests, the sideward leap, and various positional tasks such as the squat stand and head stand. Another type of balancing task involves balancing objects on the hand or head.

Kinesthesis Measures. Kinesthetic ability tests were researched quite heavily years ago. Very few studies have been done recently. Kinesthetic perception tests have included short jumps for accuracy with eyes open or closed; balancing tasks with eyes closed; throws or kicks at targets with eyes closed or the target obscured; positional tasks, such as moving the arm to a certain distance or angle; and recognizing and exerting a specific amount of force tasks such as one-half maximal hand-gripping force. The major limitation of kinesthetic tests is low reliability. Some possible reasons for this include (a) the heavy reliance on vision in normal activities which, when removed in the experimental task, greatly disrupts kinesthetic performance; and (b) the novelty of the task coupled with insufficient trials for kinesthetic ability to be demonstrated.

Coordination Measures. It is readily acknowledged that coordination is an integral component of skill-related fitness and performance. However, in accordance with the concept of specificity, there is no such thing as general, or all-around, coordination. Often-heard comments such as "so-and-so is well coordinated" are actually based on rather limited observations. Researchers gave up years ago trying to measure general coordination and motor ability.

The measurement of coordination in research studies is necessarily restricted to some observational definition of eye-hand or eye-foot coordination with respect to a particular task(s). Ball throwing, kicking, dance steps, and locomotor tasks have been used as measures of coordination for research purposes. Juggling is a classic hand-eye coordination activity which has often been used in motor-learning experiments. Elaborate testing apparatus has been devised which involves simultaneous action of the hands and feet while tracking a target. This kind of instrumentation was developed in World War II by the Air Force and used for the screening and training of pilots. Some suggest this was the beginning of research in motor learning. (See "History of Physical Education Research," Chapter 1).

Many manipulative tasks have been used in motor-learning research studies involving hand-eye coordination such as peg boards, rotary pursuit apparatus, and even children's games. Coordination measures have generally claimed logical validity. However, the nature of coordination probably lends itself well to the establishment of construct validity.

MOTOR BEHAVIOR MEASUREMENTS

Motor behavior generally deals with the acquisition and control of motor skills. Types of measurements range from tests of basic movement patterns, to sport skills tests, to laboratory measures. The distinctions among measurements within and between this part and other parts of this chapter are not nearly as clear-cut as our simplified discussion makes them appear. In addition, the measurements obtained are generally of two types—process and product. For example, in throwing, the outcome of the throw (how far, how accurate) can be measured (product) or the mechanics of the throwing movement can be analyzed (process). We will present mostly outcomes or product measurements here and discuss process or movement form (mechanics), assessment in the next section. Nevertheless, the two cannot be separated. Not only do we want to know if a movement pattern produced a quality outcome, we also want to know what about the pattern was correct and what needs to be altered.

Basic Movement Patterns. Our interest in basic movement patterns lies mostly with preschool and elementary school age children. At these ages, teachers focus on the development of movement patterns in general rather than in the specific sport context. Thus, tests frequently include throwing and kicking balls for distance and accuracy, catching, striking with implements, and jumping. Tests are constructed to measure these skills for children 9 years of age and above. Checklist and rating scales are useful for younger children because of the inconsistency of young children's performance. (For more detailed discussion, see Thomas & Thomas, 1983.) Because throwing, catching, striking, and jumping, are important skills in the sports of our culture, these skills are the most emphasized in the teaching and testing of children. The tests usually measure the outcomes of performance in time, distance, accuracy, or successful attempts. Many of the tests have been standardized and have norms as reported in books on tests and measurements in physical education (e.g., Johnson & Nelson, 1979).

Sport Skills Tests. These tests measure many of the same characteristics of performance as tests of basic movement patterns. However, performance is measured with the equipment and in the context of the specific sport; that is, any implement(s) used in the sport and in a situation that is similar to one encountered in the sport. For example, striking may be assessed in baseball as the number of successful hits out of a specific number of trials when the ball is projected by a pitching machine at 70 mph. Control of the soccer ball may be measured by a dribbling test through a series of direction changes. A kick for distance may be punting a football. Again, most tests and measurement books provide many examples of these tests with reliability and validity information and sometimes norms. In addition, AAHPERD has developed a sport skills test series for teachers' use.

Laboratory Measures. Many novel tasks have been developed for laboratory use in studying the acquisition and control of motor skills. Novelty is important in these tasks to control for prior experience. If none of the subjects has experience in performing the specific skill, then everyone begins at the same point in the skill acquisition process.

Some frequently used tasks in motor behavior laboratories are listed below:

1. *Pursuit Rotor*—a continuous tracking task much like a phonograph turntable. The task is to keep a hand-held stylus on a small circle located on the rotating disk. The stylus and disk are connected to a clock which records the amount or time the stylus remains in contact with the small circle during a specified time interval.

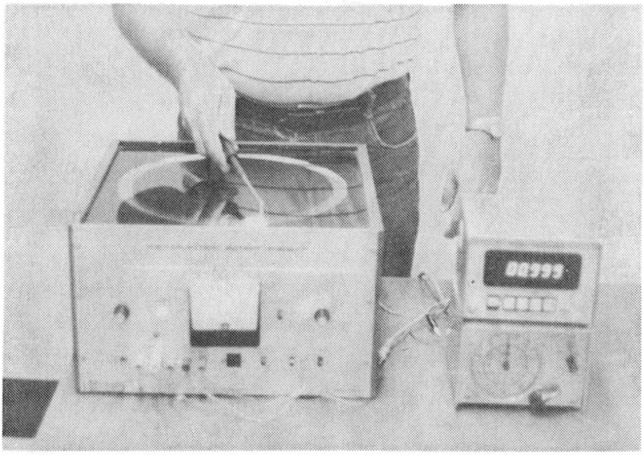

Figure 14.1 Pursuit rotor tracking. Photo courtesy of Motor Behavior Laboratory, Louisiana State University.

2. *Stabilometer*—a balance task in which a platform is centered on a fulcrum much like a child's "see-saw." The subject stands with both feet on the platform (one on either side of the fulcrum) and attempts to maintain the platform in a level (balanced) position. The score is either the number of times the platform touches the base on either side (errors), or the time the platform is kept in balance.

(a)

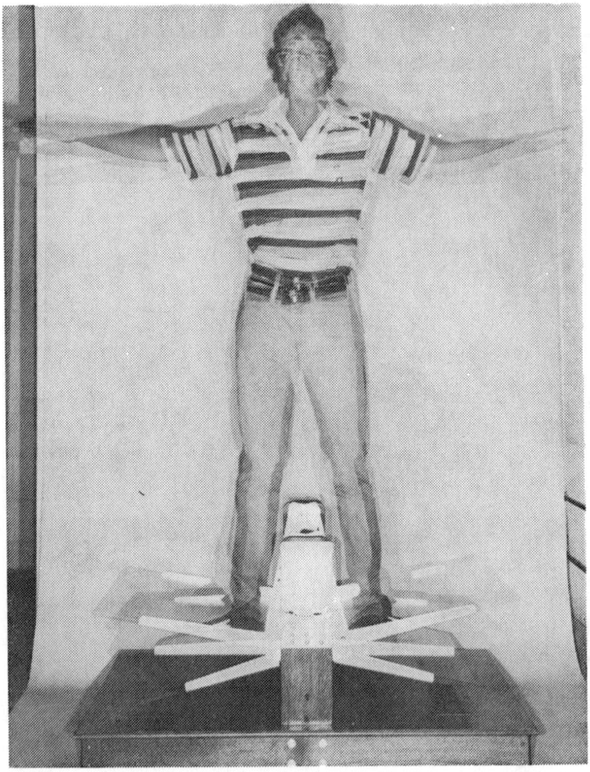

(b)

Figure 14.2 Taking the stabilometer test. Photo courtesy of Lafayette Instrument Company.

3. *Anticipation Timer*—a trackway several feet long with small lights mounted at close intervals down the trackway. A controlling device causes the lights to turn on and off consecutively down the trackway simulating movement. The speed of movement is determined by how

rapidly the lights are turned on and off. The subject's task is to press a hand-held button when the last light turns on and off (simulated movement is at the end of the trackway). The score is error in msec that the button is pressed either too early or too late.

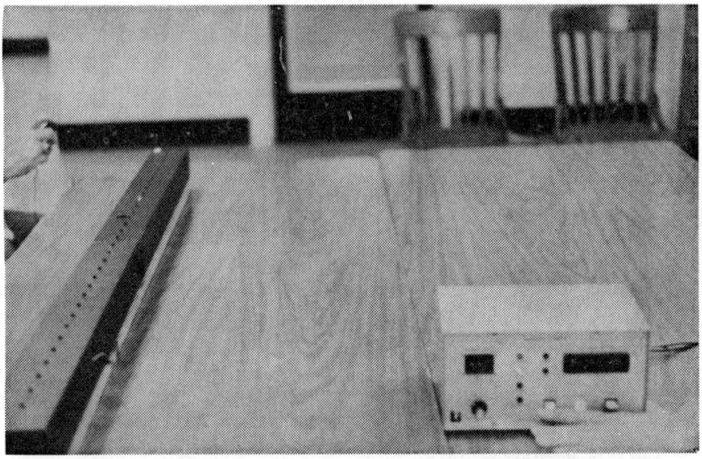

Figure 14.3 Anticipation timer. Photo courtesy of Motor Behavior Laboratory, Louisiana State University.

4. *Linear Slide*—a task where the subject moves a near frictionless handle down a trackway. The subject's task may be to move to some specified location (in which case the subject is usually blindfolded) or to move a certain distance in a criterion time (e.g., 40 cm in 400 msec). The score is error in cm (either short or long) from the location or error in msec (either fast or slow) for the time to move the specified distance.

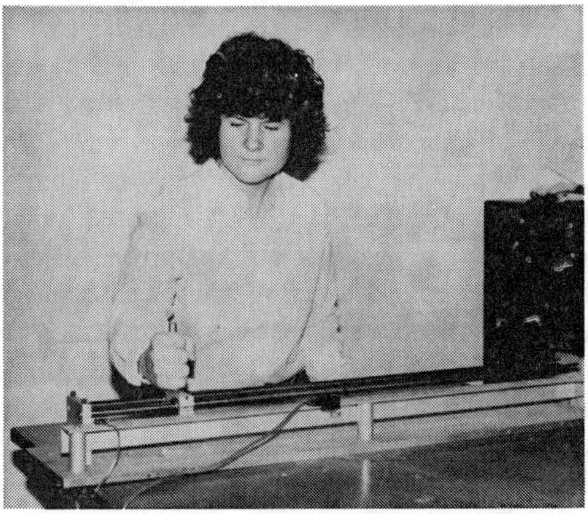

Figure 14.4 The linear slide. Photo courtesy of Peg Goyette.

5. *Tapping Board*—a task where two metal circles (can be any size but as an example, assume 2 cm in diameter) are mounted a certain distance apart (e.g., 18 cm). The subject uses a metal stylus to tap back and forth between the two circles as rapidly as possible. The circles and stylus are connected to a counter which records the number of touches during a specified time period.

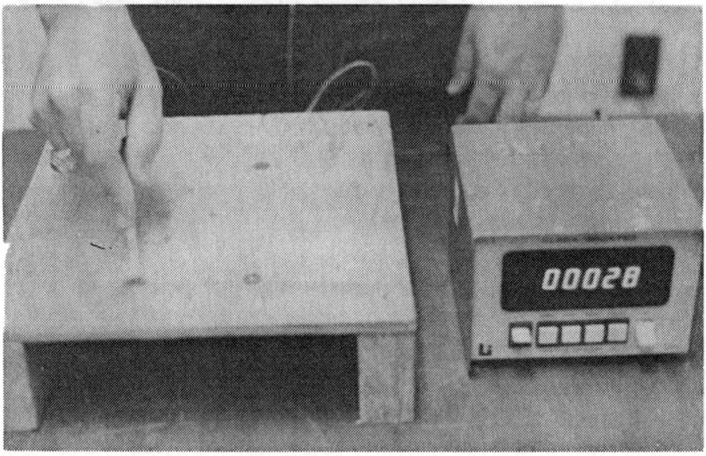

Figure 14.5 Tapping board. Photo courtesy of Motor Behavior Laboratory, Louisiana State University.

Note the outcomes from these tasks may be total time, total errors, directional error (long or short), timing error (fast or slow), or frequency of occurrence. In particular, long and short directional errors and fast or slow timing errors have generated interesting measurement issues.

If several subjects are given several trials on either the linear slide or the anticipation timer, then they are likely to have scores that are short or fast (labeled negative or minus) and long or slow (labeled positive or plus). A number of ways exist to obtain a performance estimate from these scores. Table 14.1 defines and gives an example of four common ways.

Absolute error (AE) was the most common way of reporting performance error until the paper by Schutz and Roy (1973) appeared, pointing out that AE was some undefined linear composite of constant error (CE) and variable error (VE). Schutz and Roy recommended that AE no longer be used and that CE be used to reflect bias (i.e., Did the subject tend to undershoot or overshoot the target?), and VE be used to represent variability in performance. (A low VE means consistent estimation while a high VE represents inconsistent estimation.) However, it soon became apparent that CE was not a good error estimate to average across subjects; that is, if some subjects undershoot on the average whereas others overshoot, the signs (±) of their scores tend to cancel and yield a group mean of zero. Schutz (1979) then suggested the use of absolute constant error

TABLE 14.1
WAYS OF ESTIMATING ERROR SCORES

Subject	X_1	X_2	X_3	X_4
	Trials			
Tom	+7	−4	−6	+3
Sam	−11	−2	+8	+3
Bill	−6	−3	−1	+3
John	+2	−1	−3	+1

AE—called absolute error. For each subject the scores are summed disregarding the sign and then divided by the number of scores, i.e., $AE = \Sigma|X|/N$. Thus, Tom's AE for the four trials is $(7 + 4 + 6 + 3)/4 = 20/4 = 5$.

CE—called constant error. The scores are summed (using the sign) for each subject and divided by the number of scores, i.e., $CE = \Sigma X/N$. Sam's CE is $[(-11 - 2) + (8 + 3)]/4 = (-13 + 11)/4 = -2/4 = -.50$.

/CE/—called absolute constant error. CE is calculated, then the absolute value is taken, i.e., $/CE/ = |\Sigma X|/N$. Bill's /CE/ is $|(-6 - 3 - 1 + 3)/4| = |-7/4| = 1.75$.

VE—called variable error. VE is the standard deviation of a subject's average CE score, i.e., $VE = \sqrt{\Sigma(X - M)^2/N}$. John's score is $CE = [(2 + 1) + (-1 - 3)]/4 = (3 - 4)/4$ $-1/4 = -.25$

$$VE = \sqrt{[(2 - .25)^2 + (-1 - .25)^2 + (-3 - .25)^2 + (1 - .25)^2]/4}$$

$$= \sqrt{(3.06 + 1.56 + 10.56 + .56)/4} = \sqrt{3.94} = 1.98$$

(/CE/) to solve this problem. Earlier, Henry (1974) had advocated that one error score had the advantage of simplicity, but because AE was undefined, researchers should use a defined composite error he called E, $E = \sqrt{CE^2 + VE^2}$. Beginning in the late 1970s, numerous statistical studies were done on the qualities of the error measures as dependent variables. (For example, see Gessaroli & Schutz, 1983; Safrit, Spray, & Diewert, 1980; Schutz, 1979.)

The most commonly used error scores today are /CE/ and VE, although all of them are used on occasion. Laabs (1979) suggested that CE (and thus probably /CE/) represented perceptual judgment in memory while VE represented the strength of the memory trace for a movement. Thus, VE could be used to measure learning and forgetting. VE seems to be a particularly useful measure because it represents variability of performance. Therefore, beginners should have larger VE scores than more skilled performers, and younger children should have larger VE scores than older children.

Finally, reaction time (RT), which was discussed earlier in this chapter, is also frequently used as a laboratory task. A task may be designed in which the subject is asked upon a stimulus to move from a home key to one of several other keys. The time from the stimulus until the home key is released is the RT; it has been found to vary as a function of the need for planning in the upcoming movement as to number of choices of movements, direction of movement, and length of the movement. Thus, RT seems useful as an index of motor planning or motor programming.

BIOMECHANICAL MEASUREMENTS

Biomechanics has been defined as ". . . the application of the physical laws of motion to the study of biological systems" (Burdett, 1983, p. 2). Measurements to quantify movements have resulted from three specific sources: high-speed cinematography, force transducers, and electromyography. High-speed cinematography is the most widely used with earlier studies using a single camera allowing two-dimensional analysis. More recent advances use two (or more) cameras which allow motion to be studied in three dimensions. These techniques are increasingly being applied to sport skills. Movements are then analyzed frame-by-frame for displacements of body segments as well as for their velocities and accelerations. Standard physics formulas are applied to quantify measures. More sophisticated systems are interfaced with high-speed computers for rapid and detailed analysis. Even more refined and detailed videorecording systems are now being developed.

Force transducers are used to measure the forces exerted during motor performance. These include the reactions between a runner's or jumper's feet and the ground as well as the forces exerted against equipment, such as bicycles and weight. The transducers are interfaced with computer equipment (usually by an analog-to-digital converter) for faster and more thorough analysis.

Electromyography is a technique that is bringing biomechanics and motor learning and control closer together. This technique uses skin or muscle electrodes to pick up electrical activity caused by muscle contraction during movement. This allows assessment of synchronous and asynchronous firing patterns in motor units during activity. The firing pattern determines the force exerted by the muscle as well as the timing. Of great interest is the difference in electrical patterns between skilled and novice performers, the changes that occur as a novice acquires skill over many practice trials, or the consistency of the EMG pattern during various movement speeds. Electromyographical signals are read directly into computers or can be recorded as pen displacements on a strip recorder.

OBSERVATIONAL MEASUREMENT

Most of the measures of movement discussed have been acquired in relatively constrained settings, that is, testing situations or laboratories. Sometimes measurements are made by recording observations in "real-world" settings such as during physical education classes or sport participation. This involves the use or development of some sort of coding instrument. Most frequently, the instrument has a series of categories into which the various motor behaviors may be coded. The behaviors are observed using such techniques as event recording, time sampling, and duration recording.

An example of an event recording instrument for sport is the Coaches Behavioral Assessment Scale (CBAS) developed by Smith, Smoll, and Hunt (1977). The purpose of this scale is to record the reactive and spontaneous behaviors of the coach to actions of players during games. (Football, soccer, baseball, and basketball have all been used.) The scale has eight categories of reactive behaviors and four categories of spontaneous behaviors. While watching the sport contest, the researcher codes any event of coach-player interaction that occurs. (For a more detailed description and references, see the chapter by Smoll & Smith in Thomas, 1984.)

The Academic Learning Time in Physical Education (ALT-PE) instrument developed by Siedentop, Trousignant, and Parker (1982) is an example of time sampling. The researcher observes a child for certain lengths of time at specified intervals, for example, 10 seconds of watching and 10 seconds of rest. The activities in which the child engages during the 10 seconds are coded. This allows estimates of time-on-task, time listening, and time waiting for a turn. Duration techniques are similar in format. However, the researcher's purpose is to record the length of time a subject spends on a particular event.

In these types of scales, as with any measure, validity and reliability are important. However, it is usually considerably more difficult to obtain consistency in recording children's activities in a physical education class or sport than for recording error measurements from a laboratory task such as the linear slide. The researcher must be concerned about two types of consistency—first, that an observer records an event the same way each time; and second, that two observers record the same event in the same way.

Video recording instrumentation is of tremendous value in observational research. If the activity of interest can be videotaped, then observers can be more sure of their recording techniques because performance can be viewed more than once. However, considerable cost is involved.

In observational measurement, blind and double-blind techniques are particularly useful. Observers tend to code experimental and control groups and pre- and posttests differently if they know this information. Videotapes are particularly useful here because order and group assignment can be randomized to keep the observer naive to the time period and treatment condition.

Observational researchers are always concerned about the consistency of coders. Typically, coders are trained to a criterion level of reliability, and then reliability checks are made regularly during the project. A common way of estimating reliability among coders is called interobserver agreement (IOA) and uses the following formula:

$$\text{IOA} = \text{agreements} / (\text{agreements} + \text{disagreements})$$

Where agreements = commonly coded behaviors, and disagreements = behaviors coded differently.

USING COMPUTERS IN MEASURING MOVEMENT

Whereas any type of computer can be used in measuring movement, microcomputers are the most commonly used. These computers may be used in three ways: controlling the data collection situation, recording the data, and analyzing the data.

CONTROLLING THE DATA COLLECTION SITUATION

Programs are frequently written for micros that control the testing session. In a motor behavior experiment, the task might be to make either a long or short movement when a stimulus light appears. A computer program can be written that works as follows:

1. The experimenter loads the program into the microcomputer prior to the subject's arrival in the testing situation.
2. When the subject arrives, the experimenter enters his or her name, ID number, and any other pertinent characteristics such as which group the subject is in, age, gender, and handedness.
3. The computer then displays a picture of the task and written instructions concerning how the subject is to perform.
4. The computer provides a set number of practice trials. After each trial, the subject is provided knowledge of results about his or her reaction time and movement time.
5. The computer controls all aspects of the experimental testing session including the flashing of the warning light, flashing the movement signal, randomizing the interval between the warning and movement signal, controlling the interval between trials, providing knowledge of results at a precise point between trials, and even retesting a trial if a reaction or movement time is outside a specified range.

RECORDING THE DATA

In the previously described situation, the microcomputer is also used to record the data after each trial. However, sometimes the micro might be used to record data but not control the data collection situation. For example, an observer could enter data directly into a micro while observing a physical education class. If a program were written to handle data from the ALT-PE coding instrument

(Siedentop et al., 1982), the entries could be made into a micro as easily as on to a code sheet.

ANALYZING THE DATA

The micro may also be used partly or completely to analyze the data. As shown earlier, statistical programs (see Appendix B) are available for use on microcomputers. Or, the micro can be used to send the data to a larger mainframe computer for statistical analysis. This is done by interfacing the microcomputer with the mainframe by a phone line. Normally, this requires special hardware (micromodem or acoustic coupler) and software (a special program for either the micro or mainframe). However, most computer centers at larger institutions are adaptable to this need.

Remember, these are only examples of the uses of microcomputers. Innovative researchers and technicians have found hundreds of unique ways to use micros in controlling, recording, and analyzing research. The advantages are easily seen in time saved, errors reduced, and increased sophistication of experiments. As an example, a number of errors can be made in getting the data from the instrumentation used to the analysis. If this is done by hand, the experimenter could read the instrumentation wrong, record it incorrectly, transfer it to a code sheet incorrectly, or enter it for data analysis improperly. All of these sources of error are controlled when a micro is used to record and analyze the data.

The limitations in using micro are easily observed. First, micros cost money. Second, once the micro is obtained, it must be interfaced with the equipment and programs must be written to control the experimental situation. Because these programs are unique to the experiment being conducted, they are not available commercially. Thus, the technical support must be obtained in order to use the microcomputer effectively. Finally, micros are not maintenance free and continually use supplies such as floppy disks as well as more advanced programs and additional hardware.

SUMMARY

This chapter has provided some examples of the ways movement may be measured. Included have been measurements of physical fitness, motor abilities, basic movement skills, sport skills, laboratory tasks for motor behavior, biomechanical measurements, and observational measurements. Neither the categories nor the examples within categories are meant to be inclusive. However, we feel that examples are sometimes helpful in understanding concepts.

Chapter 15

Measuring Written Responses

Much of the research conducted in HPERD involves measurement of written (and oral) responses. Research in all the fields of HPERD occasionally deals with affective behavior, which includes attitudes, interests, emotional states, and personality and psychological traits. This chapter will consider some of these affective behavior measures and will examine various types of responses that are used in such paper-and-pencil tests and some characteristics of rating scales; attention will also be given to item analysis in written tests of knowledge.

MEASUREMENT OF AFFECTIVE BEHAVIOR

A variety of behaviors fall in the category of affective behavior, including attitudes, social behavior, sportsmanship, self-concept, anxiety, and other personality measures.

ATTITUDE

A large number of attitude inventories have been developed in all fields of HPERD. Undoubtedly, the test developers feel there is a direct link between attitude and behavior. For example, if a person has a favorable attitude toward physical activities, that person will participate in such activities. Research, however, has seldom substantiated this link between attitude and behavior. However, it does seem logical.

Researchers usually try to locate an instrument that has already been validated and is an accepted measure of attitude rather than having to construct one. Finding a published test that closely pertains to the research topic is a problem. Another problem is that often the researcher wants to determine whether some treatment will bring about a change in attitude. One of the sources of invalidity in Chapter 11 is the reactive effects of testing where pretesting sensitizes the subject to the attitudes in question, which may promote a change rather than the treatment.

Still another problem is one mentioned in Chapter 10, which is inherent in any self-report inventory: whether the person is truthful. It is usually quite evident as to what a given response indicates. For example, a person is asked to indicate the degree of agreement or disagreement to the statement, "Regular exercise is an important part of our daily lives." The individual may perceive that the socially desirable response is to agree with this statement, regardless of his or her true feelings. Some respondents deliberately distort their answers to appear "good" (or "bad"). Tests sometimes use "filler" items to make the true purpose of the instrument less visible. This is especially important when social desirability considerations may be biasing factors.

When a researcher seeks to find an attitude instrument for use in his or her study, validity and reliability must, of course, be primary considerations. Unfortunately, published attitude scales have not always been constructed in a scientific manner, and limited information is provided about validity and reliability. Actually, reliability can be established rather easily as far as methodology is concerned. (We are not saying that attitude scales are easily made reliable.) Validity is usually the problem because of the failure to develop a satisfactory theoretical model for the attitude construct.

Attitudes toward physical education, sport, and exercise have been measured in numerous studies. An example of a well-constructed attitude inventory is Kenyon's Attitude Toward Physical Activity (ATPA) Inventory (1968). The theoretical model for the ATPA hinges on the premise that attitude toward activity is relatively stable, and that positive attitudes are manifested by active participation or by watching others perform (passive involvement). Content validity was established by factor analysis and expert opinion. Construct validity was also established via the group difference method.

On the other hand, the Physical Estimation and Attraction Scale (PEAS) is based on the theory that attitude toward activity is modifiable by participation in physical activity (Sonstroem, 1978). The PEAS was constructed with sound procedures, whereby construct validity has been demonstrated by a number of research studies. Thus, a researcher who is planning a study to assess changes in attitude through some planned activity would be advised to use the PEAS rather than the ATPA because the latter is based on the theoretical framework that attitude does not change.

Construct validity in attitude inventories can be established by comparing different groups who supposedly would be expected to reflect different attitudes. For example, boys of high and low fitness were found to differ significantly in both the estimation and attraction items of the PEAS test.

Although our examples of attitude measures have been in physical education, we should point out that the measurement of attitudes has occupied considerable interest in all HPERD fields. In health science, attitude studies have been conducted on such topics as drugs, rape, death and dying, smoking, menopause, alcohol, sex behaviors, handicapped persons, various diseases, and effectiveness of health instruction and services.

Research in recreation has involved attitude assessment including leisure activity preferences by various populations, the value of recreation, the effectiveness of professional preparation in recreation, recreational programs for the mentally retarded, outdoor education, industrial recreation, and fieldwork experiences in parks management.

In dance, researchers have assessed attitudes toward creativity, the contributions of various leaders in dance, mood changes through dance, the value of dance for special groups, and the place of dance in the university structure.

PERSONALITY

A large number of research studies in physical education and sport have attempted to explore the relationship between personality traits and various aspects of athletic performance. Interest in this topic can be attributed to several factors. A great deal of public attention is focused on athletics. Athletes are obviously "special" people with regard to physical characteristics. Beyond that, however, is the hypothesis that athletes have certain personality traits that distinguish them from nonathletes.

Another area of investigation has been to identify personality traits that might be uniquely characteristic of athletes in different sports. For example, do persons who gravitate toward vigorous contact sports differ in personality from those individuals who prefer noncontact sports, that is, Is there a "football-type" or a "bowler-type"? Are superior athletes different from average athletes in certain personality traits? Can participation in competitive sport modify one's personality structure? Moreover, do athletes within a sport differ on some traits, which, if known, could point to different coaching strategies, or perhaps could be used to screen and to predict those athletes who will be "hard" to coach, or who will lack certain qualities associated with success?

Persons with a strong interest in sports, such as former coaches and players, have been greatly attracted to the study of personality and athletics. Having a strong interest in athletics does not compensate for a lack of preparation and experience in psychological evaluation. Unfortunately, there have been numerous instances of ignorance about personality structure and misuse of personality-measuring instruments. Many well-intentioned but unprepared graduate students have undertaken theses and dissertations which have purported to investigate the personality structure of athletes.

We have repeatedly stressed the point that measuring instruments are not infallible; there is always the likelihood of measurement error, and when the measuring instrument is being used by someone who is not knowledgeable about the parameter being measured, the chance of error is magnified. It is true that there are some paper-and-pencil personality trait inventories that are easily administered and objectively scored. The problem arises with the interpretation.

What does it mean when groups differ significantly on traits such as *protension* or *autia*? The mere reporting of the presence or lack of significant differences in personality traits has very little meaningfulness. Alderman (1974) said, "Too often, intuitive jumps are made between very ordinary information and highly complex behavioral explanations without realizing the limitations and restrictions that many of our personality inventories possess" (p. 128).

The aspiring researcher in this area needs to know which traits can be expected to produce specific motivational states and which are not likely to have any effect. Moreover, some traits are more independent of other traits, whereas some overlap and operate in conjunction with certain others. Consistency of behaviors which manifest particular traits is impossible to achieve over a variety of situations. People simply react differently to different situations, and while a person may exhibit self-confidence or dominance in some instances, that same individual may be quite the opposite in other situations. Our point is that personality is very complex. Elaborate theories have been developed in attempting to explain human behavior through personality constructs. A graduate student is naive indeed to think that the scores on a single instrument given to a sample of subjects on one occasion by an untrained tester will yield a great deal of generalizable conclusions about such a complex concept as personality structure. The study of personality is not futile, however. On the contrary, there is persuasive evidence that certain special populations such as superior athletes do have unique and identifiable personality profiles. We are simply stressing the need for adequate scholarly preparation of the researcher and the complexity of personality dynamics.

Of the several pen-and-pencil personality inventories on the market, the Cattell 16 Personality Factor (PF) Questionnaire has been used most frequently in research studies concerning the personality profiles of athletes and participants in physical activity. A specific personality questionnaire for the evaluation of personality profiles of athletes, the Athletic Motivational Inventory (AMI), was developed by Tutko, Lyon, and Ogilvie (1969).

ANXIETY

The measurement of anxiety in HPERD has been concentrated primarily in the areas of sport psychology and motor learning because of the recognized implications of anxiety level and motor performance. Spielberger (1966) is generally credited with differentiating between two types of anxiety: *state* and *trait*. State anxiety is an immediate emotional state of apprehension and tension in accordance with a specific situation, whereas trait anxiety is more of a general tendency to be anxious. Thus, trait anxiety is a rather stable characteristic of an individual. Persons with high-trait anxiety are prone to perceive more situations as threatening and to respond with different degrees of state anxiety.

This distinction is important to the researcher who is planning to assess changes in anxiety produced by a particular stressful situation(s). If a trait anxiety inventory is selected, then, by definition, one should not expect a change. Until

Spielberger developed his A-state and A-trait anxiety scale, such studies were virtually doomed from the start as far as measurable changes in anxiety were concerned.

In light of the importance of specificity, Martens (1977) developed a sport-specific trait anxiety inventory, the Sport Competition Anxiety Test (SCAT), which he found to be a better predictor of trait-anxiety in a sport context when compared with general trait anxiety scales. Martens found satisfactory reliability and convincing evidence of content and construct validity for SCAT when it is used within the context of his model of competition.

SELF-CONCEPT

Self-concept is a personality trait which has prompted numerous studies in nearly all areas of HPERD. Other terms which have been used either synonymously with, or as a facet of, self-concept include self-image, self-confidence, self-esteem, and self-regard. A major premise for the interest in this area is that the manner in which persons see themselves has a high relationship with achievement. Furthermore, it is hypothesized that self-concept can be modified by certain types of experiences, especially those which provide positive reinforcement.

Of particular interest to persons in movement-oriented fields is the influence of body image on total self-concept. Researchers have attempted to assess the effects of weight loss on obese individuals as to changes in their body image. Several projective tests and self-report-type scales have been constructed to measure body image. However, the projective tests cannot be objectively scored, making them inappropriate for persons other than psychologists.

The effects of different types of recreational activities and experiences on self-concept have been investigated numerous times. For example, activities such as rock climbing and adventure programs have been studied to determine whether participation in such "risk-type" activities can bring about favorable changes in self-concept.

Some of the problems encountered are those which we have alluded to in other similar research topics. The primary consideration is in test selection. A test which is constructed on the premise that self-concept is a stable personality trait should not be used in a study in which changes in self-concept are expected. In other words, the researcher needs to select a measure which views self-concept as a dimension that is amenable to change.

SOCIAL BEHAVIOR

Interest in social behavior is logical because physical educators generally list social development as one of the objectives in physical education. However, the amount of interest in developing social behavior measuring instruments has diminished through the years. Major stumbling blocks in attempts to measure social behavior have been the lack of clear-cut definitions as to what social behavior consists of and the lack of acceptable validity and reliability coefficients.

Behavior measurement is usually performed by some type of rating scale. The problems associated with such ratings are discussed in Chapter 10 under "Observational Research," and limitations of rating scales, in general, are described later in this chapter. Consequently, we are simply acknowledging this area of research here as being within affective behavior measurement.

SPORTSMANSHIP

One of the espoused goals included under the objective of promoting desirable social qualities is the development of sportsmanship. A great amount of lip service has been given to this goal and claims have been made that physical education and sports contribute to the development of sportsmanship; however, almost no evidence exists to prove this occurs.

Investigators have used a cross-sectional approach in comparing samples of older children with younger children in an attempt to yield evidence that participation in organized physical activity and competition develops sportsmanship. Some researchers have compared professional players with amateurs, and others have looked at the effects of the size of the university on the sportsmanship of athletes within the different institutions.

The research results have been confusing, to say the least, with some evidence advanced that the longer one participates in sports, the poorer the sportsmanship. Some of the contradictions in findings may be attributed to the means of assessing sportsmanship. One method which has been used is with rating scales. Operationally defining observable sportsmanship poses a problem along with the lack of sufficient opportunities to display the behavior. Pencil-and-paper tests of sportsmanship have been mostly of the situational format in which a given situation is described, and the respondent is asked to indicate whether the course of action is appropriate.

The main drawback to the sport situation approach is that the respondent can easily pick out which answer is the desired one. In addition, the described situation is often one that may not be sportsmanlike in the strict interpretation of the act, but it is an accepted practice in the sport. For example, although blocking the base path in baseball is illegal, catchers are taught to do this when trying to tag the runner sliding into homeplate. Thus, an experienced player would not view this action as unsportsmanlike, whereas a person unfamiliar with the game would answer correctly because blocking the base path is, in fact, in violation of the rules. The situational approach is probably the most feasible for pencil-and-paper inventories, but much work needs to be done to develop really valid and reliable research instruments.

TYPES OF RESPONSES

In measuring affective behavior, a variety of scales are used to quantify the responses. Three of the more commonly used scales are the Likert scale, the Semantic Differential, and the Thurstone-type scales.

THE LIKERT SCALE

The Likert scale was referred to in Chapter 10 in connection with survey research techniques. It is usually a 5- or 7-point scale with assumed equal intervals between points. The Likert scale is used to assess the degree of agreement or disagreement with statements and is widely used in attitude inventories. An example of a Likert scale item is given below:

> I prefer quiet recreational activities such as chess, cards, or checkers rather than activities such as running, tennis, or basketball.

Strongly agree	Agree	Undecided	Disagree	Strongly disagree

A principal advantage of scaled responses such as the Likert is that it permits a wider choice of expression than items such as "always," "never," "yes," or "no." The five, seven, or more intervals help increase the reliability of the instrument. For more comprehensive information concerning the Likert scale, Semantic Differential, and other scales, refer to Edwards (1957) or Nunnaly (1978).

THE SEMANTIC DIFFERENTIAL

The Semantic Differential employs bipolar adjectives at each end of a 7-point scale. The respondent is asked to make judgments about certain concepts. The scale is based on the importance of language in reflecting a person's feelings. A sample of a semantic differential item follows.

The coach

1. creative __ : __ : __ : __ : __ : __ : __ : unoriginal
2. supportive __ : __ : __ : __ : __ : __ : __ : critical
3. fair __ : __ : __ : __ : __ : __ : __ : unfair

The 1 to 7 scale between adjectives is scored with 7 being the most positive judgment. Factor analysis studies have rather consistently identified the same three dimensions being assessed by the semantic differential technique: evaluation, potency, and activity.

THURSTONE-TYPE SCALES

In the Thurstone-type scales, the respondent expresses agreement or disagreement with a series of statements. In developing Thurstone scales, each of the items is first scaled by a panel of judges. The judges rate each statement with a numerical value. In the Thurstone-Chave method, ratings from 1 to 11 are used, with 11 reflecting the most positive attitude. The median score of the judges for each item is then used to differentially weight the statements for use in scoring.

An example of a statement as it would appear on the tester's manual is as follows:

1. Physical education should be required in the elementary school. (9.1)

Only items marked as "agree" are scored. The final score is the sum of all the weighted scores divided by the number of "agree" items. The Thurstone-type scales are more difficult to construct than the Likert and Semantic Differential scales due to the involvement of the judges.

RATING SCALES

Rating scales are sometimes used in research to evaluate performance. For example, in a study which compares different strategies in teaching dance, the dependent variable (dance skill) would most likely be derived from expert ratings because dance does not lend itself to objective skill tests. Thus, after the experimental treatments have been applied, persons knowledgeable in dance rate all the subjects on their dancing skills. In order to do this in a systematic and structured manner, the raters need to have some kind of scale with which to assess skill levels in different parts or phases of the performance. For an illustration in the area of dance, refer to Chapter 12 for a rating scale used in evaluating dance choreography.

There are different kinds of rating scales: Some scales use numerical ratings; some use checklists; some have verbal cues associated with numerical ratings; some require forced choices; and still others use rankings. Some scales are relatively simple, whereas others are rather complex. Regardless of the degree of complexity, practice in using the scale is absolutely imperative.

When more than one judge is asked to rate performances, there have to be some common standards. Training sessions with videotaped performances of persons of different levels of ability are very helpful in establishing standard frames of reference prior to judging the actual performances of the subjects in the study. Intertester agreement and reliability were discussed in Chapters 13 and 14.

RATING ERRORS

Despite efforts to make ratings as objective as possible, there are inherent pitfalls in the process. Some of the recognized errors in rating include leniency, central tendency, halo effect, proximity, observer bias, and observer expectation.

Leniency is the tendency for observers to be overly generous in their ratings. This error is less likely to occur in research than in evaluating peers, for example, co-workers. Thorough training of raters is the best means of reducing leniency.

Central tendency error is the inclination of the rater to give an inordinate number of ratings in the middle of the scale, avoiding the extremes of the scale. Several reasons are attributed to this. Sometimes it may be due in part to ego needs or status. For example, the judge is acting in the role of an expert and perhaps unconsciously may grade good performers as average to indicate that he or she is accustomed to seeing better performance. Sometimes, too, errors of central tendency are due to the observer wanting to ''leave room'' for better future performances. A common complaint in large gymnastics, diving, and skating competitions is that the performers scheduled early in the meet are scored lower for comparable performances than athletes scheduled later in the competition.

Central tendency error at the other end of the scale is the avoidance of assigning very low scores, likely due to the judge's reluctance to be too harsh; in other words, ''give the poor devil a break.'' It is, of course, a form of leniency.

Halo effect is the commonly observed tendency for a rater to allow previous impressions or knowledge about a certain individual to influence ratings on all of that individual's behaviors. For example, knowing an individual excels in one or more activities, we tend to rate that person highly on all other activities. Halo effect perhaps is not the most appropriate term because negative impressions of a person tend to lead to lower ratings in subsequent performances.

Proximity errors are often the result of overly detailed rating scales or the lack of sufficient familiarity with the rating criteria, or both. Proximity errors are manifested when the rater tends to rate behaviors which are listed close together as more nearly the same as when the behaviors are separated some distance on the scale. Of course, if the rater does not have adequate knowledge about all facets of the behavior, he or she may not be able to distinguish between different behaviors that logically should be placed close together on the scale. Thus, the different phases of behavior are rated the same.

Observer bias errors are a function of the judge's own characteristics and prejudices. For example, a person who has a low regard for movement education may also tend to rate students from such a program too low. Racial biases, sexual biases, and philosophical biases are all potential sources of rating errors. Observer bias errors are directional in that they produce errors that are consistently too high or too low.

Observer expectation errors can operate in various ways, often stemming from other sources of errors such as halo effect and observer bias. Observer expectations can contaminate the ratings in that a person who expects certain behaviors will be inclined to see evidence of those behaviors and interpret observations in the ''expected'' direction.

Research has demonstrated the powerful phenomenon of expectation in classroom situations in which teachers are told that some children are gifted or slow learners. The teachers tend to treat the pupils accordingly, giving more attention and patience to the ''gifted'' and less time and attention to the ''slow learners.''

In the research setting, potential observer expectation errors are likely when the observer knows what the experimental hypotheses are and is inclined to watch for these outcomes more closely than if he or she were unaware of the expected outcomes. The double-blind experimental technique described in Chapter 11 and elsewhere is useful in controlling for expectation errors. In the double-blind method, the observers are not aware of which subjects received which treatments.

(They also do not know which performances are the pretest and which are the posttest.)

In summary, rating errors are always potentially present. The researcher must be aware of them and strive to eliminate or reduce them. One of the ways to minimize rating errors is to have the behavior to be rated as objectively defined as possible. In other words, avoid having the observer make many value judgments. Another suggestion is to keep your observers "ignorant" of the hypotheses and of who received what. Bias and expectation can be minimized if the observer is given no information about the subjects' past achievements, intelligence, social status, and other characteristics. The most important precaution the researcher can take is to train the observers adequately to achieve high levels of accuracy and interrater reliability.

KNOWLEDGE TESTING

Obviously, the measurement of knowledge is a fundamental part of the educational thrusts in the fields within HPERD. However, the construction of knowledge tests is relevant for research purposes as well. Most paper-and-pencil measuring instruments used in research involve similar procedures in establishing validity and reliability. These procedures were summarized in Chapter 13; consequently, our attention will be directed primarily to item analysis techniques.

ITEM ANALYSIS

The purpose of item analysis is to determine which items are suitable and which need to be rewritten or discarded. Two important facets of item analysis are the difficulty of the test items and the power to discriminate between different levels of achievement.

ITEM DIFFICULTY

In most cases, the analysis of the difficulty of the test items is easily accomplished. One simply divides the number of persons who correctly answered the item by the total number of people who responded to the item. For example, if 80 people answered an item, and 60 answered it correctly, the item would have a difficulty index of .75 (60/80). A "hard" item has a low difficulty index; that is, if only 8 of 80 answered it correctly, the index is 8/80 = .10. Most test authorities recommend that questions with difficulty indexes of below .10 or over .90 should be eliminated. The best questions are those which have a difficulty index of around .50. Occasionally, a test maker may wish to set a specific difficulty index for screening purposes. For example, if only the top 30% of a group of applicants are to be chosen, this could be accomplished by using questions with a difficulty index of .30. Questions which everyone answers correctly or everyone misses do not provide any information about people differences in norm-referenced measurement scales.

ITEM DISCRIMINATION

The degree to which test items discriminate between persons who did well on the entire test from those who did poorly is an important consideration in analyzing test items. There are a number of ways to compute an Index of Discrimination. The simplest way is to divide the test papers into a high group and a low group based on their scores on the test, and then use the following formula:

$$\text{Index of Discrimination} = (NH - NL)/N$$

where NH = number of high scorers who answered the item correctly, NL = number of low scorers who answered the item correctly, and N = number in either the high or low group. To illustrate, if we have 30 in the high group and 30 in the low group, and 20 of the high scorers answered an item correctly and 10 of the low scorers answered it correctly, the Index of Discrimination would be .33.

$$(20 - 10)/30 = 10/30 = .33$$

Various percentages of high and low scorers are used in determining discrimination indices, such as the upper and lower 25%, 30%, 33%. The Flanagan method uses the upper and lower 27%. The proportion of each group who answer each item correctly is calculated; then a table of normalized biserial coefficients is consulted to obtain the item reliability coefficient. Hence, item reliability is the relationship between people's responses to each item and their total performance on the test.

If approximately the same proportion of high scorers answer an item correctly as did the low scorers, the item is not discriminating. Most test makers strive for an Index of Discrimination of .20 and higher for each item. Obviously, a negative Index of Discrimination would be unacceptable. In fact, when this happens, the question needs to be examined closely to see if there is something in the wording that is throwing off the high scorers.

TYPES OF KNOWLEDGE TEST ITEMS

The most common types of test questions are completion, essay, matching, alternate choice, and multiple choice. Each type of question has its strengths and weaknesses, which are discussed in detail in measurement and evaluation texts.

Knowledge tests have been used in research studies in HPERD concerning facts and fallacies about venereal disease, drugs, diet, game rules, and exercise, basic knowledge pertaining to different subject areas, and other topics. Knowledge testing in such research studies invariably use objective items such as multiple choice or alternate choice. Matching test items are objective, but they are time consuming and limited as to effective number of items that can be presented.

Multiple choice items are considered by testing authorities as the most reliable of the test items. Good multiple choice items are difficult to write. The stem should be presented clearly and concisely, and the alternatives have to be meaningful and attractive. Poor alternatives simply limit the choices and can reduce multiple choice items to alternate choice items.

The number of alternatives influence reliability. The more choices, the greater reliability because the likelihood of getting the correct answer by chance is reduced. However, as you increase the number of alternatives, practical considerations such as time required for testing negates the advantage. Between three and five choices are recommended.

Alternate choice items, such as true-false, are used occasionally in research studies. This type of item has been criticized for various reasons, but often the weaknesses cited can be minimized by careful test construction. Alternate choice items are less reliable than multiple choice tests of the same length. However, more alternate-choice items can be given in a set time period which can increase the test reliability. The items are easier to write than multiple choice, but considerable skill is required to develop good test questions. With care, alternate-choice tests can be employed to effectively assess knowledge.

Section V

WRITING THE RESEARCH REPORT

Section I discussed the research proposal, its purpose, and the structure of the different parts. Sections II, III, and IV provided the details needed to understand and conduct research, including statistics, types of research, and measurement. Finally, this section completes the research process with instructions on how to prepare the research report. You may also want to refer back to Chapter 2, which discussed some rules and recommendations for writing the review of literature, for this is an important part of the research report.

Chapter 16 is a brief chapter on all the parts of the research proposal which already have been discussed throughout several chapters. In addition, we offer some of our thoughts about the nature of the committee meeting to review the research proposal.

The remaining two chapters focus upon the final written research report. Up to now everything has involved how to understand other research and how to develop a plan for your own research. Chapter 17 helps you to organize and to write the results and discussion chapters (or sections) of your research. Suggestions are also provided on about how to prepare tables, figures, and illustrations, and where to place them in the research report.

Finally, Chapter 18 offers some suggestions about traditional and alternative ways of organizing and writing theses and dissertations. In addition, a brief section on writing for scientific journals and a short discourse on preparing and giving oral presentations is presented. To conclude, ethical considerations among researchers and between graduate students and their major professors are discussed.

Chapter 16

The Proposal

The research proposal essentially contains the definition, scope, and significance of the problem and the methodology that is going to be used to solve the problem. In a four-chapter thesis or dissertation (Introduction, Method, Results, and Discussion) the proposal consists of the first two chapters. In studies using a five-chapter format in which the review of literature is Chapter 2, the proposal encompasses the first three chapters.

One of the goals of this text has been to help prepare a student to develop a research proposal. Consequently, we have already discussed the contents of the proposal. For example, Chapters 2, 3, and 4 specifically pertain to the body of the research proposal. Other chapters relate to various facets of planning a study with regard to the hypotheses, measurement, design, and statistical analysis. Thus, this chapter will attempt to "bring the proposal together." We will also spend some time discussing the proposal meeting and committee actions. Finally, we will touch upon basic considerations involved in grant proposals—specifically, how they differ from thesis and dissertation proposals.

CHAPTER 1. INTRODUCTION

The student's number one task is to convince the committee (whether it be the proposal committee or a reviewing committee for a granting agency) that the problem is important and worth investigating. The first chapter is supposed to do this as well as to attract the reader's interest to the problem. The review of literature provides background information and a critique of the previous research done on the topic, pointing out weaknesses, conflicts, and areas needing study. A concise statement of the problem informs the reader exactly of the purpose—what the researcher intends to do.

Hypotheses are advanced, based on previous research and perhaps some theoretical model. Furthermore, operational definitions serve to inform the reader exactly how the researcher is using certain terms. Operational definitions must be observable and generally relate to the dependent and independent variables. Basic assumptions are also stated and serve to specify certain conditions and premises that must exist in order for the study to proceed. Limitations are possible shortcomings or influences that are acknowledged by the researcher and are generally the result of the delimitations to the study that arc imposed by the investigator. The first chapter concludes with a statement about the significance of the study, which can be judged from either a basic or applied research standpoint. The significance section stresses contradictory findings and limitations of previous research and the ways in which the proposed study will contribute to further knowledge about the research topic. (Refer to Section I of this text for elaboration.)

Chapter 3 covered most of the parts included in the proposal's introduction chapter. Chapter 2 concerns the literature review and Chapter 1 includes a discussion on the inductive and deductive reasoning processes used in developing the problem and in formulating hypotheses.

Innumerable hours are involved in preparing the first chapter, especially with respect to the literature search and the formulation of the problem. The student usually depends heavily on help from the advisor and on completed studies for examples of format and description.

To reiterate, the importance of the study and its contribution to the profession is the main focus of the first chapter in the proposal, and this constitutes the basis for approval or disapproval.

CHAPTER 2. METHOD

Assuming that the review of literature is included in Chapter 1, Chapter 2 is frequently the focus of most of the questions from committee members in the proposal meeting. (The proposal meeting will be discussed in the next section.) In the method chapter, the student must clearly describe how the data will be collected in order to solve the problem set forth in the first chapter. The student needs to specify who the subjects will be, how they will be chosen, how many subjects will be selected, any special characteristics of importance, how their rights and privacy will be protected, and how informed consent will be obtained. The measurements that are to be used are detailed, and the validity and reliability of the measures are documented. Next, the procedures are described. If, for example, the study is a survey, the measurement instruments are discussed as to the steps in construction and validation. If the study is an experimental one, the treatments, or experimental programs, are described explicitly along with the control procedures that will be exercised. Finally, the experimental design and planned statistical analysis of the data are delineated in this chapter.

We have periodically stressed the importance of pilot studies prior to the actual data gathering. If pilot work has been done, it should be described and the results reported. Often the committee members have major concerns about such questions as whether the treatments can produce meaningful changes, whether the measurements are accurate and can reliably discriminate between subjects, and whether the investigator can satisfactorily perform the measurements and administer the treatments. The pilot study should provide answers to these questions.

We recommended in Chapter 4 that the student use the literature to help determine the methodology. Answers to questions about whether certain treatment conditions are sufficiently long, intense, and frequent to produce anticipated changes in behavior can be defended by results of previous studies.

Future tense is used in the proposal. The investigator writes that so many subjects *will be* selected and that certain procedures *will be* carried out. Theoretically, if the proposal is carefully planned and well written, the student needs only to change the tense from future to past to have the first two chapters of the thesis or dissertation. Realistically, however, numerous revisions will probably be made between the proposal and the final version.

Some appendices are usually included with the proposal. Score sheets, cover letters, questionnaires, sample informed consent forms, and data from the pilot study are among the entries commonly appended to the proposal.

THE PROPOSAL PROCESS

We have reiterated the contents of the proposal—the introduction, including the review of literature, and the methods that are going to be used. Fundamentally, the proposed purpose in conjunction with pertinent background information, plausible hypotheses, operational definitions, and delimitations are the factors which will determine whether the study is worthwhile. Consequently, Chapter 1 is instrumental in stimulating interest in the problem and establishing the rationale and significance of the study. Hence, the decision to approve or disapprove rests primarily with the persuasiveness exhibited in the first chapter. Actually, however, the basic decision about the merit of the topic should already have been made before the proposal meeting. In other words, we believe that the student should consult with the advisor and most, if not all, of the committee members to the extent that there is consensus about the worth of the study before the proposal meeting is scheduled. If the majority of the committee is not convinced that the study is worthwhile, a formal proposal meeting should not be held.

Let us digress a moment here and talk about the composition of the proposal committee. The structure of committees and the number of committee members will vary from one institution to another. It is probably safe to say that most thesis committees consist of at least three members, and most dissertations are composed of at least five persons. The major and minor professors are included in these numbers, although the master's student is often not required to have a minor. Other members should be chosen on the basis of their knowledge about the subject or expertise in other aspects of the research such as design and statistical analysis. Sometimes the institution or department specifies that a certain number of the committee must be from inside or outside the department. Usually there is no maximum to the number of committee members allowed.

In regard to the topic of support prior to the meeting, we strongly recommend that the student, with the help and advice of the major professor, get general approval and support for the problem itself from at least two of the three thesis committee members (or three of the five dissertation committee members). This support is tentative, of course, and final approval is contingent upon the refinements that might be needed and on the adequacy of the methodology.

The formal committee meeting is not the place for planning the study. This should have been thoroughly done beforehand. In this regard, some graduate programs have "preproposal" meetings. These sessions are for the purpose of brainstorming and informally reaching an agreement on the efficacy of the proposed topic. This kind of meeting, in effect, functions to garner support from the committee before a great deal of time and effort might be spent on a fruitless endeavor. The student prepares and distributes an outline of the purpose and basic procedures before the meeting. The student should have spent considerable time in consultation with the advisor (and probably at least another committee member) and should have searched the literature sufficiently so as to be adequately prepared to present a sound case for the study. The preproposal meeting is not just a "bull" session in which the student is fishing for basic ideas. At the same time, the informality of the occasion does allow a good interchange of ideas and suggestions.

The formal proposal should be carefully prepared. If the proposal is poorly typed with errors of grammar, spelling, and format, an unfavorable impression is created with the committee members. This may lead to a feeling among committee members that the student lacks the interest, motivation, or desire to do the proposed research. Or, if errors are ignored at this point, the student may assume that carelessness is acceptable in data collection or in the final written thesis or dissertation. Copies of the proposal should be given to the committee members well in advance of the meeting. The number of days in advance is usually specified by the department or university.

In the typical proposal meeting, the student is asked to briefly summarize the rationale for the study, its significance, and the methodology. The remainder of the session consists of questioning by the committee members. Assuming that the topic is acceptable, the questions mostly concern the methods and the competence of the student to conduct the study. The student should exhibit tactful confidence in presenting the proposal. A common mistake students make is to be so humble and pliable that they agree to every suggestion made which could radically change the study. The advisor should help ward off these "helpful" suggestions, but the student must also be able to respectfully defend the scope of the study and the methodology. If adequate planning has gone into the proposal, the student (with the assistance of the major professor) should be able to recognize useful suggestions and defend against those that seem to offer minimal aid.

Once the proposal is approved, most institutions treat it as a contract in that the committee expects the study to be done in the manner specified in the proposal. Moreover, the student can assume that if the study is conducted and analyzed as planned, and if it is well written, it will be approved. If any unforeseen changes are required during the course of the study, they must be approved by the advisor. Substantial changes usually must be reviewed by some or all of the committee.

PROPOSALS FOR GRANTING AGENCIES

All sources of grants, whether governmental agencies or private foundations, require research proposals so that the agency can decide which projects to fund and to what extent. The granting agencies nearly always publish guidelines for applicants to follow in preparing proposals.

The writing of the proposal is of paramount importance. The researcher rarely gets a chance to explain or to defend the purpose or procedures. Thus, the decision is based entirely on the written proposal. The basic format for a grant proposal is similar to the thesis or dissertation proposal. However, some additional types of information are required, as well as some procedural deviations.

We cannot emphasize too strongly the importance of following the guidelines. Granting agencies tolerate little if any deviations from their directions. All sections of the application must be addressed and deadlines strictly followed. Frequently, a statement of intent to submit a proposal is required a month or so before the proposal is filed.

Grant proposals include a statement of the problem, its relevance to one of the specified priorities of the granting agency, and the methodology to be followed. A limited review of literature is often required to demonstrate familiarity with previous research. Occasionally, the funding agency will impose some restrictions with regard to design and methods. For example, it is not uncommon for an agency to prohibit control groups if the treatment is hypothesized to be effective. In other words, the agency may not want any persons to be denied treatment. This can pose some problems for the researcher in scientifically evaluating the outcomes of the project.

Because every granting agency has stipulations about what kinds of things can and cannot be funded, a detailed budget is required, along with a justification for each budget item.

In addition, the competence of the researcher(s) has to be documented. Each researcher must attach a vita, and often a written statement is required pertaining to appropriate preparation, experiences, and accomplishments. The adequacy of facilities and sources of support must also be addressed.

Letters of support are occasionally encouraged. These are included in the appendix. Numerous copies of the proposal are usually required. The proposal is evaluated by a panel of reviewers in accordance with certain criteria regarding relevance, significance, and soundness of design and methodology.

The preparation of a grant proposal is a time-consuming and exacting process. Several types of information are specified and time is needed to gather the information and state it in the manner prescribed by the guidelines. One is advised to begin preparing the proposal as soon as the guidelines are available.

Finally, it is usually wise to contact the granting agency prior to preparing and submitting a proposal. Seldom are proposals funded that are submitted without some prior contact with the granting agency. Finding out the agency's interest and needs is a time-saving venture for the researcher. Often a trip to visit or an extended phone conversation with the research officer is advisable. Looking at proposals previously funded by the agency or seeking guidance from researchers who have been funded is helpful.

Chapter 17

Results and Discussion

Results mean what you found and *discussion* explains what the results mean. In theses and dissertations, the results and discussion are usually separate chapters. Sometimes in journal papers, they are combined. We will discuss them as if they are separate chapters or sections in a research report.

THE RESULTS

The results report what your research has found. This is the most important part of the research report. The introduction and literature review indicated why you conducted the research; the method explained how you did it; the results are your contribution to knowledge, that is, what you found. The results should be concise and effectively organized with the inclusion of appropriate tables and figures.

Because there is no one correct way for all results sections, the results may be organized in various ways. Sometimes the best way may be by addressing each of the tested hypotheses. On other occasions, the results may be organized around the dependent variables of interest. In some cases, you may want to show that certain standard and expected effects have been replicated before going on to more unique findings. For example, in developmental studies of motor performance tasks, older children are better than younger ones. The researcher may want to report the replication of this effect before going on to other results.

Some items should always be reported in the results. The means and standard deviations for all dependent variables under all conditions should be included. This is basic descriptive data which allows other researchers to evaluate your findings and should be presented in one table if possible. Sometimes only the means and standard deviations of important findings are included in the results chapter. However, all the remaining means and standard deviations should be included in the appendix.

The results chapter should also use tables and figures to display appropriate findings. Figures are particularly useful for percentage data, interactions, or summarizing related findings. Only the important tables and figures should be included in the results chapter; the remaining ones should be placed in the appendix.

Statistical information should be summarized in the text where possible. ANOVA and MANOVA statistics should always be summarized in the text with complete tables relegated to the appendix. Above all, the statistics reported should be meaningful. Day (1979, p. 31) reports a classic case which read:

> 33⅓% of the mice used in this experiment were cured by the test drug; 33⅓% of the test population were unaffected by the drug and remained in a moribund condition; the third mouse got away.

Sometimes tables are a better way to present this information. However, this does not mean that the results chapter should be comprised mostly of tables and figures. It is very disconcerting to have to thumb through eight tables and figures in between two pages of text. But even worse is to have to turn 50 pages to the appendix to find a necessary table or figure. Read what you have written. Are the important facts all there? or Have you provided more information than the reader can absorb?

Do not be redundant and repetitive in the results. A common error is to include a table or figure in the results and then repeat it in the text. It is appropriate to describe tables and figures in a general way, or to point out particularly important facts, but not to repeat every finding. However, as Day (1979, p. 32) reports, some writers are so concerned with reducing verbage that they lose track of antecedents, particularly "it":

> "The left leg became numb at times and she walked it off . . . On her second day, the knee was better, and on the third day it had completely disappeared." The antecedent for both its was presumably "the numbness," but I rather think that the wording in both instances was a result of dumbness.

THE DISCUSSION

While the results are the most important part of the research report, the discussion is the most difficult to write. There are no cute tricks or "pat" ways to organize the discussion, but there are some rules which define what should be included.

1. Discuss your results—not what you wish they were but what they are.
2. Relate your results back to the introduction, previous literature, and hypotheses.
3. Explain how your results fit within theory.
4. Interpret your findings.
5. Recommend or suggest applications of your findings.
6. Summarize and state your conclusions with appropriate supporting evidence.

In particular, the discussion should point out factual relationships among variables and situations, thus leading to a presentation of the significance of the research. If after reading your discussion, the reader says "so what," then you have failed in your research reporting.

The discussion should also point out any methodological problems which occurred in the research. However, a methodological "cop out" to explain the results is unacceptable. If you did not find predicted outcomes, and you resort to methodological failure as an explanation, you did not do sufficient pilot work.

MULTIPLE EXPERIMENTS

Increasingly, graduate students are conducting research that involves multiple experiments. These experiments may ask several related questions about a particular problem or may be built on each other with the outcomes of the first leading to questions for the second. This is a very positive trend but sometimes leads to problems within the traditional thesis or dissertation format. In the next chapter traditional and alternative ways of organizing theses and dissertations will be discussed. However, within the traditional framework, multiple experiments are probably best handled by separate chapters.

The first chapter includes the introduction, theoretical framework, literature review, general statement of the research problem, and related definitions and delimitations. Subsequent chapters present each experiment. Each of these chapters includes a brief introduction, specific problem and hypotheses, method, results, and discussion. Finally, the last chapter is a general discussion in which the experiments are tied together and contains the features of the discussion previously presented.

PREPARING TABLES

The first question is "Do you need a table?" There is no easy answer to this question, but two characteristics are important: Is the material more easily understood in a table? Does the table interfere with reading the results? Once you decide you need a table (all numbers *do not* require tables), follow these basic rules:

1. Like characteristics should read vertically in the table.
2. Make the headings of tables clear.
3. A table should be understandable without referring to the text.

Table 17.1 is an example of a useless table that is more easily presented in the text. This table can be handled in one sentence: The experimental group ($M = 17.3$, $s = 4.7$) was significantly better than the control group ($M = 12.1$, $s = 3.9$), $t(28) = 3.31$, $p < .05$.

TABLE 17.1
USELESS TABLE NUMBER 1

Table 1. Means, Standard Deviations, and *t* Test for Distance Cartwheeled While Blindfolded

Groups	N	*M*	*s*	*t*
Exper	15	17.3 m	4.7 m	3.31*
Cont	15	12.1 m	3.9 m	

*$p < .05$

TABLE 17.2
USELESS TABLE NUMBER 2

Table 1. Scheffé's Test for Differences Among Age Levels in Ability to Wiggle Their Ears

Age	7	9	11	13	15
7	—	1.20	1.08	1.79	8.63*
9		—	1.32	1.42	1.57
11			—	1.58	1.01
13				—	0.61
15					—

*$p < .05$

Table 17.2 is also unnecessary. From the 10 comparisons among group means, only 1 was significant. The values in the table are the equivalent of *t* tests. This table can also be presented in one sentence: The Scheffé test was used to make comparisons among the age group means, and the only significant difference was between the youngest (7-year-olds) and oldest (15-year-olds) groups, $t = 8.63$, $p < .05$.

We have borrowed an example of a useful table (17.3) from Safrit and Wood (1983). As you can see, like characteristics appear vertically, and an extensive amount of text would be required to present these same results, yet they are easy to understand from this brief table.

One final point involves reporting numbers in either tables or in the text. Report numerical information only to the precision to which it was measured. For ex-

TABLE 17.3
EXAMPLE OF A USEFUL TABLE

Characteristics of Users and Nonusers
HRFT Pilot Survey

	Users	Nonusers
1. Gender		
Male	4 (36.4%)	33 (62.3%)
Female	7 (63.6%)	20 (37.7%)
2. Age		
20-25	1 (09.1%)	2 (03.8%)
25-30	1 (09.1%)	8 (15.1%)
30-35	5 (45.5%)	9 (17.0%)
35-40	1 (09.1%)	7 (13.2%)
40 and over	3 (27.2%)	27 (50.9%)
3. Type of school		
Elementary	1 (09.1%)	18 (34.0%)
Middle	0 (00.0%)	18 (34.0%)
Junior-senior high	1 (09.1%)	0 (00.0%)
High	9 (81.8%)	17 (32.0%)
4. Student population		
0-100	0 (00.0%)	0 (00.0%)
100-500	1 (09.1%)	17 (33.3%)
500-1000	0 (00.0%)	16 (31.4%)
1000-1500	1 (09.1%)	1 (02.0%)
over 1500	9 (81.8%)	17 (33.3%)

Note. From "The health-related fitness test opinionnaire—A pilot survey" by M.J. Safrit and T.M. Wood, 1983, *Research Quarterly for Exercise and Sport*, **54**, 204-207, Reston, VA: AAHPERD. Reprinted with permission.

ample, if you measure a jump to the nearest cm, to report that on the average, subjects jumped 34.753 cm is unnecessary. This reflects only mindless copying of numbers from computer printouts or calculator readouts. At most you would report the number as 34.8 cm, but we prefer rounding to the preciseness of measurement, that is, 35 cm. While jumping could have been measured to a more precise level than the nearest cm, it was not. Sometimes researchers' attempts at preciseness become humorous, bringing to mind the report that says the average American family has 2.4 children. (We thought children only came in whole units.) In the first example, the jump could have been measured in more precise units. In the latter example, a single child is the smallest (most discrete) unit of measurement available.

The same mindless reporting of statistical numbers also occurs. Because computer printouts carry the statistics and probabilities to five or more places beyond the decimal does not mean the numbers should be reported to that level. Two and at most three places is adequate. This, however, results in occasional reporting of probabilities that are rather odd: $t(22) = 14.73$, $p < .000$. Now, a $p < .000$ means no chance of error and cannot occur. If there is no chance of error, how can it be a probability? What happened is that the exact probability was something like $p < .00023$ and the researcher rounded it back to $p < .000$. You cannot do this. As indicated earlier, we believe it is more appropriate to report whether or not the probability exceeded the alpha set for the experiment (e.g., $p < .05$). However, if the researcher insists on reporting the probability to some level beyond alpha, a 1 or a higher number must always end the probability. In the above example, $p < .00023$, if reported to three decimals, should read $p < .001$.

While the mindless use of numbers frequently occurs, sometimes items are reported that are just as mindless. In reviewing for a research journal, one of us encountered a study in which a group of children were given a 12-week treatment. The author reported the mean age and standard deviation of the children before and after the 12-week treatment. Not surprisingly, the children had all aged 12 weeks. In addition, the author calculated a t test between the pre- and posttreatment means for age, which was, of course, significant. That is, the fact that the children had aged 12 weeks during the 12-week period was a reliable finding.

PREPARING FIGURES AND ILLUSTRATIONS

Many of the suggestions about construction of tables also apply to figures and illustrations because a figure is only another way to present a table. In fact, the important distinction between whether to use a table or a figure is, "Does the reader need the actual numbers or is a picture of the results more useful?" A more important question may be, "Do you need either?" Can the data be presented more concisely and easily in the text? Including figures and tables does not add scientific validity to your research report. In fact, it may only clutter the results. Day (1979, p. 51) suggests a reasonable means for deciding whether to use a table or a figure: "If the data show pronounced trends making an interesting picture, use a graph. If the numbers just sit there, with no exciting trend in evidence, a table should be satisfactory. . . ."

Several other considerations are important in preparing figures. Selection of the type of figure is somewhat arbitrary. Bar graphs seem particularly useful to present percentage and frequency data. Also bar graphs lend themselves to presenting more information without appearing so cluttered. Figures are quite useful in presenting interactions and data points which change over time (or across multiple trials).

Of course, the dependent variable is placed on the *y*-axis and some independent or categorical variable on the *x*-axis. If you have more than one independent variable, how do you decide which to put on the *x*-axis? We have already partially answered that question. If time or multiple trials are used, put them on the *x*-axis. For example, if a study found an interaction on the dependent variable between age level (7-, 9-, 11-, 13-, and 15-year-old males) and the treatment (experimental versus control), age with five levels is usually the more appropriate choice for the *x*-axis. Note this is a general rule, but specific circumstances may dictate otherwise. A good example of the use of a figure to present an interaction is shown in Figure 17.1. Note both age and time are independent variables, so time is placed on the *x*-axis.

Figure 17.2 is a good example of an unneeded figure. The results can be summarized in two sentences: During acquisition, all three groups reduced their

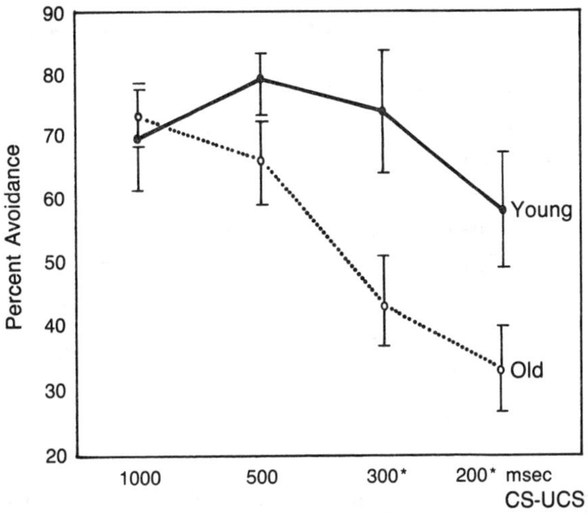

Figure 17.1 Appropriate use of a figure to depict an interaction. From "Exercise and the aging brain" by W.W. Spirduso, 1983, *Research Quarterly for Exercise and Sport*, **54**, 211, Reston, VA: AAHPERD. Reprinted with permission.

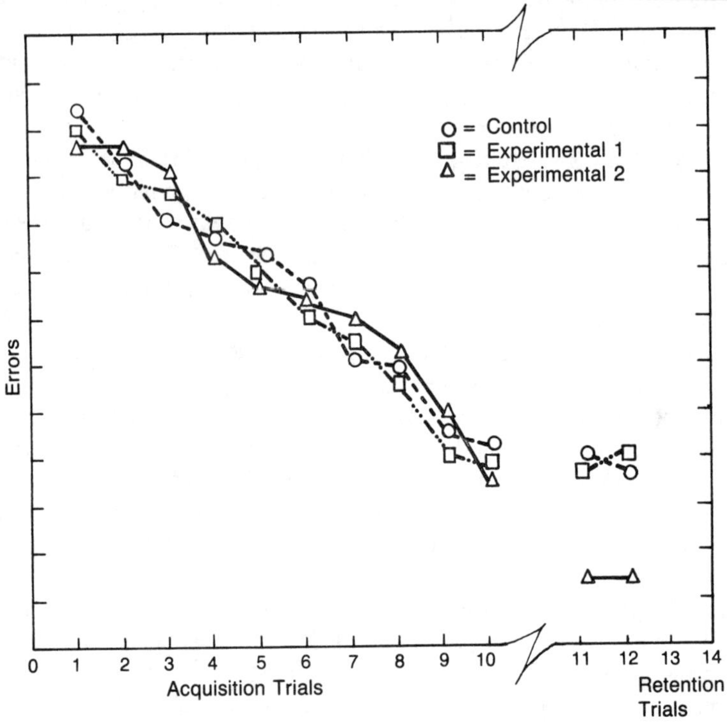

Figure 17.2. Example of a useless figure.

frequency of errors but did not differ significantly from each other. At retention, Experimental Group 2 further reduced its number of errors while Experimental Group 1 and the Controls remained at the same level. Also, when results of different groups follow a very similar pattern, a figure frequently appears cluttered.

One final consideration is the construction of the *y*-axis. In general, 8-12 intervals encompassing the range of means is useful. Do not extend the *y*-axis outside the range of means as this wastes space. Again though, consider if you need a figure at all. Often, theses and dissertations include a drawing like Figure 17.3. In looking at that figure, you immediately see a strong and significant interaction between knowledge of results (KR) and goal setting. Now look at the *y*-axis on which the dependent variable is shown. Note that the scores are given to the nearest hundredth of a second. Actually there is less than ½ second (0.50) difference among the four groups on a task in which average performance is about 18 seconds. In fact, this interaction is not significant and clearly accounts for little variance. It should merely be reported as nonsignificant with no figure included. The researcher only made the interaction appear important by the scale used on the *y*-axis.

Illustrations (photographs and line drawings) are also used in research reporting. Most frequently, illustrations are of the experimental arrangements and

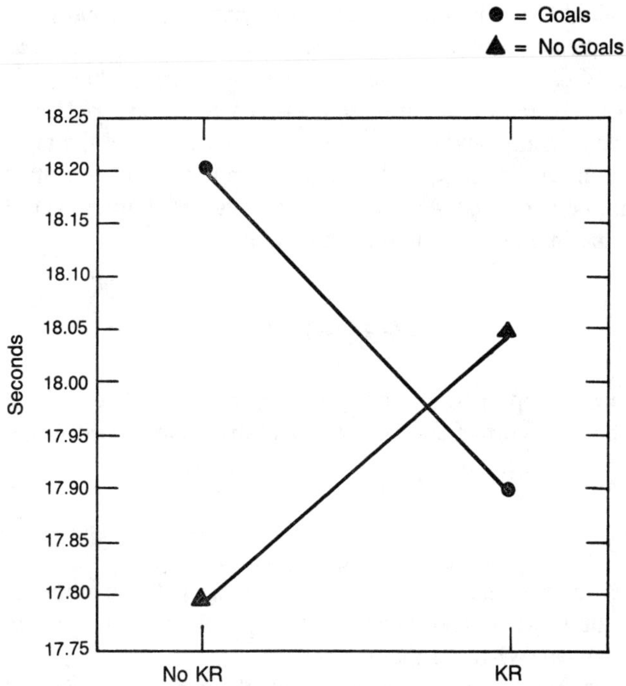

Figure 17.3. A nonsignificant interaction made to appear significant by the scale of the dependent variable.

equipment. They should not be used when the equipment is of a standard design or make. A brief description will suffice. Any unusual arrangement or novel equipment should be described and either a picture or line drawing included. If specifications and relationships are important to include within the illustration rather than in the text, a line drawing is preferable because it can be more easily labeled.

Remember, as a general rule, tables, figures, and illustrations are appropriate for the results chapter or section, but not the discussion. An exception to this rule is a report of multiple experiments in which the general discussion chapter or section could contain a table or figure to display common findings or a summary across several experiments.

To review, when determining where tables, figures, and illustrations should appear—in the text or in the appendix—consider the following recommendations:

1. Put important tables, figures, and illustrations in the text and put all others in the appendix.
2. Try not to clutter the results with too many tables, figures, and illustrations.
3. Do not put summary tables for ANOVA and MANOVA in the results. Place the important statistics from these tables in the text and put the tables in the appendix.

Remember also that all journals have a prescribed format and style for writing articles submitted to them, such as the *American Psychological Association* (*APA*) or the *Index Medicus*. These instructions for authors include directions for preparing tables and figures. Many of these decisions are arbitrary. Read and look at what you have written and then use common sense. Select the tables, figures, and illustrations that are needed to read and to understand the results. Everything else goes in the appendix. Appropriate use of tables, figures, and illustrations can add to the interest and motivation of the reader.

PROBLEMS

Select a research report from a refereed journal in your area of interest. Read the paper, but concentrate on the results and discussion. Answer the following questions in a brief report.

1. Results:
   a. How is the results section organized?
   b. Compare the order of reported findings with the introduction, literature review, and statement of the problem. Do you see any relationships? What are they?
   c. What other way might the results have been organized? Would this be better or worse? Why?
2. Tables, figures, and illustrations:
   a. Are there any? How many of each?
   b. Why are they used? Could the data have been reported more easily in the text? When either a table or figure is used, would the other have been as good? Better? Why?
3. Discussion:
   a. How is the discussion organized?
   b. Are all results discussed?
   c. Is the discussion accurate in terms of the results?
   d. Are previous findings and theory woven into the discussion?
   e. Are all conclusions and supporting evidence clearly presented?
   f. Did the author(s) use any methodological "cop outs"?

Chapter 18

Ways of Reporting Research

Our favorite author, Day (1979, p. 133), appropriately introduces this chapter on ways of reporting research with the following quote:

> Scientific research is not complete until the results have been published. Therefore, a scientific paper is an *essential* part of the research process. Therefore, the writing of an accurate, understandable paper is just as important as the research itself. Therefore, the words in the paper should be weighed as carefully as the reagents in the laboratory. Therefore, the scientist must know how to use words. Therefore, the education of a scientist is not complete until the ability to publish has been established.

Chapter 16 covered the research proposal—how to write the introduction, the literature review, the problem statement, and the methodology for the thesis or dissertation. Chapter 17 explained how to organize and write the results and discussion. Effectively coordinating all of this information into a thesis or dissertation will be the topic of concern in this section. Both the traditional style of organization and an alternative model, which we have developed for use at Louisiana State University, will be presented. In addition, information about writing for publication in research journals, preparing abstracts, and presenting papers orally (including in poster format) is included in this section.

PLAGIARISM

Plagiarism means using the ideas, concepts, writings, and drawings of others as your own. Of course, this is completely unacceptable in the research process (including writing). Plagiarism carries severe penalties at all institutions. A researcher who plagiarizes work carries a stigma for life in his or her profession. No reward is worth the risk involved.

On occasion a graduate student or faculty member can inadvertently be involved in plagiarism. This generally occurs on work that is co-authored. If one author plagiarizes material, the other author(s) could be equally punished even though he or she is unaware of the plagiarism. While there is no "sure fire" means of protection (except never to work with anyone else), never allow a paper with your name on it to be submitted (or revised) unless you have seen the complete paper in final form.

THESES AND DISSERTATIONS

Again, we quote Day (1979, p. 106). His unwritten rule, although since he wrote it, maybe it is no longer unwritten (somewhere in that statement is a limited amount of logic), is, "Write your thesis to please your major professor, if you can figure out what turns him on." Once this basic principle is understood, we offer some guidelines. But in case of doubt or conflict return to the basic principle.

1. Collect all the documents which outline university (or college) and departmental policy for theses and dissertations. Then actually read these documents as someone at some level will eventually check to see if you have followed them.
2. Review the theses and dissertations of past graduate students whose work is well regarded by your institution. Identify common elements in their work, and pattern your work after them.
3. Allow twice as much time as you think you need. Remember Murphy's law: *Whatever can go wrong will go wrong* and its special version—*when several things can go wrong, the one that will go wrong is the one that will cause the greatest harm.*

Given all of this warning, the thesis or dissertation has basically the same parts as any scientific paper: Introduction and Literature Review, Method, Results, and Discussion, each of these parts becoming a chapter. Sometimes the Introduction and Literature Review are separate chapters leading to five rather than four chapters. This format may vary in historical papers (see Chapter 8), creative research (see Chapter 12), multiple experiments (see Chapter 17), or when your major professor says so.

ALTERNATIVE FORMAT FOR THESES AND DISSERTATIONS

We are devoting considerable space here to what we call an *alternative* format for thesis and dissertation writing. First, we want to explain why we believe an alternative format is needed. The thesis or dissertation is the culminating experience for the master's or doctoral student, demonstrating his or her ability to produce original research. Unfortunately, for the master's student, that statement is generally untrue. In our experience, master's students seldom have the knowledge base or methodological tools necessary to produce original research. Thus, the major professor usually supplies the idea, the research design, aids or finds aid for the statistical analysis, and does considerable writing (and much editing) for the thesis. This is not meant to be derogatory toward master's students, but many are part-time, and even full-time students usually fail to acquire the knowledge and research tools to pursue original research. (Unfortunately, as wonderful as this book is, even it does not supply everything you need to know.)

What does all this have to do with thesis format anyway? The ultimate goal of producing new knowledge is to publish it. When the master's student completes his or her work, there is seldom the time or interest to convert the thesis into a form acceptable for a refereed research journal. If the research is to be published, the major professor must rewrite the thesis into journal style. For this reason, a thesis format to promote easy publication of the master's thesis is needed.

Why is the traditional style not the best for doctoral dissertations? In today's doctoral programs, prior to receiving the degree, the typical student will have several publications jointly with his or her major professor, other professors, other graduate students, or alone. Why should a student who has successfully learned to write in research journal style be forced to return to the traditional dissertation format? That seems counterproductive. When we force the traditional format, the new doctoral recipient must spend several months rewriting the dissertation for publication. Since the new doctoral recipient has probably just taken a new job (he or she hopes anyway) requiring considerable time, the publication of the dissertation is unnecessarily delayed.

Given these two reasons, we believe an alternative thesis/dissertation format is much overdue in HPERD. The format we propose has two characteristics: First, it produces a paper ready to submit to a research journal; and second, it retains the concept of more complete reporting of research typically expected in a thesis or dissertation. This format has three parts: the material required for any thesis or dissertation, the research report, and appendices.

REQUIRED MATERIAL

All universities or colleges require specific materials. This usually includes the title page, abstract, table of contents, sometimes a vita, and certain forms. The exact set of materials is specific to every institution and must be followed exactly. As already mentioned, materials of this type are available from the graduate school or department.

RESEARCH REPORT

The body of the thesis or dissertation is prepared in the form of a research report for a scholarly journal. The style to be used in the report (e.g., APA) may be specified by the institution or left to the decision of the graduate student and major professor depending on the journal to which it is to be submitted.

This paper has the standard features of any good research paper: Introduction and Review, Method, Results, and Discussion. It may accommodate multiple or single studies. The length of the paper should reflect the limitations of the journal to which it will be submitted (usually 15-25 pages). The text is followed by references and the appropriate tables, figures, and illustrations. The title page and abstract should be the only additions required to have the paper ready for journal submission. The advantages of this format should be readily apparent to the new doctoral recipient or the major professor directing a publishable master's thesis.

APPENDICES

Three appendices are required in this format. The first appendix is a more thorough coverage of the literature on which the thesis or dissertation is based. The literature review for this appendix should probably be written prior to the research report and then reduced to appropriate size for the research report. This review should have the properties of a good literature analysis as discussed in Chapter 9 and a complete literature search as suggested in Chapter 2. In fact, for the aspiring doctoral student, this could serve as a second paper to submit, particularly if a meta-analysis were used to do the literature analysis.

The second appendix is a more thorough description of methodology. Any materials omitted or that require an additional explanation from the Method of the research report can be included here. Because this appendix tends to be rather disjointed, an introduction identifying the various items and to what they refer should be included.

The third appendix is the tables, figures, and illustrations omitted from the results. Either an introduction or complete identification should be included to indicate what these items represent. Of course, any number of additional appendices can be included as needed.

We believe this alternative format is much better than the traditional one for theses and dissertations. We have been pleased with the results as have our graduate students. While we do not require that this format be used, we do offer it as an option for students. For two examples see:

HARDY, C. J. (1983). *The mediational role of social influence in the perception of exertion*. Doctoral dissertation, Louisiana State University, Baton Rouge.

LEE, T. D. (1982). *On the locus of contextual interference in motor skill acquisition*. Doctoral dissertation, Louisiana State University, Baton Rouge.

To emphasize the value of this style to the new doctoral recipient, Lee's dissertation was lifted directly from the dissertation for submission and, with minor revisions, was published less than 15 months after the Ph. D. was granted (Lee & Magill, 1983). Of course, this format will not aid in the publication of poor quality research, but the publication of a paper in a high-quality journal in less than 15 months from graduation is an excellent recommendation for this format.

JOURNAL WRITING

We highly recommend a work to which we have frequently referred in this book: *How to write and publish a scientific paper*, Day (1979). In our opinion, this book is the researcher's best resource in preparing a paper for submission to a research journal. The book is short (160 pages), informative, readable, and funny. Although this small section cannot replace the more thorough treatment given by Day, we do offer a few suggestions.

First, decide to which journal the research paper is to be submitted. Most journals publish guidelines for authors (e.g., see the June issue of *Research Quarterly for Exercise and Sport*). Read these guidelines carefully and follow the recommended procedures. Guidelines usually explain the journal's publication style; how to prepare tables, figures, and illustrations; where to submit papers (and how many copies); acceptable lengths for papers; and sometimes estimated review time. Nearly all journals require that manuscripts not be submitted elsewhere simultaneously. To do so is unethical.

If this is your first paper, seek some advice from a more experienced author. This may be your major professor or another faculty member. Frequently papers are rejected because they fail to provide important information. More experienced authors will pick up on this immediately. Journal editors and reviewers do not have time to teach you good scientific reporting. That is the responsibility of your major professor, research methods courses, and books like this; but most of all, it is your responsibility to acquire this skill.

Do not be discouraged if your paper is rejected. All of us have had papers rejected, particularly early in our academic careers. Carefully evaluate the reviews and determine if the paper can be salvaged. If so, rewrite, taking into account the reviewer's and editor's criticisms, and submit it to another journal. If not, learn from your mistakes. Occasionally, you may feel you have received an unfair review. If so, write the editor back, point out the biases, and ask for another review by a different reviewer. Editors are generally open to this type correspondence if handled in a professional way. However, opening with the sentence, "Look what these stupid reviewers said," is unlikely to achieve success. Recognize that writing the editor is less likely to be successful if two or more reviewers have agreed on the important criticisms. Editors cannot be expert in every area and have to rely upon the reviewers' recommendations. If you find yourself resorting to this tactic very often, the problem is likely in your work.

As a final point in this part, we have noted the infrequency with which most scientific papers are read (of course, none of ours fall in the category). Some writers have speculated that only two to four people read the average paper completely. Is it possible that a different organization of the scientific paper is needed that would promote an increased audience? The answer might lie in a paper published in *Omni* and included here as Table 18.1. The author, B.A. Realist, proposes a new organization to aid potential authors of scientific papers.

TABLE 18.1

WRITING A SCIENTIFIC PAPER

Everyone knows that scientists write badly—everybody, that is, except scientists. *They* think they're merely being precise and orderly, and everyone else on the planet is either (a) illiterate, (b) sloppy, (c) a humanist, or (d) all of the above. (Ref. 1.) In some cases, of course, the individual scientist is not well acquainted with the English language. (In the opinion of English scientists, this explains the frequently unintelligible papers of Americans.)

The scientist is, by his reliance on the passive voice, hobbled, leading to sentences like this one, in which the subject is acted upon with lumpy nouns, without ever saying exactly whom the action is done by, so that the sentences get longer and longer as you read and never seem to end, even when there is clearly nothing more to say in the sentence, at which point the reader sometimes gets a meager little semicolon; this gives him a rest, so that he can go on and read another long phrase without really learning anything more, because the writer's hand has kept on moving even though his brain has long since been disengaged.

What to do? Trying to straighten a scientist's syntax is like trying to unsnarl week-old spaghetti, with some exceptions (see Ref. 2). It is far better to change the packaging of the sentences. Scientific papers are written like elaborate lab reports—first A, then B, on to C, plodding on to the conclusion. Such papers assume the reader is fascinated by the pearls of wisdom that ooze through the barnacle-laden sentences. The sad truth is that hardly anyone ever reads a paper all the way through. A study by a British physics journal shows that the *average* number who finish the whole paper is 0.5—and that includes the author. Apparently, most scientists can't bear to reread their own work, much less read anyone else's.

In this paper a new scheme for paper organizing is proposed. It does not rely on weaning scientists away from the passive-voice construction, like that last one. Instead it relies on the way scientists actually read and on their motivation for reading papers.

While reading a scientific paper, scientists are led by two needs: (a) ego and (b) desire for information. Our research shows that Need (a) always dominates. Therefore, papers should be organized to satisfy this. The preferred approach, one that makes the most of these insights, is as follows:

1. TITLE
2. AUTHOR'S NAME
3. REFERENCES. These must contain a broad spectrum of sources, mostly to ensure the greatest probability of naming the reader. Use as many multiauthor papers as possible to maximize the number of people who can be mentioned. A scientist will *always* pay greater attention to colleagues who cite him, if only to find where in the text he gets mentioned. Thus, the best strategy is to cite everybody you can, but then place the citations in the most unlikely places in the paper. Then the scientists have to read all or most of the paper carefully to find mention of them. They might even discover what the paper is about. A really high-risk alternative is to cite someone in the list of references *but not in the text*. Then he will read the *whole* paper, twice. The disadvantage, of course, is that he will be livid with rage and frustration by the time he finishes.

TABLE 18.1

WRITING A SCIENTIFIC PAPER (Cont.)

4. ACKNOWLEDGMENTS. An important ego feeding ground. Thank the big names in your field, even if your sole contact with them was over coffee at some conference three years ago. The list should be lavish, implying close connections with the movers and shakers, but avoid mentioning dead people. They can do you no more good, and their rivals are still around. Finally, if space permits, include those who actually helped you. This part of the acknowledgments is purely optional.
5. GRANT REFERENCE. Your grant-monitoring officer will always look for this. So stick it in early. Also, others will want to know what agency got suckered into paying for this stuff, so they can hit it up for grant money themselves.
6. INTRODUCTION. Here you explain what you plan to do. Promise a lot. Few will actually read the MAIN TEXT (see below) to find out whether you actually do it. Fewer still will care.
7. CONCLUSIONS. Always overstate your results. Claim certainty where you have only the vaguest of suspicions.
8. MAIN TEXT. With any luck, there won't be any need to write this section. Everyone will have turned to the next paper to resume the search for his or her own name.

REFERENCES

1. "Professorial Pathology," by E.U. Reka, A.B. Surd, and I.M. Pedant, *Journal of Academic Backstabbing*, Vol. 3, 1980.
2. *Explaining Asimov* (12 volumes), by the National Academy of Sciences, 1981.

Note. From "Last Word" by B.A. Realist (G. Benford), 1982, *Omni*, March, p. 130. Reprinted with permission.

ABSTRACTS

Abstracts are of three general types: abstracts of theses and dissertations, abstracts for published papers, and abstracts for conferences. All require slightly different orientations. But nearly all abstracts have constraints on length and form.

The abstract for your thesis or dissertation will have several specific constraints. These probably include length, form, style, and location. First, consult your university or college regulations. Then follow these carefully. With dissertations, this nearly always includes the form for submission to *Dissertation Abstracts International*. The exact headings, length, and margins are provided in a handout available from your graduate school office. In writing this abstract, consider who will read it. It will be located in computer searches by the title and key words. (The importance of these have been already discussed in an earlier chapter.) Write the abstract so the person reading it can determine if he or she needs to look at the total thesis or dissertation. Important features are the theoretical framework, clear identification of the problem, who the subjects were, how measurements were made, and important and meaningful findings. Do not take all the space writing about your sophisticated statistical analysis or minor methodological problems.

An abstract for a published paper is much more brief. Usually, the length is 100-150 words. The important consideration is *get to the point*: What was the problem? Who were the subjects? What did you find? The most useless statement encountered in these abstracts is "Results were discussed." Would anyone have expected that results would *not* be discussed?

Abstracts for conferences are slightly different. Usually you are allowed a little more space because the reviewer must be convinced to accept your paper for presentation. In these abstracts, you should follow these procedures:

1. Write a short introduction to set up the problem statement.
2. State the problem.
3. Describe the methodology briefly, including
   a. subjects
   b. instrumentation
   c. procedures
   d. design and analysis.
4. Summarize the results.
5. Conclude with why the results are important.

A critical part of this abstract is the results and their importance. If you do this in a vague and nondescript way, the reviewer may conclude that you have not completed the study. This is generally grounds for rejection. The conference cannot turn down other completed research when it is possible that yours will not be finished. Finally, most conferences require that the paper be presented prior to publication. So if you have a paper in review at a journal, it could be hazardous to submit it to a conference that is 8 to 12 months away. Also, many conferences require that the paper has not been previously presented. Be aware of this and follow regulations. Violating these guidelines will never enhance your professional status, and other scholars will quickly become aware of it.

ORAL PRESENTATIONS

Once your conference paper is accepted, you are then faced with presenting it. The presentation will be one of two types—oral or in a poster session.

Oral presentations usually cause panic among graduate students and new faculty members. First, there is no way to get over this except to give several papers. But you can help assuage the feeling of apprehension and dread. Usually the time allowed for oral research reports is 10 to 20 minutes depending on the conference. You will be notified of the time limit when your paper is accepted. Because you must stay within the time limit, and there is no way to present a complete report within this time limit, what do you do? We suggest that you present the essential features of the report using the following divisions for a 15-minute presentation:

Introduction with citation of a few important studies	3 minutes
Statement of the problem	1 minute
Method	3 minutes
Results	3 minutes
Discussion	2 minutes
Questions and discussion	3 minutes
	15 minutes

The most frequent errors in oral presentations are (a) spending too much time on method and (b) poor presentation of results. Proper use of slides (or overheads) is the key to an effective presentation, and particularly in the results. Place a brief statement of the problem on a slide to show while you talk. A slide of the experimental arrangements reduces much of the excess verbiage in method. Always have slides prepared of the results. A picture of the results (particularly figures and graphs) is much more effective than either tables or a verbal presentation. Keep the figures and graphs simple and concise. Have a pointer available to indicate significant features. And finally, remember *Thomas' and Nelson's Five Laws of Oral Presentations* (Table 18.2).

TABLE 18.2

THOMAS' AND NELSON'S FIVE LAWS OF ORAL PRESENTATIONS

1. Something always goes wrong with the slide projector (more specifically)
   a. unless you check it beforehand, it will not work;
   b. either the electrical cord or the slide control cord (or both) will be too short;
   c. any slide not checked immediately prior to presentation will be in upside down;
   d. if the projector has worked perfectly for the three previous presenters, the bulb will burn out during your presentation;
   e. every slide will require that the projector be focused;
   f. a person getting up to leave after the previous paper will knock over the slide projector.
2. You will only drop your slide tray when you have the top off.
3. The screen will be too small for the room.
4. Your paper will be the last one scheduled during the conference. This will result in only the moderator, you, and the previous presenter being there, the latter of whom will leave on completing his or her paper. Or conversely, your paper will be scheduled at 7:30 A.M. at which time you will be hung over and everyone else will still be in bed.
5. At your first presentation, the most prestigious scholar in your field will show up, be misquoted by you, and ask you a question.

The way to avoid most of the problems associated with Thomas' and Nelson's Laws is self-evident. One that may not be is practicing your presentation. Frequently we get together the graduate students and faculty who are presenting papers at upcoming conferences. Everyone presents his or her paper and has it timed. Then the audience asks questions and offers suggestions to clarify presentations and visual aids. The quality of the graduate students' presentation is generally improved and their confidence strengthened by the practice session.

The poster session is the other way to give a paper at a conference. This involves use of a large room in which presenters place summaries of their research on the wall or on a poster stand. The session is scheduled for a specific period of time. During this time, presenters stand by their work while anyone interested walks around, reads the material, and discusses items of interest with the presenter.

We prefer this format over oral presentations. The audience can look at the papers in which they are interested and have a more detailed discussion with the author. Within 75 minutes in a large room, 15 to 20 poster presentations can be made available. In contrast, 15-minute oral presentations allow only five presentations in 75 minutes. In addition, the audience has to sit through several papers, often lacking interest or creating a disturbance by arriving or leaving.

The presenter at a poster session should follow these guidelines:

1. Know how much space is available for your materials.
2. Provide the necessary equipment for attaching your materials to the wall (even when the conference has indicated they will have supplies available).
3. Mount your posters on contrasting backgrounds so they will be easily visible and will not blend into the backboards.
4. Use figures and graphs where possible (as opposed to text and tables).
5. Use large lettering for all text, numbers and labels.

Clearly label the six parts of the poster presentation: Introduction, Statement of the Problem, Method, Results (with Figures and Graphs), Discussion and Conclusions, and Important References.

ETHICS AND THE RESEARCHER

Ethical considerations among researchers and ethical factors in the graduate student-major professor relationship are the two topics under discussion in this section. The major ethical issue among researchers involves joint research projects, but more specifically, the publication and presentation of joint research efforts. As a general rule, the order of authorship for presentations and publications should be based on the contribution of the researchers to the project. The first or senior author is usually the researcher who developed the idea and the plan for the research. Second and third authors are normally listed in the order of their contribution. Although this sounds easy enough, in reality, the decisions are sometimes difficult. Sometimes researchers make equal contributions and decide to flip a coin to determine who will be listed first. In fact, the order of authorship for this book was decided in that manner. We have team-taught the research methods course for several years here at Louisiana State University. We contributed equally to this book but used a coin toss to decide before we began who would be listed as first author. Note the statement "before we began"—this is a good procedure to follow. Make the decisions about the order of authors at the beginning of a collaborative effort. This saves hard feelings among people later when everyone may not agree on whose contribution was most important.

A second issue is, Who should be an author? Studies occasionally have more authors than subjects. In fact, sometimes the authors are also the subjects. When you look at what subjects must go through in some research studies, you can see why only a major professor's graduate students allow "that" to be done to them. Even then they insist on being an author as a reward. More seriously, here are two rules which should help define authorship:

1. Technicians do not necessarily become joint authors. Graduate students sometimes feel because they collect the data, they should be co-authors. Only when graduate students contribute to the planning, analysis, and write-up of the research report are they entitled to be listed as co-authors. Even this rule does not apply to grants where graduate students are paid for their work. A good major professor involves his or her graduate students in all aspects of his or her research program; thus, these students may frequently serve as co-authors as well as technicians.
2. Authorship should only involve people who contribute directly to the specific research project. This does not necessarily include the director of the laboratory or a graduate student's major professor. The only thing we advocate by the following chain letter in Table 18.3 is the humor.

By ethical factors in the major professor-graduate student relationship, we mean that graduate students are colleagues and should be treated as such. If we want our students to be scholars when they complete their graduate work, then we should treat them like scholars from the start, for graduate students do not become scholars on receipt of a degree. By the same token, graduate students must act like responsible scholars. This means producing *careful, thorough*, and *quality* work.

The three major concerns in this section are how to select a major professor; how to change major professors or committee members; and how to handle joint publications between you and your major professor.

First of all, selection of a major professor depends on your area of interest. Frequently, master's students attend an institution because of convenience; however, doctoral students should select the institution they attend because of the quality of program and the faculty in their area of specialization. Do not make

TABLE 18.3

CHAIN LETTER TO INCREASE PUBLICATIONS

Dear Colleague:

We are sure you are aware of the importance of publications in establishing yourself and procuring grants, awards, and good paying academic positions or chairpersonships. We have devised a way in which your curriculum vita can be greatly enhanced with very little effort.

This letter contains a list of names and addresses. Include the top two names as a co-author on your next scholarly paper. Then remove the top name and place your own name at the bottom of the list. Send the revised letter to five colleagues.

If these instructions are followed, by the time your name reaches to the top of the list, you will have claim to co-authorship of 15,625 refereed publications. If you break this chain, your next 10 papers will be rejected as lacking in relevance to "real-world" behavior. Thus, you will be labeled as ecologically invalid by your peers.

Sincerely,

Jerry R. Thomas, Professor
Jack K. Nelson, Professor

List as Co-authors
Jerry R. Thomas
Jack K. Nelson
I.M. Published
U.R. Tenured
C.D. Raise

---

a hasty decision about your major professor. If you are already at the institution, carefully evaluate the specializations that are available in your interest areas. Ask questions about faculty and whether they publish in these areas. Read some of these publications and determine your interest. What financial support such as laboratories and equipment is given to these areas? Also talk to graduate students in the areas. Finally, talk with the faculty members to determine how effectively you will be able to work with them.

However, if you are not at the institution, find out which institutions offer the specialties in which you are interested. Write their graduate schools and departments, requesting information. Read the appropriate journals (over the past 5 to 10 years) and see which faculty are publishing. After you narrow down your list, find out about financial support, and then plan a visit. Speak to the graduate coordinator for the department and the faculty in your area of interest. Sometimes you can meet some of the faculty at conventions such as National Recreation and

Parks Association, American Alliance for HPERD (national or district meetings), American College of Sports Medicine, and North American Society for Psychology of Sport and Physical Activity.

After the selection of a major professor, you must select a committee. Normally the master's or doctoral committee is selected in consultation with your major professor. The committee selected should be one who can contribute to the planning and evaluation of your work—not one who might be the easiest. It is preferable to wait a semester (quarter) or two (if you can) before selecting a final committee. This gives you the opportunity to have several potential committee members as teachers as well as allowing you to better evaluate your common interest.

What happens, however, if you have a major professor (or committee member) who is not ideal for you? First, evaluate the reason. You do not have to be best friends, but it is important that you and your major professor are striving for the same goals. Sometimes students' interests change. Sometimes people just cannot get along. If handled professionally, however, this situation should not be a problem. Go to your major professor and explain the problem as you perceive it and offer him or her an opportunity to respond. Of course, the conflict may be on a more personal level. If so, use an objective and professional approach. If you cannot, or this does not produce satisfactory results, the best recourse may be to seek the advice of the graduate coordinator or department chair.

The final concern deals with joint publications, specifically those between the major professor and graduate student. Major professors do (and should) immediately begin to involve graduate students in the major professor's research program. When this happens, the general guidelines we suggested earlier apply. However, two conflicting forces are at work: First, a professor's job is to foster and to develop the scholarly ability of students; but, second, pressure is increasing on faculty to publish in order to obtain the benefits of promotions, tenure, and merit pay. Being the first or senior author is of benefit to these endeavors. As a result, the faculty member wants to be selfless and assist the student but feels the pressure to publish. This may not be a major issue for the senior faculty, but it certainly is for the untenured assistant professor. As mentioned previously, there are no hard and fast rules other than that everyone agrees before the research is undertaken.

The thesis or dissertation is a special instance. By definition this is how the graduate student demonstrates his or her competence to receive the degree. Frequently, for the master's thesis, the major professor supplies the idea, design, and much of the writing and editing. In spite of this, we believe it should be regarded as the student's work. The dissertation should always be regarded as the student's work. However, second authorship for the major professor on either the thesis or dissertation is acceptable under certain circumstances. The American Psychological Association has defined these circumstances adequately, and we recommend the use of the guidelines reported in Table 18.4.

TABLE 18.4

APA GUIDELINES FOR JOINT AUTHORSHIP IN DISSERTATIONS

APA Statement on Authorship of Research Papers

The ethics committee of the American Psychological Association this year adopted the following policy statement, for use in weighing complaints about crediting authors of scholarly reports.

- Only second authorship is acceptable for the dissertation supervisor.
- Second authorship may be considered obligatory if the supervisor designates the primary variables or makes major interpretive contributions or provides the data base.
- Second authorship is a courtesy if the supervisor designates the general area of concern or is substantially involved in the development of the design and measurement procedures, or substantially contributes to the write-up of the published report.
- Second authorship is not acceptable if the supervisor only provides encouragement, physical facilities, financial support, critiques, or editorial contributions.
- In all instances, agreement should be reviewed before the writing for publication is undertaken and at the time of the submission. If disagreements arise, they should be resolved by a third party using these guidelines.

Note. From "The Chronicle of Higher Education," Sept. 14, 1983, **27**, 7. Reprinted with permission.

PROBLEMS

1. Writing—select a study from a journal and write a 150-word abstract in APA style (or whatever style your department uses).
2. Oral Presentations: In order to stress the importance of time limits on oral presentations, we suggest that the professor organize the following presentations in class as follows:
   a. Have each student select a published research study and prepare and present a 2-minute summary of the study.
   b. Do the same with another study but in a 5-minute summary.
3. Poster Presentation: Have each student prepare a poster presentation of a research study from a journal. Put the posters around the classroom walls. Have students critique each poster (or some percentage for large classes).

References[1]

AAHPER youth fitness test manual. (1958). Washington, D.C.: AAHPER.

AAHPERD health related physical fitness test manual. (1980). Reston, VA: American Alliance for Health, Physical Education, Recreation and Dance.

ADAMS, J.A. (1971). A closed-loop theory of motor learning. *Journal of Motor Behavior*, **3**, 111-150.

ALDERMAN, R.B. (1974). *Psychological behavior in sport.* Philadelphia: W.B. Saunders Co.

ANSHEL, M.H., & Marisi, D.Q. (1978). Effects of music and rhythm on physical performance. *Research Quarterly*, **49**, 109-115.

BAILEY, A.H. (1976). *Rhapsody in blue: A celebration of American music and dance.* Unpublished master's thesis, Texas Woman's University, Denton, TX.

BARNETT, V., & Lewis, T. (1978). *Outliers in statistical data.* New York: Wiley & Sons.

BAUMGARTNER, T.A., & Jackson, A.S. (1982). *Measurement for evaluation in physical education* (2nd ed.). Dubuque, IA: Wm. C. Brown.

BEHNKE, A.R., & Wilmore, J.H. (1974). *Evaluation and regulation of body build and composition.* Englewoods Cliffs, NJ: Prentice-Hall.

BLATTNER, S.E., & Noble, L. (1979). Relative effects of isokinetic and plyometric training on vertical jumping performance. *Research Quarterly*, **50**, 583-588.

BOND, C.F., & Titus, L.J. (1983). Social facilitation: A meta-analysis of 241 studies. *Psychological Bulletin*, **94**, 265-292.

BORG, W.R., & Gall, M.D. (1983). *Educational research* (4th ed.). New York: Longman Inc.

BROWN, J.A.C. (1954). *The social psychology of industry.* Middlesex, England: Penguin Books.

BURDETT, R.G. (1983). Status of biomechanical research in sport and physical education. *Research Consortium Newsletter* (AAHPERD), **7**(1), 2; 4.

BYRD, P.J., & Thomas, T.R. (1983). Hydrostatic weighing during different stages of the menstrual cycle. *Research Quarterly for Exercise and Sport*, **54**, 296-298.

CAMPBELL, D.T., & Stanley, J.C. (1963). *Experimental and quasi-experimental designs for research.* Chicago: Rand McNally.

---

[1]The references for Chapter 8, Historical Research, are not included in this list. They are located as footnotes (University of Chicago Style) at the end of Chapter 8.

CHEFFERS, J.T.F. (1973). The validation of an instrument design to expand the Flanders' system of interaction analysis to describe nonverbal interaction, different varieties of teacher behavior and pupil responses (Doctoral dissertation, Temple University, Philadelphia, 1972). *Dissertation Abstracts International*, **34**, 1674A.

CLARKE, H.H. (Ed.) (1967-1968, December-January). *Physical fitness newsletter*. **14**(4)(5).

CLARKE, H.H., & Clarke, D.H. (1970). *Research processes in physical education, recreation, and health*. Englewood Cliffs, NJ: Prentice-Hall.

CONOVER, W.J. (1971). *Practical nonparametric statistics*. New York: Wiley & Sons.

COOK, T.D., & Campbell, D.T. (1979). *Quasi-experimentation: Design and analysis issues for field settings*. Chicago: Rand McNally.

COTTRELL, N.B. (1972). Social facilitation. In C.G. McClintock (Ed.), *Experimental social psychology*. New York: Holt, Rinehart & Winston.

COX, R.H., & Serfass, R.C. (1981). *AAHPERD Research Consortium Papers*. Reston, VA: AAHPERD, pps. 5-60.

CRONBACH, L. (1951). Coefficient alpha and the internal structure of tests. *Psychometrika*, **16**, 297-334.

DAVIDSON, M.L. (1972). Univariate versus multivariate tests in repeated-measures experiments. *Psychological Bulletin*, **77**, 446-452.

DAY, R.A. (1979). *How to write and publish a scientific paper*. Philadelphia: ISI Press.

DECKER, J.A. (1980). *Recreation and community education directors' perceptions of recreation services for the mentally retarded in Minnesota communities*. Unpublished doctoral dissertation, University of Minnesota, Minneapolis.

DePREITAS, G.A. (1975). *Space toys—an event for dancers and audience in an electronically modifiable sound and light environment*. Unpublished master's thesis, University of Utah, Salt Lake City.

DILLMAN, D.A. (1978). *Mail and telephone survey: The total design method*. New York: Wiley & Sons.

DUNN, D.A. (1980). *The relationship of health locus of control and health value to medical self-care knowledge and attitudes of undergraduate and graduate health education majors in Oregon*. Unpublished doctoral dissertation, University of Oregon, Eugene.

ESSLINGER, A.A. (1938). A philosophical study of principles for selecting activities in physical education (Doctoral dissertation, State University of Iowa). *Health, physical education and recreation microform publications*, **1**, October 1949-March 1965, PE14.

EDWARDS, A.L. (1957). *Techniques of attitude and scale construction*. New York: Appleton-Century-Crofts.

FELTZ, D.L., & Landers, D.M. (1983). The effects of mental practice on motor skill learning and performance: A meta-analysis. *Journal of Sport Psychology*, **5**, 25-57.

FLANDERS, N.A. (1970). *Analyzing teaching behavior*. Reading, MA: Addison-Wesley.

GEISSER, S., & Greenhouse, S.W. (1958). An extension of Box's results on the use of the *F* distribution in multivariate analysis. *Annals of Mathematical Statistics*, **29**, 885-891.

GESSAROLI, M.E., & Schutz, R.W. (1983). Variable error: Variance-covariance heterogeneity, block sixe and Type I error rates. *Journal of Motor Behavior*, **15**, 74-95.

GLASS, G.V. (1976). Primary, secondary, and meta-analysis. *Educational Researcher*, **5**, 3-8.

GLASS, G.V. (1977). Integrating findings: The meta-analysis of research. *Review of Research in Education*, **5**, 351-379.

GLASS, G.V., McGraw, B., & Smith, M. (1981). *Meta-analysis in social research*. Beverly Hills, CA: Sage Publications.

GOTTFRIED, L.E. (1980). *Parabola: Documentation of an artistic collaboration in dance, music, and film*. Master's thesis, University of Iowa, Iowa City.

GRAVES, R.M., & Kahn, R.L. (1979). *Surveys by telephone: A national comparison with personal interviews*. New York: Academic Press.

HAAG, E.E. (1979). Literature searching in physical education. *Journal of Physical Education and Recreation*, **50**(1), 54-58.

HACKENSMITH, C.W. (1966). *History of physical education.* New York: Harper & Row.

HALVERSON, L.E., Roberton, M.A., & Langendorfer, S. (1982). Development of the overarm throw: Movement and ball velocity changes by seventh grade. *Research Quarterly for Exercise and Sport*, **53**, 198-205.

HARRIS, C. (1963). *Problems in measuring change.* Madison, WI: University of Wisconsin Press.

HEDGES, L.V. (1981). Distribution theory for Glass's estimator of effect size and related estimators. *Journal of Educational Statistics*, **6**, 107-128.

HEDGES, L.V. (1982). Fitting categorical models to effect sizes from a series of experiments. *Journal of Educational Statistics*, **7**, 119-137. (a)

HEDGES, L.V. (1982). Estimation of effect size from a series of independent experiments. *Psychological Bulletin*, **92**, 490-499. (b)

HEDGES, L., & Olkin, I. (1980). Vote counting methods in research synthesis. *Psychological Bulletin*, **88**, 359-369.

HEDGES, L., & Olkin, I. (1983). Regression models in research synthesis. *American Statistician*, **37**, 137-140.

HEDGES, L.V., & Olkin, I. (1985). *Statistical methods for meta-analysis.* New York: Academic Press.

HELMSTADTER, G.C. (1970). *Research concepts in human behavior.* New York: Appleton-Century-Crofts.

HENRY, F.M. (1964). Physical education: An academic discipline. *Journal of Health, Physical Education and Recreation*, **35**, 32-33; 69.

HENRY, F.M. (1974). Variable and constant performance errors within a group of individuals. *Journal of Motor Behavior*, **6**, 149-154.

HENRY, F.M., & Rogers, D.E. (1960). Increased response latency for complicated movements and a "memory drum" theory of neuromotor reaction. *Research Quarterly*, **31**, 448-458.

HERKOWITZ, J. (1984). Developmentally engineered equipment and playgrounds. In J.R. Thomas (Ed.), *Motor development during childhood and adolescence.* Minneapolis: Burgess.

HOENES, R.L., & Chissom, B.S. (1975). *A student guide for educational research* (2nd ed.). Statesboro, GA: Vog Press.

HYDE, J.S. (1981). How large are cognitive gender differences? *American Psychologist*, **36**, 892-901.

JACKSON, A.W. (1978). *The twelve minute swim as a test for aerobic endurance in swimming.* Unpublished doctoral dissertation, University of Houston.

JOHNSON, B.L., & Nelson, J.K. (1979). *Practical measurements for evaluation in physical education* (3rd ed.). Minneapolis, MN: Burgess.

JOHNSON, R.L. (1979). *The effects of various levels of fatigue on the speed and accuracy of visual recognition.* Unpublished doctoral dissertation, Louisiana State University, Baton Rouge.

KAVALE, K., & Mattson, P.D. (1983). "One jumped off the balance beam": Meta-analysis of perceptual-motor training. *Journal of Learning Disabilities*, **16**, 165-173.

KENYON, G.S. (1968). Six scales for assessing attitude toward physical activity. *Research Quarterly*, **39**, 566-574.

KIRK, R.E. (1968). *Experimental design: Procedures for the behavioral sciences.* Belmont, CA: Brooks/Cole Publishing.

KRAUS, H., & Hirschland, R.P. (1954). Minimum muscular fitness tests in school children. *Research Quarterly*, **25**, 177-188.

KROLL, W.P. (1971). *Perspectives in physical education.* New York: Academic Press.

LAABS, G.J. (1980). On perceptual processing in motor memory. In C.H. Nadeau et al., *Psychology of motor behavior and sport—1979.* Champaign, IL: Human Kinetics.

LANE, K.R. (1983). *Comparison of skinfold profiles of black and white boys and girls ages 11-13.* Unpublished master's thesis, Louisiana State University.

LEE, M. (1983). *A history of physical education and sports in the U.S.A.* New York: Wiley & Sons.

LEE, T.D., & Magill, R.A. (1983). The locus of contextual interference in motor-skill acquisition. *Journal of Experimental Psychology: Learning, Memory and Cognition*, **9**, 730-746.

LEONARD, F.G., & Affleck, G.B. (1947). *A guide to the history of physical education* (3rd ed.). Philadelphia: Lea & Febiger.

LORD, F.M. (1969). Statistical adjustments when comparing pre-existing groups. *Psychological Bulletin*, **72**, 336-337.

LORING, W. (1977). *A farewell to Lincoln Square: A choreographic thesis based on the paintings of Rafael Soyer*. Unpublished master's thesis, University of California, Los Angeles.

MABLEY, J. (January 22, 1963). Mabley's report. *Chicago American*, p. 62.

MACCOBY, E.E., & Jacklin, C.N. (1974). *The psychology of sex differences*. Stanford, CA: Stanford University Press.

MARGARIA, R., Aghems, P., & Rovelli, E. (1966). Measurement of muscular power (anaerobic) in man. *Journal of Applied Physiology*, **21**, 1662-1664.

MARTENS, R. (1973, June). People errors in people experiments. *Quest*, **20**, 16-20.

MARTENS, R. (1977). *Sport competition anxiety test*. Champaign, IL: Human Kinetics.

MARTENS, R. (1979). About smocks and jocks. *Journal of Sport Psychology*, **1**, 94-99.

MATTHEWS, P.R. (1979). The frequency with which the mentally retarded participate in recreation activities. *Research Quarterly*, **50**, 71-79.

McCLOY, C.H. (1960, Oct.). A half century of physical education. *Physical Educator*, p. 91.

MOOMAW, V. (1968). The notated creative thesis. In R. Bull (Ed.), *Research in dance: Problems and possibilities*. New York: Committee on Research in Dance.

MORLAND, R.B. (1958). A philosophical interpretation of the educational views held by leaders in American physical education (Doctoral dissertation, New York University). *Health, physical education and recreation microform publications*, **1**, October 1949-March 1965, PE394.

NOVAK, E.G. (1982). *A ceremony of carols: A program of liturgical dance*. M.S. thesis, Louisiana State University.

NUNNALY, J.C. (1978). *Psychometric theory* (2nd ed.). New York: McGraw-Hill Book Co.

PARRIS, J. (1981). *A choreographic problem: Application of the philosophies of de Stijl, Cubism, and Surrealism in the creation of three dances*. Unpublished master's thesis, Texas Woman's University, Denton, TX.

PEDHAZUR, E.J. (1982). *Multiple regression in behavioral research*. New York: Holt, Rinehart and Winston.

POPP, J.C. (1959). *Comparison of sophomore high school boys who have high and low physical fitness indices through case study procedures*. Unpublished master's thesis, University of Oregon, Eugene.

"QUIRK theory" or the universal perversity of matter (1968, December). *Illinois Technograph*, p. 59.

RAABE, J.L. (1981). *Dance is . . . ? A lecture demonstration for children*. Unpublished master's thesis, Texas Woman's University, Denton, TX.

REALIST, B.A. (Benford, G.) (1982, March). How to write a scientific paper. *Omni*, p. 130.

ROSENTHAL, R. (1966). *Experimenter effects in behavioral research*. New York: Appleton-Century-Crofts.

RUGG, H. (1941). *That men may understand*. New York: Doubleday, Doran and Co.

RYAN, E.D. (1970). The cathartic effect of vigorous motor activity on aggressive behavior. *Research Quarterly*, **41**, 542-551.

SAFRIT, M.J. (1976). (Ed.), *Reliability theory*. Washington, DC: AAHPER.

SAFRIT, M.J. (1980). (Ed.), *Research Quarterly for Exercise and Sport*, **51**(1).

SAFRIT, M.J. (1981). *Evaluation in physical education* (2nd ed.). Englewood Cliffs, NJ: Prentice-Hall.

SAFRIT, M.J., Spray, A.J., & Diewert, G. (1980). Methodological issues in short-term motor memory research. *Journal of Motor Behavior*. **12**, 13-28.

SAFRIT, M.J., & Wood, T.M. (1983). The health-related fitness test opinionnaire: A pilot survey. *Research Quarterly for Exercise and Sport*, **54**, 204-207.

SCHMIDT, R.A. (1975). A schema theory of discrete motor skill learning. *Psychological Review*, **82**, 225-260.

SCHMIDT, R.A. (1982). *Motor control and learning*. Champaign, IL: Human Kinetics.

SCHUTZ, R. (1979). Absolute, constant, and variable error: Problems and solutions. In D. Mood (Ed.), *Proceedings of the Colorado Measurement Symposium*. Boulder, CO: University of Colorado Press.

SCHUTZ, R.W., & Roy, E.A. (1973). Absolute error: The devil in disguise. *Journal of Motor Behavior*, **5**, 141-153.

SHERMAN, J. (1978). *Sex-related cognitive differences*. Springfield, IL: Charles C. Thomas.

SIDROW, C.L. (1978). *Computerized choreography*. Unpublished master's thesis, California State University, Long Beach.

SIEDENTOP, D. (1980). Two cheers for Rainer. *Journal of Sport Psychology*, **2**, 2-4.

SIEDENTOP, D., Trousignant, M., & Parker, M. (1982). *Academic learning time—Physical education: 1982 coding manual*. Columbus, OH: School of HPER, Ohio State University.

SMITH, R.E., Smoll, F.L., & Hunt, E. (1977). A system for the behavioral assessment of athletic coaches. *Research Quarterly*, **48**, 401-407.

SONSTROEM, R.J. (1978). Physical estimation and attraction scales: Rationale and research. *Medicine and Science in Sports*, **10**, 97-102.

SPARLING, P.B. (1980). A meta-analysis of studies comparing maximal oxygen uptake in men and women. *Research Quarterly for Exercise and Sport*, **51**, 542-552.

SPIELBERGER, C.D. (1966). Theory and research on anxiety. In C.D. Spielberger (Ed.), *Anxiety and behavior*. New York: Academic Press.

SPIRDUSO, W.W. (1983). Exercise and the aging brain. *Research Quarterly for Exercise and Sport*, **54**, 208-218.

STAMM, C.L., & Safrit, M.J. (1975). Comparison of significance tests for repeated measures ANOVA design. *Research Quarterly*, **46**, 403-409.

TEW, J., & Wood, M. (1980). *Proposed model for predicting probable success in football players*. Paper presented at Physical Education Measurement Symposium, AAHPERD Measurement & Evaluation Council, Houston, TX.

THOMAS, J.R. (1977). A note concerning analysis of error scores from motor-memory research. *Journal of Motor Behavior*, **9**, 251-253.

THOMAS, J.R. (1980). Half a cheer for Rainer and Daryl. *Journal of Sport Psychology*, **2**, 266-267.

THOMAS, J.R. (1984). (Ed.), *Motor development during childhood and adolescence*. Minneapolis, MN: Burgess.

THOMAS, J.R. (1984). Planning "kiddie" research: Little "kids" but big problems. In J.R. Thomas (Ed.), *Motor development during childhood and adolescence*. Minneapolis: Burgess.

THOMAS, J.R., & Thomas, K.T. (1983). Strange kids and strange numbers: Assessing children's motor development. *Journal of Physical Education, Recreation and Dance*, **54**(8), 19-20.

THOMAS, J.R., Thomas, K.T., Lee, A.M., Testerman, E., & Ashy, M. (1983). Age differences in use of strategy for recall of movement in a large scale environment. *Research Quarterly for Exercise and Sport*, **54**, 264-272.

TOLSON, H. (1980). An adjustment to statistical significance: w^2. *Research Quarterly for Exercise and Sport*, **51**, 580-584.

TRAN, Z.V., Weltman, A., Glass, G.V., & Mood, D.P. (1983). The effects of exercise on blood lipids and lipoproteins: A meta-analysis. *Medicine and Science in Sports and Exercise*, **15**, 393-402.

TRIPLETT, N.E. (1898). The dynamogenic factors in pacemaking and competition. *American Journal of Psychology*, **9**, 507-533.

TUCKMAN, B.W. (1978). *Conducting educational research* (2nd ed.). New York: Harcourt, Brace and Jovanovich.

TUTKO, T., Lyon, L.P., & Ogilvie, B. (1969). *The athletic motivational inventory*. San Jose, CA: Institute for the Study of Athletics Motivation.

VAN DALEN, D.B., & Bennett, B.L. (1971). *A history of physical education* (2nd ed.). Englewood Cliffs, NJ: Prentice Hall.

VAN TUYL, M. (1968). (Ed.), *Impulse-annual of contemporary dance*. San Francisco, CA: Impulse Publications.

VERDUCCI, F.M. (1980). *Measurement concepts in physical education*. St. Louis: C.V. Mosby.

WALL, E.L. (1981). *Lumen proprium*. Unpublished master's thesis, Louisiana State University, Baton Rouge.

WEBB, E.J., Campbell, D.T., Schwartz, R.D., & Sechrest, L. (1966). *Unobtrusive measures: Nonreactive research in the social sciences*. Chicago: Rand McNally.
WINER, B.J. (1971). *Statistical principles in experimental design*. New York: McGraw-Hill.
WORTHY, T.E. (1977). *The creative thesis: Criteria for procedural development and evaluation*. Unpublished doctoral dissertation, Texas Woman's University, Denton, TX.
ZAJONC, R.B. (1965). Social facilitation. *Science*, **149**, 269-274.
ZEIGLER, E.F. (1968). A tale of two titles. *Journal of Health, Physical Education and Recreation*, **39**, 53.

Appendix A

STATISTICAL TABLES

TABLE A.1

TABLE OF RANDOM NUMBERS

22	17	68	65	84	68	95	23	92	35	87	02	22	57	51	61	09	43	95	06	58	24	82	03	47
19	36	27	59	46	13	79	93	37	55	39	77	32	77	09	85	52	05	30	62	47	83	51	62	74
16	77	23	02	77	09	61	87	25	21	28	06	24	25	93	16	71	13	59	78	23	05	47	47	25
78	43	76	71	61	20	44	90	32	64	97	67	63	99	61	46	38	03	93	22	69	81	21	99	21
03	28	28	26	08	73	37	32	04	05	69	30	16	09	05	88	69	58	28	99	35	07	44	75	47
93	22	53	64	39	07	10	63	76	35	87	03	04	79	88	08	13	13	85	51	55	34	57	72	69
78	76	58	54	74	92	38	70	96	92	52	06	79	79	45	82	63	18	27	44	69	66	92	19	09
23	68	35	26	00	99	53	93	61	28	52	70	05	48	34	56	65	05	61	86	90	92	10	70	80
15	39	25	70	99	93	86	52	77	65	15	33	59	05	28	22	87	26	07	47	86	96	98	29	06
58	71	96	30	24	18	46	23	34	27	85	13	99	24	44	49	18	09	79	49	74	16	32	23	02
57	35	27	33	72	24	53	63	94	09	41	10	76	47	91	44	04	95	49	66	39	60	04	59	81
48	50	86	54	48	22	06	34	72	52	82	21	15	65	20	33	29	94	71	11	15	91	29	12	03
61	96	48	95	03	07	16	39	33	66	98	56	10	56	79	77	21	30	27	12	90	49	22	23	62
36	93	89	41	26	29	70	83	63	51	99	74	20	52	36	87	09	41	15	09	98	60	16	03	03
18	87	00	42	31	57	90	12	02	07	23	47	37	17	31	54	08	01	88	63	39	41	88	92	10
88	56	53	27	59	33	35	72	67	47	77	34	55	45	70	08	18	27	38	90	16	95	86	70	75
09	72	95	84	29	49	41	31	06	70	42	38	06	45	18	64	84	73	31	65	52	53	37	97	15
12	96	88	17	31	65	19	69	02	83	60	75	86	90	68	24	64	19	35	51	56	61	87	39	12
85	94	57	24	16	92	09	84	38	76	22	00	27	69	85	29	81	94	78	70	21	94	47	90	12
38	64	43	59	98	98	77	87	68	07	91	51	67	62	44	40	98	05	93	78	23	32	65	41	18
53	44	09	42	72	00	41	86	79	79	68	47	22	00	20	35	55	31	51	51	00	83	63	22	55
40	76	66	26	84	57	99	99	90	37	36	63	32	08	58	37	40	13	68	97	87	64	81	07	83
02	17	79	18	05	12	59	52	57	02	22	07	90	47	03	28	14	11	30	79	20	69	22	40	98
95	17	82	06	53	31	51	10	96	46	92	06	88	07	77	56	11	50	81	69	40	23	72	51	39
35	76	22	42	92	96	11	83	44	80	34	68	35	48	77	33	42	40	90	60	73	96	53	97	86

TABLE A.1 (cont.)

26 29 13 56 41	85 47 04 66 08	34 72 57 59 13	82 43 80 46 15	38 26 61 70 04
77 80 20 75 82	72 82 32 99 90	63 95 73 76 63	89 73 44 99 05	48 67 26 43 18
46 40 66 44 52	91 36 74 43 53	30 82 13 54 00	78 45 63 98 35	55 03 36 67 68
37 56 08 18 09	77 53 84 46 47	31 91 18 95 58	24 16 74 11 53	44 10 13 85 57
61 65 61 68 66	37 27 47 39 19	84 83 70 07 48	53 21 40 06 71	95 06 79 88 54
93 43 69 64 07	34 18 04 52 35	56 27 09 24 86	61 85 53 83 45	19 90 70 99 00
21 96 60 12 99	11 20 99 45 18	48 13 93 55 34	18 37 79 49 90	65 97 38 20 46
95 20 47 97 97	27 37 83 28 71	00 06 41 41 74	45 89 09 39 84	51 67 11 52 49
97 86 21 78 73	10 65 81 92 59	58 76 17 14 97	04 76 62 16 17	17 95 70 45 80
69 92 06 34 13	59 71 74 17 32	27 55 10 24 19	23 71 82 13 74	63 52 52 01 41
04 31 17 21 56	33 73 99 19 87	26 72 39 27 67	53 77 57 68 93	60 61 97 22 61
61 06 98 03 91	87 14 77 43 96	43 00 65 98 50	45 60 33 01 07	98 99 46 50 47
85 93 85 86 88	72 87 08 62 40	16 06 10 89 20	23 21 34 74 97	76 38 03 29 63
21 74 32 47 45	73 96 07 94 52	09 65 90 77 47	25 76 16 19 33	53 05 70 53 30
15 69 53 82 80	79 96 23 53 10	65 39 07 16 29	45 33 02 43 70	02 87 40 41 45
02 89 08 04 49	20 21 14 68 86	87 63 93 95 17	11 29 01 95 80	35 14 97 35 33
87 18 15 89 79	85 43 01 72 73	08 61 74 51 69	89 74 39 82 15	94 51 33 41 67
98 83 71 94 22	59 97 50 99 52	08 52 85 08 40	87 80 61 65 31	91 51 80 32 44
10 08 58 21 66	72 68 49 29 31	89 85 84 46 06	59 73 19 85 23	65 09 29 75 63
47 90 56 10 08	88 02 84 27 83	42 29 72 23 19	66 56 45 65 79	20 71 53 20 25
22 85 61 68 90	49 64 92 85 44	16 40 12 89 88	50 14 49 81 06	01 82 77 45 12
67 80 43 79 33	12 83 11 41 16	25 58 19 68 70	77 02 54 00 52	53 43 37 15 26
27 62 50 96 72	79 44 61 40 15	14 53 40 65 39	27 31 58 50 28	11 39 03 34 25
33 78 80 87 15	38 30 06 38 21	14 47 47 07 26	54 96 87 53 32	40 36 40 96 76
13 13 92 66 99	47 24 49 57 74	32 25 43 62 17	10 97 11 69 84	99 63 22 32 98
10 27 53 96 23	71 50 54 36 23	54 31 04 82 98	04 14 12 15 09	26 78 25 47 47
28 41 50 61 88	64 85 27 20 18	83 36 36 05 56	39 71 65 09 62	94 76 62 11 89
34 21 42 57 02	59 19 18 97 48	80 30 03 30 98	05 24 67 70 07	84 97 50 87 46
61 81 77 23 23	82 82 11 54 08	53 28 70 58 96	44 07 39 55 43	42 34 43 39 28
61 15 18 13 54	16 86 20 26 88	90 74 80 55 09	14 53 90 51 17	52 01 63 01 59
91 76 21 64 64	44 91 13 32 97	75 31 62 66 54	84 80 32 75 77	56 08 25 70 29
00 97 79 08 06	37 30 28 59 85	53 56 68 53 40	01 74 39 59 73	30 19 99 85 48
36 46 18 34 94	75 20 80 27 77	78 91 69 16 00	08 43 18 73 68	67 69 61 34 25
88 98 99 60 50	65 95 79 42 94	93 62 40 89 96	43 56 47 71 66	46 76 29 67 02
04 37 59 87 21	05 02 03 24 17	47 97 81 56 51	92 34 86 01 82	55 51 33 12 91
63 62 06 34 41	94 21 78 55 09	72 76 45 16 94	29 95 81 83 83	79 88 01 97 30
78 47 23 53 90	34 41 92 45 71	09 23 70 70 07	12 38 92 79 43	14 85 11 47 23
87 68 62 15 43	53 14 36 59 25	54 47 33 70 15	59 24 48 40 35	50 03 42 99 36
47 60 92 10 77	88 59 53 11 52	66 25 69 07 04	48 68 64 71 06	61 65 70 22 12
56 88 87 59 41	65 28 04 67 53	95 79 88 37 31	50 41 06 94 76	81 83 17 16 33

TABLE A.1 (Cont.)

02 57 45 86 67	73 43 07 34 48	44 26 87 93 29	77 09 61 67 84	06 69 44 77 75
31 54 14 13 17	48 62 11 90 60	68 12 93 64 28	46 24 79 16 76	14 60 25 51 01
28 50 16 43 36	28 97 85 58 99	67 22 52 76 23	24 70 36 54 54	59 28 61 71 96
63 29 62 66 50	02 63 45 52 38	67 63 47 54 75	83 24 78 43 20	92 63 13 47 48
45 65 58 26 51	76 96 59 38 72	86 57 45 71 46	44 67 76 14 55	44 88 01 62 12
39 65 36 63 70	77 45 85 50 51	74 13 39 35 22	30 53 36 02 95	49 34 88 73 61
73 71 98 16 04	29 18 94 51 23	76 51 94 84 86	79 93 96 38 63	08 58 25 58 94
72 20 56 20 11	72 65 71 08 86	79 57 95 13 91	97 48 72 66 48	09 71 17 24 89
75 17 26 99 76	89 37 20 70 01	77 31 61 95 46	26 97 05 73 51	53 33 18 72 87
37 48 60 82 29	81 30 15 39 14	48 38 75 93 29	06 87 37 78 48	45 56 00 84 47
68 08 02 80 72	83 71 46 30 49	89 17 95 88 29	02 39 56 03 46	97 74 06 56 17
14 23 98 61 67	70 52 85 01 50	01 84 02 78 43	10 62 98 19 41	18 83 99 47 99
49 08 96 21 44	25 27 99 41 28	07 41 08 34 66	19 42 74 39 91	41 96 53 78 72
78 37 06 08 43	63 61 62 42 29	39 68 95 10 96	09 24 23 00 62	56 12 80 73 16
37 21 34 17 68	68 96 83 23 56	32 84 60 15 31	44 73 67 34 77	91 15 79 74 58
14 29 09 34 04	87 83 07 55 07	76 58 30 83 64	87 29 25 58 84	86 50 60 00 25
58 43 28 06 36	49 52 83 51 14	47 56 91 29 34	05 87 31 06 95	12 45 57 09 09
10 43 67 29 70	80 62 80 03 42	10 80 21 38 84	90 56 35 03 09	43 12 74 49 14
44 38 88 39 54	86 97 37 44 22	00 95 01 31 76	17 16 29 56 63	38 78 94 49 81
90 69 59 19 51	85 39 52 85 13	07 28 37 07 61	11 16 36 27 03	78 86 72 04 95
41 47 10 25 62	97 05 31 03 61	20 26 36 31 62	68 69 86 95 44	84 95 48 46 45
91 94 14 63 19	75 89 11 47 11	31 56 34 19 09	79 57 92 36 59	14 93 87 81 40
80 06 54 18 66	09 18 94 06 19	98 40 07 17 81	22 45 44 84 11	24 62 20 42 31
67 72 77 63 48	84 08 31 55 58	24 33 45 77 58	80 45 67 93 82	75 70 16 08 24
59 40 24 13 27	79 26 88 86 30	01 31 60 10 39	53 58 47 70 93	85 81 56 39 38
05 90 35 89 95	01 61 16 96 94	50 78 13 69 36	37 68 53 37 31	71 26 35 03 71
44 43 80 69 98	46 68 05 14 82	90 78 50 05 62	77 79 13 57 44	59 60 10 39 66
61 81 31 96 82	00 57 25 60 59	46 72 60 18 77	55 66 12 62 11	08 99 55 64 57
42 88 07 10 05	24 98 65 63 21	47 21 61 88 32	27 80 30 21 60	10 92 35 36 12
77 94 30 05 39	28 10 99 00 27	12 73 73 99 12	49 99 57 94 82	96 88 57 17 91
78 83 19 76 16	94 11 68 84 26	23 54 20 86 85	23 86 66 99 07	36 37 34 92 09
87 76 59 61 81	43 63 64 61 61	65 76 36 95 90	18 48 27 45 68	27 23 65 30 72
91 43 05 96 47	55 78 99 95 24	37 55 85 78 78	01 48 41 19 10	35 19 54 07 73
84 97 77 72 73	09 62 06 65 72	87 12 49 03 60	41 15 20 76 27	50 47 02 29 16
87 41 60 76 83	44 88 96 07 80	83 05 83 38 96	73 70 66 81 90	30 56 10 48 59

*Table A.1 is taken from Table XXXIII of Fisher, *Statistical Methods for Research Workers*, published by Oliver and Boyd, Ltd., Edinburgh, and by permission of the author and the publisher.

TABLE A.2
CRITICAL VALUES OF CORRELATION COEFFICIENTS

	Level of significance for one-tailed test				
	.05	.025	.01	.005	.0005
	Level of significance for two-tailed test				
$df = N-2$	.10	.05	.02	.01	.001
1	.9877	.9969	.9995	.9999	1.0000
2	.9000	.9500	.9800	.9900	.9990
3	.8054	.8783	.9343	.9587	.9912
4	.7293	.8114	.8822	.9172	.9741
5	.6694	.7545	.8329	.8745	.9507
6	.6215	.7067	.7887	.8343	.9249
7	.5822	.6664	.7498	.7977	.8982
8	.5494	.6319	.7155	.7646	.8721
9	.5214	.6021	.6851	.7348	.8471
10	.4973	.5760	.6581	.7079	.8233
11	.4762	.5529	.6339	.6835	.8010
12	.4575	.5324	.6120	.6614	.7800
13	.4409	.5139	.5923	.6411	.7603
14	.4259	.4973	.5742	.6226	.7420
15	.4124	.4821	.5577	.6055	.7246
16	.4000	.4683	.5425	.5897	.7084
17	.3887	.4555	.5285	.5751	.6932
18	.3783	.4438	.5155	.5614	.6787
19	.3687	.4329	.5034	.5487	.6652
20	.3598	.4227	.4921	.5368	.6524
25	.3233	.3809	.4451	.4869	.5974
30	.2960	.3494	.4093	.4487	.5541
35	.2746	.3246	.3810	.4182	.5189
40	.2573	.3044	.3578	.3932	.4896
45	.2428	.2875	.3384	.3721	.4648
50	.2306	.2732	.3218	.3541	.4433
60	.2108	.2500	.2948	.3248	.4078
70	.1954	.2319	.2737	.3017	.3799
80	.1829	.2172	.2565	.2830	.3568
90	.1726	.2050	.2422	.2673	.3375
100	.1638	.1946	.2301	.2540	.3211

*Table A.2 is taken from Table VII of Fisher, *Statistical Methods for Research Workers*, published by Oliver and Boyd, Ltd., Edinburgh, and by permission of the author and the publisher.

TABLE A.3
CRITICAL VALUES OF *t*

df	Level of significance for one-tailed test					
	.10	.05	.025	.01	.005	.0005
	Level of significance for two-tailed test					
	.20	.10	.05	.02	.01	.001
1	3.078	6.314	12.706	31.821	63.657	636.619
2	1.886	2.920	4.303	6.965	9.925	31.598
3	1.638	2.353	3.182	4.541	5.841	12.941
4	1.533	2.132	2.776	3.747	4.604	8.610
5	1.476	2.015	2.571	3.365	4.032	6.859
6	1.440	1.943	2.447	3.143	3.707	5.959
7	1.415	1.895	2.365	2.998	3.499	5.405
8	1.397	1.860	2.306	2.896	3.355	5.041
9	1.383	1.833	2.262	2.821	3.250	4.781
10	1.372	1.812	2.228	2.764	3.169	4.587
11	1.363	1.796	2.201	2.718	3.106	4.437
12	1.356	1.782	2.179	2.681	3.055	4.318
13	1.350	1.771	2.160	2.650	3.012	4.221
14	1.345	1.761	2.145	2.624	2.977	4.140
15	1.341	1.753	2.131	2.602	2.947	4.073
16	1.337	1.746	2.120	2.583	2.921	4.015
17	1.333	1.740	2.110	2.567	2.898	3.965
18	1.330	1.734	2.101	2.552	2.878	3.922
19	1.328	1.729	2.093	2.539	2.861	3.883
20	1.325	1.725	2.086	2.528	2.845	3.850
21	1.323	1.721	2.080	2.518	2.831	3.819
22	1.321	1.717	2.074	2.508	2.819	3.792
23	1.319	1.714	2.069	2.500	2.807	3.767
24	1.318	1.711	2.064	2.492	2.797	3.745
25	1.316	1.708	2.060	2.485	2.787	3.725
26	1.315	1.706	2.056	2.479	2.779	3.707
27	1.314	1.703	2.052	2.473	2.771	3.690
28	1.313	1.701	2.048	2.467	2.763	3.674
29	1.311	1.699	2.045	2.462	2.756	3.659
30	1.310	1.697	2.042	2.457	2.750	3.646
40	1.303	1.684	2.021	2.423	2.704	3.551
60	1.296	1.671	2.000	2.390	2.660	3.460
120	1.289	1.658	1.980	2.358	2.617	3.373
∞	1.282	1.645	1.960	2.326	2.576	3.291

*Table A.3 is abridged from Table III of Fisher, *Statistical Methods for Research Workers*, published by Oliver and Boyd, Ltd., Edinburgh, and by permission of the author and the publisher.

TABLE A.4
CRITICAL VALUES OF F

n_2	n_1 degrees of freedom (for greater mean square): 1	2	3	4	5	6	7	8	9	10	11	12	14	16	20	24	30	40	50	75	100	200	500	∞
1	161	200	216	225	230	234	237	239	241	242	243	244	245	246	248	249	250	251	252	253	253	254	254	254
	4,052	4,999	5,403	5,625	5,764	5,859	5,928	5,981	6,022	6,056	6,082	6,106	6,142	6,169	6,208	6,234	6,258	6,286	6,302	6,323	6,334	6,352	6,361	6,366
2	18.51	19.00	19.16	19.25	19.30	19.33	19.36	19.37	19.38	19.39	19.40	19.41	19.42	19.43	19.44	19.45	19.46	19.47	19.47	19.48	19.49	19.49	19.50	19.50
	98.49	99.00	99.17	99.25	99.30	99.33	99.34	99.36	99.38	99.40	99.41	99.42	99.43	99.44	99.45	99.46	99.47	99.48	99.48	99.49	99.49	99.49	99.50	99.50
3	10.13	9.55	9.28	9.12	9.01	8.94	8.88	8.84	8.81	8.78	8.76	8.74	8.71	8.69	8.66	8.64	8.62	8.60	8.58	8.57	8.56	8.54	8.54	8.53
	34.12	30.82	29.46	28.71	28.24	27.91	27.67	27.49	27.34	27.23	27.13	27.05	26.92	26.83	26.69	26.60	26.50	26.41	26.35	26.27	26.23	26.18	26.14	26.12
4	7.71	6.94	6.59	6.39	6.26	6.16	6.09	6.04	6.00	5.96	5.93	5.91	5.87	5.84	5.80	5.77	5.74	5.71	5.70	5.68	5.66	5.65	5.64	5.63
	21.20	18.00	16.69	15.98	15.52	15.21	14.98	14.80	14.66	14.54	14.45	14.37	14.24	14.15	14.02	13.93	13.83	13.74	13.69	13.61	13.57	13.52	13.48	13.46
5	6.61	5.79	5.41	5.19	5.05	4.95	4.88	4.82	4.78	4.74	4.70	4.68	4.64	4.60	4.56	4.53	4.50	4.46	4.44	4.42	4.40	4.38	4.37	4.36
	16.26	13.27	12.06	11.39	10.97	10.67	10.45	10.27	10.15	10.05	9.96	9.89	9.77	9.68	9.55	9.47	9.38	9.29	9.24	9.17	9.13	9.07	9.04	9.02
6	5.99	5.14	4.76	4.53	4.39	4.28	4.21	4.15	4.10	4.06	4.03	4.00	3.96	3.92	3.87	3.84	3.81	3.77	3.75	3.72	3.71	3.69	3.68	3.67
	13.74	10.92	9.78	9.15	8.75	8.47	8.26	8.10	7.98	7.87	7.79	7.72	7.60	7.52	7.39	7.31	7.23	7.14	7.09	7.02	6.99	6.94	6.90	6.88
7	5.59	4.74	4.35	4.12	3.97	3.87	3.79	3.73	3.68	3.63	3.60	3.57	3.52	3.49	3.44	3.41	3.38	3.34	3.32	3.29	3.28	3.25	3.24	3.23
	12.25	9.55	8.45	7.85	7.46	7.19	7.00	6.84	6.71	6.62	6.54	6.47	6.35	6.27	6.15	6.07	5.98	5.90	5.85	5.78	5.75	5.70	5.67	5.65
8	5.32	4.46	4.07	3.84	3.69	3.58	3.50	3.44	3.39	3.34	3.31	3.28	3.23	3.20	3.15	3.12	3.08	3.05	3.03	3.00	2.98	2.96	2.94	2.93
	11.26	8.65	7.59	7.01	6.63	6.37	6.19	6.03	5.91	5.82	5.74	5.67	5.56	5.48	5.36	5.28	5.20	5.11	5.06	5.00	4.96	4.91	4.88	4.86
9	5.12	4.26	3.86	3.63	3.48	3.37	3.29	3.23	3.18	3.13	3.10	3.07	3.02	2.98	2.93	2.90	2.86	2.82	2.80	2.77	2.76	2.73	2.72	2.71
	10.56	8.02	6.99	6.42	6.06	5.80	5.62	5.47	5.35	5.26	5.18	5.11	5.00	4.92	4.80	4.73	4.64	4.56	4.51	4.45	4.41	4.36	4.33	4.31
10	4.96	4.10	3.71	3.48	3.33	3.22	3.14	3.07	3.02	2.97	2.94	2.91	2.86	2.82	2.77	2.74	2.70	2.67	2.64	2.61	2.59	2.56	2.55	2.54
	10.04	7.56	6.55	5.99	5.64	5.39	5.21	5.06	4.95	4.85	4.78	4.71	4.60	4.52	4.41	4.33	4.25	4.17	4.12	4.05	4.01	3.96	3.93	3.91
11	4.84	3.98	3.59	3.36	3.20	3.09	3.01	2.95	2.90	2.86	2.82	2.79	2.74	2.70	2.65	2.61	2.57	2.53	2.50	2.47	2.45	2.42	2.41	2.40
	9.65	7.20	6.22	5.67	5.32	5.07	4.88	4.74	4.63	4.54	4.46	4.40	4.29	4.21	4.10	4.02	3.94	3.86	3.80	3.74	3.70	3.66	3.62	3.60
12	4.75	3.88	3.49	3.26	3.11	3.00	2.92	2.85	2.80	2.76	2.72	2.69	2.64	2.60	2.54	2.50	2.46	2.42	2.40	2.36	2.35	2.32	2.31	2.30
	9.33	6.93	5.95	5.41	5.06	4.82	4.65	4.50	4.39	4.30	4.22	4.16	4.05	3.98	3.86	3.78	3.70	3.61	3.56	3.49	3.46	3.41	3.38	3.36
13	4.67	3.80	3.41	3.18	3.02	2.92	2.84	2.77	2.72	2.67	2.63	2.60	2.55	2.51	2.46	2.42	2.38	2.34	2.32	2.28	2.26	2.24	2.22	2.21
	9.07	6.70	5.74	5.20	4.86	4.62	4.44	4.30	4.19	4.10	4.02	3.96	3.85	3.78	3.67	3.59	3.51	3.42	3.37	3.30	3.27	3.21	3.18	3.16

TABLE A.4 (Cont.)

n_2	n_1 degrees of freedom (for greater mean square)																							
	1	2	3	4	5	6	7	8	9	10	11	12	14	16	20	24	30	40	50	75	100	200	500	∞
14	4.60	3.74	3.34	3.11	2.96	2.85	2.77	2.70	2.65	2.60	2.56	2.53	2.48	2.44	2.39	2.35	2.31	2.27	2.24	2.21	2.19	2.16	2.14	2.13
	8.86	6.51	5.56	5.03	4.69	4.46	4.28	4.14	4.03	3.94	3.86	3.80	3.70	3.62	3.51	3.43	3.34	3.26	3.21	3.14	3.11	3.06	3.02	3.00
15	4.54	3.68	3.29	3.06	2.90	2.79	2.70	2.64	2.59	2.55	2.51	2.48	2.43	2.39	2.33	2.29	2.25	2.21	2.18	2.15	2.12	2.10	2.08	2.07
	8.68	6.36	5.42	4.89	4.56	4.32	4.14	4.00	3.89	3.80	3.73	3.67	3.56	3.48	3.36	3.29	3.20	3.12	3.07	3.00	2.97	2.92	2.89	2.87
16	4.49	3.63	3.24	3.01	2.85	2.74	2.66	2.59	2.54	2.49	2.45	2.42	2.37	2.33	2.28	2.24	2.20	2.16	2.13	2.09	2.07	2.04	2.02	2.01
	8.53	6.23	5.29	4.77	4.44	4.20	4.03	3.89	3.78	3.69	3.61	3.55	3.45	3.37	3.25	3.18	3.10	3.01	2.96	2.89	2.86	2.80	2.77	2.75
17	4.45	3.59	3.20	2.96	2.81	2.70	2.62	2.55	2.50	2.45	2.41	2.38	2.33	2.29	2.23	2.19	2.15	2.11	2.08	2.04	2.02	1.99	1.97	1.96
	8.40	6.11	5.18	4.67	4.34	4.10	3.93	3.79	3.68	3.59	3.52	3.45	3.35	3.27	3.16	3.08	3.00	2.92	2.86	2.79	2.76	2.70	2.67	2.65
18	4.41	3.55	3.16	2.93	2.77	2.66	2.58	2.51	2.46	2.41	2.37	2.34	2.29	2.25	2.19	2.15	2.11	2.07	2.04	2.00	1.98	1.95	1.93	1.92
	8.28	6.01	5.09	4.58	4.25	4.01	3.85	3.71	3.60	3.51	3.44	3.37	3.27	3.19	3.07	3.00	2.91	2.83	2.78	2.71	2.68	2.62	2.59	2.57
19	4.38	3.52	3.13	2.90	2.74	2.63	2.55	2.48	2.43	2.38	2.34	2.31	2.26	2.21	2.15	2.11	2.07	2.02	2.00	1.96	1.94	1.91	1.90	1.88
	8.18	5.93	5.01	4.50	4.17	3.94	3.77	3.63	3.52	3.43	3.36	3.30	3.19	3.12	3.00	2.92	2.84	2.76	2.70	2.63	2.60	2.54	2.51	2.49
20	4.35	3.49	3.10	2.87	2.71	2.60	2.52	2.45	2.40	2.35	2.31	2.28	2.23	2.18	2.12	2.08	2.04	1.99	1.96	1.92	1.90	1.87	1.85	1.84
	8.10	5.85	4.94	4.43	4.10	3.87	3.71	3.56	3.45	3.37	3.30	3.23	3.13	3.05	2.94	2.86	2.77	2.69	2.63	2.56	2.53	2.47	2.44	2.42
21	4.32	3.47	3.07	2.84	2.68	2.57	2.49	2.42	2.37	2.32	2.28	2.25	2.20	2.15	2.09	2.05	2.00	1.96	1.93	1.89	1.87	1.84	1.82	1.81
	8.02	5.78	4.87	4.37	4.04	3.81	3.65	3.51	3.40	3.31	3.24	3.17	3.07	2.99	2.88	2.80	2.72	2.63	2.58	2.51	2.47	2.42	2.38	2.36
22	4.30	3.44	3.05	2.82	2.66	2.55	2.47	2.40	2.35	2.30	2.26	2.23	2.18	2.13	2.07	2.03	1.98	1.93	1.91	1.87	1.84	1.81	1.80	1.78
	7.94	5.72	4.82	4.31	3.99	3.76	3.59	3.45	3.35	3.26	3.18	3.12	3.02	2.94	2.83	2.75	2.67	2.58	2.53	2.46	2.42	2.37	2.33	2.31
23	4.28	3.42	3.03	2.80	2.64	2.53	2.45	2.38	2.32	2.28	2.24	2.20	2.14	2.10	2.04	2.00	1.96	1.91	1.88	1.84	1.82	1.79	1.77	1.76
	7.88	5.66	4.76	4.26	3.94	3.71	3.54	3.41	3.30	3.21	3.14	3.07	2.97	2.89	2.78	2.70	2.62	2.53	2.48	2.41	2.37	2.32	2.28	2.26
24	4.26	3.40	3.01	2.78	2.62	2.51	2.43	2.36	2.30	2.26	2.22	2.18	2.13	2.09	2.02	1.98	1.94	1.89	1.86	1.82	1.80	1.76	1.74	1.73
	7.82	5.61	4.72	4.22	3.90	3.67	3.50	3.36	3.25	3.17	3.09	3.03	2.93	2.85	2.74	2.66	2.58	2.49	2.44	2.36	2.33	2.27	2.23	2.21
25	4.24	3.38	2.99	2.76	2.60	2.49	2.41	2.34	2.28	2.24	2.20	2.16	2.11	2.06	2.00	1.96	1.92	1.87	1.84	1.80	1.77	1.74	1.72	1.71
	7.77	5.57	4.68	4.18	3.86	3.63	3.46	3.32	3.21	3.13	3.05	2.99	2.89	2.81	2.70	2.62	2.54	2.45	2.40	2.32	2.29	2.23	2.19	2.17
26	4.22	3.37	2.98	2.74	2.59	2.47	2.39	2.32	2.27	2.22	2.18	2.15	2.10	2.05	1.99	1.95	1.90	1.85	1.82	1.78	1.76	1.72	1.70	1.69
	7.72	5.53	4.64	4.14	3.82	3.59	3.42	3.29	3.17	3.09	3.02	2.96	2.86	2.77	2.66	2.58	2.50	2.41	2.36	2.28	2.25	2.19	2.15	2.13

TABLE A.4 (Cont.)

n_2	n_1 degrees of freedom (for greater mean square)																							
	1	2	3	4	5	6	7	8	9	10	11	12	14	16	20	24	30	40	50	75	100	200	500	∞
27	4.21 7.68	3.35 5.49	2.96 4.60	2.73 4.11	2.57 3.79	2.46 3.56	2.37 3.39	2.30 3.26	2.25 3.14	2.20 3.06	2.16 2.98	2.13 2.93	2.08 2.83	2.03 2.74	1.97 2.63	1.93 2.55	1.88 2.47	1.84 2.38	1.80 2.33	1.76 2.25	1.74 2.21	1.71 2.16	1.68 2.12	1.67 2.10
28	4.20 7.64	3.34 5.45	2.95 4.57	2.71 4.07	2.56 3.76	2.44 3.53	2.36 3.36	2.29 3.23	2.24 3.11	2.19 3.03	2.15 2.95	2.12 2.90	2.06 2.80	2.02 2.71	1.96 2.60	1.91 2.52	1.87 2.44	1.81 2.35	1.78 2.30	1.75 2.22	1.72 2.18	1.69 2.13	1.67 2.09	1.65 2.06
29	4.18 7.60	3.33 5.42	2.93 4.54	2.70 4.04	2.54 3.73	2.43 3.50	2.35 3.33	2.28 3.20	2.22 3.08	2.18 3.00	2.14 2.92	2.10 2.87	2.05 2.77	2.00 2.68	1.94 2.57	1.90 2.49	1.85 2.41	1.80 2.32	1.77 2.27	1.73 2.19	1.71 2.15	1.68 2.10	1.65 2.06	1.64 2.03
30	4.17 7.56	3.32 5.39	2.92 4.51	2.69 4.02	2.53 3.70	2.42 3.47	2.34 3.30	2.27 3.17	2.21 3.06	2.16 2.98	2.12 2.90	2.09 2.84	2.04 2.74	1.99 2.66	1.93 2.55	1.89 2.47	1.84 2.38	1.79 2.29	1.76 2.24	1.72 2.16	1.69 2.13	1.66 2.07	1.64 2.03	1.62 2.01
32	4.15 7.50	3.30 5.34	2.90 4.46	2.67 3.97	2.51 3.66	2.40 3.42	2.32 3.25	2.25 3.12	2.19 3.01	2.14 2.94	2.10 2.86	2.07 2.80	2.02 2.70	1.97 2.62	1.91 2.51	1.86 2.42	1.82 2.34	1.76 2.25	1.74 2.20	1.69 2.12	1.67 2.08	1.64 2.02	1.61 1.98	1.59 1.96
34	4.13 7.44	3.28 5.29	2.88 4.42	2.65 3.93	2.49 3.61	2.38 3.38	2.30 3.21	2.23 3.08	2.17 2.97	2.12 2.89	2.08 2.82	2.05 2.76	2.00 2.66	1.95 2.58	1.89 2.47	1.84 2.38	1.80 2.30	1.74 2.21	1.71 2.15	1.67 2.08	1.64 2.04	1.61 1.98	1.59 1.94	1.57 1.91
36	4.11 7.39	3.26 5.25	2.86 4.38	2.63 3.89	2.48 3.58	2.36 3.35	2.28 3.18	2.21 3.04	2.15 2.94	2.10 2.86	2.06 2.78	2.03 2.72	1.98 2.62	1.93 2.54	1.87 2.43	1.82 2.35	1.78 2.26	1.72 2.17	1.69 2.12	1.65 2.04	1.62 2.00	1.59 1.94	1.56 1.90	1.55 1.87
38	4.10 7.35	3.25 5.21	2.85 4.34	2.62 3.86	2.46 3.54	2.35 3.32	2.26 3.15	2.19 3.02	2.14 2.91	2.09 2.82	2.05 2.75	2.02 2.69	1.96 2.59	1.92 2.51	1.85 2.40	1.80 2.32	1.76 2.22	1.71 2.14	1.67 2.08	1.63 2.00	1.60 1.97	1.57 1.90	1.54 1.86	1.53 1.84
40	4.08 7.31	3.23 5.18	2.84 4.31	2.61 3.83	2.45 3.51	2.34 3.29	2.25 3.12	2.18 2.99	2.12 2.88	2.07 2.80	2.04 2.73	2.00 2.66	1.95 2.56	1.90 2.49	1.84 2.37	1.79 2.29	1.74 2.20	1.69 2.11	1.66 2.05	1.61 1.97	1.59 1.94	1.55 1.88	1.53 1.84	1.51 1.81
42	4.07 7.27	3.22 5.15	2.83 4.29	2.59 3.80	2.44 3.49	2.32 3.26	2.24 3.10	2.17 2.96	2.11 2.86	2.06 2.77	2.02 2.70	1.99 2.64	1.94 2.54	1.89 2.46	1.82 2.35	1.78 2.26	1.73 2.17	1.68 2.08	1.64 2.02	1.60 1.94	1.57 1.91	1.54 1.85	1.51 1.80	1.49 1.78
44	4.06 7.24	3.21 5.12	2.82 4.26	2.58 3.78	2.43 3.46	2.31 3.24	2.23 3.07	2.16 2.94	2.10 2.84	2.05 2.75	2.01 2.68	1.98 2.62	1.92 2.52	1.88 2.44	1.81 2.32	1.76 2.24	1.72 2.15	1.66 2.06	1.63 2.00	1.58 1.92	1.56 1.88	1.52 1.82	1.50 1.78	1.48 1.75
46	4.05 7.21	3.20 5.10	2.81 4.24	2.57 3.76	2.42 3.44	2.30 3.22	2.22 3.05	2.14 2.92	2.09 2.82	2.04 2.73	2.00 2.66	1.97 2.60	1.91 2.50	1.87 2.42	1.80 2.30	1.75 2.22	1.71 2.13	1.65 2.04	1.62 1.98	1.57 1.90	1.54 1.86	1.51 1.80	1.48 1.76	1.46 1.72
48	4.04 7.19	3.19 5.08	2.80 4.22	2.56 3.74	2.41 3.42	2.30 3.20	2.21 3.04	2.14 2.90	2.08 2.80	2.03 2.71	1.99 2.64	1.96 2.58	1.90 2.48	1.86 2.40	1.79 2.28	1.74 2.20	1.70 2.11	1.64 2.02	1.61 1.96	1.56 1.88	1.53 1.84	1.50 1.78	1.47 1.73	1.45 1.70

TABLE A.4 (Cont.)

n_2	n_1 degrees of freedom (for greater mean square)																							
	1	2	3	4	5	6	7	8	9	10	11	12	14	16	20	24	30	40	50	75	100	200	500	∞
50	4.03	3.18	2.79	2.56	2.40	2.29	2.20	2.13	2.07	2.02	1.98	1.95	1.90	1.85	1.78	1.74	1.69	1.63	1.60	1.55	1.52	1.48	1.46	1.44
	7.17	5.06	4.20	3.72	3.41	3.18	3.02	2.88	2.78	2.70	2.62	2.56	2.46	2.39	2.26	2.18	2.10	2.00	1.94	1.86	1.82	1.76	1.71	1.68
55	4.02	3.17	2.78	2.54	2.38	2.27	2.18	2.11	2.05	2.00	1.97	1.93	1.88	1.83	1.76	1.72	1.67	1.61	1.58	1.52	1.50	1.46	1.43	1.41
	7.12	5.01	4.16	3.68	3.37	3.15	2.98	2.85	2.75	2.66	2.59	2.53	2.43	2.35	2.23	2.15	2.06	1.96	1.90	1.82	1.78	1.71	1.66	1.64
60	4.00	3.15	2.76	2.52	2.37	2.25	2.17	2.10	2.04	1.99	1.95	1.92	1.86	1.81	1.75	1.70	1.65	1.59	1.56	1.50	1.48	1.44	1.41	1.39
	7.08	4.98	4.13	3.65	3.34	3.12	2.95	2.82	2.72	2.63	2.56	2.50	2.40	2.32	2.20	2.12	2.03	1.93	1.87	1.79	1.74	1.68	1.63	1.60
65	3.99	3.14	2.75	2.51	2.36	2.24	2.15	2.08	2.02	1.98	1.94	1.90	1.85	1.80	1.73	1.68	1.63	1.57	1.54	1.49	1.46	1.42	1.39	1.37
	7.04	4.95	4.10	3.62	3.31	3.09	2.93	2.79	2.70	2.61	2.54	2.47	2.37	2.30	2.18	2.09	2.00	1.90	1.84	1.76	1.71	1.64	1.60	1.56
70	3.98	3.13	2.74	2.50	2.35	2.23	2.14	2.07	2.01	1.97	1.93	1.89	1.84	1.79	1.72	1.67	1.62	1.56	1.53	1.47	1.45	1.40	1.37	1.35
	7.01	4.92	4.08	3.60	3.29	3.07	2.91	2.77	2.67	2.59	2.51	2.45	2.35	2.28	2.15	2.07	1.98	1.88	1.82	1.74	1.69	1.62	1.56	1.53
80	3.96	3.11	2.72	2.48	2.33	2.21	2.12	2.05	1.99	1.95	1.91	1.88	1.82	1.77	1.70	1.65	1.60	1.54	1.51	1.45	1.42	1.38	1.35	1.32
	6.96	4.88	4.04	3.56	3.25	3.04	2.87	2.74	2.64	2.55	2.48	2.41	2.32	2.24	2.11	2.03	1.94	1.84	1.78	1.70	1.65	1.57	1.52	1.49
100	3.94	3.09	2.70	2.46	2.30	2.19	2.10	2.03	1.97	1.92	1.88	1.85	1.79	1.75	1.68	1.63	1.57	1.51	1.48	1.42	1.39	1.34	1.30	1.28
	6.90	4.82	3.98	3.51	3.20	2.99	2.82	2.69	2.59	2.51	2.43	2.36	2.26	2.19	2.06	1.98	1.89	1.79	1.73	1.64	1.59	1.51	1.46	1.43
125	3.92	3.07	2.68	2.44	2.29	2.17	2.08	2.01	1.95	1.90	1.86	1.83	1.77	1.72	1.65	1.60	1.55	1.49	1.45	1.39	1.36	1.31	1.27	1.25
	6.84	4.78	3.94	3.47	3.17	2.95	2.79	2.65	2.56	2.47	2.40	2.33	2.23	2.15	2.03	1.94	1.85	1.75	1.68	1.59	1.54	1.46	1.40	1.37
150	3.91	3.06	2.67	2.43	2.27	2.16	2.07	2.00	1.94	1.89	1.85	1.82	1.76	1.71	1.64	1.59	1.54	1.47	1.44	1.37	1.34	1.29	1.25	1.22
	6.81	4.75	3.91	3.44	3.14	2.92	2.76	2.62	2.53	2.44	2.37	2.30	2.20	2.12	2.00	1.91	1.83	1.72	1.66	1.56	1.51	1.43	1.37	1.33
200	3.89	3.04	2.65	2.41	2.26	2.14	2.05	1.98	1.92	1.87	1.83	1.80	1.74	1.69	1.62	1.57	1.52	1.45	1.42	1.35	1.32	1.26	1.22	1.19
	6.76	4.71	3.88	3.41	3.11	2.90	2.73	2.60	2.50	2.41	2.34	2.28	2.17	2.09	1.97	1.88	1.79	1.69	1.62	1.53	1.48	1.39	1.33	1.28
400	3.86	3.02	2.62	2.39	2.23	2.12	2.03	1.96	1.90	1.85	1.81	1.78	1.72	1.67	1.60	1.54	1.49	1.42	1.38	1.32	1.28	1.22	1.16	1.13
	6.70	4.66	3.83	3.36	3.06	2.85	2.69	2.55	2.46	2.37	2.29	2.23	2.12	2.04	1.92	1.84	1.74	1.64	1.57	1.47	1.42	1.32	1.24	1.19
1000	3.85	3.00	2.61	2.38	2.22	2.10	2.02	1.95	1.89	1.84	1.80	1.76	1.70	1.65	1.58	1.53	1.47	1.41	1.36	1.30	1.26	1.19	1.13	1.08
	6.66	4.62	3.80	3.34	3.04	2.82	2.66	2.53	2.43	2.34	2.26	2.20	2.09	2.01	1.89	1.81	1.71	1.61	1.54	1.44	1.38	1.28	1.19	1.11
∞	3.84	2.99	2.60	2.37	2.21	2.09	2.01	1.94	1.88	1.83	1.79	1.75	1.69	1.64	1.57	1.52	1.46	1.40	1.35	1.28	1.24	1.17	1.11	1.00
	6.64	4.60	3.78	3.32	3.02	2.80	2.64	2.51	2.41	2.32	2.24	2.18	2.07	1.99	1.87	1.79	1.69	1.59	1.52	1.41	1.36	1.25	1.15	1.00

*Reprinted by permission from *Statistical Methods* by George W. Snedecor and William G. Cochran, sixth edition © 1967 by Iowa State University Press, Ames, Iowa.

TABLE A.5
CRITICAL VALUES OF THE STUDENTIZED RANGE STATISTIC

		k = number of means or steps between ordered means								
df for S_w^2	$1-\alpha$	2	3	4	5	6	7	8	9	10
1	.95	18.0	27.0	32.8	37.1	40.4	43.1	45.4	47.4	49.
	.99	90.0	135	164	186	202	216	227	237	246
2	.95	6.09	8.3	9.8	10.9	11.7	12.4	13.0	13.5	14.
	.99	14.0	19.0	22.3	24.7	26.6	28.2	29.5	30.7	31.
3	.95	4.50	5.91	6.82	7.50	8.04	8.48	8.85	9.18	9.
	.99	8.26	10.6	12.2	13.3	14.2	15.0	15.6	16.2	16.
4	.95	3.93	5.04	5.76	6.29	6.71	7.05	7.35	7.60	7.
	.99	6.51	8.12	9.17	9.96	10.6	11.1	11.5	11.9	12.
5	.95	3.64	4.60	5.22	5.67	6.03	6.33	6.58	6.80	6.
	.99	5.70	6.97	7.80	8.42	8.91	9.32	9.67	9.97	10.
6	.95	3.46	4.34	4.90	5.31	5.63	5.89	6.12	6.32	6.
	.99	5.24	6.33	7.03	7.56	7.97	8.32	8.61	8.87	9.
7	.95	3.34	4.16	4.69	5.06	5.36	5.61	5.82	6.00	6.
	.99	4.95	5.92	6.54	7.01	7.37	7.68	7.94	8.17	8.
8	.95	3.26	4.04	4.53	4.89	5.17	5.40	5.60	5.77	5.
	.99	4.74	5.63	6.20	6.63	6.96	7.24	7.47	7.68	7.
9	.95	3.20	3.95	4.42	4.76	5.02	5.24	5.43	5.60	5.
	.99	4.60	5.43	5.96	6.35	6.66	6.91	7.13	7.32	7.
10	.95	3.15	3.88	4.33	4.65	4.91	5.12	5.30	5.46	5.
	.99	4.48	5.27	5.77	6.14	6.43	6.67	6.87	7.05	7.
11	.95	3.11	3.82	4.26	4.57	4.82	5.03	5.20	5.35	5.
	.99	4.39	5.14	5.62	5.97	6.25	6.48	6.67	6.84	6.
12	.95	3.08	3.77	4.20	4.51	4.75	4.95	5.12	5.27	5
	.99	4.32	5.04	5.50	5.84	6.10	6.32	6.51	6.67	6
13	.95	3.06	3.73	4.15	4.45	4.69	4.88	5.05	5.19	5
	.99	4.26	4.96	5.40	5.73	5.98	6.19	6.37	6.53	6
14	.95	3.03	3.70	4.11	4.41	4.64	4.83	4.99	5.13	5
	.99	4.21	4.89	5.32	5.63	5.88	6.08	6.26	6.41	6
16	.95	3.00	3.65	4.05	4.33	4.56	4.74	4.90	5.03	5
	.99	4.13	4.78	5.19	5.49	5.72	5.92	6.08	6.22	6
18	.95	2.97	3.61	4.00	4.28	4.49	4.67	4.82	4.96	5
	.99	4.07	4.70	5.09	5.38	5.60	5.79	5.94	6.08	6
20	.95	2.95	3.58	3.96	4.23	4.45	4.62	4.77	4.90	5
	.99	4.02	4.64	5.02	5.29	5.51	5.69	5.84	5.97	6
24	.95	2.92	3.53	3.90	4.17	4.37	4.54	4.68	4.81	4
	.99	3.96	4.54	4.91	5.17	5.37	5.54	5.69	5.81	5
30	.95	2.89	3.49	3.84	4.10	4.30	4.46	4.60	4.72	4
	.99	3.89	4.45	4.80	5.05	5.24	5.40	5.54	5.56	5
40	.95	2.86	3.44	3.79	4.04	4.23	4.39	4.52	4.63	4
	.99	3.82	4.37	4.70	4.93	5.11	5.27	5.39	5.50	5
60	.95	2.83	3.40	3.74	3.98	4.16	4.31	4.44	4.55	4
	.99	3.76	4.28	4.60	4.82	4.99	5.13	5.25	5.36	5
120	.95	2.80	3.36	3.69	3.92	4.10	4.24	4.36	4.48	4
	.99	3.70	4.20	4.50	4.71	4.87	5.01	5.12	5.21	[illegible]
∞	.95	2.77	3.31	3.63	3.86	4.03	4.17	4.29	4.39	[illegible]
	.99	3.64	4.12	4.40	4.60	4.76	4.88	4.99	5.08	[illegible]

*This table is abridged from Table II.2 in *The probability integrals of the range and of the Studentized range*, prepared by H. Leon Harter, Donald S. Clemm, and Eugene H. Guthrie. These tables are published in WADC tech. Rep. 58—484, vol. 2, 1959, Wright Air Development Center, and are reproduced with the kind permission of the authors.

Appendix B

STATISTICAL COMPUTER PROGRAMS FOR THE APPLE II (II+ OR IIe)

INTRODUCTION

SOURCE OF COMPUTER PROGRAMS

The programs listed here have been used with the consent of the persons who wrote them. The *Random Numbers* program was written by Stephen Silverman from the University of Texas, Austin. The *Omega Squared* program was written by Tim Lee from McMaster University (Canada). The remaining six programs are taken from a more complete statistical package written by:

> Steinmetz, J.E., Romano, A.G., & Patterson, M.M. (1981). Statistical programs for the Apple II microcomputer. *Behavior Research Methods & Instrumentation*, **15**(5), 702.

We want to thank each of these people, but, in particular, we express our appreciation to Joe Steinmetz, Department of Psychology, Stanford University, for allowing us to take these programs from his package. A complete copy of the package for the Apple II (II+ or IIe) with 48K and at least one disk drive can be obtained without charge by sending an unformatted blank 5.25″ floppy disk to:

> Michael M. Patterson
> Director of Research Affairs
> College of Osteopathic Medicine
> Ohio University
> Athens, OH 45701

HOW TO USE THESE PROGRAMS

If you want to enter these programs on your Apple, use the following procedure:

1. Place an initialized floppy disk in the disk drive and turn on the Apple.
2. Type in the program statements exactly as listed.
3. Type "SAVE" and then the name you want to save the program under (for example, SAVE DESCRIPTIVE STATISTICS).
4. To use the program, type "LOAD" and then the name of the program (LOAD DESCRIPTIVE STATISTICS).
5. Then type "RUN."

The monitor will display the program name and features. All you need to do to use the program is follow the instructions on the monitor.

COMPUTER PROGRAMS

The eight computer programs follow. For each one we provide the following:

1. The name of the program
2. A brief description
3. The listing of program statements
4. A sample run on data from this text

The programs are written in BASIC and should run without adjustment on an Apple II (II+ or IIe) with at least one disk drive and 48K memory. Most of the programs offer the option of displaying the data on the monitor and/or printing the data if you have a printer. Once you have the programs correctly entered and saved on a disk, you should write-protect the disk to avoid inadvertently erasing the programs. If you are going to store data, we suggest using a separate disk.

If you want to use these programs on micros other than the Apple, some symbols in BASIC will need to be changed. While the changes are time consuming (depending on your level of skill), they are relatively minor.

(*NOTE:* The ANOVA programs place an asterisk after significant *F* ratios. The routine used to evaluate the *F* ratios is only an estimate, hence, the *F* ratios should be verified against a table of *F* values.)

Programs 2, 3, 4, 5, 7, and 8 all have internal options which will allow printing of the data. For programs 1 and 6, you must use the PR#1 command to turn your printer on prior to running the program if you want a printed copy.

DOCUMENTATION FOR APPLE STATISTICAL PROGRAMS

Program 1: Random Numbers. This program provides for either the random selection of a sample from a population or the random assignment of a sample of subjects to groups. For the *random selection* program, you enter the number of subjects in the population and the sample size desired. The program then lists the number-name of the randomly selected subjects. For *random assignment*, you enter the sample size and the number of cells (groups) to which subjects are to be assigned. The program will ask if you have equal cell size. If you answer no, it will balance the cells as nearly as possible. This program does not have an option to print, so if you want to print a copy of the output, turn your printer on prior to running the program (use the "PR#1" command, or the number for the slot your printer is in). All of the remaining programs use a sample run from data in the text. The sample run from the random selection program involved selecting 50 subjects from a population of 500 while the random assignment example placed 45 subjects into 5 groups of 9 subjects each.

PROGRAM 1

RANDOM NUMBERS

```
10  HOME
20  HTAB 5
30  PRINT "RANDOM SELECTION AND ASSIGNMENT"
32  HTAB 92
33  PRINT "STEPHEN SILVERMAN"
34  HTAB 7
35  PRINT "LOUISIANA STATE UNIVERSITY"
40  HTAB 87
50  PRINT "WHICH PROCEDURE WOULD YOU"
60  HTAB 12
70  PRINT "LIKE TO PERFORM?"
80  HTAB 45
90  PRINT "A. RANDOM SELECTION"
100  HTAB 5
110  PRINT "B. RANDOM ASSIGNMENT"
120  HTAB 5
130  PRINT "X. EXIT THE PROGRAM"
140  INPUT A$
150  IF A$ = "A" THEN  GOTO 1000
160  IF A$ = "B" THEN  GOTO 2000
170  IF A$ = "X" THEN  GOTO 9000
1000  HOME
1010  HTAB 3
1020  INPUT "WHAT IS THE POPULATION SIZE?    ";P
1040  HTAB 81
1050  INPUT "HOW MANY SUBJECTS DO YOU WANT SELECTED?  ";S1
1052  HTAB 81
1058  HTAB 81
1059  PRINT "PLEASE INPUT ANY NUMBER"
1060  INPUT N
1061  HTAB 81
1062  PRINT "PLEASE WAIT......"
1065 N1 = 0
1070  DIM A%(S1)
1080  FOR X = 1 TO S1
1090 N = N + 1
1100 R =  RND (N)
1110 R1 = R * 1000
```

PROGRAM 1 (Cont.)

```
1120 R2 =  INT (R1)
1130  IF R2 > P THEN  GOTO 1090
1131  IF R2 = 0 THEN  GOTO 1090
1132 N1 = N1 + 1
1135  IF N1 = 1 THEN A%(1) = R2
1137  IF N1 = 1 THEN  GOTO 1190
1140  FOR Z = 1 TO S1
1150  IF A%(Z) = R2 THEN  GOTO 1090
1160  NEXT Z
1170 A%(X) = R2
1190  NEXT X
1200  HOME
1210  HTAB 1
1220  PRINT "THE SUBJECTS YOU SHOULD SELECT ARE:"
1230  HTAB 81
1240  FOR W = 1 TO S1
1260  PRINT A%(W),
1270  NEXT W
1280  PRINT "  "
1290  PRINT "DO YOU WANT TO CONTINUE? (Y/N)"
1300  INPUT AN$
1310  IF AN$ = "Y" THEN  GOTO 10
1320  IF AN$ = "N" THEN  GOTO 9000
2000  HOME
2010  HTAB 2
2020  PRINT "HOW MANY CELLS DO YOU WANT TO FILL?"
2030  INPUT I1
2040  HTAB 86
2050  PRINT "WHAT IS YOUR TOTAL SAMPLE SIZE?"
2060  INPUT I2
2070  HTAB 81
2080  PRINT "WILL THE CELL SIZES BE EQUAL? (Y/N)"
2090  INPUT E$
2100  IF E$ = "Y" THEN  GOTO 2200
2110  IF E$ = "N" THEN  GOTO 3000
2200 CS = I2 / I1
2210  DIM B%(I1,CS)
2220  HTAB 81
2230  PRINT "PLEASE INPUT ANY NUMBER"
2240  INPUT N
2250  HTAB 81
2260  PRINT "PLEASE WAIT -- THIS MAY TAKE A MINUTE OR TWO"
2270 N1 = 0
2280  FOR X = 1 TO I1
2290  FOR Y = 1 TO CS
2300 N = N + 1
2310 R =  RND (N)
2320 R1 = R * 100
2330 R2 =  INT (R1)
2340  IF R2 > I2 THEN  GOTO 2300
2350  IF R2 = 0 THEN  GOTO 2300
2360 N1 = N1 + 1
2370  IF N1 = 1 THEN B%(1,1) = R2
2380  IF N1 = 1 THEN  GOTO 2300
2390  FOR Z = 1 TO X
2400  FOR U = 1 TO CS
2410  IF R2 = B%(Z,U) THEN  GOTO 2300
2420  NEXT U
```

PROGRAM 1 (Cont.)

```
2430  NEXT Z
2440 B%(X,Y) = R2
2450  NEXT Y
2460  NEXT X
2470  HOME
2500  HTAB 4
2510  PRINT "ASSIGNMENTS ARE LISTED BELOW - "
2520  FOR V1 = 1 TO I1
2522  HTAB 81
2525  PRINT "CELL ";V1
2527  HTAB 41
2530  FOR V2 = 1 TO CS
2540  PRINT B%(V1,V2),
2550  NEXT V2
2552  HTAB 81
2553  IF V1 = I1 THEN  GOTO 2600
2554  PRINT "PRESS RETURN TO CONTINUE"
2556  INPUT T$
2560  NEXT V1
2590  HTAB 81
2600  PRINT "DO YOU WANT TO CONTINUE? (Y/N)"
2610  INPUT AN$
2620  IF AN$ = "Y" THEN  GOTO 10
2630  IF AN$ = "N" THEN  GOTO 9000
3000  HTAB 81
3010  INPUT "WHAT IS THE SMALLEST CELL SIZE? ";CZ
3020 I5 = CZ * I1
3030 I6 = I2 - I5
3040 C3 = CZ + 1
3050  DIM C%(I1,C3)
3060  HTAB 81
3070  INPUT "PLEASE INPUT ANY NUMBER   ";N
3080  HTAB 81
3090  PRINT "PLEASE WAIT -- THIS MAY TAKE A MINUTE OR TWO"
3100 N1 = 0
3110  FOR X = 1 TO I1
3120  FOR Y = 1 TO CZ
3130 N = N + 1
3140 R =  RND (N)
3150 R1 = R * 100
3160 R2 =  INT (R1)
3170  IF R2 > I2 THEN  GOTO 3130
3180  IF R2 = 0 THEN  GOTO 3130
3190 N1 = N1 + 1
3200  IF N1 = 1 THEN C%(1,1) = R2
3210  IF N1 = 1 THEN  GOTO 3130
3220  FOR Z = 1 TO X
3230  FOR U = 1 TO CZ
3240  IF R2 = C%(
          Z,U) THEN  GOTO 3130
3250  NEXT U
3260  NEXT Z
3270 C%(X,Y) = R2
3280  NEXT Y
3290  NEXT X
3300  FOR X = 1 TO I1
3305  IF I5 = I2 THEN  GOTO 3700
3310 Y = C3
```

PROGRAM 1 (Cont.)

```
3320 N = N + 1
3330 R =  RND (N)
3340 R1 = R * 100
3350 R2 =  INT (R1)
3360  IF R2 > I2 THEN  GOTO 3320
3370  IF R2 = O THEN  GOTO 3320
3380  FOR Z = 1 TO I1
3390  FOR U = 1 TO C3
3400  IF R2 = C%(Z,U) THEN  GOTO 3320
3410  NEXT U
3420  NEXT Z
3430 C%(X,Y) = R2
3445 I5 = I5 + 1
3450  NEXT X
3700  HOME
3710  HTAB 4
3720  PRINT "ASSIGNMENTS ARE LISTED BELOW -- "
3730  FOR V1 = 1 TO I1
3740  HTAB 81
3750  PRINT "CELL ";V1
3755  HTAB 41
3760  FOR V2 = 1 TO C3
3770  PRINT C%(V1,V2),
3780  NEXT V2
3782  HTAB 81
3783  IF V1 = I1 THEN  GOTO 3800
3784  PRINT "PRESS RETURN TO CONTINUE"
3785  INPUT T$
3790  NEXT V1
3800  HTAB 81
3810  PRINT "DO YOU WANT TO CONTINUE? (Y/N)"
3820  INPUT AN$
3830  IF AN$ = "Y" THEN  GOTO 10
3840  IF AN$ = "N" THEN  GOTO 9000
```

PROGRAM 1

SAMPLE RUN

```
PR#1
]RUN
    RANDOM SELECTION AND ASSIGNMENT

           STEPHEN SILVERMAN
      LOUISIANA STATE UNIVERSITY

      WHICH PROCEDURE WOULD YOU
           LIKE TO PREFORM?

     A. RANDOM SELECTION
     B. RANDOM ASSIGNMENT
     X. EXIT THE PROGRAM
?A
  WHAT IS THE POPULATION SIZE?   500

HOW MANY SUBJECTS DO YOU WANT SELECTED?  50
```

PROGRAM 1 SAMPLE RUN (Cont.)

```
PLEASE INPUT ANY NUMBER
?4


PLEASE WAIT......
THE SUBJECTS YOU SHOULD SELECT ARE:


103                 17                  131
268                 419                 368
123                 280                 115
427                 22                  128
289                 91                  68
246                 256                 433
169                 129                 37
99                  212                 161
203                 429                 197
367                 399                 375
253                 497                 481
182                 175                 374
90                  469                 318
225                 216                 282
369                 494                 243
247                 198                 395
275                 221
DO YOU WANT TO CONTINUE? (Y/N)
?N



]RUN
    RANDOM SELECTION AND ASSIGNMENT


          STEPHEN SILVERMAN
      LOUISIANA STATE UNIVERSITY


      WHICH PROCEDURE WOULD YOU
           LIKE TO PREFORM?

    A. RANDOM SELECTION
    B. RANDOM ASSIGNMENT
    X. EXIT THE PROGRAM
?B
 HOW MANY CELLS DO YOU WANT TO FILL?
?5


     WHAT IS YOUR TOTAL SAMPLE SIZE?
?45


WILL THE CELL SIZES BE EQUAL? (Y/N)
?Y


PLEASE INPUT ANY NUMBER
?7
```

PROGRAM 1 SAMPLE RUN (Cont.)

```
PLEASE WAIT --- THIS MAY TAKE A MINUTE OR TWO
   ASSIGNMENTS ARE LISTED BELOW -


CELL 1

43                  11                  10
36                  31                  40
32                  45                  18


PRESS RETURN TO CONTINUE
?


CELL 2

4                   28                  24
26                  37                  15
20                  17                  41


PRESS RETURN TO CONTINUE


CELL 3

6                   44                  16
30                  2                   19
27                  34                  5


PRESS RETURN TO CONTINUE
?


CELL 4

3                   23                  13
29                  8                   38
25                  22                  33


PRESS RETURN TO CONTINUE
?


CELL 5

21                  39                  14
7                   1                   9
42                  12                  35


DO YOU WANT TO CONTINUE? (Y/N)
?N
```

Program 2: Descriptive Statistics. This program calculates the mean, variance, standard deviation, and standard error of the mean for a set of data points. A routine for converting raw scores to *z*-scores is also included.

PROGRAM 2
DESCRIPTIVE STATISTICS (M, s, s^2)

```
1Ø  REM     DESCRIPTIVE STATISTICS
2Ø  REM          VERSION IA
3Ø  REM       JOSEPH E. STEINMETZ
4Ø  REM        OHIO UNIVERSITY
5Ø  REM           OCT., 1981
6Ø  REM
7Ø  HOME : PRINT "THIS PROGRAM CALCULATES DESCRIPTIVE": PRINT "STATISTICS.": PRINT : PRINT "AVAILABLE STATISTICS:": PRINT "--
    -----------------"
8Ø  PRINT "(1) MEAN": PRINT "(2) VARIANCE AND STANDARD DEVIATION": PRINT "(3) STANDARD ERROR"
9Ø  PRINT : PRINT "AVAILABLE OPTIONS:": PRINT "-----------------": PRINT "(1) DATA ENTRY CORRECTION ROUTINE": PRINT "(2) SAVE
     DATA TO DISK": PRINT "(3) GET DATA FROM DISK"
1ØØ  GOSUB 52Ø
11Ø  CLEAR : HOME :D$ =  CHR$ (4)
12Ø  INPUT "ENTER A VARIABLE NAME: ";F$: PRINT : PRINT : PRINT
13Ø  INPUT "HOW MANY DATA POINTS ? ";N: PRINT : PRINT : PRINT : PRINT
14Ø  DIM X(N): DIM Y(N): DIM Z(N)
15Ø  PRINT : PRINT : PRINT "WOULD YOU LIKE THE RESULTS": INPUT "PRINTED (Y/N) ? ";ANSWER$: IF ANSWER$ = "Y" THEN V2 = 1
16Ø  IF V2 = 1 THEN  PRINT : PRINT : INPUT "PRINTER SLOT# ? ";PS%
17Ø  HOME : PRINT "WOULD YOU LIKE TO USE DATA THAT IS": INPUT "STORED ON A DISK (Y/N) ? ";ANSWER$: IF ANSWER$ = "Y" THEN  GOSUB
     53Ø: GOSUB 59Ø
18Ø  HOME : IF V1 = 1 THEN  INPUT "ANY CHANGES (Y/N) ? ";ANSWER$: IF ANSWER$ = "Y" THEN  GOSUB 44Ø
19Ø  IF V1 = 1 THEN  GOTO 23Ø
2ØØ  PRINT "ENTER THE "N" DATA POINTS:": PRINT : PRINT : PRINT
21Ø  FOR I = 1 TO N: INPUT X(I): NEXT I
22Ø  GOSUB 59Ø: HOME : INPUT "ANY CHANGES (Y/N) ? ";ANSWER$: IF ANSWER$ = "Y" THEN  GOSUB 44Ø
23Ø  FOR I = 1 TO N:Y(I) = X(I) * X(I)
24Ø SUM = SUM + X(I):SQSUM = SQSUM + Y(I): NEXT I
25Ø MN = SUM / N
26Ø SS = (SQSUM - SUM * SUM / N)
27Ø VAR = SS / (N - 1):V6 = SS / N
28Ø SD =  SQR (VAR):S6 =  SQR (V6)
29Ø  FOR I = 1 TO N:D = X(I) - MN:AA = AA + D * D:D = Ø: NEXT I:SE =  SQR (AA / (N * (N - 1)))
```

PROGRAM 2 (Cont.)

```
300  HOME
310  IF V2 = 1 THEN  PRINT D$;"PR#";PS%: PRINT : PRINT
320  PRINT "****DESCRIPTIVE STATISTICS SUMMARY****  ": PRINT : PRINT "VARIABLE NAME: "F$: PRINT : PRINT
330  PRINT "MEAN = "MN: PRINT
340  PRINT "VARIANCE = "VAR: PRINT
350  PRINT "STANDARD DEVIATION = "SD: PRINT
360  PRINT "STANDARD ERROR = "SE: PRINT : PRINT "***************************************"
370  PRINT : PRINT : PRINT : PRINT : PRINT : PRINT : PRINT
380  IF V2 = 1 THEN  PRINT D$;"PR#0"
390  GOSUB 520
400  HOME : PRINT "WOULD YOU LIKE TO STORE THIS DATA": INPUT "DATA TO DISK (Y/N) ?";ANSWER$: IF ANSWER$ = "Y" THEN  GOSUB 610
410  HOME : VTAB 13: PRINT "WOULD YOU LIKE THE RAW DATA CONVERTED": INPUT "TO STANDARD (Z) SCORES (Y/N) ? ";ANSWER$: IF ANSWE
     R$ = "Y" THEN  GOSUB 660
420  HOME : INPUT "RUN ANOTHER ANALYSIS (Y/N) ? ";ANSWER$: IF ANSWER$ = "Y" THEN  GOTO 110
430  GOTO 500
440  HOME : PRINT "***DATA CORRECTION ROUTINE***": PRINT : PRINT : PRINT
450  INPUT "WHICH DATA POINT WAS INCORRECTLY ENTERED ? ";ZZ
460  PRINT : PRINT : PRINT "CURRENT DATA POINT IS "X(ZZ)
470  PRINT : PRINT : INPUT "ENTER CORRECT DATA POINT: ";X(ZZ): PRINT : PRINT
480  INPUT "ANY MORE CHANGES (Y/N) ? ";ANSWER$: IF ANSWER$ = "Y" THEN  GOTO 440
490  RETURN
500  HOME : PRINT "RETURNING TO MENU": PRINT D$;"RUN HELLO"
510  END
520  VTAB 23: INPUT "PRESS <RETURN> TO CONTINUE ";OK$: RETURN
530  REM    DATA RETRIEVAL
540 V1 = 1: VTAB 12: PRINT "PLACE DATA DISK IN DRIVE 1 AND PRESS": INPUT "<RETURN> TO CONTINUE ";OK$
550  VTAB 22: INPUT "ENTER FILE NAME (TYPE '?' FOR CATALOG)  ";ID$: IF ID$ = "?" THEN  GOSUB 790
560  PRINT D$;"OPEN ";ID$: PRINT D$;"READ ";ID$
570  FOR I = 1 TO N: INPUT X(I): NEXT I
580  PRINT D$;"CLOSE ";ID$: RETURN
590  REM    DATA DISPLAY
600  HOME : PRINT "DATA": PRINT : FOR I = 1 TO N: PRINT X(I): NEXT I: PRINT : INPUT "PRESS <RETURN> TO CONTINUE ";OK$: RETURN
```

PROGRAM 2 (Cont.)

```
610  REM    DATA STORAGE TO DISK
620  VTAB 12: PRINT "INSERT DATA DISK IN DRIVE 1 AND": INPUT "PRESS <RETURN> ";OK$: VTAB 24: INPUT "ENTER A FILE NAME: ";ID$
630  PRINT D$;"OPEN ";ID$: PRINT D$;"WRITE ";ID$
640  FOR I = 1 TO N: PRINT X(I): NEXT I
650  PRINT D$;"CLOSE ";ID$: RETURN
660  REM    Z-SCORE CONVERSION
670  FOR I = 1 TO N:Z(I) = (X(I) - MN) / S6: NEXT I
680  IF V2 = 1 THEN  PRINT D$;"PR#";PS%
690  HOME : PRINT : PRINT : PRINT "CONVERSION FROM RAW TO Z SCORES": PRINT : PRINT
700  PRINT "RAW SCORES","Z-SCORES"
710  PRINT "==========","========": PRINT
720  FOR I = 1 TO N: PRINT X(I),Z(I): NEXT I
730  IF V2 = 1 THEN  PRINT D$;"PR#0"
740  VTAB 23: INPUT "PRESS <RETURN> TO CONTINUE ";OK$
750  HOME : PRINT "WOULD YOU LIKE TO SAVE THE Z-SCORES": INPUT "TO DISK (Y/N) ? ";ANSWER$: IF ANSWER$ = "Y" THEN Z% = 1
760  IF Z% = 1 THEN  VTAB 12: PRINT "PLACE DATA DISK IN DRIVE 1 ": VTAB 23: INPUT "ENTER A FILE NAME: ";NAME$
770  IF Z% = 1 THEN  PRINT D$;"OPEN ";NAME$: PRINT D$;"WRITE ";NAME$: FOR I = 1 TO N: PRINT Z(I): NEXT I: PRINT D$;"CLOSE ";N
     AME$
780  RETURN
790  PRINT D$;"CATALOG": PRINT : INPUT "PRESS <RETURN> ";OK$: HOME : INPUT "ENTER FILE NAME: ";ID$: RETURN
```

PROGRAM 2
SAMPLE RUN

```
****DESCRIPTIVE STATISTICS SUMMARY****

VARIABLE NAME: M &SD


MEAN = 4

VARIANCE = 2.5

STANDARD DEVIATION = 1.58113883

STANDARD ERROR = .707106781

**************************************




CONVERSION FROM RAW TO Z SCORES


RAW SCORES          Z-SCORES
==========          ========

2                   -1.41421356
4                   0
3                   -.707106781
5                   .707106781
6                   1.41421356
```

Program 3: Correlation. Both Pearson's *r* and Spearman *rho* correlation coefficients can be calculated with this program. In addition, an option is provided for the regression equation in which predicted Y's are given for any X.

PROGRAM 3
CORRELATION (*r*, REGRESSION, SPEARMAN'S rho)

```
10  REM       CORRELATION PROGRAMS
20  REM             VERSION IC
30  REM       JOSEPH E. STEINMETZ
40  REM         OHIO UNIVERSITY
50  REM               MAY, 1983
60  REM
70  HOME
80  PRINT "THIS PROGRAM CALCULATES EITHER A": PRINT "PEARSON'S 'R' OR SPEARMAN'S RHO": PRINT "CORRELATION COEFFICIENT."
90  PRINT : PRINT : PRINT
100  PRINT "AVAILABLE OPTIONS:": PRINT : HTAB 5: PRINT "(1) DATA ENTRY CORRECTION ROUTINE": HTAB 5: PRINT "(2) INPUT DATA FRO
     M DISK": HTAB 5: PRINT "(3) SAVE DATA TO DISK": HTAB 5: PRINT "(4) GENERATE REGRESSION EQUATION"
105  HTAB 9: PRINT "USING PEARSON'S R"
110  GOSUB 780
120  HOME : CLEAR :D$ =  CHR$ (4):REPLY$ = "Y"
130  HOME : PRINT "WHICH CORRELATION COEFFICIENT DO YOU": PRINT "WANT TO CALCULATE ?"
140  PRINT : HTAB (5): PRINT "(1) PEARSON'S R": HTAB (5): PRINT "(2) SPEARMAN'S RHO"
150  PRINT : PRINT : INPUT "(ENTER A 1 OR 2) ";AA
160  HOME : INPUT "HOW MANY PAIRS OF SCORES ARE INVOLVED   IN THE CORRELATION ? ";N
170  DIM X(N): DIM Y(N): DIM D(N)
180  HOME
190  HOME : PRINT "WOULD YOU LIKE TO USE DATA THAT IS": INPUT "STORED ON A DISK (Y/N)? ";ANSWER$: IF ANSWER$ = REPLY$ THEN GOSUB
     790
200  IF V1 = 1 THEN  GOTO 320
210  HOME : PRINT "ENTER THE "N" PAIRS OF SCORES:": PRINT : PRINT "--------------------------": PRINT "SCORE X       SCORE
     Y": PRINT "-------          -------": FOR I = 1 TO N: INPUT " ";X(I):JS% =  PEEK (37):
```

PROGRAM 3 (Cont.)

```
220  HTAB 16: VTAB JS%: INPUT " ";Y(I): GOSUB 1Ø64: NEXT I
32Ø  HOME : PRINT "WOULD YOU LIKE THE DATA": INPUT "DISPLAYED (Y/N) ? ";ANSWER$: IF ANSWER$ = REPLY$ THEN  GOSUB 9ØØ
33Ø  HOME : INPUT "ANY CHANGES (Y/N) ? ";ANSWER$: IF ANSWER$ = "Y" THEN  GOSUB 97Ø: GOTO 32Ø
34Ø  IF AA = 1 GOTO 36Ø
35Ø  IF AA = 2 GOTO 59Ø
36Ø  FOR I = 1 TO N
37Ø XSUM = XSUM + X(I)
38Ø YSUM = YSUM + Y(I)
39Ø PSUM = PSUM + (X(I) * Y(I))
4ØØ SXSUM = SXSUM + (X(I) * X(I))
41Ø SYSUM = SYSUM + (Y(I) * Y(I))
42Ø  NEXT I
425 MX = XSUM / N:MY = YSUM / N
43Ø NUM = PSUM - ((XSUM * YSUM) / (N))
44Ø SSX = SXSUM - ((XSUM * XSUM) / N)
45Ø OSS = SYSUM - ((YSUM * YSUM) / N)
455 E1 =  SQR (SSX / (N - 1)):E2 =  SQR (OSS / (N - 1))
46Ø Q = SSX * OSS
47Ø DEN =  SQR (Q)
48Ø R = NUM / DEN
49Ø  GOSUB 93Ø
5ØØ  HOME
51Ø  IF QQ = 2 THEN  PRINT D$;"PR#";PS%
52Ø  PRINT "***PEARSON'S R COEFFICIENT***": PRINT : PRINT : PRINT
53Ø  PRINT "X = "LABEL$"  (MEAN = "MX")": PRINT : PRINT "Y = "LIBEL$"  (MEAN = "MY")"
54Ø  PRINT : PRINT : PRINT "R = "R: PRINT : PRINT : PRINT "******************************": PRINT D$;"PR#Ø": VTAB 24: GOSUB 78
     Ø
55Ø  PRINT D$;"PR#";PS%: PRINT : PRINT : PRINT : HOME : PRINT "DATA FOR VARIABLES X AND Y:": PRINT : FOR I = 1 TO N: PRINT X(
     I),Y(I): NEXT I
56Ø  PRINT : PRINT : PRINT
57Ø  PRINT D$;"PR#Ø"
58Ø  GOTO 73Ø
59Ø  FOR I = 1 TO N
```

PROGRAM 3 (Cont.)

```
600 D(I) = D(I) + (X(I) - Y(I))
610 SQD = SQD + (D(I) * D(I))
620  NEXT I
630 NUM = 6 * SQD
640 DEN = N * (N * N - 1)
650 TT = NUM / DEN
660 RHO = 1 - TT
670  GOSUB 930
680  HOME : IF QQ = 2 THEN  PRINT D$;"PR#";PS%
690  PRINT "***SPEARMAN'S RHO COEFFICIENT***": PRINT : PRINT : PRINT
700  PRINT "X = "LABEL$: PRINT : PRINT "Y = "LIBEL$
710  PRINT : PRINT : PRINT "RHO = "RHO: PRINT : PRINT : PRINT "*******************************": PRINT D$;"PR#0": VTAB 24:
     GOSUB 780
720  PRINT D$;"PR#";PS%: PRINT : PRINT : PRINT : HOME : PRINT "DATA FOR VARIABLES X AND Y:": PRINT : FOR I = 1 TO N: PRINT X(
     I),Y(I): NEXT I: PRINT : PRINT : PRINT : PRINT D$;"PR#0"
730  GOSUB 780: GOSUB 1070
740  HOME : INPUT "SAVE THIS DATA TO DISK (Y/N) ?";ANSWER$: IF ANSWER$ = REPLY$ THEN  GOSUB 850
750  HOME : INPUT "ANOTHER CORRELATION ANALYSIS (Y/N) ? ";ANSWER$: IF ANSWER$ = REPLY$ THEN  GOTO 120
760  HOME : PRINT "RETURNING TO MENU": PRINT D$;"RUN HELLO"
770  END
780  VTAB 23: INPUT "PRESS <RETURN> TO CONTINUE ";OK$: RETURN
790  REM   RETRIEVE DATA FROM DISK
800 V1 = 1: VTAB 12: PRINT "PLACE DATA DISK IN DRIVE 1 AND PRESS": INPUT "<RETURN> ";OK$: VTAB 22: INPUT "ENTER FILE NAME (TY
    PE '?' FOR CATALOG)  ";ID$: IF ID$ = "?" THEN  GOSUB 1060
810  PRINT D$;"OPEN ";ID$: PRINT D$;"READ ";ID$
820  FOR I = 1 TO N: INPUT X(I): NEXT I: FOR J = 1 TO N: INPUT Y(J): NEXT J
830  PRINT D$;"CLOSE ";ID$
840  RETURN
850  REM     DATA STORAGE ROUTINE
860  VTAB 15: PRINT "PLACE A DISK IN DRIVE 1 AND PRESS": INPUT "<RETURN> ";OK$: VTAB 23: INPUT "FILE NAME: ";ID$
870  PRINT D$;"OPEN ";ID$: PRINT D$;"WRITE ";ID$
880  FOR I = 1 TO N: PRINT X(I): NEXT I: FOR J = 1 TO N: PRINT Y(J): NEXT J
890  PRINT D$;"CLOSE ";ID$: RETURN
```

PROGRAM 3 (Cont.)

```
900  REM    DATA DISPLAY ROUTINE
910  HOME : PRINT "DATA FOR VARIABLE X AND Y: ": PRINT E$: PRINT : PRINT : FOR I = 1 TO N: PRINT X(I),Y(I): NEXT I: PRINT :
     PRINT : INPUT "PRESS <RETURN> TO CONTINUE ";OK$
920  RETURN
930  HOME : PRINT "THE CALCULATIONS HAVE BEEN COMPLETED. ": PRINT "HOW SHOULD THE RESULTS BE REPORTED ?": PRINT : PRINT : HTAB
     5: PRINT "(1) VIDEO DISPLAY ONLY": HTAB 5: PRINT "(2) PRINTER AND VIDEO"
940  PRINT : INPUT "(ENTER A 1 OR 2): ";QQ: PRINT : PRINT : INPUT "VARIABLE X LABEL: ";LABEL$: PRINT : INPUT "VARIABLE Y LABE
     L: ";LIBEL$
950  IF QQ = 2 THEN  PRINT : PRINT : INPUT "ENTER PRINTER SLOT#  ";PS%
960  RETURN
970  REM    DATA CORRECTION ROUTINE                      FOR DISK DATA
980  HOME : HTAB 9: PRINT "DATA CORRECTION ROUTINE": PRINT : PRINT
990  PRINT "WHICH VARIABLE (X OR Y) HAS THE ": INPUT "INCORRECT DATA POINT ? ";CR$
1000  PRINT : PRINT : IF CR$ = "X" THEN  PRINT "WHICH OBSERVATION WITHIN VARIABLE 'X'": INPUT "IS ENTERED INCORRECTLY ? ";ZZ:
      PRINT : PRINT "THE CURRENT DATA POINT IS "X(ZZ): GOTO 1020
1010  PRINT : PRINT : IF CR$ = "Y" THEN  PRINT "WHICH OBSERVATION WITHIN VARIABLE 'Y'": INPUT "IS ENTERED INCORRECTLY ? ";ZZ:
      PRINT : PRINT : PRINT "THE CURRENT DATA POINT IS "Y(ZZ): GOTO 1030
1020  PRINT : PRINT : INPUT "ENTER THE CORRECT DATA POINT ";X(ZZ): GOTO 1040
1030  PRINT : PRINT : INPUT "ENTER THE CORRECT DATA POINT ";Y(ZZ)
1040  VTAB 24: INPUT "ANY MORE CHANGES (Y/N) ?";ANSWER$: IF ANSWER$ = "Y" THEN  GOTO 970
1050  RETURN
1060  PRINT D$;"CATALOG": PRINT : INPUT "PRESS <RETURN> ";OK$: HOME : INPUT "ENTER FILE NAME: ";ID$: RETURN
1064  IF JS% = 23 THEN  CALL  - 912: VTAB 23
1066  RETURN
1070  REM      REGRESSION EQUATION
1080  HOME : IF AA = 1 THEN  PRINT "WOULD YOU LIKE TO USE THE REGRESSION": INPUT "EQUATION FOR PREDICTING Y FROM X (Y/N)? ";A
     N$: IF AN$ = "Y" THEN  GOTO 1100
1090  RETURN
1100  PRINT : PRINT : PRINT "THE GENERAL FORM OF THE EQUATION IS: ": PRINT " Y' = YMEAN + R*(SY/SX)*(X-MEANX)": GOSUB 780
1110 I1 = R * (E2 / E1):E3 = E2 * ( SQR (1 - (R * R)))
1115  IF QQ = 2 THEN  PRINT D$;"PR#";PS%
1120  HOME : PRINT : PRINT "****************************************": PRINT : PRINT " YOUR REGRESSION EQUATION IS:": PRINT :
      PRINT "   Y' = "MY" + ("I1")(X - "MX")"
```

PROGRAM 3 (Cont.)

```
1122  PRINT : PRINT "SX = "E1" AND SY = "E2: PRINT : PRINT "STANDARD ERR OF PREDICTION = "E3: PRINT : PRINT "****************
     ***********************": PRINT : IF QQ = 2 THEN  PRINT D$;"PR#Ø"
1125  GOSUB 78Ø
113Ø  HOME : PRINT "ENTER YOUR PREDICTOR VALUES (TERMINATE": PRINT "PROCESSING BY ENTERING A -999)": PRINT "----------------
     ----------------------"
1135  POKE 34,4
114Ø Y = Ø: PRINT : PRINT : INPUT "ENTER VALUE OF X: ";X: IF X =  - 999 GOTO 117Ø
115Ø Y = MY + I1 * (X - MX): IF QQ = 2 THEN  PRINT D$;"PR#";PS%
116Ø  PRINT : PRINT "    WHEN X = "X", Y' = "Y: IF QQ = 2 THEN  PRINT D$;"PR#Ø"
1165  GOTO 114Ø
117Ø  TEXT : NORMAL : RETURN
```

PROGRAM 3
SAMPLE RUN

```
* **PEARSON'S R COEFFICIENT***


X = BODY WEIGHT   (MEAN = 98)

Y = STRENGTH   (MEAN = 167)


R = .681300908


****************        ********


DATA FOR VARIABLES X AND Y:

112             215
98              210
104             190
105             180
110             170
92              175
86              150
91              130
86              125
96              125


*************************        ********

 YOUR REGRESSION EQUATION IS:

   Y' = 167 + (2.41895262)(X - 98)

SX = 9.43986818 AND SY = 33.5161653

STANDARD ERR OF PREDICTION = 24.5339491

*******************************        **


      WHEN X = 100, Y' = 171.837905

      WHEN X = 110, Y' = 196.027431

      WHEN X = 91, Y' = 150.067332
```

Program 4: *t* Tests. Routines for t *tests for independent or correlated (dependent) groups are available. Unequal group sizes can be used in the independent t* analysis but group sizes must be equal when performing the correlated *t* calculation.

PROGRAM 4
t TESTS (DEPENDENT AND INDEPENDENT)

```
10  REM       T-TEST PROGRAMS
20  REM           VERSION IB
30  REM       JOSEPH E. STEINMETZ
40  REM         OHIO UNIVERSITY
50  REM           MARCH, 1982
60  HOME
70  PRINT "THIS PROGRAM CALCULATES THE T-STATISTIC": PRINT "(INDEPENDENT OR CORRELATED).": PRINT : PRINT : PRINT
80  PRINT "AVAILABLE OPTIONS:": PRINT : HTAB 5: PRINT "(1) DATA ENTRY CORRECTION ROUTINE": HTAB 5: PRINT "(2) INPUT DATA FROM
      DISK": HTAB 5: PRINT "(3) SAVE DATA TO DISK"
90  GOSUB 1280
100  CLEAR : HOME :D$ =  CHR$ (4)
110  PRINT "WHICH TYPE OF T-TEST DO YOU WANT": PRINT : HTAB 10: PRINT "(1) INDEPENDENT": HTAB 10: PRINT "(2) CORRELATED": PRINT
     : PRINT
120  INPUT "(ENTER A 1 OR 2) ";QB
130  HOME : INPUT "HOW MANY DATA POINTS IN GROUP 1 ? ";N1
140  PRINT : PRINT
150  INPUT "HOW MANY DATA POINTS IN GROUP 2 ? ";N2
160  DIM X(N1): DIM Y(N2): DIM SX(N1): DIM SY(N2): DIM D(N1)
170  HOME : PRINT "WOULD YOU LIKE TO USE DATA THAT IS": INPUT "STORED ON A DISK (Y/N) ? ";ANSWER$: IF ANSWER$ = "Y" THEN GOSUB
     1290: GOSUB 1050: GOSUB 1090
180  IF V1 = 1 THEN  GOTO 290
190  HOME : PRINT "ENTER SCORES FOR GROUP 1": PRINT
200  FOR I = 1 TO N1
210  INPUT X(I)
```

PROGRAM 4 (Cont.)

```
220  NEXT I
230  HOME
240  HOME : PRINT "ENTER SCORES FOR GROUP 2": PRINT
250  FOR J = 1 TO N2
260  INPUT Y(J)
270  NEXT J
280  HOME : GOSUB 1050: GOSUB 1090
290  IF QB = 2 GOTO 690
300  FOR I = 1 TO N1:XTT = XTT + X(I):SX(I) = X(I) * X(I)
310 XSRTT = XSRTT + SX(I): NEXT I
320  FOR J = 1 TO N2
330 YTT = YTT + Y(J)
340 SY(J) = Y(J) * Y(J)
350 YSRTT = YSRTT + SY(J)
360  NEXT J
370 MX = XTT / N1
380 MY = YTT / N2
390 A = XTT * XTT
400 B = YTT * YTT
410 SA = XSRTT - (A / N1):S1 =  SQR (SA / (N1 - 1)): FOR I = 1 TO N1:S3 = X(I) - MX:S5 = S5 + S3 * S3:S3 = 0: NEXT I:S3 =  SQR
     (S5 / (N1 * (N1 - 1)))
420 SB = YSRTT - (B / N2):S2 =  SQR (SB / (N2 - 1)): FOR I = 1 TO N2:S4 = Y(I) - MY:S6 = S6 + S4 * S4:S4 = 0: NEXT I:S4 =  SQR
     (S6 / (N2 * (N2 - 1)))
430 DRF = MX - MY
440 SSTT = SA + SB
450 DF = N1 + N2 - 2
460 DEN = (1 / N1) + (1 / N2)
470 C = SSTT / DF
480 TDEN = C * DEN
490 D =  SQR (TDEN)
500  IF D = 0 THEN 1260
510 T = DRF / D
520  GOSUB 1390
```

PROGRAM 4 (Cont.)

```
530  HOME : IF QQ = 2 THEN  PRINT D$;"PR#";PS%
540  PRINT "*********************************": PRINT : PRINT : HTAB (4): PRINT "SUMMARY FOR INDEPENDENT-T": PRINT : PRINT :
     PRINT "X = "LABEL$: PRINT "Y = "LIBEL$: PRINT : PRINT
550  PRINT "MEAN 1 = "MX"  S.D.= "S1"  S.E.M.= "S3
560  PRINT
570  PRINT "MEAN 2 = "MY"  S.D.= "S2"  S.E.M.= "S4
580  PRINT
590  PRINT "THE VALUE OF THE T-STATISTIC IS"
600  PRINT : PRINT
610  HTAB 15: PRINT T: PRINT : PRINT "DF = "DF
620  PRINT : PRINT : PRINT "*********************************"
630  PRINT D$;"PR#0": GOSUB 1280
640  IF QQ = 2 THEN  HOME : INPUT "WOULD YOU LIKE THE DATA PRINTED (Y/N)? ";ANSWER$: IF ANSWER$ = "Y" THEN  GOSUB 1110
650  HOME : INPUT "SAVE THIS DATA TO DISK (Y/N) ? ";ANSWER$: IF ANSWER$ = "Y" THEN  GOSUB 1340
660  HOME : INPUT "ANOTHER ANALYSIS (Y/N) ?";ANSWER$: IF ANSWER$ = "Y" THEN 100
670  HOME : PRINT "RETURNING TO MENU": PRINT D$;"RUN HELLO"
680  END
690  FOR I = 1 TO N1:XTT = XTT + X(I):YTT = YTT + Y(I):D(I) = X(I) - Y(I): NEXT I
700  FOR I = 1 TO N1:XSRTT = XSRTT + X(I) * X(I):YSRTT = YSRTT + Y(I) * Y(I)
710  NEXT I
720 SA = XSRTT - ((XTT * XTT) / N1):SB = YSRTT - ((YTT * YTT) / N1):S1 =  SQR (SA / (N1 - 1)):S2 =  SQR (SB / (N1 - 1))
730  FOR I = 1 TO N1
740 DD = DD + D(I)
750 EE = EE + D(I) * D(I)
760  NEXT I
770 MX = XTT / N1:MY = YTT / N2: FOR I = 1 TO N1:S3 = X(I) - MX:S4 = Y(I) - MY:S5 = S5 + S3 * S3:S6 = S6 + S4 * S4:S3 = 0:S4 =
     0: NEXT I:S3 =  SQR (S5 / (N1 * (N1 - 1))):S4 =  SQR (S6 / (N1 * (N1 - 1)))
780 JOE = EE - ((DD * DD) / N1)
790 NI = (JOE / (N1 * (N1 - 1)))
800 NI =  SQR (NI)
810  IF NI = 0 THEN 1260
820 ZB = (DD / N1) / NI
830  GOSUB 1390
```

PROGRAM 4 (Cont.)

```
840  HOME : IF QQ = 2 THEN  PRINT D$;"PR#";PS%
850  PRINT "***************************************"
860  PRINT : PRINT : HTAB (10): PRINT "SUMMARY FOR CORRELATED T": PRINT : PRINT : PRINT "X = "LABEL$: PRINT "Y = "LIBEL$: PRINT
     : PRINT
870  PRINT "MEAN 1 = "MX"  S.D.= "S1"  S.E.M.= "S3
880  PRINT "MEAN 2 = "MY"  S.D.= "S2"  S.E.M.= "S4
890  PRINT : PRINT : PRINT "THE VALUE OF THE T-STATISTIC IS ": PRINT : PRINT
900  HTAB (15): PRINT ZB: PRINT : PRINT "DF = "N1 - 1
910  PRINT : PRINT : PRINT "***************************************"
920  PRINT D$;"PR#0": GOSUB 1280
930  IF QQ = 2 THEN  HOME : INPUT "WOULD YOU LIKE THE DATA PRINTED (Y/N) ?";ANSWER$: IF ANSWER$ = "Y" THEN  GOSUB 1110
940  HOME : INPUT "SAVE THIS DATA TO DISK (Y/N) ? ";ANSWER$: IF ANSWER$ = "Y" THEN  GOSUB 1340
950  HOME : INPUT "ANOTHER ANALYSIS ? ";ANSWER$: IF ANSWER$ = "Y" THEN 100
960  HOME : PRINT "RETURNING TO MENU": PRINT D$;"RUN HELLO"
970  END
980  HOME : PRINT " *** DATA CORRECTION ROUTINE ***": PRINT : PRINT "IN WHICH GROUP (X OR Y) IS THE DATA": INPUT "POINT ENTER
     ED INCORRECTLY? ";CR$
990  PRINT : PRINT : IF CR$ = "X" THEN  PRINT "WHICH DATA POINT ("1" TO "N1") WAS": INPUT "ENTERED INCORRECTLY ? ";ZZ: PRINT
     : PRINT "THE CURRENT DATA POINT IS "X(ZZ): GOTO 1010
1000  PRINT : PRINT : IF CR$ = "Y" THEN  PRINT "WHICH OBSERVATION ("1" TO "N2") WAS": INPUT "ENTERED INCORRECTLY ? ";ZZ: PRINT
     : PRINT "THE CURRENT DATA POINT IS "Y(ZZ): GOTO 1020
1010  PRINT : PRINT : INPUT "ENTER THE CORRECT DATA POINT ";X(ZZ): GOTO 1030
1020  PRINT : PRINT : INPUT "ENTER THE CORRECT DATA POINT ";Y(ZZ)
1030  VTAB 24: INPUT "ANY MORE CHANGES (Y/N) ? ";ANSWER$: IF ANSWER$ = "Y" THEN  GOTO 980
1040  RETURN
1050  REM  DATA DISPLAY ROUTINE
1060  HOME : PRINT "DATA FOR VARIABLE X:": PRINT : FOR I = 1 TO N1: PRINT X(I): NEXT I: PRINT : INPUT "PRESS <RETURN> TO CONT
     INUE ";OK$
1070  HOME : PRINT "DATA FOR VARIABLE Y: ": PRINT : FOR I = 1 TO N2: PRINT Y(I): NEXT I: PRINT : INPUT "PRESS <RETURN> TO CON
     TINUE ";OK$
1080  RETURN
1090  HOME : INPUT "ANY CHANGES (Y/N) ?";ANSWER$: IF ANSWER$ = "Y" THEN  GOSUB 980
1100  RETURN
```

PROGRAM 4 (Cont.)

```
1110  IF QQ = 2 THEN  PRINT D$;"PR#";PS%
1120  PRINT "RAW DATA USED IN THIS T-TEST": PRINT : PRINT
1130  PRINT "DATA FROM GROUP X"
1140  PRINT "================="
1150  FOR I = 1 TO N1
1160  PRINT X(I)
1170  NEXT I
1180  PRINT "DATA FROM GROUP Y"
1190  PRINT "================="
1200  FOR J = 1 TO N2
1210  PRINT Y(J)
1220  NEXT J: PRINT : PRINT : PRINT
1230  PRINT D$;"PR#Ø"
1240  HOME
1250  RETURN
1260 BELL$ =  CHR$ (7): FOR I = 1 TO 5: PRINT BELL$: NEXT I: HOME : PRINT "YOUR STANDARD ERROR TERM IS EQUAL": PRINT "TO Ø, A
     N ANALYSIS IS IMPOSSIBLE!!!"
1270  VTAB 24: GOSUB 128Ø: GOTO 95Ø
1280  VTAB 23: INPUT "PRESS <RETURN> TO CONTINUE ";OK$: RETURN
1290  REM  DATA RETRIEVAL ROUTINE
1300 V1 = 1: VTAB 12: PRINT "PLACE DATA DISK IN DRIVE 1 AND PRESS": INPUT "<RETURN>. ";OK$: VTAB 22: INPUT "ENTER FILE NAME (
     TYPE '?' FOR CATALOG)  ";ID$: IF ID$ = "?" THEN  GOSUB 143Ø
1310  PRINT D$;"OPEN ";ID$: PRINT D$;"READ ";ID$
1320  FOR I = 1 TO N1: INPUT X(I): NEXT I: FOR J = 1 TO N2: INPUT Y(J): NEXT J
1330  PRINT D$;"CLOSE ";ID$: RETURN
1340  REM    DATA STORAGE TO DISK
1350  VTAB 12: PRINT "PLACE DATA DISK IN DRIVE 1 AND PRESS": INPUT "<RETURN> ";OK$
1360  VTAB 24: INPUT "ENTER A FILE NAME: ";ID$: PRINT D$;"OPEN ";ID$: PRINT D$;"WRITE ";ID$
1370  FOR I = 1 TO N1: PRINT X(I): NEXT I: FOR J = 1 TO N2: PRINT Y(J): NEXT J
1380  PRINT D$;"CLOSE ";ID$: RETURN
1390  HOME : PRINT "THE CALCULATIONS HAVE BEEN COMPLETED. ": PRINT "HOW SHOULD THE RESULTS BE REPORTED ?": PRINT : PRINT : HTAB
     5: PRINT "(1) VIDEO DISPLAY": HTAB 5: PRINT "(2) PRINTER AND VIDEO"
```

PROGRAM 4 (Cont.)

```
1400  PRINT : INPUT "(ENTER A 1 OR 2) ";QQ: PRINT : PRINT : INPUT "VARIABLE X LABEL: ";LABEL$: PRINT : INPUT "VARIABLE Y LABE
    L: ";LIBEL$
1410  IF QQ = 2 THEN  PRINT : PRINT : INPUT "ENTER PRINTER SLOT# ";PS%
1420  RETURN
1430  PRINT D$;"CATALOG": PRINT : INPUT "PRESS <RETURN> ";OK$: HOME : INPUT "ENTER FILE NAME: ";ID$: RETURN
```

PROGRAM 4
SAMPLE RUN

```
*************************************

         SUMMARY FOR CORRELATED T

X = PRE
Y = POST

MEAN 1 = 16.5  S.D.= 3.02765036  S.E.M.= .957427108
MEAN 2 = 19.7  S.D.= 3.12872002  S.E.M.= .989388139

THE VALUE OF THE T-STATISTIC IS

             -4.82418151

DF = 9

*************************************


*******************************

   SUMMARY FOR INDEPENDENT-T

X = GROUP1
Y = GROUP2

MEAN 1 = 3  S.D.= 1.58113883  S.E.M.= .707106781

MEAN 2 = 8  S.D.= 1.58113883  S.E.M.= .707106781

THE VALUE OF THE T-STATISTIC IS

             -5

DF = 8
```

PROGRAM 4 SAMPLE RUN (Cont.)

```
*********************************
RAW DATA USED IN THIS T-TEST


DATA FROM GROUP X
=================
1
2
3
4
5
DATA FROM GROUP Y
=================
6
7
8
9
10
```

Program 5: One-way ANOVA. This is a completely randomized design for two or more groups of subjects. Only one score per subject may be used. Although not necessary, an equal number of subjects per group is desirable.

PROGRAM 5
ONE-WAY (SIMPLE) ANOVA

```
1  REM        ONEWAY ANOVA
2  REM          VERSION IB
3  REM      JOSEPH E. STEINMETZ
4  REM        OHIO UNIVERSITY
5  REM          JAN., 1982
6  REM
7  REM
8  REM
10  HOME
20  PRINT "  *** ONE-WAY ANALYSIS OF VARIANCE ***"
30  PRINT : PRINT : PRINT "THIS PROGRAM EXECUTES A ONE-WAY ANOVA"
40  PRINT "(NON-REPEATED MEASURES)."
50  PRINT : PRINT : PRINT "AVAILABLE OPTIONS: ": PRINT : HTAB 5: PRINT "(1) AN INPUT CORRECTION ROUTINE": HTAB 5: PRINT "(2)
    INPUT DATA FROM DISK": HTAB 5: PRINT "(3) SAVE DATA TO DISK"
60  VTAB (24): INPUT "PRESS <RETURN> TO CONTINUE ";OK$
70  CLEAR : HOME :D$ =  CHR$ (4):M$ = "Y"
80  PRINT : PRINT
90 C$ = "======================================================================"
100 E$ = "----------------------------------------"
110  INPUT "ENTER TOTAL NUMBER OF OBSERVATIONS:  ";N
120  PRINT : PRINT E$
130  INPUT "ENTER TOTAL NUMBER OF GROUPS:  ";G
140  DIM X(G,N): DIM Y(G,N): DIM GSUM(G): DIM MEAN(G): DIM ZQ(G)
150  PRINT : PRINT E$: PRINT "ARE THE "G" GROUPS EQUAL IN SIZE (Y/N) ": INPUT ANSWER$: IF ANSWER$ = M$ THEN  GOTO 200
160  PRINT : PRINT E$: PRINT "YOUR DESIGN HAS "N" SUBJECTS UNEQUALLY": PRINT "DIVIDED AMONG "G" GROUPS."
```

PROGRAM 5 (Cont.)

```
170  VTAB 24: INPUT "PRESS <RETURN> TO CONTINUE ";OK$
180  FOR I = 1 TO G: HOME : PRINT "ENTER NUMBER OF OBSERVATIONS IN": PRINT "GROUP "I: PRINT : PRINT : INPUT ZQ(I): NEXT I
190  GOTO 230
200 N1 = N / G
210  FOR I = 1 TO G:ZQ(I) = N1: NEXT I: PRINT : PRINT E$: PRINT "THIS ANALYSIS HAS "N" TOTAL OBSERVATIONS": PRINT "EQUALLY DI
     STRIBUTED AMONG "G" GROUPS."
220  VTAB 24: INPUT "PRESS <RETURN> TO CONTINUE ";OK$
230  HOME : PRINT "WOULD YOU LIKE TO USE DATA THAT IS": INPUT "STORED ON A DISK (Y/N) ? ";ANSWER$: IF ANSWER$ = M$ THEN  GOSUB
     1020
240  IF H1 = 1 THEN  GOTO 300
250  FOR I = 1 TO G: HOME
260  PRINT "ENTER SCORES FOR GROUP "I: PRINT
270  FOR J = 1 TO ZQ(I)
280  INPUT X(I,J)
290  NEXT J: NEXT I
300  HOME : PRINT "WOULD YOU LIKE THE DATA": INPUT "DISPLAYED (Y/N) ? ";ANSWER$: IF ANSWER$ = M$ THEN  GOSUB 1130
310  HOME : INPUT "ARE THERE ANY CHANGES (Y/N) ? ";ANSWER$: IF ANSWER$ = M$ THEN  GOSUB 850: GOTO 300
320  HOME : PRINT "PROCESSING......."
330  FOR I = 1 TO G: FOR J = 1 TO ZQ(I)
340 Y(I,J) = X(I,J) * X(I,J)
350 YSUM = YSUM + Y(I,J)
360 GSUM(I) = GSUM(I) + X(I,J)
370  NEXT J
380  NEXT I
390  FOR I = 1 TO G:MEAN(I) = GSUM(I) / ZQ(I): NEXT I
400  FOR I = 1 TO G
410 GDTL = GDTL + GSUM(I)
420  NEXT I
430 CT = (GDTL * GDTL) / N
440 TSS = YSUM - CT
450  FOR I = 1 TO G
460 Z = Z + (GSUM(I) * GSUM(I)) / ZQ(I)
470  NEXT I
```

PROGRAM 5 (Cont.)

```
480 BSS = Z - CT
490 WSS = TSS - BSS
500 TDF = N - 1
510 BDF = G - 1
520 WDF = TDF - BDF
530 TMS = TSS / TDF
540 BMS = BSS / BDF
550 WMS = WSS / WDF
560 F = BMS / WMS
570  HOME : PRINT "THE CALCULATIONS HAVE BEEN COMPLETED.": PRINT : PRINT : PRINT
580  PRINT "HOW WOULD YOU LIKE YOUR RESULTS": PRINT "REPORTED ? ": PRINT
590  HTAB (5): PRINT "  (1) VIDEO DISPLAY"
600  HTAB (5): PRINT "  (2) PRINTER"
610  PRINT : INPUT "(ENTER A 1 OR 2): ";FLAG
620  PRINT : IF FLAG = 2 THEN  INPUT "PRINTER SLOT ? ";PS%
630  PRINT : PRINT : IF FLAG = 2 THEN  PRINT "ENTER A LABEL FOR THE TREATMENT": INPUT "VARIABLE:  ";G$
640  IF FLAG = 2 THEN  GOSUB 1000
650  HOME : PRINT "SUMMARY TABLE FOR ONE-WAY ANOVA"
660  PRINT C$
664  IF FLAG = 2 THEN  PRINT "TREATMENT VARIABLE = "G$: PRINT C$
668  GOSUB 1250
670  PRINT : PRINT "BETWEEN:    SS= "BSS"  DF= "BDF"    MS= "BMS"    F= "F" "T$
680  PRINT : PRINT "WITHIN:     SS= "WSS"  DF= "WDF"    MS="WMS
690  PRINT C$
700  PRINT "TOTAL:      SS= "TSS"  DF= "TDF
710  PRINT C$: PRINT "** P<.01      * P<.05": PRINT : PRINT : PRINT : PRINT
720  GOSUB 1010
730  VTAB (24): INPUT "PRESS <RETURN> TO CONTINUE ";OK$
740  IF FLAG = 2 THEN  GOSUB 1000
750  HOME : PRINT E$: PRINT "*** SUMMARY OF GROUP MEANS ***": PRINT : PRINT : FOR I = 1 TO G: PRINT "GROUP "I" MEAN = "MEAN(I
     ): NEXT I
760  PRINT : PRINT : PRINT E$: GOSUB 1010
770 M$ = "Y"
```

PROGRAM 5 (Cont.)

```
78Ø  VTAB (24): INPUT "WOULD YOU LIKE THE DATA PRINTED (Y/N)?";ANSWER$
79Ø  IF ANSWER$ = M$ THEN  GOSUB 91Ø
8ØØ  HOME : INPUT "SAVE THIS DATA TO DISK (Y/N) ? ";ANSWER$: IF ANSWER$ = M$ THEN  GOSUB 1Ø8Ø
81Ø  HOME : INPUT "RUN ANOTHER ONE WAY ANOVA (Y/N) ?";ANSWER$
82Ø  IF ANSWER$ = M$ THEN 7Ø
83Ø  HOME : PRINT "RETURNING TO MENU": PRINT D$;"RUN HELLO"
84Ø  END
85Ø  HOME : PRINT " *** DATA CORRECTION ROUTINE ***": PRINT : PRINT : INPUT "IN WHICH GROUP WAS THE MISTAKE MADE? ";VV
86Ø  PRINT : PRINT : PRINT : INPUT "WHICH SUBJECT WAS ENTERED INCORRECTLY?";VW
87Ø  PRINT : PRINT : PRINT "PRESENT DATA POINT = "X(VV,VW)
88Ø  PRINT : PRINT : INPUT "ENTER CORRECT DATA POINT: ";X(VV,VW)
89Ø  VTAB (24): INPUT "ANY MORE CHANGES (Y/N) ?";ANSWER$: IF ANSWER$ = M$ THEN 85Ø
9ØØ  RETURN
91Ø  IF FLAG = 2 THEN  GOSUB 1ØØØ: PRINT "RAW DATA USED IN THIS ONE-WAY ANOVA.": PRINT : PRINT
92Ø  FOR I = 1 TO G
93Ø  PRINT "DATA FROM GROUP "I
94Ø  FOR J = 1 TO ZQ(I)
95Ø  PRINT X(I,J)
96Ø  NEXT J: NEXT I
97Ø  PRINT : PRINT : PRINT
98Ø  GOSUB 1Ø1Ø
99Ø  RETURN
1ØØØ  PRINT D$;"PR#";PS%: RETURN
1Ø1Ø  PRINT D$;"PR#Ø": RETURN
1Ø2Ø  REM    INPUT FROM DISK
1Ø3Ø H1 = 1: VTAB 12: PRINT "PLACE DATA DISK IN DRIVE 1 AND": INPUT "PRESS <RETURN> ";OK$
1Ø4Ø  VTAB 23: INPUT "FILE NAME ? ";ID$
1Ø5Ø  PRINT D$;"OPEN ";ID$: PRINT D$;"READ ";ID$
1Ø6Ø  FOR I = 1 TO G: FOR J = 1 TO ZQ(I): INPUT X(I,J): NEXT J: NEXT I
1Ø7Ø  PRINT D$;"CLOSE ";ID$: RETURN
1Ø8Ø  REM        SAVE DATA TO DISK
1Ø9Ø  HOME : INPUT "ENTER A FILE NAME: ";ID$
11ØØ  PRINT D$;"OPEN ";ID$: PRINT D$;"WRITE ";ID$
```

PROGRAM 5 (Cont.)

```
1110  FOR I = 1 TO G: FOR J = 1 TO ZQ(I): PRINT X(I,J): NEXT J: NEXT I
1120  PRINT D$;"CLOSE ";ID$: RETURN
1130  REM       DATA DISPLAY
1140  HOME : FOR I = 1 TO G: HOME : PRINT "DATA FROM GROUP "I: PRINT : FOR J = 1 TO ZQ(I): PRINT X(I,J): NEXT J: PRINT : PRINT
    : INPUT "PRESS <RETURN> TO CONTINUE ";OK$: NEXT I: RETURN
1250  REM     F-DISTRIBUTION
1260 Y2 = 1: IF F < 1 THEN 1280
1270 Y3 = BDF:Y4 = WDF:Y5 = F: GOTO 1290
1280 Y3 = WDF:Y4 = BDF:Y5 = 1 / F
1290 Y6 = 2 / 9 / Y3:Y7 = 2 / 9 / Y4
1300 Y8 =  ABS ((1 - Y7) * Y5 ^ (1 / 3) - 1 + Y6) /  SQR (Y7 * Y5 ^ (2 / 3) + Y6)
1310  IF Y4 > 4 THEN 1340
1320 Y2 = .5 / (1 + Y8 * (.196854 + Y8 * (.115194 + Y8 * (.000344 + Y6 * .019527)))) ^ 4
1330 Y2 =  INT (Y2 * 10000 + .5) / 10000: GOTO 1350
1340 Y8 = Y8 * (1 + .08 * Y8 ^ 4 / Y4 ^ 3): GOTO 1320
1350  IF F >  = 1 THEN 1370
1360 Y2 = 1 - Y2
1370 Y9 = 1 - Y2
1380  IF Y9 < .9241 THEN T$ = " "
1390  IF Y9 >  = .9341 THEN T$ = "*"
1400  IF Y9 >  = .9733 THEN T$ = "**"
1410  RETURN
```

PROGRAM 5
SAMPLE RUN

```
SUMMARY TABLE FOR ONE-WAY ANOVA
==========================================================================
TREATMENT VARIABLE = TEACHING METHOD
==========================================================================

BETWEEN:     SS= 90   DF= 2    MS= 45    F= 10 **

WITHIN:      SS= 54   DF= 12    MS=4.5
==========================================================================
TOTAL:       SS= 144   DF= 14
==========================================================================
** P<.01       * P<.05



---------------------------------------
*** SUMMARY OF GROUP MEANS ***


GROUP 1 MEAN = 10
GROUP 2 MEAN = 7
GROUP 3 MEAN = 4


---------------------------------------
RAW DATA USED IN THIS ONE-WAY ANOVA.


DATA FROM GROUP 1
12
10
11
7
10
DATA FROM GROUP 2
9
7
6
9
4
DATA FROM GROUP 3
6
7
2
3
2
```

Program 6: Omega Squared. This program calculates w^2 for a one-way ANOVA. You must provide the sum of squares (SS) for Total, sum of squares (SS) for treatment (Between), degrees of freedom (*df*) for treatment, and the mean square (MS) for error (Within). This program does not have an option to print, so you must turn your printer on prior to running the program.

PROGRAM 6
OMEGA SQUARED (FOR ONE-WAY ANOVA)

```
10  HOME
23  HOME : PRINT A$
25  PRINT  TAB( 13)"OMEGA SQUARED"
30  PRINT A$
35  PRINT : PRINT
100  INPUT "ENTER SS(TOTAL) ";ST
120  INPUT "ENTER SS (TREAT.) ";SR
125  INPUT "ENTER DF(TREAT.) ";DF
130  INPUT "ENTER MS(ERROR) ";MS
140  REM  CAL.
150 W2 = (SR - (DF * MS)) / (ST + MS):W2 = W2 * 100
155  CALL  - 936
160  PRINT : PRINT
170  PRINT "VARIANCE ACCOUNTED FOR = ";W2;"%"
180  PRINT : INPUT "RUN ANOTHER W2 (Y/N)? ";Y$
190  IF Y$ = "Y" THEN 23
195  PRINT : PRINT
200  PRINT "***PROCESSING COMPLETE***"
```

PROGRAM 6
SAMPLE RUN

```
]RUN W2

             OMEGA SQUARED


ENTER SS(TOTAL) 144
ENTER SS (TREAT.) 90
ENTER DF(TREAT.) 2
ENTER MS(ERROR) 4.5


VARIANCE ACCOUNTED FOR = 54.5454546%

RUN ANOTHER W2 (Y/N)? N


***PROCESSING COMPLETE***
```

Program 7: Two-way ANOVA. This is a factorial design involving two factors. There can be only one score for each subject in each group. It is best to have an equal number of subjects in each of the groups. If unequal cell sizes are present, an unweighted means analysis is performed.

PROGRAM 7
TWO-WAY (FACTORIAL) ANOVA

```
10  REM      TWOWAY ANOVA
20  REM        VERSION IB
30  REM   JOSEPH E. STEINMETZ
40  REM     OHIO UNIVERSITY
50  REM          JAN., 1982
60  REM
70  REM
80  HOME : PRINT " *** TWO-WAY ANALYSIS OF VARIANCE ***"
90  PRINT : PRINT : PRINT "THIS PROGRAM EXECUTES A TWO-WAY ANOVA": PRINT "(NO REPEATED MEASURES)."
100  PRINT : PRINT : PRINT "AVAILABLE OPTIONS:": PRINT : HTAB 5: PRINT "(1) INPUT CORRECTION ROUTINE": HTAB 5: PRINT "(2) UNW
     EIGHTED MEANS ANALYSIS": HTAB 5: PRINT "(3) INPUT  DATA  FROM DISK": HTAB 5: PRINT "(4) OUTPUT DATA TO DISK"
110  VTAB (24): INPUT "PRESS <RETURN> TO CONTINUE ";OK$
120  CLEAR : HOME :D$ =  CHR$ (4):REPLY$ = "Y":H$ =  CHR$ (12):B$ =  CHR$ (4)
130  PRINT : PRINT
140 C$ = "================================================================================"
150 E$ = "-----------------------------------"
160  PRINT "HOW MANY LEVELS OF THE ROW"
170  INPUT "VARIABLE ARE THERE ? ";R
180  PRINT : PRINT E$: PRINT "HOW MANY LEVELS OF THE COLUMN"
190  INPUT "VARIABLE ARE THERE ? ";C
200  PRINT : PRINT E$: PRINT "IS THERE AN EQUAL NUMBER OF": INPUT "OBSERVATIONS IN EACH CELL (Y/N) ?";ANSWER$: IF ANSWER$ = R
     EPLY$ THEN  GOTO 420
210 XF = 1
220  DIM N(R,C)
```

PROGRAM 7 (Cont.)

```
230  VTAB 24: INPUT "PRESS <RETURN> TO CONTINUE";OK$
240  HOME
250  FOR I = 1 TO R: FOR J = 1 TO C
260  HOME : PRINT "HOW MANY OBSERVATIONS ARE IN"
270  PRINT "ROW "I" COLUMN "J: PRINT : PRINT : INPUT N(I,J)
280 N = N + N(I,J)
290  NEXT J: NEXT I
300  HOME : PRINT "THIS ANALYSIS HAS "N" TOTAL": PRINT "OBSERVATIONS DISTRIBUTED": PRINT "IN A "R" X "C" DESIGN.": PRINT: PRINT
     "SINCE CELL SIZES ARE NOT EQUAL, AN ": PRINT "UNWEIGHTED MEANS ANALYSIS WILL BE": PRINT "EXECUTED."
310  VTAB 24: INPUT "PRESS <RETURN> TO CONTINUE ";OK$
320  DIM X(25,R,C): DIM Y(25,R,C): DIM CE(R,C): DIM MEAN(R,C): DIM QZ(R): DIM W(R): DIM QV(C): DIM L(C)
330  DIM B(C): DIM BB(C): DIM A(R): DIM AA(R): DIM RM(R): DIM CM(C): DIM MR(R): DIM MC(C)
340  HOME : PRINT "WOULD YOU LIKE TO USE DATA STORED": INPUT "ON A DISK (Y/N) ? ";ANSWER$: IF ANSWER$ = REPLY$ THEN  GOSUB 16
     20
350  IF X9 = 1 GOTO 480
360  FOR I = 1 TO R: FOR J = 1 TO C
370  HOME : PRINT "ENTER SCORES FOR ROW "I" COLUMN "J" :": PRINT
380  FOR K = 1 TO N(I,J)
390  INPUT X(K,I,J)
400  NEXT K: NEXT J: NEXT I
410  GOTO 480
420  DIM N(R,C): PRINT : PRINT E$: INPUT "ENTER NUMBER OF OBSERVATIONS PER CELL:   ";N1
430  FOR I = 1 TO R: FOR J = 1 TO C:N(I,J) = N1: NEXT J: NEXT I
440 N = R * C * N1
450  PRINT : PRINT E$: PRINT "THIS ANALYSIS HAS "N" TOTAL": PRINT "OBSERVATIONS DISTRIBUTED EQUALLY": PRINT "IN A "R" X "C" D
     ESIGN."
460  VTAB 23: INPUT "PRESS <RETURN> TO CONTINUE ";OK$
470  GOTO 320
480  HOME : PRINT "WOULD YOU LIKE THE DATA": INPUT "DISPLAYED (Y/N) ? ";ANSWER$: IF ANSWER$ = REPLY$ THEN  GOSUB 1490
490  HOME : INPUT "ARE THERE ANY CHANGES (Y/N) ? ";ANSWER$: IF ANSWER$ = REPLY$ THEN  GOSUB 1220: HOME : PRINT "WOULD YOU LIK
     E THE DATA": INPUT "REDISPLAYED (Y/N) ";ANSWER$: IF ANSWER$ = REPLY$ THEN  GOSUB 1490
500  HOME : PRINT "PROCESSING........."
510  FOR I = 1 TO R
```

PROGRAM 7 (Cont.)

```
520  FOR J = 1 TO C
530  FOR K = 1 TO N(I,J)
540 Y(K,I,J) = X(K,I,J) * X(K,I,J)
550 CE(I,J) = CE(I,J) + X(K,I,J)
560 A = A + Y(K,I,J)
570  NEXT K
580 MEAN(I,J) = CE(I,J) / N(I,J)
590 U = U + CE(I,J)
600  NEXT J: NEXT I
610  GOSUB 1500
620  IF XF = 1 THEN  GOSUB 1370
630  IF XF = 1 THEN  GOTO 790
640 CT = (U * U) / N
650 TSS = A - CT
660  FOR I = 1 TO R: FOR J = 1 TO C
670 QZ(I) = QZ(I) + CE(I,J):W(I) = W(I) + N(I,J)
680  NEXT J: NEXT I
690  FOR I = 1 TO R:D = D + (QZ(I) * QZ(I)) / W(I): NEXT I
700 DSS = D - CT
710  FOR J = 1 TO C: FOR I = 1 TO R:QV(J) = QV(J) + CE(I,J):L(J) = L(J) + N(I,J): NEXT I: NEXT J
720  FOR J = 1 TO C:B = B + (QV(J) * QV(J)) / L(J): NEXT J
730 BSS = B - CT
740  FOR I = 1 TO R: FOR J = 1 TO C
750 ZG = ZG + ((CE(I,J) * CE(I,J)) / N(I,J))
760  NEXT J: NEXT I
770 ISS = ZG - CT - DSS - BSS
780 ESS = TSS - DSS - BSS - ISS
790 TDF = N - 1
800 RTPPDF = R - 1
810 CZPPDF = C - 1
820 XNUMDF = RTPPDF * CZPPDF
830 EDF = TDF - RTPPDF - CZPPDF - XNUMDF
840 ROWMS = DSS / RTPPDF
```

PROGRAM 7 (Cont.)

```
850 COLMS = BSS / CZPPDF
860 IACMS = ISS / XNUMDF
870 EROMS = ESS / EDF
880 FROWS = ROWMS / EROMS
890 FCOLS = COLMS / EROMS
900 FIAC = IACMS / EROMS
910  REM

     REPORT SECTION

920  HOME : PRINT "THE CALCULATIONS HAVE BEEN COMPLETED.": PRINT : PRINT : PRINT
930  PRINT "HOW WOULD YOU LIKE YOUR RESULTS": PRINT "REPORTED ? ": PRINT
940  HTAB 5: PRINT "(1) VIDEO DISPLAY
950  HTAB 5: PRINT "(2) PRINTER
960  PRINT : INPUT "(ENTER A 1 OR 2): ";FLAG
970  PRINT : IF FLAG = 2 THEN  INPUT "PRINTER SLOT ? ";PS%
980  PRINT : IF FLAG = 2 THEN  INPUT "ROW VARIABLE LABEL: ";R$
990  PRINT : IF FLAG = 2 THEN  INPUT "COLUMN VARIABLE LABEL: ";Z$
1000  IF FLAG = 2 THEN  GOSUB 1350
1010  HOME : PRINT "SUMMARY TABLE FOR TWO-WAY ANOVA"
1020  PRINT C$
1030  IF FLAG = 2 THEN  PRINT "ROW VARIABLE = "R$: PRINT "COLUMN VARIABLE = "Z$: PRINT C$
1040  GOSUB 1680: PRINT : PRINT "ROW VARIABLE:      SS= "DSS"  DF= "RTPPDF"   MS= "ROWMS"   F = "FROWS" "T$
1050  GOSUB 1685: PRINT : PRINT "COLUMN VARIABLE:   SS= "BSS"  DF= "CZPPDF"   MS= "COLMS"   F= "FCOLS" "T$
1060  GOSUB 1690: PRINT : PRINT "INTERACTION:       SS= "ISS"  DF= "XNUMDF"   MS= "IACMS"   F= "FIAC" "T$
1070  PRINT : PRINT "ERROR-W:            SS= "ESS"  DF= "EDF"   MS = "EROMS
1080  PRINT C$
1090  PRINT "TOTAL:       SS= "TSS"   DF= "TDF
1100  PRINT C$
1105  PRINT "** P<.01": PRINT "*  P<.05"
1110  GOSUB 1360
1120  INPUT "PRESS <RETURN> TO CONTINUE ";OK$: IF FLAG = 2 THEN  GOSUB 1350
1130  PRINT : PRINT : PRINT : HOME : PRINT E$: PRINT " *** SUMMARY OF CELL MEANS *** ": PRINT : PRINT
```

PROGRAM 7 (Cont.)

```
1140  FOR I = 1 TO R: FOR J = 1 TO C: PRINT "ROW "I" COLUMN "J" = "MEAN(I,J): NEXT J: NEXT I
1150  PRINT E$: PRINT : PRINT : GOSUB 1360: INPUT "PRESS <RETURN> TO CONTINUE ";OK$: GOSUB 1550
1160  PRINT : PRINT : PRINT
1170  PRINT : INPUT "WOULD YOU LIKE THE DATA PRINTED (Y/N) ?";ANSWER$: IF ANSWER$ = REPLY$ THEN  GOSUB 1280
1180  HOME : INPUT "SAVE THE DATA TO DISK (Y/N) ? ";ANSWER$: IF ANSWER$ = REPLY$ THEN  GOSUB 1590
1190  HOME : INPUT "RUN ANOTHER TWO-WAY ANOVA (Y/N) ?";ANSWER$: IF ANSWER$ = REPLY$ THEN  GOTO 120
1200  HOME : PRINT "RETURNING TO MENU": PRINT D$;"RUN HELLO"
1210  END
1220  HOME : PRINT " *** DATA CORRECTION ROUTINE ***": PRINT : PRINT : PRINT "IN WHICH CELL WAS THE ENTRY ERROR MADE?": PRINT
     : INPUT "ROW = ";UD: INPUT "COLUMN = ";UE
1230  PRINT : PRINT "WHICH SUBJECT WAS ENTERED INCORRECTLY ?": INPUT "SUBJECT = ";UF
1240  PRINT : PRINT "CURRENT DATA POINT = "X(UF,UD,UE)
1250  PRINT : PRINT : INPUT "ENTER CORRECT DATA POINT: ";X(UF,UD,UE)
1260  VTAB 24: INPUT "ANY MORE CHANGES (Y/N) ? ";ANSWER$: IF ANSWER$ = REPLY$ THEN  GOTO 1220
1270  RETURN
1280  IF FLAG = 2 THEN  GOSUB 1350: PRINT "RAW DATA USED IN THIS TWO-WAY ANALYSIS:": PRINT : PRINT
1290  FOR I = 1 TO R: FOR J = 1 TO C
1300  PRINT "DATA FROM ROW "I" COLUMN "J":"
1310  FOR K = 1 TO N(I,J)
1320  PRINT X(K,I,J)
1330  NEXT K: NEXT J: NEXT I
1340  GOSUB 1360: RETURN
1350  PRINT B$;"PR#";PS%: RETURN
1360  PRINT B$;"PR#Ø": RETURN
1370  REM   UNWEIGHTED MEANS SOLUTION
1380  FOR I = 1 TO C: FOR J = 1 TO R:B(I) = B(I) + MEAN(J,I): NEXT J: NEXT I
1390  FOR I = 1 TO C:BB(I) = BB(I) + (B(I) * B(I)) / R: NEXT I
1400  FOR I = 1 TO R: FOR J = 1 TO C:A(I) = A(I) + MEAN(I,J):D = D + (CELL(I,J) * CELL(I,J)) / N(I,J):B = B + MEAN(I,J):ZG =
     ZG + (MEAN(I,J) * MEAN(I,J)): NEXT J: NEXT I
```

PROGRAM 7 (Cont.)

```
1410  FOR I = 1 TO R:AA(I) = AA(I) + (A(I) * A(I)) / C: NEXT I
1420 CT = (B * B) / (R * C)
1430  FOR I = 1 TO R:AV = AV + AA(I): NEXT I
1440  FOR I = 1 TO C:AQ = AQ + BB(I): NEXT I
1450 GN = R * C: FOR I = 1 TO R: FOR J = 1 TO C:GD = GD + (1 / N(I,J)): NEXT J: NEXT I
1460 UM = GN / GD
1470 DSS = UM * (AV - CT):BSS = UM * (AQ - CT):ISS = UM * (ZG - AV - AQ + CT):ESS = A - D:TSS = A - CT
1480  RETURN
1490  FOR I = 1 TO R: FOR J = 1 TO C: HOME : PRINT "SCORES ENTERED FOR ROW "I" COLUMN "J: PRINT E$: PRINT : FOR K = 1 TO N(I,
     J): PRINT X(K,I,J): NEXT K: VTAB 24: INPUT "PRESS <RETURN> TO CONTINUE ";OK$: NEXT J: NEXT I: RETURN
1500  FOR I = 1 TO R: FOR J = 1 TO C:RM(I) = RM(I) + MEAN(I,J): NEXT J: NEXT I
1510  FOR I = 1 TO C: FOR J = 1 TO R:CM(I) = CM(I) + MEAN(J,I): NEXT J: NEXT I
1520  FOR I = 1 TO R:MR(I) = RM(I) / C: NEXT I
1530  FOR I = 1 TO C:MC(I) = CM(I) / R: NEXT I
1540  RETURN
1550  HOME : IF FLAG = 2 THEN  GOSUB 1350
1560  PRINT E$: PRINT " *** SUMMARY OF MARGINAL MEANS *** ": PRINT : PRINT
1570  FOR I = 1 TO R: PRINT "MEAN OF ROW "I" = "MR(I): NEXT I: PRINT : FOR I = 1 TO C: PRINT "MEAN OF COLUMN "I" = "MC(I): NEXT
     I
1580  PRINT : PRINT : PRINT E$: GOSUB 1360: RETURN
1590  HOME : INPUT "ENTER A FILE NAME: ";ID$: PRINT D$;"OPEN ";ID$: PRINT D$;"WRITE ";ID$
1600  FOR I = 1 TO R: FOR J = 1 TO C: FOR K = 1 TO N(I,J): PRINT X(K,I,J): NEXT K: NEXT J: NEXT I
1610  PRINT D$;"CLOSE ";ID$: RETURN
1620 X9 = 1: VTAB 10: PRINT "PLACE DATA DISK IN DRIVE AND PRESS": INPUT "<RETURN>  ";OK$: VTAB 20
1630  INPUT "ENTER FILE NAME (TYPE '?' FOR CATALOG)  ";ID$: IF ID$ = "?" THEN  GOSUB 1670
1640  PRINT D$;"OPEN ";ID$: PRINT D$;"READ ";ID$
1650  FOR I = 1 TO R: FOR J = 1 TO C: FOR K = 1 TO N(I,J): INPUT X(K,I,J): NEXT K: NEXT J: NEXT I
1660  PRINT D$;"CLOSE ";ID$: RETURN
1670  PRINT D$;"CATALOG": PRINT : INPUT "PRESS <RETURN> ";OK$: HOME : INPUT "ENTER FILE NAME: ";ID$: RETURN
1680 Y3 = RTPPDF:Y4 = EDF:Y5 = FROWS: GOSUB 1700: RETURN
1685 Y3 = CZPPDF:Y4 = EDF:Y5 = FCOLS: GOSUB 1700: RETURN
1690 Y3 = XNUMDF:Y4 = EDF:Y5 = FIAC: GOSUB 1700: RETURN
1700 Y2 = 1: IF Y5 < 1 THEN T$ = " ": RETURN
```

PROGRAM 7 (Cont.)

```
1705 Y6 = Ø:Y7 = Ø:Y8 = Ø:Y9 = Ø
171Ø Y6 = 2 / 9 / Y3:Y7 = 2 / 9 / Y4
172Ø Y8 =  ABS ((1 - Y7) * Y5 ^ (1 / 3) - 1 + Y6) /  SQR (Y7 * Y5 ^ (2 / 3) + Y6)
173Ø  IF Y4 < 4 THEN 176Ø
174Ø Y2 = .5 / (1 + Y8 * (.196854 + Y8 * (.115194 + Y8 * (.ØØØ344 + Y6 * .Ø19527)))) ^ 4
175Ø Y2 =  INT (Y2 * 1ØØØØ + .5) / 1ØØØØ: GOTO 177Ø
176Ø Y8 = Y8 * (1 + .Ø8 * Y8 ^ 4 / Y4 ^ 3): GOTO 174Ø
177Ø Y9 = 1 - Y2
178Ø  IF Y9 < .9341 THEN T$ = " "
179Ø  IF Y9 >  = .9341 THEN T$ = "*"
18ØØ  IF Y9 >  = .9733 THEN T$ = "**"
181Ø  RETURN
```

PROGRAM 7
SAMPLE RUN

```
SUMMARY TABLE FOR TWO-WAY ANOVA
==============================================================================
ROW VARIABLE = INTEN OF EXER
COLUMN VARIABLE = FREQ OF EXER
==============================================================================

ROW VARIABLE:       SS= 1443831.75  DF= 2   MS= 721915.875   F = 161.577739 **

COLUMN VARIABLE:    SS= 2004667.63  DF= 1   MS= 2004667.63   F= 448.680621 **

INTERACTION:        SS= 1010354.88  DF= 2   MS= 505177.438   F= 113.067784 **

ERROR-W:            SS= 107230  DF= 24   MS = 4467.91667
==============================================================================
TOTAL:      SS= 4566084.25   DF= 29
==============================================================================
** P<.01
*  P<.05



-----------------------------------
 *** SUMMARY OF CELL MEANS ***


ROW 1 COLUMN 1 = 3017
ROW 1 COLUMN 2 = 3040
ROW 2 COLUMN 1 = 3038
ROW 2 COLUMN 2 = 3664
ROW 3 COLUMN 1 = 3111
ROW 3 COLUMN 2 = 4013
-----------------------------------
```

PROGRAM 7 SAMPLE RUN (Cont.)

```
-----------------------------------
 *** SUMMARY OF MARGINAL MEANS ***

MEAN OF ROW 1 = 3028.5
MEAN OF ROW 2 = 3351
MEAN OF ROW 3 = 3562

MEAN OF COLUMN 1 = 3055.33333
MEAN OF COLUMN 2 = 3572.33333
-----------------------------------

RAW DATA USED IN THIS TWO-WAY ANALYSIS:

DATA FROM ROW 1 COLUMN 1:
2940
3070
3100
2925
3050
DATA FROM ROW 1 COLUMN 2:
2980
3160
3025
3045
2990
DATA FROM ROW 2 COLUMN 1:
3150
3020
2990
3050
2980
DATA FROM ROW 2 COLUMN 2:
3720
3630
3570
3690
3710
DATA FROM ROW 3 COLUMN 1:
3170
3120
3050
3110
3105
DATA FROM ROW 3 COLUMN 2:
3920
4040
4110
4005
3990
```

Program 8: One-way ANOVA (Repeated Measures). This is a randomized block or repeated measures design in which all subjects are measured more than once. Missing observations on subjects should be avoided whenever possible. If one or two observations are missing, however, a routine is provided to estimate the data points.

PROGRAM 8
REPEATED MEASURES (ONE-WAY) ANOVA

```
1  REM     RANDOMIZED BLOCK
2  REM        VERSION IB
3  REM    JOSEPH E. STEINMETZ
4  REM      OHIO UNIVERSITY
5  REM          JAN., 1982
6  REM
7  REM
100  HOME
110  PRINT "** ONE WAY ANOVA - REPEATED MEASURES **"
120  PRINT : PRINT : PRINT "THIS PROGRAM EXECUTES A ONE-WAY ANOVA": PRINT "(RANDOMIZED-BLOCK DESIGN)"
130  PRINT : PRINT : PRINT : PRINT "AVAILABLE OPTIONS:": PRINT : HTAB 5: PRINT "(1) DATA CORRECTION ROUTINE": HTAB 5: PRINT "
     (2) MISSING OBSERVATION ESTIMATION": HTAB 5: PRINT "(3) INPUT DATA FROM DISK": HTAB 5: PRINT "(4) SAVE DATA TO DISK"
140  VTAB (24): INPUT "PRESS <RETURN> TO CONTINUE ";OK$
150  CLEAR : HOME :D$ =  CHR$ (4):REPLY$ = "Y"
```

PROGRAM 8 (Cont.)

```
160 C$ = "==========================================================================="
170 E$ = "----------------------------------------"
180  HOME : INPUT "ENTER TOTAL NUMBER OF SUBJECTS: ";N: PRINT : PRINT E$
190  PRINT "ENTER NUMBER OF LEVELS OF THE REPEATED": INPUT "MEASURE: ";R: PRINT : PRINT E$
200 OBS = N * R
210  DIM X(N,R): DIM CSUM(R): DIM RSUM(N): DIM MN(R)
220  PRINT "ARE THERE ANY MISSING OBSERVATIONS (Y/N)": INPUT ANSWER$: IF ANSWER$ = REPLY$ THEN MAC = 1
230  IF MAC = 1 THEN  GOSUB 1080
240  HOME : PRINT "WOULD YOU LIKE TO USE DATA THAT IS": INPUT "STORED ON A DISK (Y/N) ? ";ANSWER$: IF ANSWER$ = REPLY$ THEN
     GOSUB  1230
250  IF H1 = 1 THEN  GOTO 320
260  FOR I = 1 TO N
270  HOME : PRINT E$: PRINT "ENTER THE "R" MEASURES FOR SUBJECT "I":"
280  PRINT E$: PRINT : PRINT
290  FOR J = 1 TO R
300  INPUT X(I,J)
310  NEXT J: NEXT I
320  HOME : PRINT "WOULD YOU LIKE THE DATA": INPUT "DISPLAYED (Y/N) ? ";ANSWER$: IF ANSWER$ = REPLY$ THEN  GOSUB 1310
330  HOME :REPLY$ = "Y": INPUT "ANY CHANGES ? ";ANSWER$: IF ANSWER$ = REPLY$ THEN  GOSUB 960: GOTO 320
340  IF MAC = 1 THEN  GOSUB 1110
350  HOME : PRINT "PROCESSING........"
360  FOR I = 1 TO N:RSUM(I) = O: NEXT I: FOR J = 1 TO R:CSUM(J) = 0: NEXT J:SUM = 0
370  FOR I = 1 TO R
380  FOR J = 1 TO N
390 CSUM(I) = CSUM(I) + X(J,I)
400  NEXT J: NEXT I
410  FOR I = 1 TO N: FOR J = 1 TO R:SQSUM = SQSUM + X(I,J) * X(I,J): NEXT J: NEXT I
420  FOR I = 1 TO R
430 MN(I) = CSUM(I) / N
440 SUM = SUM + CSUM(I)
450  NEXT I
460 CT = (SUM * SUM) / OBS
470 TSS = SQSUM - CT
```

PROGRAM 8 (Cont.)

```
480  FOR I = 1 TO N
490  FOR J = 1 TO R
500 RSUM(I) = RSUM(I) + X(I,J)
510  NEXT J: NEXT I
520  FOR I = 1 TO N
530 A = A + (RSUM(I) * RSUM(I)) / R
540  NEXT I
550 NSS = A - CT
560  FOR I = 1 TO R
570 C = C + (CSUM(I) * CSUM(I)) / N
580  NEXT I
590 ASS = C - CT
600 ERSS = TSS - NSS - ASS
610 TDF = OBS - 1
620  IF MAC = 1 THEN TDF = TDF - XA
630 NDF = N - 1
640 ADF = R - 1
650 EDF = TDF - NDF - ADF
660  IF MAC = 1 THEN EDF = EDF - XA
670  IF EDF = 0 THEN EDF = EDF + XA
680 AMS = ASS / ADF
690 NMS = NSS / NDF
700 EMS = ERSS / EDF
710 F = AMS / EMS
720 F2 = NMS / EMS
730  HOME : PRINT "THE CALCULATIONS HAVE BEEN COMPLETED.": PRINT : PRINT : PRINT : PRINT "HOW WOULD YOU LIKE YOUR RESULTS":
     PRINT "REPORTED ?": PRINT
740  HTAB 5: PRINT "(1) VIDEO DISPLAY"
750  HTAB 5: PRINT "(2) PRINTER"
760  PRINT : INPUT "(ENTER A 1 OR 2): ";FLAG
770  VTAB 15: IF FLAG = 2 THEN  INPUT "PRINTER SLOT ? ";PS%: VTAB 20: INPUT "TREATMENT LABEL: ";LABEL$
774  IF FLAG = 2 THEN  GOSUB 1050
780  HOME : PRINT "SUMMARY TABLE FOR RANDOMIZED BLOCK ANOVA": PRINT C$
```

PROGRAM 8 (Cont.)

```
782  IF FLAG = 2 THEN  PRINT "TREATMENT = "LABEL$
784  IF FLAG = 2 THEN  PRINT C$
79Ø  GOSUB 297Ø: PRINT : PRINT "TREATMENT  SS = "ASS"  DF = "ADF"  MS = "AMS"  F = "F" "T$
8ØØ  GOSUB 2975: PRINT : PRINT "SUBJECTS: SS = "NSS"  DF = "NDF"  MS = "NMS"  F = "F2" "T$
81Ø  PRINT : PRINT "ERROR: SS = "ERSS"  DF = "EDF"  MS = "EMS
82Ø  PRINT C$
83Ø  PRINT "TOTAL: SS = "TSS"  DF = "TDF
84Ø  PRINT C$: PRINT "** P<.Ø1     * P<.Ø5": PRINT : PRINT : PRINT : PRINT : GOSUB 1Ø6Ø
85Ø  GOSUB 1Ø7Ø
86Ø  IF FLAG = 2 THEN  GOSUB 1Ø5Ø
87Ø  HOME : PRINT E$: PRINT "*** SUMMARY OF GROUP MEANS ***": PRINT : PRINT
88Ø  FOR I = 1 TO R
89Ø  PRINT "MEAN OF TREATMENT LEVEL "I" = "MN(I): NEXT I
9ØØ  PRINT : PRINT : PRINT E$: GOSUB 1Ø6Ø: GOSUB 1Ø7Ø
91Ø  HOME : IF FLAG = 2 THEN  INPUT "WOULD YOU LIKE THE DATA PRINTED (Y/N) ?";ANSWER$: IF ANSWER$ = REPLY$ THEN  GOSUB 1Ø2Ø
92Ø  HOME : INPUT "SAVE THE DATA TO DISK (Y/N) ? ";ANSWER$: IF ANSWER$ = REPLY$ THEN  GOSUB 128Ø
93Ø  HOME :REPLY$ = "Y": INPUT "ANOTHER RANDOMIZED BLOCK ANALYSIS (Y/N) ? ";ANSWER$: IF ANSWER$ = REPLY$ THEN 15Ø
94Ø  HOME : PRINT "RETURNING TO MENU": PRINT D$;"RUN HELLO"
95Ø  END
96Ø  HOME : PRINT " *** DATA CORRECTION ROUTINE ***": PRINT : PRINT
97Ø  PRINT "ENTER THE SUBJECT NUMBER AND TREATMENT": PRINT "LEVEL IN WHICH THE ERROR WAS MADE": PRINT : PRINT : HTAB 5: INPUT
     "SUBJECT = ";NN: HTAB 5: INPUT "TREATMENT LEVEL = ";RR
98Ø  PRINT : PRINT : PRINT "DATA POINT PRESENTLY STORED = "X(NN,RR)
99Ø  PRINT : PRINT : INPUT "ENTER CORRECT DATA POINT: ";X(NN,RR)
1ØØØ  PRINT : PRINT : VTAB 24: INPUT "ANY MORE CHANGES ? ";ANSWER$: IF ANSWER$ = REPLY$ THEN 96Ø
1Ø1Ø  RETURN
1Ø2Ø  IF FLAG = 2 THEN  GOSUB 1Ø5Ø: PRINT : PRINT : PRINT : PRINT "RAW DATA USED IN THIS ANALYSIS:": PRINT : PRINT
1Ø3Ø  FOR I = 1 TO N: PRINT "DATA FOR SUBJECT "I: FOR J = 1 TO R: PRINT X(I,J): NEXT J: NEXT I
1Ø4Ø  PRINT : PRINT : PRINT : GOSUB 1Ø6Ø: RETURN
1Ø5Ø  PRINT D$;"PR#";PS%: RETURN
```

PROGRAM 8 (Cont.)

```
1060  PRINT D$;"PR#0": RETURN
1070  VTAB 24: INPUT "PRESS <RETURN> TO CONTINUE ";OK$: RETURN
1080  HOME : PRINT "YOUR ANALYSIS CONTAINS MISSING ": PRINT "OBSERVATIONS.  THEY WILL BE DEALT WITH": PRINT "LATER IN THE PRO
     GRAM.": PRINT : PRINT : PRINT "FOR NOW, PLEASE ENTER A '0' FOR THESE": PRINT "MISSING OBSERVATIONS."
1090  VTAB 10: INPUT "HOW MANY MISSING VALUES ARE THERE ? ";XA
1100  GOSUB 1070: RETURN
1110  HOME : PRINT E$: PRINT "** ESTIMATION OF MISSING OBSERVATIONS **": PRINT E$
1120  PRINT : PRINT : PRINT "ANALYSIS PROCEDURES FOR A RANDOMIZED": PRINT "BLOCK DESIGN REQUIRE THAT THE NUMBER": PRINT "OF O
     BSERVATIONS IN EACH BLOCK MUST BE": PRINT "EQUAL.  THUS WHEN MISSING DATA OCCUR,": PRINT "THEY MUST BE ESTIMATED IN ORDE
     R TO"
1130  PRINT "CARRY OUT THE ANALYSIS.": PRINT : PRINT
1140  PRINT "THIS PROGRAM USES YATES' ESTIMATION": PRINT "PROCEDURE TO ESTIMATE THE MISSING": PRINT "VALUES.": GOSUB 1070
1150  HOME : PRINT "ENTER THE SUBJECT AND TREATMENT LEVEL": PRINT "THAT IS MISSING:": PRINT : HTAB 5: INPUT "SUBJECT = ";ZY: HTAB
     5: INPUT "TREATMENT LEVEL = ";ZX
1160  FOR I = 1 TO N:RSUM(I) = 0: NEXT I: FOR J = 1 TO R:CSUM(J) = 0: NEXT J:SUM = 0
1170  FOR I = 1 TO R: FOR J = 1 TO N:CSUM(I) = CSUM(I) + X(J,I):SUM = SUM + X(J,I): NEXT J: NEXT I
1180  FOR I = 1 TO N: FOR J = 1 TO R:RSUM(I) = RSUM(I) + X(I,J): NEXT J: NEXT I
1190 NUM = (N * RSUM(ZY)) + (R * CSUM(ZX)) - SUM:DEN = (N - 1) * (R - 1):X(ZY,ZX) = NUM / DEN
1200  VTAB 18: PRINT "THE VALUE OF THIS MISSING OBSERVATION": PRINT "HAS BEEN ESTIMATED TO BE "X(ZY,ZX)
1210  VTAB 24: INPUT "ANY MORE MISSING OBSERVATIONS (Y/N) ? ";ANSWER$: IF ANSWER$ = REPLY$ THEN  GOTO 1150
1220  RETURN
1230 H1 = 1: VTAB 10: PRINT "PLACE DATA DISK IN DRIVE AND PRESS": INPUT "<RETURN>  ";OK$: VTAB 20
1240  INPUT "ENTER FILE NAME (TYPE '?' FOR CATALOG)  ";ID$: IF ID$ = "?" THEN  GOSUB 1400
1250  PRINT D$;"OPEN ";ID$: PRINT D$;"READ ";ID$
1260  FOR I = 1 TO N: FOR J = 1 TO R: INPUT X(I,J): NEXT J: NEXT I
1270  PRINT D$;"CLOSE ";ID$: RETURN
1280  HOME : INPUT "ENTER A FILE NAME:  ";ID$: PRINT D$;"OPEN ";ID$: PRINT D$;"WRITE ";ID$
1290  FOR I = 1 TO N: FOR J = 1 TO R: PRINT X(I,J): NEXT J: NEXT I
1300  PRINT D$;"CLOSE ";ID$: RETURN
1310  FOR I = 1 TO N: HOME : PRINT "SCORES ENTERED FOR SUBJECT "I":": PRINT E$: PRINT : PRINT : FOR J = 1 TO R: PRINT X(I,J):
      NEXT J: GOSUB 1070: NEXT I: RETURN
1400  PRINT D$;"CATALOG": PRINT : INPUT "PRESS <RETURN> ";OK$: HOME : INPUT "ENTER FILE NAME: ";ID$: RETURN
```

PROGRAM 8 (Cont.)

```
2970 Y3 = ADF:Y4 = EDF:Y5 = F: GOSUB 3000: RETURN
2975 Y3 = NDF:Y4 = EDF:Y5 = F2: GOSUB 3000: RETURN
3000 Y2 = 1: IF Y5 < 1 THEN T$ = " ": RETURN
3010 Y6 = 0:Y7 = 0:Y8 = 0:Y9 = 0
3020 Y6 = 2 / 9 / Y3:Y7 = 2 / 9 / Y4
3030 Y8 =  ABS ((1 - Y7) * Y5 ^ (1 / 3) - 1 + Y6) /  SQR (Y7 * Y5 ^ (2 / 3) + Y6)
3040  IF Y4 < 4 THEN 3070
3050 Y2 = .5 / (1 + Y8 * (.196854 + Y8 * (.115194 + Y8 * (.000344 + Y6 * .019527)))) ^ 4
3060 Y2 =  INT (Y2 * 10000 + .5) / 10000: GOTO 3080
3070 Y8 = Y8 * (1 + .08 * Y8 ^ 4 / Y4 ^ 3): GOTO 3050
3080 Y9 = 1 - Y2
3090  IF Y9 < .9341 THEN T$ = " "
3100  IF Y9 >  = .9341 THEN T$ = "*"
3110  IF Y9 >  = .9733 THEN T$ = "**"
3120  RETURN
```

PROGRAM 8
SAMPLE RUN

```
SUMMARY TABLE FOR RANDOMIZED BLOCK ANOVA
=======================================================================
TREATMENT = TRIALS
=======================================================================

TREATMENT SS = 16.9333334  DF = 2  MS = 8.4666667  F = 18.1428571 **

SUBJECTS: SS = 28.2666666  DF = 4  MS = 7.06666666  F = 15.1428571 **

ERROR: SS = 3.73333335  DF = 8  MS = .466666669
=======================================================================
TOTAL: SS = 48.9333334  DF = 14
=======================================================================
** P<.01     * P<.05



-----------------------------------------------
*** SUMMARY OF GROUP MEANS ***


MEAN OF TREATMENT LEVEL 1 = 4.6
MEAN OF TREATMENT LEVEL 2 = 6
MEAN OF TREATMENT LEVEL 3 = 7.2


-----------------------------------------------



RAW DATA USED IN THIS ANALYSIS:


DATA FOR SUBJECT 1
5
7
9
DATA FOR SUBJECT 2
3
4
4
DATA FOR SUBJECT 3
4
6
7
DATA FOR SUBJECT 4
5
5
7
DATA FOR SUBJECT 5
6
8
9
```

PROGRAM 8 SAMPLE RUN (Cont.)

```
SUMMARY TABLE FOR RANDOMIZED BLOCK ANOVA
=====================================================================
TREATMENT = TRIALS
=====================================================================

TREATMENT SS = 7.60000003  DF = 2  MS = 3.80000001  F = 6.00000003 *

SUBJECTS: SS = 14.9333333  DF = 4  MS = 3.73333333  F = 5.89473685 *

ERROR: SS = 5.06666666  DF = 8  MS = .633333333
=====================================================================
TOTAL: SS = 27.6  DF = 14
=====================================================================
** P<.01     * P<.05



-----------------------------------------
*** SUMMARY OF GROUP MEANS ***


MEAN OF TREATMENT LEVEL 1 = 2.4
MEAN OF TREATMENT LEVEL 2 = 3.8
MEAN OF TREATMENT LEVEL 3 = 4


-----------------------------------------



RAW DATA USED IN THIS ANALYSIS:


DATA FOR SUBJECT 1
3
3
4
DATA FOR SUBJECT 2
4
6
6
DATA FOR SUBJECT 3
2
3
4
DATA FOR SUBJECT 4
1
3
4
DATA FOR SUBJECT 5
2
4
2
```

PROGRAM 8 SAMPLE RUN (Cont.)

```
SUMMARY TABLE FOR RANDOMIZED BLOCK ANOVA
=======================================================================
TREATMENT = TRIALS
=======================================================================

TREATMENT SS = .0999999643  DF = 1  MS = .0999999643  F = .117647016

SUBJECTS: SS = 11.4  DF = 4  MS = 2.85  F = 3.35294114

ERROR: SS = 3.40000004  DF = 4  MS = .850000009
=======================================================================
TOTAL: SS = 14.9  DF = 9
=======================================================================
** P<.01     * P<.05



----------------------------------------
*** SUMMARY OF GROUP MEANS ***


MEAN OF TREATMENT LEVEL 1 = 3.8
MEAN OF TREATMENT LEVEL 2 = 4


----------------------------------------



RAW DATA USED IN THIS ANALYSIS:


DATA FOR SUBJECT 1
3
4
DATA FOR SUBJECT 2
6
6
DATA FOR SUBJECT 3
3
4
DATA FOR SUBJECT 4
3
4
DATA FOR SUBJECT 5
4
2
```

Appendix C

DESCRIPTIONS OF STATISTICAL PACKAGES FOR MAINFRAME COMPUTERS

SAS—STATISTICAL ANALYSIS SYSTEM

SAS Institute Inc. (1982). ***SAS users guide: Statistics (1982 ed.).*** **Cary, NC: SAS Institute Inc.**

SAS is an acronym for Statistical Analysis System. It has developed into an all-purpose data analysis system that provides tools for information storage and retrieval, data modification and programming, report writing, statistical analysis, and file handling. However, in this book we are mainly concerned with the statistical analysis part of the system.

The SAS statistical manual is divided into sections: Regression, Analysis of Variance, Categorical Data Analysis, Multivariate Methods, Discriminant Analysis, Clustering, Scoring, and MATRIX. Within each major section, an introductory chapter describes the procedures. Then, each procedure is a separate chapter. Each chapter is divided into abstract, introduction, specifications, details, examples, and references.

The section on regression serves as a good example. The first chapter is "Introduction to SAS Regression Procedures." This is followed by separate chapters called:

NLIN—builds nonlinear regression models

REG—performs general purpose regression with many diagnostics and input/output capabilities

RSQUARE—builds models and shows fitness measures for all possible models

RSREG—builds quadradic response-surface regression models

STEPWISE—implements several stepping methods for selecting models

SAS runs interactively (communicates back and forth with a terminal) or in batch (all programming and data read in without stopping). The data can be input from cards, disks, or tape and organized into a SAS data set. Of course, all options may not be available at all computer centers.

SPSS—STATISTICAL PACKAGE FOR THE SOCIAL SCIENCES SPSS Inc. (1983). *SPSS user's guide (1983 ed.)*. Chicago, IL: SPSS Inc.

SPSS is an acronym for Statistical Package for the Social Sciences. While older editions were not as flexible as SAS, the latest edition is quite flexible and usable. SPSS has features that allow data verification and updating, development of tables and reports, and graphics, as well as comprehensive statistical procedures.

The SPSS manual is divided by sections according to statistical procedures. Suggested statistical guides and bibliographies are also included to aid the user in appropriate application. The statistical sections include:

Frequency Distributions and Descriptive Statistics

Relationships Between Two or More Variables (CROSSTABS)

Correlation Coefficients and Scatterplots

Multiple Regression Analysis

Factor Analysis

Discriminant Analysis

Survival Analysis

Analysis of Additive Scales

Nonparametric Statistics

Log-Linear Models

Univariate and Multivariate Analysis of Variance

Box-Jenkins Analysis of Time Series Data

Again to use regression as an example, SPSS allows six equations-building methods including:

FORWARD—forward entry of variables with an entry criterion

BACKWARD—backward elimination of variables with a removal criterion

STEPWISE—stepwise selection with both entry and removal criteria

ENTER—an option to control the order of entering variables

REMOVE—an option to force the order of variables removed

TEST—a means of testing specific subsets of variables for the maximum R^2

SPSS may be used interactively or through the batch mode if your computer center is set up for both.

BIMED—BIOMEDICAL COMPUTER PROGRAMS, P-SERIES (BMDP)

Dixon, W.J. & Brown, M.B. (1981). *BMDP statistical software 1981 manual*. Berkeley, Ca: University of California Press.

BMDP (or BIMED) is an acronym for Biomedical Computer Programs, P-Series. BIMED is one of the oldest (began in 1961) and probably the most widely used mainframe statistical package. While the programs have their own internal control language (which is very consistent across programs), BMDP also allows user-specified FORTRAN (widely used computer language) statements.

The BMDP manual has seven introductory chapters to teach the use of the stystem. These are followed by the statistical section (each containing chapters for the various techniques):

Data Description

Data Into Groups

Plots and Histograms

Frequency Tables

Missing Values

Regression

Nonlinear Regression (maximum likelihood estimation)

Analysis of Variance and Covariance

Nonparametric Analysis

Survival Analysis

Time Series

Again using the regression section as an example, BMDP has five techniques for developing regression equations:

P1R—multiple linear regression using all the predictor variables

P2R—stepwise regression using either forward or backward stepping with specified criteria

P4R—regression on the principal components derived from the set of predictor variables

P5R—used when the criterion variable has a nonlinear relationship to the predictors

P9R—regression using all possible subsets of predictor variables

While BMDP is not as flexible for data management as SAS, the newer version is much improved. BMDP may be used interactively or in batch depending on the capabilities of your computer center.

Subject Index

C

D

E

K

L

M

N

O

P

Author Index